The publisher gratefully acknowledges the generous support of the Humanities Endowment Fund of the University of California Press Foundation.

THE LAST GASP

OTHER BOOKS BY SCOTT CHRISTIANSON

With Liberty for Some: 500 Years of Imprisonment in America
Condemned: Inside the Sing Sing Death House
Innocent: Inside Wrongful Conviction Cases
Notorious Prisons: Inside the World's Most Feared Institutions
Bodies of Evidence: Forensics and Crime
Great Escapes: The Stories Behind 50 Remarkable Journeys to Freedom
Freeing Charles: The Struggle to Free a Slave on the Eve of the Civil War

THE LAST GASP

THE RISE AND FALL OF THE AMERICAN GAS CHAMBER

Scott Christianson

UNIVERSITY OF CALIFORNIA PRESS
BERKELEY LOS ANGELES LONDON

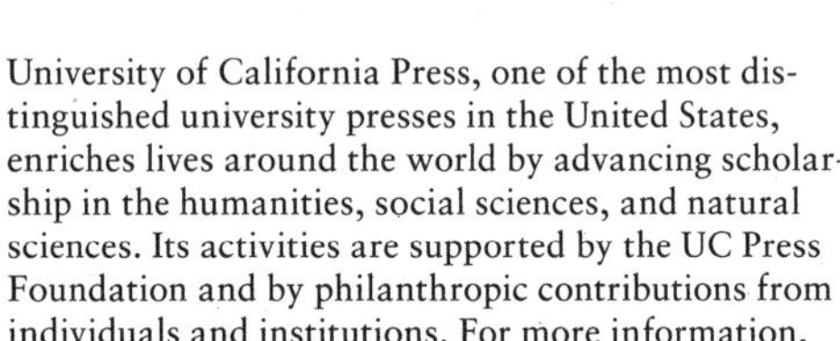

University of California Press, one of the most distinguished university presses in the United States, enriches lives around the world by advancing scholarship in the humanities, social sciences, and natural sciences. Its activities are supported by the UC Press Foundation and by philanthropic contributions from individuals and institutions. For more information, visit www.ucpress.edu.

University of California Press
Berkeley and Los Angeles, California

University of California Press, Ltd.
London, England

Library of Congress Cataloging-in-Publication Data

Christianson, Scott.
The last gasp : the rise and fall of the American gas chamber / Scott Christianson.
p. cm.
Includes bibliographical references and index.
ISBN 978-0-520-25562-3 (cloth : alk. paper)
1. Gas chambers—United States—History.
2. Capital punishment—United States—History—20th century. I. Title.

HV8699.U5C415 2010
364.66—dc22 2009052476

Manufactured in the United States of America

19 18 17 16 15 14 13 12 11 10
10 9 8 7 6 5 4 3 2 1

This book is printed on Cascades Enviro 100, a 100% post consumer waste, recycled, de-inked fiber. FSC recycled certified and processed chlorine free. It is acid free, Ecologo certified, and manufactured by BioGas energy.

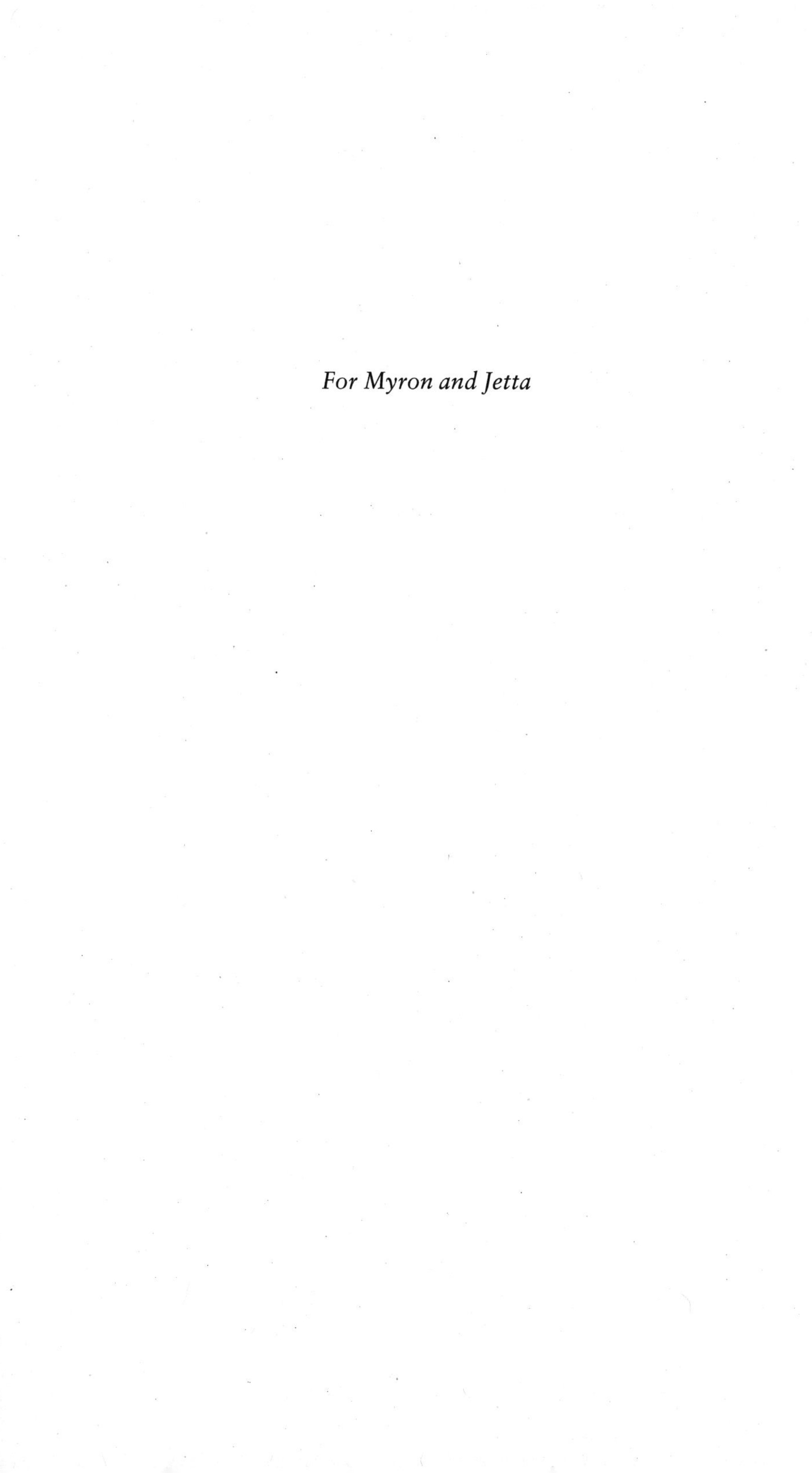

For Myron and Jetta

Contents

Illustrations

Acknowledgments

With a project of this sort, there are countless individuals to thank for many things. I can only single out a few persons for acknowledgment, while attesting to the fact that I alone am responsible for any errors or other shortcomings.

I am especially thankful to Michael Laurence of the Habeas Corpus Resource Center in San Francisco for providing access to the voluminous materials compiled as part of his historic constitutional challenge to lethal gas executions known as *Fierro v. Gomez*, and also for sharing with me some of his personal observations and experiences involving California's gas chamber. This study could not have been completed without his assistance. However, he had no editorial control over the final product. I have also benefited from the lifework and generosity of the great Anthony Amsterdam, who graciously served as an advisor to one of my earlier death penalty documentation projects, just as in the 1970s I gained much from my discussions with Jack Boger, David Kendall, and other brilliant lawyers who were then staff attorneys at the NAACP Legal Defense and Educational Fund, Inc., as well as from my frequent exchanges with the late Henry Schwarzschild of the American Civil Liberties Union Capital Punishment Project. A tiny but committed cadre of brilliant lawyers changed history in those years.

More recently I drew upon the tremendous work done on capital punishment by Deborah W. Denno of Fordham University Law School, Dick Dieter at the Death Penalty Information Center, Professor

James Acker and Charles S. Lanier of the University at Albany Capital Punishment Research Initiative, David Kaczynski and Ronald Tabak of New Yorkers Against the Death Penalty, Jonathan Gradess of the New York State Defenders Association, and Michael L. Radelet of the University of Colorado, to name only a few people. I also drew from the works of Hugo Adam Bedau, William Bowers, Craig Haney, and Austin Sarat. My participation in a series of programs for the History Channel in 2000–2001 spurred me to expand my research on the American gas chamber and other execution methods.

My long-term interest in the eugenics movement, anti-Semitism, and the Holocaust were brought together by consulting the writings of Edwin Black, Stefan Kühl, the late Carey McWilliams (one of my former editors), Joseph W. Bendersky, Robert J. Lifton, Robert Jan van Pelt, Michael Thad Allen, and many others. I was deeply affected by my visit to Auschwitz-Birkenau and Germany in September 2009. The staff of the Museum of Auschwitz-Birkenau were exceptionally kind and helpful. Discussions with Myron and Jetta Gordon, Dr. Felix Bronner, and Rabbi Bill Strongin also added to my understanding. I further benefited from interviews of Nicole Rafter as well as Jan Witkowski, Paul Lombardo, Garland Allen, Elof Axel Carlson, and other scholars associated with the Cold Spring Harbor Eugenics Archives, interviews I conducted when writing a piece about the Jukes for the *New York Times*.

While working on this book I was aided by archivists and librarians from several institutions, including the staffs of the state archives of Arizona, California, Colorado, Missouri, New Mexico, Nevada, North Carolina, and Wyoming, and the National Archives and Records Administration in College Park, Maryland, as well as librarians at the New York State Library, New York Public Library, California State Library, Bancroft Library of the University of California, Nevada Historical Society, Washington and Lee University Library and Archives, Cañon City Public Library, University of Oregon Library and Archives, Hagley Museum and Library, Denver Public Library, Princeton University Library, and Nevada Department of Corrections and Arizona Department of Corrections. Among the historians who enhanced my knowledge of Nevada's first gassing were Guy Rocha, Phill Earl, and Bob Nylen. Robert Perske helped educate me about the Joe Arridy case in Colorado, and Dean Marshal shared his observations based on his long experience as a correction officer in Cañon City. Former Eaton

Metal Products Company employee Nancy Thompson described that firm's history as the world's first gas chamber builder.

I am indebted to Howard Brodie for permission to publish his extraordinary eyewitness drawing of Aaron Mitchell's execution, and I appreciate the assistance provided by his son, Bruce Brodie. Hagley Museum and Library in Wilmington, Delaware, contains extensive information about E.I. DuPont de Nemours and Company and other chemical companies that proved very illuminating. Sam Knight of the *Financial Times* in London and Jane Wylen (daughter of Wallace Hume Carothers) also provided welcome assistance. Professor Anthony S. Travis of Hebrew University and the Leo Baeck Institute in London and author John V.H. Dippel kindly shared knowledge about German and American relationships in the chemical industry. Will Allen educated me about pesticides. My collaboration with the author and filmmaker Egmont R. Koch of Bremen, with whom I made a documentary film commissioned by the Arte and WDR television networks, has proven enormously valuable—in part because it enabled me to visit many of the locations named in this book.

For background about the Zinssers and John J. McCloy (whom I had the privilege to meet in 1975), I wish to thank Alan Brinkley of Columbia University, Kai Bird, Jules Witcover; the law firm of Cravath, Swaine & Moore; and Muriel Olsson, Fatima Mahdi, and their colleagues at the Hastings Historical Society.

I learned something about North Carolina from Paul M. Green of Durham, who shared information about his grandfather, the playwright Paul Green; Marshall Dyan, a longtime capital defender who represented David Lawson; Norman B. Smith, Esq., of Greensboro; Gerda Stein; Adam Stein; and Mary Ann Tally. During my visits to California I appreciated the hospitality provided by Bill and Linda Babbitt, Richard Jacoby, and Judith Tannenbaum. The staff at the Museum of Colorado Prisons in Cañon City provided special access to an Eaton gas chamber that was used in some of the executions described in this book.

Those who read one or more versions of the proposal and manuscript and offered constructive criticism include Tamar Gordon, Chuck Grench, Philip Turner, Iris Blasi, Ralph Blumenthal, Richard Jacoby, Charles Lanier, Ronald Tabak, Austin Sarat, Deborah Denno, Egmont Koch, Mike Allen, and two anonymous reviewers. Their input was invaluable. Early in the process I was most fortunate to connect with

Niels Hooper, my savvy editor at the University of California Press, who offered several cogent and insightful suggestions and guided this work to fruition with great skill and good cheer. I am indebted to him and his colleagues for bringing this work into print. Suzanne Knott oversaw its production and Sharron Wood served as copy editor; together they helped clean up what was a messy manuscript.

The nature of the subject has made this project deeply challenging emotionally as well as intellectually. As always, I wouldn't have been able to pursue this work without the steadfast support and encouragement of my beloved: buddy Kenny Umina; my parents-in-law, Myron and Jetta Gordon; my Hastings hosts, Eve Gordon and Michael Gardner; my siblings, Susie Ouellette, Peter Christianson, and Carol Archambault; my daughters in California, Kelly Whitney and Emily Christianson; my son, Jonah; my son-in-law, Scott Whitney; and my father, Keith R. Christianson. My dear mother, Joyce Fraser Christianson, passed away as I was starting to write this book, but her spirit remains strong in its pages. Without the extraordinary patience and intelligence of my wife, Tamar Gordon, none of my scattered literary efforts would have ever reached completion.

Pursuing this haunted path has brought great sadness; my battered heart grieves in memory of those lost.

INTRODUCTION

The huge literature about the Holocaust has assumed that, in the words of one leading historian, "The creation of the gas chamber was a unique invention of Nazi Germany."[1] In fact, however, the lethal chamber, later called the execution gas chamber or homicidal gas chamber, was originally envisioned before Adolf Hitler was born, and the first such apparatus claimed its initial human victim nine years before the Nazis rose to power and more than sixteen years before they executed anyone by lethal gas.

The earliest gas chamber for execution purposes was constructed in the Nevada State Penitentiary at Carson City and first employed on February 8, 1924, with the legislatively sanctioned and court-ordered punishment of Gee Jon, a Chinese immigrant who had been convicted of murdering another Chinese immigrant, amid a wave of anti-immigrant and racist hysteria that gripped the country at that time.

America's and the world's first execution by gas arose as a byproduct of chemical warfare research conducted by the U.S. Army's Chemical Warfare Service and the chemical industry during the First World War. Embraced by both Democrats and Republicans, including many progressives, and touted by both the scientific and legal establishments as a "humane" improvement over hanging and electrocution, the gas chamber was also considered a matter of practical social reform. Its adherents claimed that the gas chamber would kill quickly and painlessly, without the horrors of the noose or the electric chair, and in a much more orderly and peaceful fashion. But they were quickly proven wrong. Technocrats nevertheless kept tinkering with its workings for seventy-five years in a vain attempt to overcome the imperfections of lethal gas.

Eventually adopted by eleven states as the official method of execution, lethal gas claimed 594 lives in the United States from 1924 to 1999, until it was gradually replaced by another, supposedly more humane, method of capital punishment, lethal injection (see table 1). Along the way, the specter of the gas chamber evoked revulsion throughout the world and eventually contributed to the ongoing decline in America's resort to the death penalty.

Beginning in the late 1930s, and with unparalleled ferocity immediately after the outbreak of World War II, the Nazi regime began using every conceivable means to murder prisoners: beatings, starvation, the guillotine, lethal injection, and firing squads, to name a few. The gas chamber turned out to be their most efficient form of mass slaughter. The Third Reich took the practice of gas-chamber executions from the Americans and expanded upon it, developing a huge industrial system to systematically slaughter millions of innocent men, women, and children in an effort to carry out genocide against the Jewish people and Gypsies and eliminate mentally handicapped persons, homosexuals, and political radicals. Unlike other execution methods, the gas chamber—sealed off and removed from witnesses' sight and hearing—finally proved to be the preferred way for the Nazis to efficiently exterminate large groups of persons and with the least threat of exposure; it enabled the killers to better conceal their atrocious crimes against humanity, thereby reducing the dangers of resistance, reprisals, and self-incrimination. At the same time it offered the pretense of quick and painless euthanasia.

This book is the first in-depth attempt to trace the dreadful history of the gas chamber, providing both a step-by-step account of its operations and an analysis of the factors that contributed to its rise and fall.[2] I recount some of the scientific, political, and legal background leading up to the adoption of lethal gas, describe the executions, and outline the struggle to abolish the use of gas-chamber executions, all within the social, political, and legal context of the day. Although the Holocaust figures prominently in this history, forever shattering the gas chamber's image as a "humane" method of execution, most of this book focuses on its reign in the United States. There too its operation can hardly be described as painless or kind.

Table 1 AMERICAN GAS CHAMBER EXECUTIONS, 1924–1999

State	Asian/Pacific Islander	Black	Hispanic	Native American	Not Listed	White	Total
Arizona Ariz. Const. art. XXII, Sect. 22 (1933)	0	10	5	0	0	22	37
California 1937 Cal. Stat. 172 Sect. 1 (lethal gas)	4	43	15	2	4	128	196*
Colorado 1933 Colo. Sess. Laws 61 Sect. 1 (lethal gas)	0	0	6	0	6	20	32
Maryland 1955 Md. Laws 625 Sect. 1 (lethal gas)	0	3	0	0	0	0	3
Mississippi 1954 Miss. Laws 220 Sect. 1 (lethal gas)	0	28	0	0	0	7	35
Missouri 1937 Mo. Laws p. 222 Sect. 1 (lethal gas)	0	24	0	0	0	15	39
Nevada 1921 Nev. Stat. 246 Sect. 1 (lethal gas)	1	1	3	0	8	18	31
New Mexico 1955 N.M. Laws 127 Sect. 1 (lethal gas)	0	0	0	0	0	1	1
North Carolina 1935 N.C. Sess. Laws 294 Sect. 1 (lethal gas)	0	149	0	5	0	43	197
Oregon 1937 Or. Laws 274 Sect. 1 (lethal gas)	0	3	1	0	0	14	18
Rhode Island 1973 R.I. Pub. Laws 280 Sect. 1 (lethal gas)	0	0	0	0	0	0	0
Wyoming 1935 Wyo. Sess. Laws 22 Sect. 1 (lethal gas)	0	1	1	0	0	3	5
Total	**5**	**262**	**31**	**7**	**18**	**271**	**594**

SOURCE: M. Watt Espy and John Ortiz Smykla, *Executions in the United States, 1608–2002: The Espy File* [computer file], compiled by M. Watt Espy and John Ortiz Smykla, University of Alabama (Ann Arbor, MI: Inter-University Consortium for Political and Social Research, 2004), and other sources.

*Includes 3 executed under federal authority

As hard as it may be to believe today, given what we know about Auschwitz-Birkenau and other death camps, the gas chamber originated as a grand but practical utopian idea. Like gas itself, the sinuous rise of what was first called the lethal chamber led (though not always intentionally) to other variants, although its sometime chaotic movements later proved difficult to track.

The lethal chamber was a construct of modernity. Charles Darwin's formulation in *Origin of Species* (1859) of natural selection as the survival process of living things in a world of limited resources and changing environments transformed humankind's relationship to nature and supplied a coherent discourse for Western capitalism. At first Darwin was writing about the natural world without reference to man, but many of his contemporaries and followers saw his model as having profound religious, social, and political implications for humankind as well as meaning for the lower animal and vegetable kingdoms, and Darwin himself later extended some of his musings into those realms as well. However, it wasn't so much what Darwin intended or initially wrote as what others made from it that later caused so much trouble, particularly as his readers combined his theory with another notion gaining currency at that time.

The English philosopher Herbert Spencer popularized the term "the survival of the fittest," envisioning a form of class warfare between the impoverished "unfit," who were doomed to failure, and the privileged elite, whom he and many of his peers saw as worthy persons destined to succeed. "The whole effort of nature," according to Spencer, was to "get rid of" the pauper classes "and to make room for the better. . . . If they are not sufficiently complete to live, they die, and it is best they should die."[3] For some, then, after Darwin's *Origin of Species* appeared, the notion of a battle for the "survival of the fittest" among lower forms of life gave rise to notions of human racial supremacy and imperialism that came to be called (rather unfairly) "social Darwinism" and "scientific racism."

As Victorians raced to come to terms with some of these ramifications, a constellation of Britain's intellectual elite—scientists, medical titans, visionaries, and social reformers—gathered around the newfound ethos known as *eugenics*. Its originator, Sir Francis Galton (who was Darwin's first cousin), had coined the term in 1883 to signify the scientific betterment of the human race and the supremacy of one race and species over the others. He defined the word as referring to "the science which deals with all the influences that improve the inborn qualities of a race; also with those that develop them to the utmost advantage."[4]

Believing that *degeneracy* or *degeneration* posed a serious problem for humankind, many of these eugenicists scrambled to devise solutions they thought would advance the human race, in large measure by eliminating the defective or degenerate aspects of humankind. Such notions proved so powerful that within just a few years, by the turn of the twentieth century, eugenics took on the righteousness of a religion and became a growing social movement whose members longed to change the world. In short order the eugenicists' discriminating beliefs about hereditarily superior and inferior classes would contribute to calls for immigration control, intelligence testing, birth control, involuntary sterilization, racial segregation, large-scale institutionalization, and euthanasia. Intoxicated by such ideas, some eugenicists soon began to envision what came to be known as the "lethal chamber," a modern mechanism to cull the gene pool of its defective germ plasm and free civilized society from unwanted burdens. It would be a quality-control appliance that would remove society's unwanted pests and detritus as humanely and painlessly as possible.

Such visions were more than just idle thinking. Within a few years they had combined with other forces to make the lethal chamber a reality. Much of the materiel and technology behind the specific gases capable of killing human beings came from the military-scientific-and-industrial complex during the First World War. Moreover, during the next quarter-century, scientists, physicians, writers, industrialists, warriors, politicians, reformers, managers, and bureaucrats on both sides of the Atlantic would all make their contributions to the gas chamber's conceptual development, many of them scarcely imagining that their utopian dreams would ultimately become implicated in the greatest crime of the twentieth century.

The thinking behind eugenics seemed to dovetail nicely with the American way, as evidenced in part by how the country had handled Native Americans and blacks. "What in England was the biology of class," one historian has written, "in America became the biology of racial and ethnic groups. In America, class was, in large measure, racial and ethnic."[5] Despite its origins in progressive social thought, American eugenics by the 1920s had become virtually synonymous with biological racism and modern degenerationism. During that period American eugenicists achieved what one historian has identified as two great political victories: the passage of the Johnson-Reed Immigration Act

(1924), which set a quota holding that no more than 2 percent of all immigrants to the United States could come from southern and eastern Europe and closed the gates to practically all newcomers from Asia; and the ruling by the U.S. Supreme Court in *Buck v. Bell* (1927), which upheld the involuntary sterilization of a "mentally defective" inmate in Virginia.[6] Following this line of thinking, one could also count Gee's gassing as a third such "triumph," for it turned out to have incalculable precedent-setting ramifications.

Enthusiasm for eugenics was by no means limited to the United States and Great Britain. By the early 1930s its influence was also being felt in Italy, Germany, Spain, Soviet Russia, Japan, and various South American nations. At the time—when fascists were remaking Germany, Italy, and Spain, threatening to sweep the globe as the "wave of the future," and America was deep in the throes of its Great Depression, with the continued survival of its democratic institutions greatly imperiled—radical theories of "race" and "racial superiority" were reaching their most extreme conclusion.

It was during this politically hazardous period, from 1933 to 1937, that seven additional states in the American West, South, and Midwest followed Nevada by legally adopting lethal gas as their official method of execution, and they too commenced building gas chambers. This first wave of construction took place in the United States shortly before Germany began erecting its gas chambers. After some initial experimentation a small and obscure American company, Eaton Metal Products Company of Denver and Salt Lake City, became the world's leading designer and maker of specially constructed gas chambers for prison executions. The U.S. government patented two models of the company's death-dealing apparatus and aided the states to put them into use.

From the start, the American gas chambers utilized deadly cyanide gas—specifically, some form of hydrogen cyanide (HCN), also known as hydrocyanic acid or Prussic acid. With each new addition to its product line Eaton made various modifications and improvements. Additional patents for the lethal gas and gas-delivery systems for killing insects or "warm-blooded obnoxious animals"[7] were filed in Europe and the United States by a bevy of German and American firms, including Deutsche Gold & Silber Scheideanstalt (DEGUSSA) in Frankfurt am Main, Germany; Imperial Chemical Industries (ICI) in Great Britain; and Roessler & Hasslacher Chemical Company, E.I. DuPont de Nemours and Company, and American Cyanamid and Chemical Corporation in North America, all of which were members of an international cartel with IG Farben (Interessen Gemeinschaft Farbenindustrie Aktiengesellschaft, or the Community of Interests of Dye-Making Companies) of Frankfurt am Main. Hundreds of other companies often worked with them in close cooperation across the globe. Hence the advancement of gas-chamber technology was a joint effort involving players from several different countries and spheres.

Detailed news reports, articles in scientific journals, and industry sources describing America's early lethal-gas executions circulated across the globe. The first reports reached Hitler in Germany at the crucial moment when he was on trial or in prison writing *Mein Kampf*. Fifteen or so years later, he latched onto the gas-chamber idea as a more efficient and "humane" method of mass extermination. As the Nazi dictator put into action his long-threatened genocide against the Jews, his underlings devised many practical enlargements of its design and operations, building upon what the Americans had recently done and were still doing.

The Nazis appropriated the evolving American method of gas-chamber executions and embellished upon it with unfettered ferocity, adding new ways to "lure the victims to the chambers, to kill them on an assembly line, and to process their corpses"—grand-scale refinements that enabled them to gas and cremate more than a million human beings with astonishing speed and efficiency.[8] Under the Nazis the gas chamber evolved into the most efficient technique ever invented for wholesale extermination—a high-volume methodology that was less messy than shooting individuals and shoveling them into pits, chopping off heads one by one, or slowly starving them, and much less time consuming than hanging, injecting, or electrocuting each terrified victim.

After first employing carbon monoxide as their lethal agent, the Nazis ultimately settled upon using a brand of hydrocyanic acid known as Zyklon-B, a compound that had been invented shortly after World War I and patented as an insecticide in Germany in 1922 as an offshoot from that nation's continuing chemical warfare research. Its inventor had actually worked for an American company in California's burgeoning fumigation industry. Hydrogen cyanide gas already had been used to execute prisoners in the United States, where the method had been upheld by American courts as not constituting cruel and unusual punishment and was accepted by most members of the American public. The U.S. Public Health Service, among other official bodies, also had been issuing public reports about Zyklon-B and other combinations involving hydrocyanic acid for several years prior to its introduction in German death camps. Embracing and perfecting the gas chamber enabled the Nazis to marshal the apparatuses and techniques of modernity on an unprecedented scale. Unlike the Americans, who required witnesses and public reports for their executions, the Germans went to extreme lengths to implement their gas executions with great secrecy. By the time they were through, they had slaughtered millions of hapless prisoners. As much as possible, they tried to cover up their crimes by dynamiting many of their crematoria and gas chambers, murdering the witnesses, incinerating the corpses, destroying the records, and professing ignorance about anything that might prove their culpability.

The Final Solution claimed more than six million Jewish men, women, and children from 1941 to 1945, more than three million of them by various lethal gases (carbon monoxide and later hydrogen cyanide), whereas the Americans would end up gassing about six hundred convicted adult criminals over a span of seventy-five years, making it unreasonable to compare the two experiences. This book in no way equates the Holocaust with what was done in the United States, nor does it blame the Americans for the Nazi atrocities. Yet it is interesting to note that it was Americans who designed and built the first prison gas chambers, American scientists who selected cyanide gas as the poison of choice for executions, and American firms with close ties to German chemical corporations that provided the deadly gas (and paid the Germans for patents and licensing), as well as Americans who devised many of the basic killing procedures and bureaucratic modi operandi for putting to death helpless human beings by that means. American prisons functioned as the first laboratory for carrying out gas executions. Initially, it was American chemists, legislators, governors, prosecutors and defense counsels, prison wardens, public health officials, physicians, guards, executioners, prisoners, clergymen, business executives and sales personnel, technicians, clerks, political opponents, representatives of the news media, local residents, and members of the general public who were confronted with the issue of the gas chamber. Two American firms—Roessler & Hasslacher (which DuPont purchased in 1930) and American Cyanamid—also manufactured Zyklon-B under license from the Germans, and they helped to advance its image as well as its application. It was Americans who initially provided a scientific, ethical, and legal rationale and justification for gas executions and who trumpeted their actions across the globe. The Nazis took it from there, ultimately making gas-chamber executions and hydrogen cyanide their preferred tools for mass extermination, using it to carry out what many advocates of the lethal chamber had long espoused—the eradication of the "unfit" who were "unworthy of life."

The Americans and Germans may not have been the first to use poison gas to execute prisoners. According to one historical footnote, in 1791, in an effort to put down the bloody Santo Domingo slave revolt, one of Napoleon Bonaparte's ruthless colonial commanders had packed Haitian rebel prisoners into ships' holds and pumped in sulfur dioxide gas produced from burning oil, thereby intentionally killing as many as 100,000 slaves by asphyxiation and hence creating what some historians have called "history's first primitive gas chamber," although the episode did not become widely known until 2005.[9] Napoleon's crude effort was merely a prelude, however. Gas chambers specifically designed for execution purposes were a product of twentieth-century thinking.

The Nazis' programs to exterminate prisoners using gas chambers were authorized, engineered, and carried out with utmost secrecy, yet British and American government officials almost immediately began to receive detailed intelligence reports about what was happening. They did nothing, however, to intervene other than to continue waging war. As the fighting in Europe ground to a close and victorious Allied troops began to liberate the German death camps, however, graphic and irrefutable proof of the true horrors finally emerged, leaving no doubt that the Nazis had committed mass murder on an unprecedented scale. Although Hitler's forces had committed genocide by every conceivable means, their ultimate weapon of choice was revealed to have been lethal gas, most notably hydrogen cyanide.

Following Germany's defeat were more public disclosures, and there were even some war crimes trials to judge not only some of the executioners, but also a few of the German executives and chemical firms that had supplied the gas and built the gas chambers and ovens. Some culpability was established and a handful of individuals were convicted and executed or imprisoned, although many later had their sentences reduced. But many of those involved in providing gas for the death camps were never pursued, in part, perhaps, because members of the German military and chemical company executives had destroyed the incriminating records, and also because the victors may not have relished what might come out from a thorough investigation. Most of the German companies and executives who had helped equip the death camps and war machine were let off lightly, and many corporations resumed their business.

Although the Germans had dominated the cyanide business worldwide for many years, one murky link that was never explored was that American as well as German firms had manufactured and sold vast quantities of cyanide for various purposes, including the patented poison Zyklon-B, for "pest removal." More than ten years before the Nazis began ordering huge quantities of the poison from German sources for use in their concentration camps, Roessler & Hasslacher (which was acquired by E.I. DuPont de Nemours and Company in 1930) and the American Cyanamid Company in New York had also been licensed to manufacture Zyklon-B, and they had done so at a considerable profit for both themselves and Germany's IG Farben. Indeed, prior to the war the bulk of the profits the Germans derived from Zyklon's sale came from abroad, particularly from the United States. To this day, neither DuPont nor American Cyanamid has come clean about this depressing history. Until now, this American involvement and its disturbing implications have been largely overlooked. Historians have also neglected to explore what German cartel executives and Nazis in the 1920s and 1930s knew about the progress of American gas executions, how closely they monitored the evolution of the gas chamber in the United States, and whether German-controlled companies may have actually provided the lethal cyanogen and potassium cyanide used to execute American prisoners until late 1940, when the United States finally halted German cyanide imports. Might the earlier American development of lethal-gas executions have influenced the Nazis to take the approach further to much greater extremes?

A number of postwar trials brought criminal charges against a few German chemical executives and crematorium makers as well as SS executioners for their actions involving the gas chamber. But the American experience of the gas chamber was scrupulously kept out of the trials and the ensuing discussion about Nazi war crimes. No witnesses testified about the prior development of lethal-gas executions in the United States, or about the role of the U.S. military in promoting American gas executions, or the collaboration of American chemical companies with their German counterparts in the worldwide cyanide cartel. All such collusion was kept out of the discussion. Nobody brought up the development of gas-chamber technology by the Eaton Metal Products Company or the adoption by several states of lethal gas statutes for executions in the 1930s. Nor did anyone point out the prevailing U.S. argument that killing by lethal gas amounted to a "quick and painless" and "humane" method of execution. Some executives who were convicted and imprisoned had their sentences commuted to very brief terms, after which they resumed their lives and in some cases their careers. In the years that followed the war, critics of the German public's complicity in the genocidal policies of the Nazi regime failed to examine the complacent response by the American public—especially the press, criminologists, members of the bar, and medical professionals—to their own gas-chamber executions and the merchandizing of death-dealing technologies. American and British military commanders were informed about the Nazis' ongoing extermination efforts, yet they did nothing to intervene or attempt to disrupt the genocide other than to try to win the war. Then, when the conflict was won, most of the German companies and executives who had helped equip the death camps and war machine were let off lightly, and many corporations resumed their business. With a few exceptions, the commentators and historians also played down the failure—indeed, the refusal—of Allied policymakers to try to disrupt or diminish the Nazi death camps.

Although this book breaks some new ground regarding the American and German adoption of the gas chamber, the extent to which German officials and companies were monitoring or assisting America's gas executions before the entry of the United States into the war still remains unclear. More investigation needs to be done to establish whether any American corporations or individuals contributed, wittingly or unwittingly, to Germany's gas-chamber genocide. But this book raises some serious questions about American-German gas-chamber collaboration.

The horrors of Auschwitz stripped the mask of humaneness from gas-chamber executions and ruined the image of gassing as a form of painless euthanasia. A growing realization about the horrors of the Holocaust contributed to the decline of the death penalty in Europe and probably hastened its fall from favor in the United States as well. But eleven American states continued to maintain gas chambers. Notwithstanding the issues raised by the war crimes trials, America's struggle over lethal gas was remarkably subdued. Finally, however, agitation against the death penalty itself gradually intensified in the media and the courts.

In the late 1950s and early '60s, reports of suffering from lethal gas executions and highly publicized cases such as Caryl Chessman's ordeal in California at last resulted in the suspension of executions in the United States, a moratorium that lasted for ten years. But even this milestone proved to mark only a temporary end for the gas chamber.

In the 1970s conservatives escalated their campaign for the restoration of capital punishment. To convince undecided voters, some of those demanding the death penalty's return suggested the adoption of a new form of execution that would avert the criticisms of such distasteful methods as electrocution and lethal gas. After the U.S. Supreme Court in 1976 appeared to open the door to "improved" death penalty statutes, lethal gas as a method of legal execution was for the first time seriously contested on constitutional grounds. In the 1990s a federal court received a substantial body of scientific evidence showing how human beings had actually suffered and died from cyanide executions. It convinced both a federal district court and the Ninth Circuit Court of Appeals to conclude for the first time that death by lethal gas amounted to cruel and unusual punishment under the Eighth Amendment.

A few legal loopholes, however, remained until 1999, when at last the final American gas execution was carried out in Arizona. Ironically, the gas chamber's final victim was a German national, and the World Court later condemned the execution as a violation of international law. Even after Auschwitz, it still took more than fifty years for gas-chamber executions to cease in the United States. At the close of the twentieth century, seventy-five years after the first lethal gas execution, the American gas chamber appeared to have reached the end of the line. One by one, the strange-looking steel-and-glass contraptions that had taken hundreds of lives were either consigned to museums or parking lots, or converted into lethal-injection chambers with hospital gurneys instead of chairs.

Even today some observers wonder if the gas chamber might be brought back. As I was writing this book, the Nebraska Supreme Court ruled in *State v. Mata* that execution by the electric chair is cruel and unusual punishment, finding that the "evidence here shows that electrocution inflicts intense pain and agonizing suffering."[10] Shortly thereafter the U.S. Supreme Court in *Baze v. Rees* considered whether Kentucky's execution by a three-drug protocol of lethal injection violated the Eighth Amendment ban on cruel and unusual punishment. The action was historic because the only time the court had ever ruled directly on a method of execution was in 1878, when it upheld the use of the firing squad. Until *Baze,* the court had scrupulously avoided dealing with the nuts and bolts of specific execution methods.[11] A leading capital-punishment scholar who testified in the case, Professor Deborah W. Denno, commented that the courts' lack of Eighth Amendment guidance had "unraveled" the death penalty in the United States, contributing to a recent moratorium on executions as several states awaited the Supreme Court's ruling.[12]

But when the Supreme Court finally did rule, in April of 2008, validating the three-drug "cocktail," Chief Justice John Roberts Jr. wrote for the 7–2 majority, "Simply because an execution method may result in pain, either by accident or as an inescapable consequence of death, does not establish the sort of 'objectively intolerable risk of harm' that qualifies as cruel and unusual." Nevertheless, the ruling was so divided and convoluted that six individual justices wrote their own opinions, and legal observers concluded that the decision had generated more questions than answers, leaving open many possible future challenges to lethal injection and the death penalty in general.[13]

So, with two of America's dominant methods of execution subject to ongoing constitutional assault, some legal scholars have wondered if lethal gas might somehow reemerge to fill the vacuum. That doesn't appear very likely—for reasons this book makes plain. Simply put, the gas chamber has lost its legitimacy.

The nature of a society's system of criminal punishment reveals a great deal about that society's values and power structure. Several books have examined the strange birth of the electric chair as a gimmick in the epic battle between Thomas Edison and George Westinghouse for dominance in the electrical power industry, and scores of articles and monographs probe the strange history of the even more medicalized alternative execution method of lethal injection (which was first implemented by the Nazis).[14] Yet no such attention has been given to the American invention of the gas chamber, even though its unfolding is more illuminating and far-reaching. Surprisingly, even death-penalty scholars have neglected lethal gas. I hope that this book will stimulate further study.

Very few penologists have offered any hypotheses to explain why a society tends to adopt a specific form and degree of criminal punishment at a certain time. Some of the more persuasive theories have focused on the nature of the social structure in which the new punishment was introduced. Georg Rusche and Otto Kirchheimer in *Punishment and Social Structure* (1939) contended that fiscal motives have shaped the punishments developed in modern society, arguing that "every system of production tends to discover punishments which correspond to its productive relationships." In another related work, Rusche, a Jewish Communist who had fled Nazi Germany, went so far as to claim that "the history of the penal system is . . . the history of relations [between] the rich and the poor."[15]

Theories of class struggle and capitalist profit seeking may help to explain the origin of the electric chair at the dawn of the electrical age in tumultuous industrial America. Such interpretations might also serve to account in part for the rise of the lethal chamber that had been championed by upper-class intellectuals for use against the "unfit" at a time when powerful chemical companies were dominating the modern industrial age, changing the nature of warfare, and championing the extermination of pests. But as far as the introduction of the gas chamber is concerned, Rusche and Kirchheimer's approach seems to be too economically deterministic and neat to fully explain why and how the new execution method of lethal gas originated, spread, and died out.

What is clear is that neither punishment, the electric chair nor the gas chamber, arose simply as a response to crime, and indeed, there appears to have been little relationship between the nature of the penalties and the crimes that they were meant to punish. As Rusche and Kirchheimer have pointed out, "Punishment is neither a simple consequence of crime, nor the reverse side of crime, nor a mere means which is determined by the end to be achieved." Their writing proved prophetic. The Nazis rendered individual guilt irrelevant. For the victims of the Holocaust, there was no connection between crime and punishment; the prisoners had not committed any criminal offense, and many were helpless children. According to Rusche and Kirchheimer, "Punishment must be understood as a social phenomenon freed from both its juristic concept and its social ends. We do not deny that punishment has specific ends, but we do deny that it can be understood from its ends alone."[16]

Rusche and Kirchheimer were rightly skeptical that humanitarian motives had ever been primarily responsible for determining changes in punishments such as methods of execution. Such wariness seems warranted, even though in the case of the lethal chamber much of the early impetus for its use came in the shape of calls for euthanasia that would end needless suffering and rid society of unwanted animals or persons who were deemed to be better off dead. Notions of "humane" treatment, humanitarianism, benevolence, tenderheartedness, philanthropy, and the effort to ease the pain and suffering of the oppressed gained considerable respectability in the early twentieth century—particularly as the world was reeling from the effects of the Great War and other traumas that were antithetical to these qualities.

This movement toward "humane executions" did not occur in a vacuum. At the precise moment when reformers in Nevada were enacting the "Humane Execution Law" to put criminals to death by means of poison gas, the renowned Alsatian philosopher and physician Albert Schweitzer was delivering his first lectures and publications introducing his philosophy of "reverence for life." And in 1936, as intellectual support for gas euthanasia was high, the great humanist Schweitzer was characterizing the "modern age [as a time] when there are abundant possibilities for abandoning life, painlessly and without agony."[17]

The rise of the gas chamber also grew out of the birth of modern warfare, with its growing willingness to decimate civilian populations by chemical warfare and other means as part of a program of total war. Confronted by the fact that civilian noncombatants were relatively innocent and therefore shouldn't be subjected to the same treatment as warriors, some military and political leaders advocated chemical attacks that would exterminate the enemy civilian population, but in a "kind" way that would reduce pain and suffering.

Likewise, in industry at that time, the purveyors of deadly chemicals sought to employ their manufactured poisons in every conceivable way, particularly as pesticides that would eradicate insects and rodents that destroyed crops and spread disease. Adverse consequences for human beings or the ecosystem were never seen as a problem.

The particular lethal gases selected for executions in the twentieth century were originally billed as "humane" agents that would kill very quickly without causing the person being killed pain and suffering, and thus would finally spare the executioners and witnesses as well—something that had not previously been achieved by any other method of execution. That cyanide was already used to extract gold, toughen steel, and exterminate pests—vermin and insects that were subhuman and contrary to the interests of man—further enhanced its penal appeal. This was not only because the poison supposedly killed quickly and painlessly, but also because it put condemned humans in the same category as bothersome insects and rats, for which polite society was not bound to feel any sympathy, and because it conjured up images of producing pure gold or manufacturing the strongest steel. And yet, from the time of its earliest use, experience showed that cyanide was not nearly as quick, painless, or humane as was originally claimed; it also polluted the environment and poisoned the body politic. But states would nevertheless continue to use it, and the Nazis embraced it as an optimal tool for genocide.

The gas chamber, then, represented a great social laboratory in which one could control and study the mechanisms of death and dying, possibly leading to new discoveries that would remove the element of painful suffering and maybe even enable scientists to find the key to life itself. In short, gassing provided a gateway into all sorts of areas that had nothing to do with responding to crime.

• • •

Postmodern philosophers and social theorists have injected more penetrating insight into the philosophical discussion about criminal punishment. In the 1970s Michel Foucault's critique of the ways in which new modes of criminal punishment became rationalized as technologies of power within modernity began to offer a way to analyze changing historical definitions of the "proper" relationship between the individual and the state. In *Discipline and Punish* (1977) Foucault examined the birth of the prison from the perspective of the body as social subject, arguing that the move from corporal punishment to imprisonment that occurred after the Enlightenment reflected an important change by which the direct infliction of pain was replaced by an increased spiritualization of punishment. Foucault characterized the "disappearance of torture as a public spectacle" and the "elimination of pain" (a "gentle way in punishment") as specific features of post-Enlightenment modernity and governmentality, features that were subsumed in new discursive regimes of criminality, science, and the self.

Although Foucault didn't mention lethal gas per se, many of these discourses formed the underpinning for twentieth-century visions of the lethal chamber. Who were its designated "beneficiaries" of humane punishment? They were the criminal and defective classes, whose lives were not worth living, whose elimination would preserve the health of the social body, and whose deaths could conceivably be carried out without pain or suffering through medical regulation and scientific execution. Some executioners rationalized their use of lethal gas as the agent of needed "cleansing" and "euthanasia"—not as a form of retributive execution.

As if building on Franz Kafka's great short story "In the Penal Colony," Foucault immersed himself in what David Garland has described as "the minutiae of penal practice and the intricacies of institutional life in a way which recalls—and goes beyond—the classic [sociological] studies of prison life offered by [Donald] Clemmer,

[Gresham] Sykes and [Erving] Goffman."[18] In doing so, Foucault raised, among other things, an important issue for the study of capital punishment: that modern legal executions of prisoners are carried out in prisons, not in the public square. Foucault's close attention to the environmental aspects of the formalized killing process and the meticulous regulatory practices whereby modern criminal subjects are created has opened important new pathways for thought. His analysis not only captures the essence of the modern penal apparatus. It also indicates why the notion of capital punishment as a "commonsense" solution for crime is inherently flawed.

Foucault introduced into the discussion more attention to the essential notion of resistance. Prior to Foucault, most discussions of penal systems and capital punishment completely left out any consideration of resistance. In doing so, they denied agency on the part of prisoners and their supporters and even their executioners. Foucault's understanding of the intrinsic link between power and resistance was complex and evolving. He famously said, "Where there is power, there is resistance, and yet, or rather consequently, this resistance is never in a position of exteriority in relation to power."[19] Simply put, he did not ascribe much agency to modern subjects, and many philosophers have taken him to task on this score.

In this history of the rise and fall of the American gas chamber, on the other hand, acts of resistance are an integral part of the story. What Bryan G. Garth and Austin Sarat in another context have called "the tactics of resistance of disempowered persons" can be seen as taking many forms, including on the prisoners' part such actions as work stoppages, hunger strikes, attempted escapes and revolts, volunteering to take the place of another condemned person, issuing impassioned speeches and writings, making defiant gestures, and mounting protracted legal appeals, to name a few. Resistance on the part of their allies and advocates is also described. Some of these actions include picketing the prison and governor's mansion, waging constant legal battles through the courts and legislatures, and organizing movements against capital punishment. Some types of resistance occurred from the beginning; others appear to have increased over time, until finally states were compelled to abandon their use of the gas chamber.

Resistance to the gas chamber ultimately unmasked hegemonic notions of state-sponsored killing as being naturally just and humane, and finally destroyed its legitimacy as a method of execution. But the fall of the gas chamber went beyond that. In the end the resistance not only destroyed the moral legitimacy of the gas chamber; it also challenged the fundamental legitimacy of capital punishment itself.

This rise and fall of the gas chamber is problematic and incomplete because the defenders of capital punishment substituted another "rational" technique—lethal injection—in place of the discredited methods, and this replacement method of the poison needle is similarly shrouded in the trappings of bureaucratic management and medical ceremonialization. Lethal injection is hideous in its own right, but it is not a practical tool for mass murder. Unlike gassing, it is too unwieldy and individualized for carrying out genocide.

Social theories have their strengths and weaknesses. One might say, for example, that Rusche and Kirchheimer's orthodox Marxist approach overestimates the importance of economic forces in shaping penal practice and underestimates the influence of political and ideological factors, giving little attention to the symbols and social messages conveyed.[20] Foucault's work is less a history of the birth of the prison than it is a structural analysis of the state's power to discipline and punish, and he devotes considerable attention to knowledge and the body while ignoring other angles of interpretation. Instead of underestimating the role of politics in punishment, Foucault goes so far as to define punishment as "a political technology" and "a political tactic."[21]

Another social theorist whose work is especially pertinent here is the German philosopher and sociologist Jürgen Habermas, who in his youth actually lived in Nazi society. Habermas went on to write of "the cruel features of an age which 'invented' gas chambers and total war, state-conducted genocide and terrorism, death camps, brain-washing, and panoptical control of whole populations." He also noted that the twentieth century "'produced' more victims, more dead soldiers, more murdered citizens, more killed civilians and displaced minorities, more dead by torture, maltreatment, hunger, and cold, more political prisoners and refugees than previously were even imaginable. Phenomena of violence and barbarism define the signature of the age."[22] Habermas's main aim was to develop social theory that would advance the goals of human emancipation while maintaining an inclusive universalist moral framework. His work squarely recognized the horrors of the Holocaust, yet he also held out hope that Germans and others who lived through it may have learned something beneficial from the disasters of the first half of the century.

Historians criticize many of these aforementioned theories on the basis that their broad generalities are not historically grounded and supported by detailed historical research that is particular to time and place. My own study—although influenced by the general theoretical work of Rusche and Kirchheimer, the classical sociologists, Albert Schweitzer, Foucault, Habermas, and other social theorists and writers about punishment and the Holocaust—essentially takes this position. I have opted for a historical approach rather than offering what might have been primarily a social theory of punishment: the book presents the results of detailed historical research into the rise and fall of the American gas chamber in specific states during the later three-quarters of the twentieth century. I have tried to pay attention to historical antecedents, ideological and political underpinnings, and changing political status over time. I've also sought to place these developments in their economic and social context, showing how the technology of gas-chamber executions evolved in response to scientific and political concerns.

Until now there has not been a book or even a single major article exploring this dreadful history. This book tells the story of the American gas chamber from its early imaginings to its nightmarish last gasp, with an attempt to place the developments in a historical context. The investigation takes us into several different arenas of modern science, war, industry, medicine, law, politics, and human relations, marshaling evidence from many quarters.

There remains much to learn for those willing to probe for it. Studying this subject has been a painful and demanding experience, but criminal punishments and crimes against humanity, I have long believed, can reveal many things about a civilization, and the tragic saga of the rise and fall of the lethal chamber is full of the stuff philosophers and tragedians dwell upon—and fools ignore at their own peril.

PART ONE

THE RISE OF THE LETHAL CHAMBER

CHAPTER 1

ENVISIONING THE LETHAL CHAMBER

The history of the gas chamber is a story of the twentieth century.

But an earlier event that would subsequently figure into its evolution occurred one day in 1846, when a French physiologist, Claude Bernard, was in his laboratory studying the properties of carbon monoxide (CO), a colorless, odorless, and tasteless gas that would eventually be recognized as the product of the incomplete combustion of carbon-containing compounds. By that time the substance was already suspected of somehow being responsible for many accidental deaths, but nothing was known about the *mechanism* of its poisoning. Bernard therefore set out to explore its mysterious lethality by means of scientific experiment.

Bernard forced a dog to breathe carbon monoxide until it was dead, and immediately afterward opened the creature's body to examine the result. The Frenchman observed the blood of the lifeless canine spilling onto the table. As he examined the state of the organs and the fluids, what instantly attracted his attention was that all of the blood appeared crimson. Bernard later repeated this experiment on rabbits, birds, and frogs, always finding the same general crimson coloration of the blood.

A decade later Bernard conducted additional experiments with the gas in his laboratory–turned–killing chamber, carefully recording each of his actions as he proceeded. In one instance he passed a stream of hydrogen through the crimson venous blood taken from an animal poisoned by carbon monoxide, but he could not displace the oxygen in the dead creature's venous blood. What could have happened to the oxygen in the blood, he wondered?

Bernard continued with other experiments designed to determine the manner in which the carbon monoxide could have made the oxygen disappear. Since gases displace one another, he naturally thought that the carbon monoxide could have displaced the oxygen and driven it from the blood. In order to confirm this, he tried to place the blood in controlled conditions, which would permit him to recover the displaced oxygen. He then studied the action of carbon monoxide on the blood by *artificial poisoning*. To do this he took a quantity of arterial blood from a healthy animal and placed it under mercury in a test tube containing carbon monoxide. He then agitated the entire setup in order to poison the blood while protecting it from contact with the outside air. After a period of time he looked to see if the air in the test tube that was in contact with the poisoned blood had been modified, and he determined that it was notably enriched with oxygen, at the same time that the proportion of carbon monoxide was diminished. It appeared to Bernard after repeating these experiments under the same conditions that there had been a simple exchange, volume for volume, between the carbon monoxide and the oxygen in the blood. But the carbon monoxide that had displaced the oxygen in the blood remained fixed in the blood corpuscles and could no longer be displaced by oxygen or any other gas, so that death occurred by the death of the blood corpuscles, or, to put it another way, by the cessation of the exercise of their physiological property that is essential to life.[1] Not long after performing one of these experiments, Bernard's health suddenly deteriorated, perhaps, in part, as a consequence of the poison carbon monoxide gas to which he was exposed during his morbid experiments.

Bernard's fate was all too common among early research chemists, who often made a practice of smelling, tasting, and otherwise coming into close contact with the gases they were studying. Such a premature death had also befallen another great explorer of deadly gases, Carl Wilhelm Scheele, the Swedish chemist and pharmacist who had perished after tasting too much of his hydrogen cyanide in mercury.[2]

Both Scheele and Bernard had focused their attention on the effect of gases *on the blood*—work that later would become central to understanding the lethal power of the gas chamber. Following in their footsteps, other scientists explored the effects of still more gases, conducting various experiments on small animals to test each gas's peculiar lethality.

By the mid-nineteenth century, several scientists were seriously exploring the lethal effects of all kinds of substances. As Bernard was conducting his initial experiments with carbon monoxide, others were discovering the properties of carbon dioxide—CO_2—a heavy, odorless, colorless gas formed during respiration and during the decomposition of organic substances. In 1874 CO_2 was pumped into a chamber in the London pound to asphyxiate dogs, though not with very neat results, until the method was improved by inserting the animal into a chamber that had already been filled with the gas, at which time the killing was achieved with commendable humanity, according to the newspapers.[3]

In 1884 Sir Benjamin Ward Richardson, a British pioneer in anesthesiology, delivered a lecture to London's Society of Arts entitled "On the Painless Extinction of Life in the Lower Animals," in which he traced the history of gases and vapors that could be used to carry out the humane slaughter of dogs and cats. Richardson designed a wood-and-glass container, large enough to hold a Saint Bernard or several smaller animals, which was connected to a slender tank full of carbonic acid gas and a heating apparatus. At the time, unwanted horses, dogs, and other animals were a pressing social problem, seen as contributing to disease and other maladies, and animal euthanasia seemed to offer many benefits. Gases were already on everyone's mind, particularly in London, the world's largest city at the time and known for its filthy fog and foul vapors that belched forth from hundreds of thousands of coal-burning chimneys and steam engines. In one four-month stretch alone, the winter of 1879 to 1880, an estimated three thousand people perished from aggravated lung conditions, as the day-time air became so dark that pedestrians stumbled to their death in the Thames.[4] Residents coughed and choked in a sulfurous haze. It was precisely then and there, amid such foul pollution, that notions of a lethal gas chamber assumed greater currency, and "humane societies" throughout Europe adopted Richardson's lethal chamber to remove unwanted animals.[5] Scientists tested carbon dioxide as a possible cure to the animal overpopulation problem, oblivious to the fact that its use would only make the air worse for everyone.

At first such use was reserved for small animals, who were "put to sleep" behind closed doors, away from inquiring eyes, but soon many prominent eugenicists openly remarked about what others had only privately imagined: why not try it out on humans?[6] Writing at the dawn of the twentieth century, H. G. Wells often mentioned "lethal chambers for the insane" and mused that the "swarms of black, brown, and dirty-white, and yellow people . . . have to go."[7] Another British eugenicist of that time, Robert Rentoul, called for "degenerates" convicted of murder to be executed in a "lethal chamber."[8] The novelist D.H. Lawrence gave "three cheers for the inventors of poison gas," saying, "If I had my way, I would build a lethal chamber as big as the Crystal Palace, with a military band playing softly, and a Cinematograph working brightly, and then I'd go out in back streets and main streets and bring them all in, all the sick . . . the maimed; I would lead them gently, and they would smile me a weary thanks."[9] The dramatist George Bernard Shaw also favored mass use of the lethal chamber.[10] Such talk became so prevalent that some commentators even began using the noun as a verb, saying so-and-so ought to be "lethal chambered."

Yet although *eugenics* ("good birth") and *euthanasia* ("good death") were closely interrelated in language and thought, not all eugenics advocates supported euthanasia. Debates about the morality of eliminating mental defectives and other types of the "unfit" widened some major schisms within the eugenics movement. In the meantime, however, notions of using a lethal chamber for large-scale euthanasia nevertheless had become part of the public discourse.[11]

Another significant development in the discussion that would turn into the eugenics movement was set in motion in July 1874, when a frail and chronically ill gentleman from New York City, Richard Louis Dugdale, visited a dingy local jail in New York's Hudson Valley as a volunteer inspector for the New York Prison Association. Dugdale was shocked to learn that six persons under four family names, all of them blood relatives to some degree, were incarcerated in the same Ulster County institution, and that of twenty-nine males who were their "immediate blood relations," seventeen had been arrested and fifteen were convicted of various crimes. He decided to examine the family in order to determine how they had come to be so criminal. The sheriff directed Dugdale to two longtime residents of the area, one of them an eighty-four-year-old former town physician who obligingly provided detailed personal information about the prisoners' kin, most of whom were his former patients. The researcher also culled data from local poorhouse records, court and prison files, and interviews with local residents, which he wrote up in the *Boston Medical and Surgical Journal* and in a little book on the subject, *The Jukes: A Study in Crime, Pauperism, Disease, and Heredity,* which was published by G.P. Putnam's Sons in 1877.

In his book he claimed that the six prisoners "belonged to a long lineage, reaching back to the early colonists, and had intermarried so slightly with the emigrant population of the old world that they may be called a strictly American family. They had lived in the same locality for generations, and were so despised by the reputable community that their family name *had come to be used generically as a term of reproach*." Dugdale said he had traced the family's Hudson Valley roots back seven generations to a colonial frontiersman named Max, a descendant of the early Dutch settlers who lived in the backwoods as a "hunter and fisher, a hard drinker, jolly and companionable, averse to steady toil." His genealogical research indicated that different branches of the family had experienced characteristic types of failure. One branch that appeared to have produced an inordinate number of criminals was traced back to a woman "founder," Margaret, whom Dugdale called the "Mother of Criminals," who had married one of Max's sons. Presenting large genealogical charts and descriptions of each family member, each listed only by first name or code, Dugdale concluded that of 709 Jukes or persons married to Jukes, more than 200 had been on relief and 64 ended up in the poorhouse, indicating a tendency that was several times greater than that of other New Yorkers. Eighteen had kept brothels, 128 had been prostitutes, and more than 76 were convicted criminals. The author estimated their social problems had cost the public, through relief, medical care, police arrests, and imprisonment, a total of $1,308,000 (about $20.9 million in today's dollars)—a figure that astounded and appalled many taxpayers.

Dugdale's strange study was hailed as a landmark work in social science, in part because he had conducted extensive field research to attempt to address the question of whether hereditary or environmental factors were more responsible for pauperism, crime, and other social maladies. Although the author did not definitively ascribe the Jukes' social pathology solely to heredity, and had left open the possibility that what they had actually inherited was a common environment, subsequent writers used Dugdale's book to buttress their claims about biological or innate inferiority. The study made the Jukes the most notorious and despised clan in the world, but few persons outside Ulster County knew their true identity because Dugdale had used a pseudonymous surname. Although he had explained the name that he had chosen—it was derived from the slang "to juke," which referred to the erratic nesting behavior of chickens, which deposited their eggs wherever it was convenient—some readers may have also thought the name sounded like "Jews."

Forty years after Dugdale's study first appeared, a field worker employed by the Eugenics Record Office in Cold Spring Harbor, New York, Arthur H. Estabrook, conducted a follow-up study using Dugdale's original records and code sheet. In it, Estabrook claimed to have traced 1,402 additional members of the Jukes clan and found that they were as "unredeemed" and as plagued by "feeblemindedness, indolence, licentiousness, and dishonesty" as their predecessors. Dugdale's report, the Estabrook update, and other related works all helped to build an empirical foundation for views about "degenerate" classes and what needed to be done about them. It would not be for many more decades that people would begin to expose the studies' methodological flaws.[12]

Eugenics rapidly caught on all over the Western world, including the United States. America had only recently ended its practice of slavery, and it continued to treat blacks as second-class citizens. It was also still cleaning up from its policies of genocide, relocation, imprisonment, and ethnic cleansing directed against the Native Americans. Eugenics dovetailed readily with other already established American notions such as manifest destiny, racial segregation, and a reliance on capital punishment.

Max Weber characterized the modern state as monopolizing the means of legitimate physical violence in the enforcement of its order. Coincidentally, discussions in the United States regarding eugenics, euthanasia, and the lethal chamber occurred just as the modern state was taking over the execution process from local powers that heretofore had entrusted their hangings to lynch mobs or the local sheriff.[13] Prior to 1900, lynching was more common than official execution as the predominant mode of the death penalty in the United States, claiming more lives over the course of American history than legal capital punishment. Of 3,224 Americans lynched between 1889 and 1918, 702 were white and 2,522 were black; many of those killed were strung up for such crimes as talking boldly to a white man or eyeing a white girl, and all of them were killed without the benefit of due process.[14] During the same period, 1,080 convicted defendants were officially put to death under state authority, of which slightly fewer than half were white.[15]

In New York, one way that the consolidation of state power was manifested involved a sweeping change in the entire manner of official executions. In 1885 a new governor, David B. Hill, rode into office, saying, "The present mode of executing criminals by hanging has come down to us from the dark age and it may well be questioned whether the science of the present day cannot provide a means for taking the life of such as are condemned to die in a less barbarous manner."[16] Determined to find a better method of execution, he appointed to study the matter a blue-ribbon commission consisting of a prominent lawyer, a physician, and a descendant of one of the signers of the Declaration of Independence who was counsel to the Society for the Prevention of Cruelty to Animals. The commission circulated a questionnaire asking respondents if they favored a substitute to hanging, and added that the following options had been proposed: 1) electricity; 2) Prussic acid (also known as hydrogen cyanide, hydrocyanic acid, or HCN) or other poison; 3) the guillotine; 4) the garrote. For further assistance the commission called on the New York Medico-Legal Society, an influential body of medical and legal experts involved in shaping medical jurisprudence. In 1878 the society had hosted a lecture by Professor J.H. Packard of Philadelphia, who recommended that hanging be replaced by the most painless method available, which he claimed was sulfuric oxide gas, administered by means of the lethal chamber.[17] (Sulfuric dioxide was the gas Napoleon's army allegedly used to murder captive slaves in Haiti.)

As the commission went about its task, Dr. J. Mount Bleyer, a New York physician and self-proclaimed opponent of the death penalty, emerged as one of the New York Medico-Legal Society's most energetic advocates of chemical execution. Bleyer carefully assessed a number of never-before-administered alternatives to hanging, including lethal injection, electrocution, and the lethal chamber, but his proposal that a hypodermic needle might be used to inject a fatal dose of morphine did not go over well with other members of the medical community. The notion of utilizing an electrical device received much more favorable reception, in part because it was viewed as a more powerful deterrent to crime. He also proposed that a large dose of chloroform might be held over the condemned prisoner's mouth and nostrils, but this, too, was rejected because it was considered to seem like a mercy killing or euthanasia rather than capital punishment. Besides, it might prove difficult to administer to a struggling convict, and also, to be effective it would require that the execution be carried out on an empty stomach, and some thought this violated the time-honored custom of allowing the condemned to enjoy a last meal of his choice.[18]

In addition to Bleyer, other members of the medical community also weighed in. One of these was Allan McLane Hamilton, M.D., a prominent alienist and forensic specialist and a direct descendant (and biographer) of Alexander Hamilton whose work treating nervous diseases had led him to experiment with a number of innovative approaches, including electro-therapeutics and the use of nitrous oxide. Hamilton, who had also studied criminals' brains and attended numerous executions and autopsies, favored the lethal chamber. He proposed sentencing a prisoner to be put to death during a certain week, without specifying the precise date. Unbeknownst to the condemned, the condemned prisoner's cell would be "hermetically sealed" and fitted with pipes leading to a furnace or engine. Carbon dioxide or carbon monoxide could then be pumped in while he was asleep. The unsuspecting convict would never awaken, thereby being spared the fear and pain of an ordinary execution. The witnesses would also avoid the usual distasteful public spectacle, and yet justice would be done.[19]

One New Yorker who liked Hamilton's idea of using lethal gas instead of electrocution was J. Sloat Fassett, a Republican state senator from Elmira who had studied at the University of Heidelberg in Germany (and who later would serve as a congressman and secretary of the Republican National Committee).[20] Fassett was among those who favored gas execution. But Hamilton's idea didn't catch on initially, in part because not everyone was convinced that gas technology was up to the task yet. As a result, the commission rejected the proposal for the lethal chamber in favor of electrocution, although the place in the prison where the executions were carried out came to be called the "death chamber" rather than the gallows.[21]

New York wasn't the only state to consider gas executions. In 1886 the Medical Society of Allegheny County, Pennsylvania, completed its own study of death-penalty methods by concluding that the "most humane method is to extinguish the life of the criminal sentenced to death by the use of gas." It contended that "the gas chamber will be at once more effective, cheaper, and less repugnant to the gentler sentiments than the electric chair."[22] Henry M. Boies, a penologist for the Pennsylvania Board of Public Charities, went further by saying that it was "established beyond controversy that criminals and paupers, both, are degenerate; the imperfect, knotty, knurly, worm-eaten, half-rotten fruit of the race." Society, he said, needed to take a multifaceted approach that included preventive and reformative measures. In his view, "The 'unfit,' the abnormals, the sharks, the devil-fish, and other monsters, ought not to be liberated to destroy, and multiply, but must be confined and secluded until they are exterminated."[23]

Such calls were taken seriously, and some sought to make them a reality. In 1899 W. Duncan McKim, a prominent New York physician and eugenics advocate, argued, "The surest, the simplest, the kindest, and most humane means for preventing reproduction among those whom we deem unworthy of this high privilege [of human reproduction], is a gentle, painless death." McKim aimed his plan at "the *very* weak and the *very* vicious, *who fall into the hands of the State, for maintenance, reformation, or punishment*"—idiots, imbeciles, most epileptics, insane or incorrigible criminals, and a few other classes. To eliminate them, he recommended the use of carbonic acid gas (also known as carbon dioxide, the gas that had been widely used to euthanize animals).[24] At the time, McKim's view was widely shared in the United States; *The Nation* magazine of November 1, 1900, recommended his work to "all good citizens interested in human progress." But still, gas executions remained just an idea whose time hadn't come.

By 1916 the public discourse regarding the lethal chamber seemed to have entered a new phase. Much of the talk about it increasingly straddled the boundaries governing "putting stray animals to sleep," sterilization, and other forms of birth control, and the moral imperative of devising "humane methods" to execute criminals and "euthanize" mental defectives and other members of the "unfit" classes. Americans seemed to have become more comfortable with lethal-chamber technology. In 1915 the Society for the Prevention of Cruelty to Animals in New York City announced that it had eliminated 276,683 animals; during the first three weeks of that year alone, responding in part to reports that germs from infected animals might lead to infantile paralysis, it gassed an astonishing 72,000 cats and 8,000 dogs.[25]

But removing unwanted animals was one thing; addressing the human being was another matter. Popular anxiety about class, immigration, and race mixing came together in 1916 when the blue-blood American conservationist and eugenicist (and director of the Bronx Zoo) Madison Grant brought out his popular book *The Passing of the Great Race: The Racial Basis of European History,* a work that would exert considerable influence over the next twenty-five years, particularly in Germany. "Mistaken regard for what are believed to be divine laws," he wrote, "and a sentimental belief in the sanctity of human life tend to prevent both the elimination of defective infants and the sterilization of such adults as are themselves of no value to the community." Instead, Grant insisted, the "laws of nature require the obliteration of the unfit"—the extermination of defectives—because "human life is valuable only when it is of use to the community or race."[26]

In his popular book, the most explicit statement of racist ideology ever published in the United States, Grant's hatred for democracy and the immigration of "inferior peoples" knew no bounds. He expressed special disdain for "the Polish Jew . . . with his dwarf stature, peculiar mentality and ruthless concentration on self-interest." According to Grant, "a cross between any of the three European races and a Jew is a Jew." But Jews were not his only targets. His categories of inferiority extended to other races as well—indeed, to anyone who did not meet his definition of white Anglo-Saxon.[27]

Grant's views were widely shared among a hard core of leading eugenicists such as the biologist and American eugenics organizer Charles Davenport and Lothrop Stoddard, the Boston Brahmin political scientist and leading anti-Bolshevik who labeled the Jew as "the cause of world unrest." Many such ideas also enjoyed support among many liberals, such as the government chemist and Pure Food and Drug Act pioneer Dr. Harvey W. Wiley, birth control advocate Margaret Sanger, and civil rights lawyer Clarence Darrow, who said it was *just* to "chloroform unfit children . . . [and] show them the same mercy that is shown beasts that are no longer fit to live."[28] William J. Robinson, a New York urologist and leading authority on birth control, eugenics, and marriage, wrote that the best solution would be for society to "gently chloroform" the children of the unfit or "give them a dose of potassium cyanide." Robinson also insisted that splitting hairs about any of their "individual rights" should never be allowed to trump the preservation of the race. "It is the acme of stupidity," he wrote, "to talk in such cases of individual liberty, of the rights of the individual. Such individuals have no rights. They have no right in the first instance to be born, but having been born, they have no right to propagate their kind."[29]

Grant's views helped provide more of a political foundation for the lethal chamber. Across the country his friend Paul Popenoe, the leader of California's powerful eugenics movement, also endorsed the lethal chamber as a sensible response to society's woes. "From an historical point of view," he wrote in his popular text *Applied Eugenics* (1918), "the first method which presents itself is execution. . . . Its value in keeping up the standard of the race should not be underestimated."[30]

In 1916, the same year that Grant's book appeared, Allan McLane Hamilton released a memoir in which he recounted having witnessed a grisly double execution in Sing Sing prison's famous electric chair several years earlier. The first inmate, he wrote, had been "a degenerate Italian" who was quickly reduced to "a limp thing," although a convulsion had caused the prisoner's right hand to "coincidentally" raise the crucifix he had been clutching. The second condemned convict was a burly German who had strangled his wife in a fit of jealousy. The execution did not go as smoothly, for it required the warden to order a second jolt, thereby causing the "distressingly perceptible and horrid" smell of burning flesh to permeate the execution chamber. "It was not long," wrote Hamilton, "before my nervous system and stomach rebelled and I hurried to the cool outer air and left Sing Sing as soon as I could." The famous physician said that for years afterward, he remained haunted by the brutality of the electrical execution he had witnessed, adding that it made him wish that the more humane alternative of gas had been used instead.[31]

Hamilton's words arrived just as humankind was experiencing another impetus for the realization of early visions of the lethal chamber. That new crucible was the battlefield of modern war.

CHAPTER 2

FASHIONING A FRIGHTFUL WEAPON OF WAR

The Great War that began in August 1914 ushered in deadly new weapons, including modern artillery, tanks, airplanes, and machine guns. It was the moment when Franz Kafka in Prague wrote his prescient short story "In the Penal Colony," in which he describes the unveiling of a terrifying new execution apparatus.

Eight months into the fighting, the nature of warfare took yet another horrific turn. On April 22, 1915, Allied soldiers—French Algerians and territorial division troops—were dug into their trenches around the village of Langemarck, in Flanders, facing four German divisions that were hunkered down a few hundred yards away. At five o'clock in the afternoon, three red rockets streaked into the sky, signaling the start of a deafening artillery barrage, and some of the high-explosive shells began pounding the deserted town of Ypres and surrounding villages. From their distant vantage point, Allied officers observed two curious greenish-yellow clouds arise from the German line and get picked up by the approaching wind, gradually merging to form a single bank of blue-white mist, such as schoolboys might see over a swamp on a frosty night.[1]

According to one British soldier's eerie eyewitness account, the French divisions were "utterly unprepared for what was to come." They gazed spellbound at the strange specter they saw creeping slowly toward them. Within a few seconds the sweet-smelling stuff tickled their nostrils, without any effect. "Then, with inconceivable rapidity, the gas worked, and blind panic spread." Hundreds fought for air and fell dying, suffering "a death of hideous torture, with the frothing bubbles gurgling in their throats and the foul liquid welling up in their lungs." One after another, they drowned. Others staggered and lurched, trying to move away from the gas. As they did so, many were shot down in a hail of fire and shrapnel, leaving their defensive line broken. Suddenly their flank was exposed, and the northeast corner of the salient around Ypres had been pierced.

Six miles away, Anthony R. Hossack of the Queen Victoria Rifles observed a low cloud of yellow-gray vapor hanging over the area struck by the bombardment. Suddenly, from the Yser Canal down the road galloped a team of horses, lashed by riders making a frenzied retreat. "Plainly something terrible was happening," Hossack thought, wondering what could have caused such a panicked reaction. Officers and staff stood staring at the scene, dumbfounded not only by the sight but also assailed by a pungent nauseating smell that tickled their throats and stung their eyes. As horses and men poured down the road, Hossack noticed two or three men clinging to one mount, while many soldiers cast off their equipment, tunics, and rifles in order to hasten their retreat. As Hossack later recalled about one man who came stumbling through their lines, "An officer of ours held him up with leveled revolver, 'What's the matter, you bloody lot of cowards?' says he. The Zouave was frothing at the mouth, his eyes started from their sockets, and he fell writhing at the officer's feet."[2] "It was the most fiendish, wicked thing I have ever seen," another British veteran later exclaimed.[3] After about fifteen minutes, the German troops rose from their trenches and cautiously but freely advanced across ground that until recently had been fiercely contested, stepping over enemy corpses as they moved ahead.[4]

History had been made. The terror of modern chemical warfare had been unleashed on the world. Under the cover of darkness, German troops had clandestinely buried thousands of canisters along the lines at Ypres. When the wind was right, the Germans had moved with perfect precision to simultaneously open the valves on 5,700 high-pressure steel tanks containing four hundred tons of deadly chlorine gas, a highly poisonous substance that strips the bronchial tubes and lungs, blocks the windpipe with fluid that fills the lungs, and causes its stricken victims to gasp for breath and fall dead.[5]

The Germans estimated that by the time the attack was over they had inflicted fifteen thousand casualties, five thousand of them deaths—a significant toll. Two days later the Germans mounted a second devastating gas attack. The use of gas provided the Germans with the advantage of being able to render battlefields uninhabitable for six to twenty-four hours after an assault, thereby enabling them to stall likely Allied advances. But its greatest impact was psychological: the specter of poison gas constituted the most powerful weapon of mass destruction and terror yet devised. Although gas ultimately didn't prove to be the breakthrough weapon that some had hoped, it still changed the nature of warfare.

Since antiquity armies had occasionally tried to employ poisonous or noisome gases, vapors, and smoke to defeat or incapacitate their enemies. In the fifth century B.C. Thucydides wrote that the Spartans used arsenic smoke during the Peloponnesian War. In the fifteenth century, Leonardo da Vinci sketched plans for smoke weapons formed of sulfur and arsenic dust. In the sixteenth century, an Austrian chemist, Veit Wulff von Senftenberg, wrote about stink bombs containing horrid mixtures of feces and blood, saying, "It is a terrible thing. Christians should not use it against Christians, but it may be used against the Turks and other unbelievers to harm them."[6] In modern times before World War I, however, the use of gas and poisons generally had been regarded as dishonorable under the laws of warfare. During the American Civil War, a Confederate officer, Brigadier General W.N. Pendleton, had considered manufacturing "stink shells" to utilize the "suffocating effect of certain offensive gases," but he decided against it; even in that bloody conflict the combatants opted against introducing such weapons.[7] International conventions of 1899 and 1907 had banned their use. The Hague signatories, including Germany and the Allied powers (except Great Britain and the United States), had pledged to "abstain from the use of projectiles the object of which is the diffusion of asphyxiating or deleterious gases." (Technically speaking, the Germans' cylinders were not "projectiles.")

In the wake of the Ypres attack the Allies discussed what to do in response, but in the end they "realized there was no choice on their part and that they had to retaliate in like manner."[8] As a result of Germany's actions at Ypres, previous agreements had gone out the window, and the resulting arms race to devise more and deadlier gases would transform the nature of war itself and have many profound implications for the development of the gas chamber.

Germany's first use of poison gas in World War I reflected its global dominance in the field of chemistry. German chemical productive capacity, so vital to the manufacture of explosives and other military items, was unmatched, and Germany had a corps of top-flight chemists. They included Fritz Haber, the scientific genius who had personally directed the Ypres attack, which the Germans had code-named Operation Disinfection.[9]

Haber was an extraordinarily ambitious German patriot of Jewish descent who had converted to Christianity. In 1905 he published his most important book, *Thermodynamik technischer Gasreaktionen* (The Thermodynamics of Technical Gas Reactions), a pioneering work that exerted considerable influence in teaching and research. In 1911 Haber had been appointed to direct the world-leading Kaiser-Wilhelm Institut für physikalische Chemie in Berlin-Dahlem, a government-sponsored and privately funded research organization that was modeled after the Carnegie Institution in the United States. Haber's invention with Carl Bosch of a process to produce ammonia from the nitrogen in the air not only benefited the manufacture of fertilizer, but it also had enormous strategic value, because ammonia was essential in the production of nitric acid, which was necessary for making explosives.[10] When the fighting started, Haber threw himself into the war effort. He was, one German who knew him wrote, "above all concerned with the effectiveness of the new weapon; science, he once said, belonged to humanity in peacetime and to the fatherland in war."[11] Haber didn't invent the use of poison gas as a weapon of war, but he took the idea to new levels.[12] "We could hear the tests that Professor Haber was carrying out at the back of the institute," one of his colleagues said, "with the military authorities, who in their steel-gray cars came to Haber's Institute every morning. . . . The work was pushed day and night, and many times I saw activity in the building at eleven o'clock in the evening. It was common knowledge that Haber was pushing these men as hard as he could." (His laboratory assistant died in an explosion during one of these experiments.)[13]

At a firing range near Berlin in mid-December 1914, Haber attended a test of artillery shells filled with tear gas, but finding the gas was too widely dispersed to have any effect, he suggested using chlorine instead, noting that it would immediately produce violent coughing; corrode the eyes, nose, mouth, throat, and lungs; and finally asphyxiate the person who inhaled it. If blown in the wind toward the enemy lines, he theorized, the gas, which was heavier than air, would sink into their trenches and either kill them there like dogs or drive the soldiers into the open, where they could easily be mowed down. The German high command embraced the gas idea as a possible super-weapon. Following a successful test demonstration outside Cologne that sealed the deal, a dinner party was planned to celebrate. But Haber's wife, Clara Immerwahr (the first woman in her university to have earned a doctoral degree in chemistry), was deeply troubled by the immoral nature of this project, and she accused her husband of perverting science, to which he responded by branding her a traitor. That night Immerwahr took her husband's army pistol and shot herself through the heart. The couple's embittered youngest son, Ludwig, later wrote, "In Haber the [High Command] found a brilliant mind and an extremely energetic organizer, determined, and possibly unscrupulous." Soon his work catapulted him to a position of great power within the German war machine, eventually earning him the title of "father of chemical warfare."[14] The budget of his institute grew fifty times larger.

Following Fritz Haber's example, Germany's scientists worked in close cooperation with the military as part of a highly centralized system.[15] Researchers often conducted experiments on animals and humans to explore how best to treat gas casualties, and much of their study of this sort was assigned to the Kaiser Wilhelm Institute's Department E (Pharmacology and Work Pathology), headed by toxicologist Ferdinand Flury.[16] The full-scale exploration of lethal gases had begun.

Confronted with such a hideous new weapon, the British, French, and Italians immediately responded by frantically starting their own chemical warfare programs. Less than five months after the Germans' first gas attack, the British unleashed their own chlorine cloud at Loos, but a change in the wind turned the poison back on them, causing 2,639 self-inflicted casualties (although only seven actually died) and prompting what would become a deep-seated hatred of gas on the part of many British troops.[17]

Not to be outdone by the Germans, the British set up a massive chemical warfare center at Porton Down. Their researchers plunged into designing new gas masks and decontamination procedures and began investigating every sort of poisonous substance known to man. The Allies also established gas schools in France to train every soldier in chemical warfare tactics. The instructors could hardly keep up with the frenzied developments in respirator equipment, warning procedures, and tutorials about all the latest gases being used by one side or the other.

Each new gas appeared more deadly than the last: phosgene (or carbonyl chloride, a compound that had originally been identified by

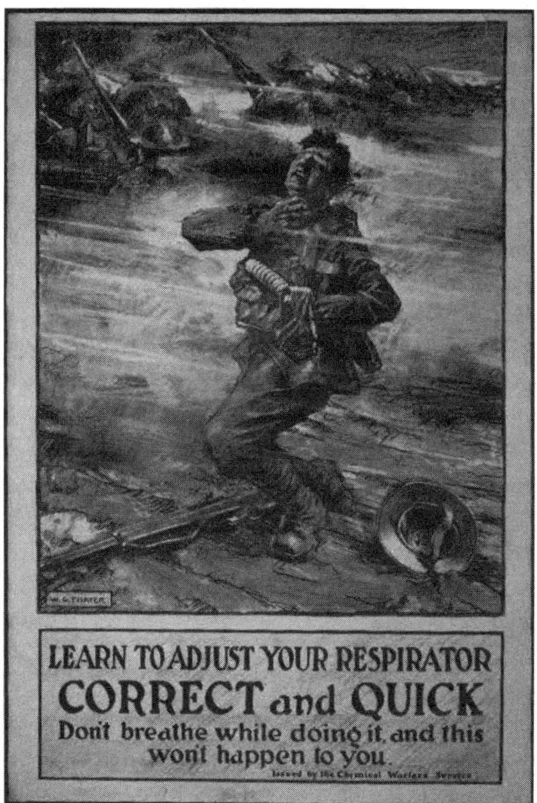

LEARN TO ADJUST YOUR RESPIRATOR
CORRECT and QUICK
Don't breathe while doing it, and this
won't happen to you.

Figure 1 Poster of World War I battlefield gassing (U.S. Chemical Warfare Service). Unknown artist. Courtesy of Library of Congress.

John Davy in 1812) was said to be eighteen times more powerful than chlorine and more difficult to detect, and mustard gas, a vesicant (skin irritant), was deemed five times more lethal than phosgene. Mustard gas was considered "the most powerful casualty producing agent yet devised," in part because "even minute traces could insinuate clothing, including rubber boots and gloves, to incapacitate victims" with huge red welts and other ailments for several days, leading to its emergence as "an almost perfect battle gas."[18] Each kind of poison offered its unique advantages and disadvantages: phosgene, for example, proved extremely deadly until soldiers learned to detect its telltale odor (like freshly cut hay) and color, and masks were devised to ward off its worst effects. Another lung and eye irritant, chloropicrin, was more difficult

Figure 2 French soldiers entering a gas chamber, World War I. Unknown photographer. From *The Great War: The Standard History of the All-Europe Conflict,* vol. 4, ed. H.W. Wilson and J.A. Hammerton (London: Amalgamated Press, 1915).

to defend against without gas masks containing charcoal. It took only 60 pounds of mustard gas to produce one casualty, compared to 230 pounds of lung irritant or 500 pounds of high explosives.[19]

Inventors devised frightful new delivery systems such as the Livens Projector and the Stokes Mortar, and starry-eyed tacticians extolled the enormous potential of air power for dropping gas bombs on hapless German troops and cities—just as their enemy plotted its own glorious triumphs. The effects of all these poisons upon the environment were simply ignored.[20]

One of the early innovations developed at the War Department Experimental Ground at Porton Down was a state-of-the-art "gas chamber" for testing various poison gases. Soldiers volunteered to serve as human guinea pigs (called "observers" in Porton's terminology), subjecting themselves to any one of a range of poisonous substances that were being tested in the contraption. Typically they stood for protracted periods wearing gas masks as the vapor swirled around them, and some were required to expose areas of their skin to see how it might respond to the chemical agent.[21]

Cyanide gases were among the poisons studied under laboratory conditions. John Barcroft headed the unit's physiology department. Previously French scientists had tested one such gas on dogs, which had died, but the British had tried it on goats, which survived, leaving the question of its effectiveness open to debate. Barcroft, an intrepid Quaker, decided he would personally intervene to settle the matter. One night, when everyone had gone to bed, he instructed a corporal to witness his experiment. Barcroft then flooded the gas chamber with a one in two thousand concentration of hydrogen cyanide and, without donning a mask, he entered the gas-filled chamber along with a dog. The air had a distinctive almond smell. "In order that the experiment might be as fair as possible and that my respiration should be relatively as active as that of the dog," Barcroft wrote,

> I remained standing, and took a few steps from time to time while I was in the chamber. In about thirty seconds the dog began to get unsteady, and in fifty-five seconds it dropped to the floor and commenced the characteristic distressing respiration which heralds death from cyanide poisoning. One minute out [and] thirty-five seconds after the commencement the animal's body was carried out, respiration having ceased and the dog being apparently dead. I then left the chamber. As regards the result upon myself, the only real effect was a momentary giddiness when I turned my head quickly. This lasted about a year, and then vanished. For some time it was difficult to concentrate on anything for any length of time.[22]

Based on his first-hand observations, Barcroft and his colleagues concluded that hydrocyanic acid at higher concentrations was indeed lethal. His Quaker sensibilities may have been offended by the deadly uses to which this knowledge was put, for shortly afterward, in July 1916, the Allies introduced hydrogen cyanide and cyanogen chloride, or CC (later called CK), which the French called *mauguinite* or HCN, which was also known as *forestite*.[23] The French used hydrogen cyanide in artillery shells in the Battle of the Somme and afterward. Both sides also used additional cyanide mixtures including cyanogen bromide (French name *campilite,* German name *E-Stoff*) and bromobenzyl cyanide (*camite* to the French and White Cross to the Germans).

A Swiss human rights writer, Gertrud Woker, later reported, "On the Austrian Alpine front, trenches were frequently found in which all the soldiers had died from the poison [cyanide] gas of the Italians. No less horrifying are the reports of the doctors who went with the Austrian troops into the Italian lines where poison gases were employed; this was at the time when cyanide gases were first used. The dead held the exact positions they were in when attacked by the cyanide gas. There sat men turned to stone at the games, the cards in their hands, motionless; an indescribable picture!"[24] Woker couldn't know it at the time, but similar images involving cyanide gas would later come back to haunt the world a generation later.

The United States didn't enter the war until April 1917. By then the military standoff had lasted for thirty-three agonizing months and millions of combatants and civilians had perished. Large areas of Europe lay in waste, its soil, water, and air poisoned by toxic chemicals "where ignorant armies clashed by night." The United States remained ill prepared for waging such a war. Few American officials had grasped the importance that would be attached to poison gases. When one of the nation's leading chemists had contacted the secretary of war, Newton D. Baker, to offer his services, Baker replied the help would be "unnecessary" because the War Department "already had a chemist."[25] Only a few observers initially realized what it would mean, but they would come to find out soon enough. As one representative of the American chemical industry exhorted his colleagues, "The holocaust now raging in Europe has forced opportunities upon American chemists and has correspondingly increased our responsibilities."[26]

At the time, the United States already had become the world's leading industrial power, but the state of its chemical industry didn't compare to Germany's.[27] German scientists had achieved many of the recent breakthroughs in research; German firms dominated the production of synthetic organic chemicals such as dyes and related pharmaceuticals; and German chemistry school programs were without peer. When America entered the war, the U.S. Army had "no gas masks, no supply of offensive chemicals, and its troops received no gas training."[28] Virtually overnight the nation found itself embroiled in what was increasingly being called "the chemist's war."[29]

But that was about to change. American authorities immediately halted the supply of German chemicals into the United States and seized many vital German assets; agents confiscated 4,800 German dyestuff and chemical patents, for everything from aspirin to munitions, and eventually made them available to American firms. Chemical companies that were run by German Americans but linked to German interests rushed to proclaim their allegiance to the United States. The American Chemical Society, representing American chemical interests, offered its services to the U.S. government and conducted a nationwide census of chemists who could be called upon to assist the nation in war.[30] Much of the funding for research came from private sources such as the Rockefeller and Carnegie Foundations.[31] To obtain chemicals and equipment for its new research laboratory, the military turned to Chester G. Fisher, the president of the Fisher Scientific Materials Company of Pittsburgh, which previously had relied on producers in Bavaria for its supplies.[32] The federal Bureau of Mines, by virtue of its prior experience dealing with hazardous respiratory conditions in mining, assumed primary responsibility for U.S. development of poison gas, with James F. Norris of the Massachusetts Institute of Technology as its director of chemical research.[33] Many university chemistry departments across the country virtually became part of the War Department. "In view of the present emergency the Catholic University of America has the honor to offer itself to you for such services as the Government of the United States may desire from it," its rector, Thomas Shahan, wrote to President Woodrow Wilson.[34] Shahan informed his students, "This war itself is a scientific war; and before it ends we shall need, as other nations have already found, to continue unremittingly at the task of research and preparation."[35] By end of May 1917 the Bureau of Mines had enlisted the aid of laboratories in twenty-one colleges and universities, including the University of Michigan, University of Chicago, and Western Reserve University; it also drew on three industrial companies and three government agencies. Yandell Henderson of Yale, the nation's foremost expert on poison gases and automobile exhaust, personally tested his new gas mask design in a specially constructed chlorine gas chamber.[36] George Burrell, who before the war had studied such phenomena as the effects of carbon monoxide on small animals, became the new chief of the Research Division. A researcher on the use of chemicals to maintain swimming pools became engaged in developing lethal poisons.[37] According to some accounts, of all the chemists in the nation who were asked to join in the government's war gas research, only one chemist refused.[38] "War, the destroyer," wrote the executive secretary of the American Chemical Society, "has been . . . the incentive to marvelous chemical development with a speed of accomplishment incomprehensible in normal times."[39] Within a few months of entering the war, America's chemical industry was thriving so much that American chemists had "accomplished in two years what it had taken Germany forty years to attain."[40]

Immediately upon America's entry into the war, a colonel from the Army Corps of Engineers, Amos A. Fries, was ordered to France as director of road building. Then forty-three years old, the former West

Pointer already had made a name for himself as a talented, no-nonsense administrator who had engineered the construction of the Dalles-Celilo Canal in Oregon, directed all harbor work in Southern California and the Colorado River, developed the plans for the Los Angeles harbor, and helped to carve out Yellowstone National Park. Three days after his arrival in Paris, the immaculately groomed Fries appeared before the commander of the American Expeditionary Forces, General John J. "Blackjack" Pershing, and snapped to attention. Pershing, who remembered him from their service together in the Philippines, put him at ease and told him in his Missouri drawl, "We're going to have a gas service, and you're going to head it."

Fries proved to be an excellent choice. Promoted to brigadier general, he moved with remarkable speed, helping to set up a major research laboratory, working feverishly with several top scientific and industrial leaders to develop America's chemical warfare program, and launching a training program to prepare his troops for the terrifying realities of gas warfare.[41] He received permission from the French government to convert a former tuberculosis research laboratory at Puteaux, near Paris, into a chemical warfare laboratory, and he created a test field near Chaumont.[42] In January 1918 contingents of American chemists began to arrive with supplies. They included Gilbert N. Lewis of the University of California, one of the world's top physical chemists; Joel H. Hildebrand, the future president of the American Chemical Society; and Frederick G. Keyes, later of MIT.[43]

On May 11, 1918, the War Department ordered famed Major General William L. Sibert to draw up plans for a new gas service structure. Sibert, of Alabama, had served in the Philippines and was best known for having superintended the epic building of the Panama Canal. In June 1918, just as the Allies were first employing their own mustard gas against the Germans, President Wilson signed Executive Order 2894 approving Sibert's plan for the Chemical Warfare Service.[44] The Americans' military-industrial-scientific-educational complex already had gone into high gear.

Back in the states, the U.S. government had established its chemical research at American University on the northwestern outskirts of Washington. Over the next 600 days it would grow from a single building to 153 facilities employing more than 1,700 chemists and 700 service assistants, as it became the largest federal scientific research project yet undertaken and the prototype for the later project that would build the atomic bomb a generation later.[45] Its director was Captain

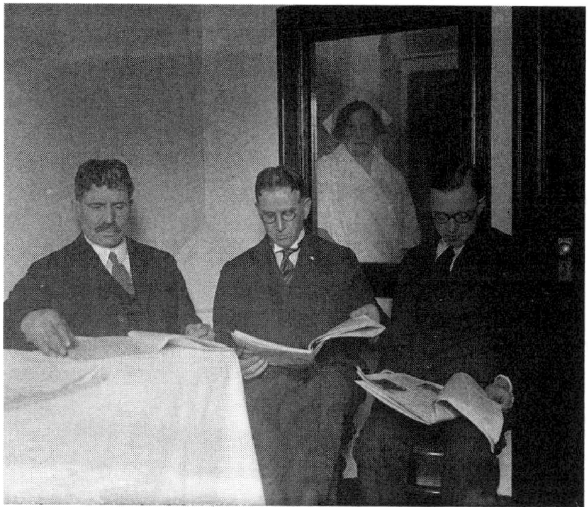

Figure 3 General Amos Fries (left) of the Chemical Warfare Service tries out new chlorine gas chamber at Veterans Bureau, 1925. National Photo Company Collection. Courtesy of the Library of Congress.

James B. Conant, a young organic chemist from Harvard University (who later would become its president and play a key role in organizing the Manhattan Project, which built the atomic bomb).[46] Conant and his colleagues would end up testing the effects of more than 1,600 compounds on mice, rats, dogs, and other animals, as well as on American soldiers.

One of their first priorities was to assess previous research. In 1903, at a laboratory at the University of Notre Dame, a Roman Catholic priest, Julius Aloysius Nieuwland, had combined arsenic trichloride in the presence of aluminum chloride to cause a highly toxic compound (dichloro-2-chlorovinyl arsine) to form. Notes about his work had been filed away for more than a decade. Then, during the war, the chemist Captain Winford Lee Lewis of Northwestern University, working at Catholic University, learned of Nieuwland's previous discoveries and purified the compound into a substance that came to be called methyl or lewisite.[47]

A highly explosive oily amber liquid, the compound carried the gentle fragrance of geranium blossoms but burst into flame when combined with water. Lewisite also proved extremely deadly with the slightest contact or inhalation and was rated seventy-two times more lethal than mustard gas, making it the strongest poison ever discovered to that point. Working at American University's Experimental Station (AUES), Conant and his staff investigated it with as much caution as they could summon. They tested specimens on snails, slugs, mice, rats, guinea pigs, and canaries, and tied thousands of dogs, monkeys, and goats to stakes in nearby farmers' fields in order to expose them to chemical bombs. The animals' symptoms were carefully recorded over a period of several days, and the dead ones were subjected to postmortem examination, some of their vital organs preserved in glass jars or rendered by artists with oil paints.[48]

The Bureau of Entomology of the Department of Agriculture also collaborated with the Chemical Warfare Service to test four gases that would combat another of the army's biggest problems at the front: lice. The objective was to place soldiers wearing gas masks in a gas chamber and subject them to the right lethal gas that would "kill all cooties and their nits."[49] The researchers saw themselves as waging war against the insect world.[50]

The AUES researchers also conducted human tests in a "Man Test Laboratory" that was unluckily designated number 13, a low, squat barracks that was kept stocked with canaries to warn the soldiers of dangerous gas levels and equipped with a "vast tub of soapsuds [that] awaited the frenzied plunges of men on whom the horrid stuff had settled."[51] One serviceman who was exposed to lewisite but survived to tell the tale, Sergeant George Temple, later said he believed that more American soldiers were killed by gas at the AUES than died from gas in battle.[52] The director of the research division, Colonel George A. Burrell, said the AUES casualty rate was higher than in any other unit in the army except the infamous gas-manufacturing unit at Edgewood Arsenal.[53]

On the bright summer morning of August 3, 1918, a former United States senator from West Virginia, Nathan Bay Scott, was seated with his wife and sister on the back porch of their home, about four hundred yards away from AUES, relaxing and enjoying the breeze, when suddenly he noticed a dense cloud of yellowish gas advancing toward them. The group smelled a faint odor and felt intense burning in their eyes. After rushing inside the house and shutting the windows, they looked out and saw dead birds and small animals littering the ground. Some soldiers who were nearby were also stricken and had to be hospitalized. Despite the senator's complaints, however, the matter was hushed up. But lewisite had been the culprit.[54]

American factories played a key role in the chemical war, churning out 5,920,000 gas masks, more than 45,000 signal horns to warn troops of gas attacks, and more than 50,000 specially designed oversized fans to blow poison gas vapors out of trenches and dugouts.[55] To produce its mustard gas and other poisons, the army relied on a web of plants scattered throughout the Northeast and Midwest. Contracts were secretly arranged with chemical manufacturing facilities at Stamford, Connecticut, Hastings-on-Hudson, New York, Kingsport, Tennessee, Croyland, Pennsylvania, Niagara Falls and Buffalo, New York, Charleston, West Virginia, and Midland, Michigan, all of which were expected to produce tons of poison gas.

The largest American workshop was Edgewood Arsenal in Maryland. Specially constructed on a three-hundred-acre tract of former farmland along the Chesapeake, twenty-six miles from Baltimore, and surrounded by miles of fence and heavily guarded by soldiers with drawn bayonets, it rapidly became the largest lethal gas factory on earth, manufacturer of mustard gas, chlorine, sulfur monochloride, chloropicrin, and phosgene. Its commander was Colonel William H. Walker, a former professor of chemical engineering at MIT. Under his supervision Edgewood grew to become a city of brick kilns, high chimneys, correlated vats in innumerable series, eleven miles of high-tension electric lines, fifteen miles of roadways, twenty-eight miles of railway, countless miles of elevated pipelines, and "machinery of the finest type and the most perfect installation, housed in concrete and sheet iron, built apparently for permanence"—all of it capable of producing two hundred thousand chemical bombs and shells per day.[56]

Work in America's poison gas plants was extraordinarily dangerous. The army's official figures indicated that in the period from June to December 1918 alone Edgewood suffered 925 casualties—769 of them from August through October. Mustard gas accounted for 674 of the total, followed by stannic chloride (50), phosgene (50), chloropicrin (44), bleach chlorine (44), liquid chlorine (18), phosphorous (15), caustic soda (10), sulfur chloride (9), sulfuric acid (8), picric acid (2), and carbon monoxide (1).[57] A *New York Times* reporter who was allowed to visit the site shortly after the armistice witnessed two large dormitories that were still serving as hospitals for many of those who had suffered as a result of work-related accidents. "I saw boys who had been struck down by the fiendish gases while at work," the visitor wrote:

> some with arms and legs and trunks shriveled and scarred as by a horrible fire, some with the deep suppurations still oozing after weeks of careful nursing. In one case a drop of mustard oil had fallen from

> a conduit pipe under which a soldier had walked, hitting his shoe. He wiped it off, thinking that made him safe. The next day his flesh began to peel. Now, five weeks later, his foot looks like a charred ember. Another had accidentally kicked over what he thought an empty pipe. It contained phosphorous, which flew over his face and upper body. Now, weeks later, he is still a mass of horrible burns. Another case (one of the fatalities) was that of an officer who came in from the works to the office. He wore rubber gloves, as they all do when near the gases, but did not know he had been near enough to pick up the mustard oil. He picked up a chair and placed it in front of his desk, intending to seat himself. At that moment the telephone rang and he stepped to the wall to answer. A friend, another officer, entered and took the seat by the desk. Forty-eight hours later the second officer was dead. The first officer had accidentally rubbed mustard oil on the back of the chair. It went through the clothes and into the spine of the second.[58]

The army was eager to put lewisite to work in ways that would achieve its maximum effect. General Sibert had ordered that three thousand tons of the methyl in artillery shells and storage drums must be ready on March 1, 1919, for a massive spring offensive he was planning against Germany. Captain Conant's most important mission was to ensure this deadline was met in absolute secrecy. To carry it out, he selected a site in a tiny Cleveland suburb, Willoughby. In early 1918 he commandeered the abandoned Ben Hur Motor Company plant and instituted airtight security.[59] It was there, he hoped, that the material known by its top-secret designation of G-34 would become "the great American gas which would win the war."[60] Working through the spring and into the torrid August heat, when gases were at their most volatile, Conant and his team geared up their machinery to produce an output of ten tons a day, or one ton more than what could have "depopulated" Manhattan, a city of four million. This volume was more than ten times the Germans' total output of poison gas, and Conant's variety was also seven times more deadly—more than enough, it was said, to exterminate Berlin.[61] Remarkably, although many workers at Willoughby received serious burns as a result of their work, no soldier died, and there was no catastrophic accident.[62]

Meanwhile, in France, Fries was trying to improve the ability of American soldiers to survive chemical attacks. Knowing that many new recruits would fail to heed their instructors' call to quickly don their gas masks and keep them in place, somebody hatched the idea to win over the doughboys by using sports celebrities as their trainers. Some of those selected were baseball greats Ty Cobb, George Sisler,

Christy Mathewson, and Branch Rickey. The ball players were told to put their trainees through an ordeal that included constant gas mask drills and immersion in a specially constructed gas-filled container known as the "gas chamber."

Commissioned as a captain, the irascible Cobb reported to the Allied Expeditionary Forces headquarters in Chaumont in October 1918, assigned to the Gas and Flame Division. He and his company had hundreds of soldiers to train. "Those that gave us trouble and didn't heed orders didn't last long," he later wrote, "for we weren't fooling around with simulated death when we entered the gas chambers. The stuff we turned loose was the McCoy and meant to train a man to be on *qui vive*—or else."[63]

One of their training exercises involved marching men into an airtight underground chamber. Once the troops were inside they were given a hand signal, at which time everyone was immediately supposed to snap his mask into position. Trainees were primed to be as alert and quick as possible. "I'll never be able to forget the day when some of the men—myself included—missed the signal," Cobb later recalled.

Many screamed and panicked when they caught a strange whiff in the air. Some stampeded toward the exit and became entangled in a terrified mass. As soon as Cobb realized what had happened, but only after he and many of the others had inhaled some of the poison vapors, he fixed his mask and groped his way to the wall, struggling to work past the thrashing bodies. Leading the mob to safety proved hopeless, and it turned out to be every man for himself. "When I staggered out and gulped in fresh air, I didn't know how badly my lungs had been damaged," Cobb later recalled. He emerged to find sixteen bodies on the ground. Eight men died within hours, and more became disabled over time. For weeks, a colorless discharge drained from his chest, and he was wracked by a hacking cough. "I remember [Christy] Mathewson (baseball's all-time greatest pitcher) telling me, 'Ty, I got a good dose of the stuff. I feel terrible,'" Cobb later said. "He was wheezing and blowing out congested matter."

Mathewson was subsequently diagnosed with "tuberculosis" in both lungs and died seven years later, at the age of forty-five. After attending his friend's funeral, a grieving Cobb said, "Big Six looked peaceful in that coffin, that damned gas got him and nearly got me."[64] But the ballplayers' experience with gas was largely downplayed: once the war was won, their service to their country had exhausted its publicity value.

The army's secret plan for the spring 1919 offensive called for a stepped-up use of poison gas that would have turned the fighting largely into a chemical war. The strategy included a series of massive attacks that would unload tons of mustard gas on German strongholds and dump an even deadlier payload of lewisite (which Fries called "the dew of death") on Berlin with the aim of annihilating everyone.[65] The methyl was packed into 155-millimeter shells and drums, each carrying from 350 to 400 pounds, that were intended for bombardment from airplanes. Edgewood's commander, Colonel Walker, the nation's leading chemical engineer, later explained:

> We had been working for some time on a device whereby mustard gas could be transported in large containers by airplanes and released over fortresses of the Metz type, and at last it was perfected, fully sixty days before the armistice was signed. Mustard has been found, for all-around purposes, to be the most effective gas used in warfare, because it advances comparatively easily and also because it is the most difficult to protect against. People used to think Prussic acid was terrible. Well, the Germans discarded the use of Prussic acid because it was too mild and used mustard gas instead.
>
> Our idea was to have containers that would hold a ton of mustard gas carried over fortresses like Metz and Coblenz by plane, and released with a time fuse arranged for explosion several hundred feet above the forts. The mustard gas, being heavier than air, would then slowly settle while it also dispersed. A one-ton container could thus be made to account for perhaps an acre or more of territory, and not one living thing, not even a rat, would live through it. The planes were made and successfully demonstrated, the containers were made, and we were turning out the mustard gas in the requisite quantities in September.[66]

Walker may or may not have known about the plans to utilize lewisite from Willoughby as well. During the war the plans were never publicly revealed, nor was there any debate about their legality or morality. Whether the Germans were ever warned of the threat, or learned of it by means of espionage, remains an open question, for according to Walker:

> They capitulated, and I am sure that a very big factor in that capitulation was the knowledge they certainly possessed of our gas preparations. What we were doing here was known to the German Government. They knew that when this plant was going into full blast their last hope was gone. They knew that if they had been able to make gas in even half the quantity we could produce here they would have swept over all France long ago. If there was any final argument to help them make up their minds it was our gas production.[67]

Some historians later contended that the Allies would not have used gas bombing "unless they had to," and noted that the published record of the Supreme War Council did not discuss possible use of gas in the spring of 1919.[68] It is unclear the extent to which German intelligence knew about or believed in the power of the Allies to carry out such threats involving gas. It's possible that such calculations by the German high command may have helped to explain why Kaiser Wilhelm II abruptly surrendered effective November 11, 1918.[69] In the absence of a clear explanation, however, many vanquished German combatants simply felt betrayed.

The human cost of the war was beyond anyone's comprehension. According to some estimates, it killed 8.5 to 19 million persons and wounded 21 million others, including 1.3 million in losses from the new horror of chemical warfare. Civilians accounted for as many as 9 to 13 million casualties, marking an end to "civilized" warfare.[70] One-tenth of Germany's entire population was dead. Although about 27.3 percent of America's battlefield casualties (74,779 of 274,217) were officially attributed to gas, the real numbers were much higher, as the government didn't acknowledge the thousands of delayed but premature deaths, such as Mathewson's, which should have been attributed to gas. Had the conflict continued, the war's toll from gas certainly would have skyrocketed due to the increased lethality of the weapons and the combatants' greater desperation.

By war's end, American plants were said to have shipped 3,662 tons of gas that had been loaded into shells and used by the American troops or their allies. The *New York Times* later reported that "while American gas was not actually fired in American shell against the Germans, American gas was used against the enemy and America furnished at least as much gas as she fired." The gas was made in the United States, shipped to France, and placed in shells that had been made in England or France. America also shipped 18,600 Livens drums loaded with phosgene, containing 279 tons of gas, some of which was also fired at the enemy.

The armistice left tons of deadly lewisite in anxious American hands. "What was to be done with it, now that there was no longer any occasion for exterminating Germans?" one commentator asked. Cleveland did not want the deadly stuff dumped into Lake Erie, and there was no practical way to neutralize it. Scientists estimated there was almost enough of the poison left to kill every man, woman, and child in the United States if properly administered. The ocean seemed the only option. After hair-raising transport by rail, 364 fifty-five-gallon drums of the lethal cargo were loaded onto ships and taken fifty miles out into the Atlantic. Dumped into the sea at a depth of three miles in undisclosed and unmarked locations, it was left to await its inevitable leakage.[71]

Although Haber feared he would be treated as a war criminal for having unleashed chemical weapons upon the world, a year after the fighting stopped he was startled to find himself receiving a Nobel Prize instead, albeit for his prewar synthesis of ammonia. One of his American counterparts, Conant, later observed, "To me, the development of new and more gases seemed no more immoral than the manufacture of explosives and guns. I did not see in 1917, and I do not see in 1968, why tearing a man's guts out by a high-explosive shell is to be preferred to maiming him by attacking his lungs or skin."[72] Nobody was ever prosecuted for war crimes involving poison gas.

Many of those who initially survived being gassed went on to suffer from debilitating wounds, both physical and psychological. An Austrian corporal, Adolf Hitler, had been gassed and temporarily blinded in October 1918, shortly before the war's sudden ignominious end, and the experience left him permanently scarred and embittered.

In Germany, the vanquished titans of the chemical and munitions industry managed to evade accountability. American scientists, on the other hand, especially the chemists, were flushed with success, believing they had decided the war's final course. The big American chemical interests had become supremely powerful. And people the world over had learned about the boundless lethal potential of poisonous chemicals and political powers that had displayed no compunction about using them against enemies of all types. Gas had proved itself to be a frightful weapon of war, and the real-life horrors of injury and death by chemical poisons had stripped gas of some of its associations with painlessness. The lethal chamber, which previously had been reserved for dogs and cats, now seemed much more familiar. Some saw in it more potential for experimental and educational purposes, although anyone who had been through any manner of gas chamber or gassing during the war must have come away with an abiding dread for its unpredictable terrors.

CHAPTER 3

DEVISING "CONSTRUCTIVE PEACETIME USES"

When the war ended, America shut down its poison gas plants for a time.[1] Most soldiers and chemists went home, and the military-industrial gas complex was largely disbanded. Army chief of staff General Peyton C. Marsh said he remained haunted by witnessing children who had been gassed to death. The secretary of war said he favored ending all chemical warfare activities. Amid the war's tumultuous wake in March 1919—the time when some commanders had expected to launch their most poisonous campaign and annihilate Berlin and other cities—the Chemical Warfare Service (CWS) was set to be dissolved and General Amos Fries found himself demoted to lieutenant colonel.[2]

But Fries and the chemical industry vowed to fight the dismantling of the precious apparatus they had worked so hard to build. They would not renounce their war gases, allow the valuable stockpile to be totally destroyed, or permit research and production to be discontinued. Fries called gas "the most powerful and the most humane method of warfare ever invented," and he insisted that the United States must retain the strategic advantage it had won during the war.[3] "What we need now," he wrote to one CWS veteran, "is good, sound publicity along lines showing the importance of Chemical Warfare, its powerful and far-reaching effects in war, and its humanity when you compare the number of deaths per hundred gassed with the numbers of deaths from bullets and high explosives for each hundred injured by those means."[4]

To spread this message, Fries encouraged many of his present and former subordinates to lobby Congress and write letters to newspapers. Behind the scenes, he worked closely with the chemical manufacturers and two of his friends in Congress, Senator George E. Chamberlain Jr., a conservative Democrat from Oregon who was chairman of the Senate Committee on Military Affairs, and Representative Julius Kahn, a German-born Jewish Republican of California, to fight moves to end his Chemical Warfare Service and cease production of the valuable poisons they had developed.[5]

Due to their efforts, despite overwhelming public opinion against gas warfare and strong political opposition from his own commanders, Fries and his allies somehow succeeded in gaining passage of the National Defense Act of 1920, which not only saved the Chemical Warfare Service from extinction, but also turned it into a permanent part of the army. The feat made Fries a legendary figure in military circles. Politically, he had become unusually powerful.

Fries publicly disputed notions that poison gas was any more inhumane or dishonorable than other weapons of war. "As to non-combatants," he wrote, carefully parsing his statements, "certainly we do not contemplate using poisonous gas against them, no more at least than we propose to use high explosives in long range guns or aeroplanes against them." As for the abandonment of poison gas, "it must be remembered that no powerful weapon of war has ever been abandoned once it proved its power unless a more powerful weapon was discovered." Fries argued that poison gas would never be abandoned or effectively stopped by any international agreement. Some nations would continue to use it. "Let the world know," he urged, that Americans would "use gas against all troops that may be engaged against us, and that we propose to use it to the fullest extent of our ability." Such a stance would form a powerful deterrent, he said, and "do more to head off war than all the peace propaganda since time began." He also rejected arguments that gas should never be used against adversaries that were not also equipped with gas. "Then why did we use repeating rifles and machine guns against Negritos and Moros armed only with bows and arrows or poor muskets and knives?" he asked. "Let us apply the same common sense to the use of gas that we apply to all other weapons of war."[6]

But Fries and his allies had to face other mounting obstacles. The 1919 Treaty of Versailles forbade the "use of asphyxiating, poisonous or other gases and all analogous liquids, materials, or devices being prohibited, their manufacture and importation . . . *in Germany*" (italics added), and President Woodrow Wilson and the International Committee of the Red Cross favored banning chemical weapons. When Republican Warren Harding swept into the White House in 1921, his administration favored a position at the Washington Arms Conference that would curtail gas warfare as well as submarine and aircraft attacks.[7] A survey of the American public found 385,170 votes for the abolition of chemical weapons and only 169 for retention.

To buttress their case, Fries and the chemical lobby argued that war gases and other poisons offered countless constructive domestic benefits in peacetime. Much of this perceived value lay in expanded industrial applications. Under Fries's leadership, the CWS publicly turned its attention to undertaking cooperative enterprises with various government departments to harness the fruits of wartime gas research in constructive, peaceful ways. Soon the Bureau of Mines was exploring means to introduce some of the benefits of its wartime knowledge into the mining industry. The Department of the Interior helped test gas masks for commercial use in refrigeration plants, firefighting, and other settings. The Treasury Department fumigated ships at port with HCN gas, and public health and agriculture officials employed deadly phosgene to kill rats and gophers.

The U.S. Public Health Service was especially supportive. President Wilson's final appointee as surgeon general, Dr. Hugh S. Cumming of Virginia, demonstrated a knack for politics that enabled him to get along with many different interest groups. A former Marine officer who maintained excellent relations with the military, members of Congress, leaders of the eugenics movement, the medical profession, and the chemical industry, Cumming was also a staunch believer in states' rights, white supremacy, and immigration restriction—and he proved a key ally for Fries. Their common beliefs converged. Cumming and his staff vastly expanded the use of gas to fumigate ships in all of America's major ports. (One of the most obvious problems posed by using hydrocyanic acid in that way entailed how to determine that the highly poisonous gas had been removed from all parts of the vessel, so as not to accidentally kill longshoremen or seamen.)[8] On his watch the federal government became the biggest single user of cyanide for fumigation purposes. Through the good graces of the Pan American Sanitary Code (1924), Cumming also got all republics in the Americas to require HCN fumigation in their ports. His agents carried the fumigation message throughout the world.

Although the war was over, the chemical industry was conducting additional research to devise alternate uses for its deadly war gases. Scientists were now testing them for every use, from exterminating pests to fighting fires.[9] Phosgene, for example, was already known to be useful in making dye, and the war experience had enabled industry to reduce its price from $1.50 to 15 cents a pound. Now chemical industry spokesmen said housewives could also use phosgene for a variety of other tasks, such as adding color to rustling silk or polishing the family's valuable crystal. Chlorine as well had many applications for cleaning.[10] Chemical scientists hadn't yet figured out any beneficial uses for mustard gas, but within a few years Fries would claim it was an effective tool against marine borers that were destroying docks and other waterfront structures.[11] He also proclaimed that a perfected gas mask would soon protect Americans from every known type of poison gas and prove invaluable for the nation's fire fighters.[12] The mission of the Chemical Warfare Service, he said, had changed; now the agency was simply doing "peace work principally."[13]

Fries especially touted the use of war gases for "insect and animal extermination." "We have given a good deal of attention to [the elimination of insects and other pests]," he noted in 1922, "and expect to give a great deal more to it in the future." Then he added, with obvious scorn, "The nearly four years that have elapsed since the close of the war have shown us that the human pest is the worst of all pests to handle."[14] During the war, the military had regarded the enemy as insects; now, during peacetime, it aimed to "wage warfare against insect life."[15] L. O. Howard, chief of the Bureau of Entomology, said the insect horde seemed from "another planet, more monstrous, more energetic, more insensate, more atrocious, more infernal than ours."[16]

Fries tried his best to build national support for his policies. He told reporters the military had used some of its leftover poison gas to kill rats in seaport cities and wipe out locusts in the Philippines; next it would wage war against the pesky boll weevil, which ravaged cotton in the South.[17] When Southern senators heard this, they rushed to insert funds for that purpose into the War Department's budget. (In fact, the boll weevil proved more resistant to the poisons than expected, due to what some researchers later ascribed to the insects' "apparent ability to suspend breathing more or less at will.")[18] Turning west, Fries also bolstered political support in California by pointing out that citrus growers were using liquid cyanide gas against scale and other bugs that had endangered their fruit crops.[19]

The science of pest control and the science of chemical warfare shared much in common. "Chemists, entomologists, and military researchers knew that chemicals toxic to one species often killed others," one historian has observed, "so they developed similar chemicals to fight human and insect enemies. They also developed similar methods of dispensing chemicals to poison both."[20] Fries also understood how to win funding from Congress by appealing to various vested interests.

By December 1923 the United States Department of Agriculture had become so concerned about the possible health effects of using hydrocyanic acid gas as a fumigant on fruits and other foods that it released a study reporting the quantity of the fumigant that was absorbed by various foodstuffs. Aware of the power of the chemical lobby, however, the agency didn't dare offer any conclusions about whether fumigated foods were safe for human consumption, saying only that such conclusions "lie in the domain of the pharmacologist."[21] Indeed, no government agency ever challenged the pervasive use of poisons in the nation's food and water supply and air.

In this void, the CWS propaganda campaign cited studies concluding that there were no harmful health effects from war gas—no tuberculosis or other respiratory problems related to exposure to war gases, even though thousands of war veterans were still suffering from just such maladies.[22] Notwithstanding the veterans' complaints, Fries kept insisting that "the after effects of warfare gases are practically nothing," and he adamantly denied there was any link between poison gases and respiratory disease or other ailments.[23] Alleged environmental damage from poison gas was also denied. (Years later, a scientist revealed that the results of the government's gas experiments were kept secret, "on account of the resultant damage to vegetation" and other effects.)[24]

Instead, industry spokesmen insisted how benign or even beneficial various poison gases could be, claiming that they would rid the world of dreaded diseases. Chlorine gas, they said, would eliminate the common cold and pneumonia; mustard gas would cure tuberculosis; and lewisite might be the remedy for paresis (the final stage of syphilis) and locomotor ataxia (an inability to control one's bodily movements).[25]

Some claimed that their research findings were backed by human experimentation. For example, Dr. Arthur S. Lovenhart, a well-known pharmacologist at the University of Wisconsin, injected sodium cyanide into a severely disabled mental patient and was surprised that the previously catatonic subject suddenly relaxed, opened his eyes, and even answered a few questions.[26] Lovenhart also conducted experiments using arsenic-based water-soluble compounds (such as lewisite) to treat patients with syphilis.[27]

In 1923 a prominent article planted in the press proclaimed that "poison gases invented to slay are just completing their first year's apprenticeship to the arts of peace." Unnamed sources reported that men who had worked in the poison gas factories during the war had become immune to influenza or other germs due to their exposure to hydrogen sulfide, chloropicrin, and chlorine. The War Department offered statistics apparently showing that soldiers who had been gassed were less susceptible to tuberculosis.[28] "Inhalariums," or gassing chambers where sick patients could breathe chlorinated air, became a new craze. Fries was photographed in one of these chambers, and even President Calvin Coolidge was convinced enough to receive chlorine treatments for a cold (he later said it had "cured" him).[29] Although New York health officials later minimized chlorine's ability to fight the common cold, Fries vociferously defended it, insisting it was a miracle cure.[30]

Many historians trace the beginning of cancer chemotherapy to the aftermath of World War II, crediting two pharmacologists in particular, Louis S. Goodman and Alfred Gilman, for using mustard gas to treat lymphoma. (Goodman and Gilman had been recruited by the Department of Defense to investigate possible therapeutic applications of chemical warfare agents.) But in fact, some important preliminary work leading to such chemotherapy had occurred earlier, during and shortly after World War I. By the early 1920s, Fries was already saying that medical discoveries from chemical warfare had proved a boon to the human race, and in some respects he may have been right.[31]

Gas's appeal seemed boundless, particularly in fighting crime. Fries got himself deputized to supervise a "gas battalion" for the Philadelphia police to handle disorderly crowds using tear gas.[32] Tear-gas devices, which some security operatives mischievously referred to as "lewisite," were rigged to bank vaults to deter robberies.[33] Later, as the crime problem of the Roaring Twenties appeared more threatening to the social order, gas advocates such as Fries gave more thought to dramatizing other ways it might serve as a deterrent.

While this was going on, a fierce industrial and political battle ensued over one of the world's deadliest and more useful poisons: cyanide. Hydrogen cyanide—the gas Barcroft had encountered at Porton Down—is a chemical compound with the chemical formula HCN. Discovered in 1782, hydrogen cyanide is a colorless or pale blue liquid or gas that is highly volatile, with a bitter taste and an odor like bitter almonds, although a sizable segment of the human population is not able to detect the scent due to a genetic trait. It is also extremely poisonous. A solution of hydrogen cyanide in water is known as hydrocyanic acid, Prussic acid, or "Berlin blue acid," due to its intensely blue coloration.

If taken by mouth in salt form, such as potassium cyanide, a person's stomach acid converts the cyanide to volatile hydrogen cyanide, often making it fatal if taken in a sufficient dose. Both the liquid and vapor are acutely poisonous if absorbed through the lungs, skin, or eyes. Massive doses can cause a sudden loss of consciousness, asphyxiation, and death from respiratory arrest. Medical studies warn that cyanide can cause salivation, nausea, vomiting, hyperpnea (hyperventilation), dyspnea (labored breathing), an irregular or weak pulse, anxiety, confusion, tachypnea (rapid breathing), vertigo, giddiness, stiffness of the jaw, neurasthenia, breathlessness, bradycardia (slow heart rate), arterial hypnotonia, polycythemia, hepatic impairment, and thyroidal hypofunction. Unconsciousness is followed by violent convulsions, protruding eyeballs, dilating pupils, foaming at the mouth, paralysis, and death.[34] Whether or not it also acts as a carcinogen has not been documented; hydrogen cyanide is generally considered not to have mutagenic properties and is not considered to cause cancer, simply because there have not been any studies to test its carcinogenicity.

Despite its dangerous properties, cyanide became highly prized by modern industrial society.[35] It was widely used in photographic processing, steel hardening, electroplating, pharmaceutical production, fumigation, the killing of birds and other wildlife deemed pests, and mining, in which it served to separate ores. Prior to the early twentieth century, the Germans had long controlled its production. By the eve of World War I, the world's appetite for it had become voracious. Then the war made it even more valuable. Both of the warring sides developed and used cyanide-based chemical weapons, although not on as large a scale as they did some other poisons. Cyanides were classed as "blood agents" because they attacked the body through the blood and interfered with the metabolism of all living tissues. As weapons of war, hydrogen cyanide, cyanogen chloride, or chlorocyanogen had proved relatively ineffective on the battlefield because it was difficult to achieve a sufficient concentration of the gas in the open air to consistently kill the enemy.

For many years there was only one cyanide manufacturer and supplier in the United States. Besides importing potassium cyanide from Germany, Roessler & Hasslacher had begun to manufacture cyanide from prussiate in New Jersey in 1894.[36] Although Roessler & Hasslacher was legally based in the United States and headed by Franz Roessler, it was actually a long-established German-controlled firm that had been founded by his brother, Hector Roessler, and was part of the German chemical concern DEGUSSA (Deutsche Gold und Silber Scheideanstalt) of Frankfurt am Main, which served as the selling agent for the German cyanide producers. In fact, Roessler & Hasslacher was DEGUSSA's American subsidiary.[37]

The sale of cyanide was largely controlled by an international cyanide cartel, which aimed to restrict the supply and thereby set a price high enough to ensure the desired profits for the established firms but low enough to keep smaller or new firms in check. Because of this system, the Germans largely dominated the U.S. market prior to the war, enjoying in particular a monopoly on the supply of potassium cyanide, which was imported from Germany. By 1921 Roessler & Hasslacher had discontinued its manufacture of potassium cyanide and taken up making large quantities of sodium cyanide. The raw materials used in its manufacture were caustic soda, anhydrous ammonia, and charcoal, all of which were produced in the United States.[38] As a result of Germany's defeat in World War I, however, DEGUSSA was supposedly stripped of its American subsidiary, Roessler & Hasslacher, along with its Hoboken plant and all other foreign shareholdings and patent rights.[39] Approximately 47 percent of the shares in the company were sold at public auction under the Alien Enemy Act. But Germans somehow managed to retain control.[40]

In 1926, it was revealed that Isaac Meekins of North Carolina had received a salary as a voting trustee of Roessler & Hasslacher while he was employed as counsel to the U.S. alien property custodian, Colonel Thomas W. Miller, when the custodian was taking over the firm's holdings. Meekins was said to have used his influence to get relief for the company and its affiliated holdings.[41] It was also alleged that Miller had been appointed to his position through the influence of the DuPont Dye Trust, of which his father-in-law was an officer, and that his administration, like that of his predecessors, was dominated by the Chemical and Dye Trust, which was controlled by the du Ponts. The alien property custodian, one congressional watchdog group reported, "cooperated in an effort to have one of the DuPont Dye Trust chemists made a voting trustee of the Roessler-Hasslacher Chemical Co., an alleged enemy concern which in this particular case would have given the du Ponts not only an insight into the business of one of their competitors in the chemical industry, but control over it. Happily this plan failed because of violent opposition, but not for lack of support given by Custodian Miller to the DuPont aspirant who appears to have been represented in the negotiations by Francis P. Garvan, president of the so-called Chemical Foundation, incorporated by DuPont attorneys."[42]

The mining industry relied on cyanide's ability to separate silver, gold, copper, lead, and other ores. Some mining had been conducted in Nevada and other parts of the Southwest dating back to the Spanish period, and much of the area's history centered on mineral discoveries and boom-or-bust mining camps. In the United States Roessler & Hasslacher's potassium cyanide was known to be of high quality, and since 1916 the firm had offered various grades of cyanide based on the sodium cyanide content.[43] Shortly after the war, in 1921, the Nevada Mine Operators Association was confronted with a high price from Roessler & Hasslacher, so it purchased the chemical from a different supplier at a lower cost, thereby saving the Tonopah companies 10 cents per ton of ore they treated, for a total savings of $100,000 in just a few months—a considerable sum in those days.[44]

Roessler & Hasslacher's new competitor, American Cyanamid, had been founded in 1907 and specialized in manufacturing a compound of gray granules called cyanamid. Consisting of lime, carbide, and nitrogen, it was made by blowing nitrogen through white-hot calcium carbide. Crushed, it was suitable for use as fertilizer, which accounted for three-quarters of the firm's business. American Cyanamid's manufacture of calcium cyanamide—which used a technology different from Germany's Haber-Bosch Process, required huge amounts of electricity, which was why the company located its plant at Niagara Falls.

Because cyanamid readily lends itself to conversion into ammonia that is used to manufacture explosives, Congress in 1916 appropriated $20 million for American Cyanamid to build a plant to make nitric acid, and America's subsequent entry into the world war caused the company to focus all its capacity on government ordnance contracts, producing aqua ammonia used in the manufacture of ammonium nitrate and sulfuric acid. In 1917 the company began to manufacture a low-grade cyanide from cyanamid of lime, for the treatment of previous and base metal ores—a product that soon became competitive with Roessler & Hasslacher's brand. Big mining companies began using it. The company also produced a liquid hydrocyanic acid used for the fumigation of citrus trees in California, and cyanogas, a fumigant, insecticide and rodenticide.[45]

There was a catch, however. Although Roessler & Hasslacher was controlled by the Germans, its product was manufactured in New Jersey. American Cyanamid's form of lesser-grade cyanide, on the other hand, was actually manufactured abroad, at Niagara Falls, Canada.

In early 1921 Roessler & Hasslacher appeared before the Committee on Ways and Means in Washington, D.C., and asked for a 33⅓-cent ad valorem duty on cyanide salts.[46] The California Metal and Mineral Producers Association petitioned Congress against the proposed import duty.[47] As a result, there was a terrific fight.[48] Some industry observers believed that if the Congress put such a duty on cyanide, the business would become monopolized by the German-controlled firm and its largely American competitor would go out of business. This, in turn, would raise the cost of fumigation for the California citrus growers and Nevada silver mining interests.[49] Supporters of the mining and citrus interests as well as American chemical interests waged a fierce publicity campaign against their German competitors, claiming that Roessler & Hasslacher was largely (48 percent) under German control. The advocates also complained that the firm's "Prussian methods in its business" were "disadvantageous to the consumers."[50] Stories about the California citrus industry noted how orange growers had recently changed their cyanide fumigation method to fight scale pests, switching from the use of potassium cyanide to the cheaper sodium cyanide.[51]

While this trade battle was going on, in early 1921 another "constructive peacetime use" was suggested for poison gas. The proving ground was Nevada, the sparsely settled Western mining state with a population of only about seventy-seven thousand. During the postwar boom buyers from Los Angeles had begun to invade the state to buy up the land, only 3 percent of which was privately held.[52] Mining interests controlled the state. Nevada had also established a reputation for progressive reform: it was the first state to adopt quick divorce, indeterminate prison sentencing, rigidly enforced prohibition, and was considered a relatively infrequent user of capital punishment. In 1903 the state legislature had required that all hangings be carried out in the state prison at Carson City. In deference to Mormon preferences, the lawmakers had granted condemned convicts the right to choose being hanged or shot, though only one man (a Montenegrin, Andriza Mircovich) had opted for the latter.[53] In previous years, fifteen states had at some point abolished the death penalty for a time, though only seven were still without a capital punishment statute in 1921. Since 1911 Progressives in eight states had wiped it from the books, and Nevada might have become another, were it not for some "humane alternative."[54]

In early 1921 Frank Curran, a former district attorney who was one of U.S. Senator Key Pittman's aides, suggested that lethal gas should be substituted as the "most humane" way to end life, particularly if it were administered when the condemned was asleep or sedated with a soporific drug. Curran claimed to have been influenced by the ideas of the late Dr. Allan McLane Hamilton, the famous alienist who had recommended such a method in his memoir published in 1916.[55] Curran took the idea to two assemblymen, J.J. Hart of Lovelock (R-Pershing County) and Harry L. Bartlett (D-Elko), hoping they would introduce the appropriate legislation.[56] Near the end of the legislative session, on March 8, 1921, Hart and Bartlett introduced Assembly Bill 230. It was favorably reported out of the committee and was approved by the lower house one week later. The next day the senate received the bill and quickly approved it on March 15, sending it to Governor Emmet D. Boyle, a Democrat who had been in office since 1915 and who was also a mining engineer from Virginia City.[57]

Boyle later said the bill's supporters had claimed that the lethal gas method of inflicting the death penalty had been officially adopted in France already, and that they had cited Dr. Hamilton's writings about it. (In fact, gas hadn't been used in French executions.) Boyle also recalled that the matter had been taken up with the National Committee on Prisons and Prison Labor, a group that said it was opposed to capital punishment, yet it had "passed on the lethal gas method as more humane than any other which had been brought to its attention." Although the world had recently undergone the horrors of chemical warfare, advocates of gassing claimed that the poor soldiers on the battlefield had suffered more because of low concentrations and other conditions, whereas a lethal chamber would provide highly concentrated doses in an enclosed space, thereby ensuring a quick and painless death. Upon receiving such assurances and seeing no one presently awaiting execution in Nevada nor any death cell constructed, on March 28, 1921, Boyle signed the Humane Execution Bill, making Nevada the first state in the world to require the administration of lethal gas to legally end human life.[58]

The new law required that a suitable cell be constructed for inflicting the death penalty by gas, and it specified that the warden, a competent physician, and six other citizens must witness the execution. The news wire reported, "It is planned that when the condemned man is asleep the air valves shall be closed and others, admitting lethal gas, be opened, life being taken without the prisoner awakening."[59] Several suggestions were made for ways to carry out the gassing when the prisoner was asleep. "It is anticipated the gas will be administered much as gas is administered to a patient in a dental chair or to a person preparing for a surgical operation," one local newspaper reported. "In other words, it will be a form of anesthesia, and the administrator will probably be an expert anesthetist chosen from among physicians or male nurses. Those who favor this method of dealing death declare it is absolutely painless."[60]

Nevada's innovation received worldwide publicity. An editorial in the *New York Times* commented, "The electric chair is not modern enough for the Nevadans, apparently, or else it displeases them in some way, and their law calls for the use of putting of condemned murderers to death in what is called in euphemistic terms a 'lethal chamber'—a room that can be made airtight and into which at will can be introduced through hidden conduits a suffocating gas."[61] Nevada's lethal gas approach provided further dramatic testimony in support of Amos Fries's vision: gas would act as a powerful deterrent to America's public enemies while serving as the "most humane" weapon of war yet devised.

Meanwhile, Nevada's cyanide machinations continued to be bound up in economics and politics. In May 1922, the United States Senate was taking up the tariff issue. Senator Reed Smoot, a Republican from Utah and a Mormon apostle who was strongly protariff, attacked Roessler & Hasslacher as being the sole agent of the German cyanide cartel in the United States. Smoot said the firm had made "unconscionable" profits from its sale of cyanide; however, he still argued for the 10 percent duty proposed by the committee on the grounds that without it the cyanide industry in the United States would be destroyed, and as a result Germany and Canada would control the American market. Then, Smoot said, he had no doubt that the Germans would force the Canadian company (American Cyanamid) out of business and impose ruinous prices on American consumers as it had done in the past.

On the other hand, Senator Key Pittman (the Nevada Democrat who represented Tonopah mining interests) argued that the proposed duty was in the interest of only one company and its subsidiaries, Roessler & Hasslacher, adding that with it the firm would charge "what the citrus fruit growers and the miners of this country can afford to pay." Pittman charged that two days before the United States entered the war against Germany, Roessler & Hasslacher's owners had transferred stock to German-American citizens in order to conceal the company's true German ownership.

But Senator Theodore Frelinghuysen, a Republican from New Jersey (site of Roessler & Hasslacher's headquarters), declared that Roessler & Hasslacher was now American-owned and therefore subject to tariff protection.[62] In the end, the tariff act of 1922 brought tariff barriers to new heights, guaranteeing U.S. manufacturers in several fields a monopoly of the domestic market. But the Senate, on the motion of Senator Tasker L. Oddle, Republican of Nevada, voted to make cyanide duty-free.[63] The Fordney-McCumber Tariff signed by President Harding on September 21, 1922, created an average duty of 14 percent on all imports, and an average of 38.5 percent on dutiable imports, but cyanide was an exception, which resulted in a considerable increase in imports of that material.[64] The tariff act created a chemical division of the United States Tariff Commission to investigate production costs and other factors in the competitive situation regarding various commodities, and some of the commission's surveys contained information about trade secrets and cost data of individual manufacturers.[65] The tariff exemption saved the mining industry a great deal of money and in the process benefited American Cyanamid as well as German interests. "The action on the part of the Senate is very gratifying to the mine operators of Nevada and the entire West," said the secretary of the Nevada Mine Operators Association.[66] In its aftermath, the purveyors of cyanide jockeyed to take advantage of the changes to come.

By the time the conservative Quaker lawyer and staunch Republican William Brown Bell became head of American Cyanamid in 1922, the company had already branched out to begin making cyanide from cyanamid, and it had also started to produce hydrocyanic acid, which would prove an especially important ingredient in the vulcanization of rubber. By the mid-1920s the cyanide end of its product line had helped to propel American Cyanamid into a period of substantial growth. One of the hallmarks of Bell's administration was that he provided little information to his stockholders or anyone else about the company's activities or revenue sources, while at the same time he studied his competitors' elaborate reports as a means of sharpening his competitive edge.[67]

By 1923 the alien property custodian had been confiscating German patents and German-controlled businesses in the United States, and Roessler & Hasslacher was under intense scrutiny that prompted it to cloak its German ties. In one of its most important expanding markets, Southern California, new cyanide plants were going up. One of these plants was started near Cudahy City. Its manufacturer was the newly established California Cyanide Company, a corporation chartered in Delaware in April 1923. The company was a subsidiary of the Air Reduction Company, an enterprise that sold oxygen and other gases, and which had been started by Percy A. Rockefeller, a nephew of John D. Rockefeller. The directors of the California Cyanide Company included a collection of East Coast and West Coast industrialists and bankers: Charles Edward Adams, a banker (and later a member of the Federal Reserve) who headed the Air Reduction Company; Samuel F. Pryor, the president of Remington Arms and a director of the German Hamburg-Amerika Line, who would later be called before a congressional committee to testify about his involvement with the IG Farben cartel; Colonel Leonor Fresnel Loree, the railroad tycoon; and Frederick W. Braun of Los Angeles, a prominent California businessman and developer who had long served as the West Coast sales agent for Roessler & Hasslacher Chemical Company and the Pacific R & H Chemical Corporation in Los Angeles.[68]

Deaths caused by the rampant introduction of poisons into so many sectors of American society were now and then reported, as when cyanide-laced mooring ropes cost seamen their lives, or when citizens inspired by what they read in the newspaper turned on the gas to commit suicide or laced their husband's coffee with cyanide.[69] But in an era before strict government regulation, incidents such as these were often overlooked, and they seldom resulted in any serious follow-up.

Fries and his supporters didn't seem to be troubled by the dangers chemicals posed. Instead, they railed against the "menace" resulting from a "rising tide" of nonwhite immigration. One of his former captains in the Chemical Warfare Service, Representative Albert Johnson, chairman of the powerful Committee on Immigration and Naturalization, led the charge in Congress to restrict the immigration influx. Like Fries, Johnson was a transplanted Midwesterner who had ended up in Washington state, and his politics were extremely conservative, nativist, white supremacist, and antisocialist.[70] Exclusionary immigration acts were enacted in 1921 and 1924. In 1921 China and Japan were portrayed as restless enemies of the United States, and fears of the "yellow peril" ran especially high in the Western states of California, Oregon, Washington, and Nevada.[71]

After Germany's defeat in the war, Fries focused his greatest scorn on those he considered America's newest threat—the Reds. Like Attorney General A. Mitchell Palmer, J. Edgar Hoover, and other anti-Communist zealots, Fries did his part in the Red Scare. Although the United States had signed the treaty at the Washington Conference on the Limitation of Armament, Fries also warned that other governments were secretly preparing poisonous chemicals for war purposes.[72]

In July 1922, at the same time that congressional agreement was reached on exempting cyanide from the Tariff Act, the War Department announced that the manufacture of poison gas for the army was being discontinued. Under the pact, however, limited quantities for research and development of gas-defense appliances would still be produced. The secretary of war directed General Pershing to sign the order shutting down the production of poison gas.[73] After the international treaty prohibiting the use in war of asphyxiating, poisonous, or other gases and all analogous liquids, materials, or devices, was signed, the U.S. Senate ratified it by a vote of seventy-two to zero.[74]

At the same time, General Pershing also issued an order granting officers the same right of self-expression as civilians and he encouraged them to exercise their civic duty. Fries used this newfound license to make speeches and write articles attacking pacifist organizations for being part of a worldwide Communist conspiracy. Even after later orders explicitly forbade such activities, Fries used his army resources to conduct a wide-ranging propaganda campaign against his political opponents.[75] The American Defense Society, the Lions Club, and other right-wing patriotic groups backed Fries's efforts, denouncing any critics as "disloyal" stooges of Moscow.[76] The National Council for the Prevention of War and other pacifist groups protested these allegations and denied they promoted Communism, but this didn't stop the printing presses and mailings.[77] Fries directed his office librarian, Lucia R. Maxwell, to prepare a detailed graphic using U.S. Army files that purported to show the sinister links between many of the peace organizations that lobbied against chemical warfare and in favor of the League of Nations and the Geneva Convention. Maxwell's widely circulated "spider-web chart" listed the League of Women Voters, the National Council for Prevention of War, the Women's Christian Temperance Union, and several other moderate groups as "Reds" who were secretly committed to international socialism. At the bottom of her chart she also included a polemical poem deriding "Miss Bolsheviki." The Red-baiting chart was printed in Henry Ford's newspaper as proof of the worldwide Communist conspiracy.[78]

Both the Chemical Warfare Service and the Military Intelligence Division of the War Department were instrumental in fomenting the Red Scare throughout the early 1920s. Aiding them were the Department of Justice, the American Legion, the Veterans of Foreign Wars, the American Chemical Society, and other groups.[79] Fries and his allies also lobbied against America's support for the Geneva Protocol, which sought to outlaw chemical warfare. He and the chemical industry adamantly opposed restrictions on America's chemical gas production.[80] Led by DuPont, Dow, and other large chemical concerns, the industry mounted a campaign aimed at defending gas warfare on practical and humanitarian grounds.[81] They also enlisted civic groups such as chambers of commerce, Rotary Clubs, and the Kiwanis. Together the alliance demanded continued funding of the Chemical Warfare Service, renewed government contracts and subsidies for the chemical industry, and high tariffs to prevent German and other foreign competition from challenging America's greatly enhanced chemical power. By and large, they got what they wanted.

The League of Nations at Geneva attempted to ban poison gas, and the Protocol for the Prohibition of the Use in War of Asphyxiating, Poisonous or Other Gases, and of Bacteriological Methods of Warfare, was signed in 1925, but it did not go before the Senate for a vote until late 1926. In the end, thanks to lobbying by Fries and others, the United States did not sign the Geneva Protocol.

CHAPTER 4

STAGING THE WORLD'S FIRST GAS EXECUTION

In order to serve as a deterrent and to demonstrate its humane killing power, Nevada's new weapon against crime would have to be proven effective, and that meant someone had to be executed. The opportunity arose five months after the enactment of the state's Humane Execution Law, when prosecutors identified a crime with all the makings of a readymade test case.

It occurred in Mina, a tiny copper mining boomtown gone bust, located about 175 miles south of Reno in Mineral County, not far from Toponah Junction. There on the evening of August 21, 1921, Tom Quong Kee, a seventy-four-year-old laundryman and nominal member of the Bing Kung Tong, answered a knock at his cabin door and was shot twice in the heart with a .38-caliber revolver. Within hours of receiving the report, Deputy Sheriff W. J. ("Jack") Hammill had sized up the crime scene, traced the footprints of two persons from the cabin entrance to a nearby spot yielding automobile tracks and empty beer bottles, and identified a Greek cab driver who had been spotted in the vicinity at that time buying beer for his passengers. Soon Hammill came to suspect two Chinese men who had been seen being driven toward Reno at about that time, and upon their arrival the pair were quickly apprehended.[1]

Law enforcement authorities said the killing was part of a wave of tong killings that was sweeping nearby Northern California. Most whites, particularly in the Nevada desert, knew very little about

Chinese-on-Chinese gangster violence.[2] At the time Chinese immigrants were experiencing intense discrimination, as the "yellow peril." The crime, therefore, fit the bill as a potential landmark capital case.[3]

Hughie Sing, aged nineteen, one of the pair nabbed for the Mina killing, had attended grammar school in Carson City, and authorities persuaded him to cooperate. Although he weighed only 105 pounds, he claimed to have been a member of the Hop Sing Tong and an underling in crime to an older and larger accomplice, Gee Jon.[4]

Gee understood little English, having emigrated from Canton around 1907 and having lived ever since within the confines of San Francisco's Chinatown.[5] Although the cops had no hard evidence against them nor any apparent motive, the Reno police chief managed to convince Hughie to confess and implicate his associate, which the youth did in damning detail. Afterward, the pair were transported back to Mina to be held awaiting trial. An intermediary from San Francisco, W.H. Chang, arranged for them to hire a local lawyer, James M. Frame, to represent both men (something that would not be allowed before American courts today due to a conflict of interest).[6] The district attorney, Jay Henry White (an active military official), and Sheriff Fred Balzar (who was also chairman of the Nevada Republican Party), mounted a withering prosecution.

Without question, race played a central role in the case. Many white Nevadans at the time harbored considerable prejudice against Asians, and the local press referred to the defendants as "Chinese coolies," demanding that the state make an example of the Chinese tongs from San Francisco who had brought their murderous ways to peace-loving Nevada.[7] Hughie tried to recant his confession, but his fate was sealed. After a brief trial, on December 3, 1921, a jury convicted the two men of first-degree murder. Judge J. Emmett Walsh sentenced both to death, making them the first defendants eligible for execution under the world's first lethal-gas statute.[8]

The special nature of the case, especially the required imposition of a new method of legal execution, ensured there would be lengthy appeals, and besides, no death apparatus had yet been put into place to carry out the gassings. Their lawyer moved for a new trial, but his motion was denied, after which he prepared an appeal in state supreme court, arguing that execution by lethal gas constituted cruel and unusual punishment in violation of the Eighth Amendment of the United States Constitution.[9] Whether the punishment thus inflicted was "cruel" was open to debate, a writer for the *New York Times* commented, "but that it is 'unusual' seems undeniable. Is it therefore unconstitutional? The counsel of the condemned Nevadans say it is, but the electric chair also was 'unusual' a few years ago, and yet it has come and remained with the sanction of the courts."[10] Until the courts could sort this out, their executions were delayed, pending the outcome of the appeals. In January 1923 the state court affirmed the convictions and held that execution by lethal gas was not cruel and unusual punishment.[11] To satisfy the Constitution, one commentator observed, all that was needed was for the gas chamber to be "modern and scientific."[12]

Frame filed another appeal in state supreme court, which was also denied. So he and his partner, Fiore Raffetto, applied for a writ of certiorari in the U.S. Court of Appeals in San Francisco, on multiple grounds.[13] But these actions, too, went nowhere.[14] As a last resort, the legal team presented a petition for a writ of error to Associate Justice Joseph McKenna and then to Chief Justice William Howard Taft of the U.S. Supreme Court, but they refused to permit the petition to be filed, indicating that the nation's highest court wished to wash its hands of the matter of death by lethal gas.[15]

Eventually the lawyers appealed to the state board of pardons to spare the lives of the two condemned men, arguing that there were mitigating factors and adding, "We feel the extreme penalty should not be exacted and think that commutation of the sentence to life imprisonment would fully vindicate the law and subserve public good and avoid the horror of taking human life by administration of lethal gas, a new and untried method."[16] To support their campaign they gathered more than five hundred letters of support from prominent citizens and civic organizations, including the League of Women Voters in Reno, and sent them in to the pardon board and newspapers.[17]

With Boyle gone from the governor's office in 1922, Nevada's new chief executive was another Democrat, James G. Scrugham, the former state engineer. His opponents called him "Gasoline Jimmy." Scrugham had served in the war as a lieutenant colonel in the army reserves. He was also one of the founders of the American Legion, of which he had served as the national vice commander in 1920, a position that had put him in close contact with General Amos Fries, Senator Key Pittman, and representatives of the American Chemical Society.[18]

Years earlier, one of Scrugham's political rivals had been acting governor Denver S. Dickerson, a fellow Democrat, Spanish-American War veteran, and former staff member at Leavenworth Federal Penitentiary, who represented a Colorado-based contingent in Nevada politics. Since

Figure 4 Putting the finishing touches on the rear of Nevada's new prison death house, 1924. Unknown photographer. Courtesy of the Nevada State Archives.

leaving the governor's office and later holding the position of inspector of pharmacies, in late December 1923 Dickerson had been serving as warden of the state prison in Carson City, where all of Nevada's legal executions were supposed to be carried out.[19] His predecessor as warden, R.B. Henrichs, had been openly opposed to capital punishment. But Dickerson was not an abolitionist. At least, not yet.

In January 1924, a third prisoner—Thomas Russell, a Mexican American convicted of murdering his sweetheart, a Native American girl named Mamie Johnny—was also scheduled to die by lethal gas within the next thirty days, unless the board of pardons acted to save his life.[20] Although the Humane Execution Law had been in effect for almost three years, Warden Dickerson had made no preparations to carry out a gas execution, since the law and the death sentences were still under legal review.[21] On January 7, however, Dickerson said he could have the death cell ready for the executions in early February. Although some details remained to be worked out, he said he thought all three men might be executed together, and he didn't anticipate any problems. He expected to prepare an airtight room where the execution would be conducted in full view of the assembled witnesses. Once the sentence had been carried out, the gas would be drawn from the

Figure 5 Workers at the nearly completed Nevada prison death house, 1924. Unknown photographer. Courtesy of the Nevada State Archives.

room and fresh air would be injected to enable a physician to enter and pronounce death.[22]

With the date of the pardon review fast approaching, the governor's office began to take the necessary steps to see that the law's requirements were met. On January 22 state officials announced that construction of the death cell was underway at the prison. Later it was revealed that five convicts had to be placed in solitary confinement—the "black hole"—after refusing to participate in the building of the death chamber.[23] Some said their leaders were two members of the International Workers of the World (IWW), who had been rounded up in the Red Scare.[24]

Nevada's history-making death house turned out to be extremely primitive: officials had simply converted the prison's forty-year-old barbershop for the task. The single-story stone building was eleven feet long, ten feet wide, and eight feet high. Merely a stone-and-concrete shack with a small tank and a tangle of pipes against one wall and an exhaust fan on the roof, it had a single glass window on each side and an oval one in the back, as well as two windows and a door in front.[25] The main renovation consisted of filling in noticeable cracks to prevent the poison gas from leaking out.

Figure 6 Nevada death house, front view, 1924. Unknown photographer. Courtesy of the Nevada State Archives.

Inside the sealed room, two shiny, high-backed wooden chairs with armrests had been positioned a couple of feet away from each other. They appeared to be almost exact replicas of the electric chairs used at Sing Sing, absent the wires, electrodes, and other electrical apparatus. In front of and between them, only a few feet away, stood a small metal device that resembled a mailbox on sticks—the spraying contraption that would dispense the poison gas.

State officials announced to the world that the agent of death would be a form of hydrocyanic acid (HCN), commercially known as cyanogen. A state spokesman described it as being "invisible," saying it would paralyze any condemned man's respiratory organs, displace all of the oxygen in his body, and cause instant and painless death after one deep breath. Witnesses would be spared any painful outcries.

The initial plan called for lethal gas to be piped from metal cylinders to the floors of two airtight cells. (From the start, the designers anticipated carrying out multiple gas executions at once.) Each cell was to have a glass observation window. The gas would quickly spread to all parts of the cell, rise to the ceiling, and eventually be discharged through a pipe that would be high enough to prevent injury to the witnesses. Three cylinders of gas and two cylinders of compressed air would be used. At the warden's signal five guards would open the respective valves, each with the option of believing that his tank contained the harmless substance and thereby saving everyone from potential feelings of guilt.[26]

On January 28, Frank Curran, the former district attorney who had written the Nevada lethal gas legislation in 1921, spoke out against the planned execution. He said the use of hydrogen cyanide gas would be as brutal as clubbing a man to death.[27]

On January 30, Major Charles R. Alley, chief of the Technical Division of the Chemical Warfare Service in Washington and an aide to General Fries, wrote to Nevada's attorney general to let him know that he was aware of news reports that "certain criminals" were slated to be executed soon by lethal gas. "As this is in line with the work of the Chemical Warfare Service," he wrote, "it is requested that a report of these executions, covering the kind of gas used, the method of its application, and the physiological effects as noted by the physicians in attendance, be furnished."[28] State officials quickly moved to honor General Fries's request.

As the execution date drew near, controversy continued to surround the case's racial aspects. The *Fallon Standard* said that Hughie Sing would not have been sentenced to death if he were white.[29] Racism also suffused many of the news stories, such as an Associated Press report that claimed, "Gee Jon . . . [the] Chinese tong gunman, looks forward to the death behind a wrinkled, yellow mask of oriental indifference."[30] Even the pair's own lawyer appealed for mercy partly due to their "racially inferior mental ability" that precluded their ability to distinguish between right and wrong. After weighing the evidence and appeals, the clemency board ruled to spare Hughie Sing's life, but not Gee Jon's.[31] The Mexican-American youth Russell was still expected to die as well, so it seemed that the first two persons gassed would both be nonwhite.

Once the pardon board made its decision, on January 27, Hughie was transferred from death row to a cell among the prison's general population and assigned to work in the institution's laundry.[32] On Gee's behalf, however, his lawyer was now reduced to trying a last-ditch series of pleas of insanity, none of which proved successful.[33] After weeks of frantic efforts to stop the execution based on his mental state, on February 7, 1924, Frame ran out of legal avenues.

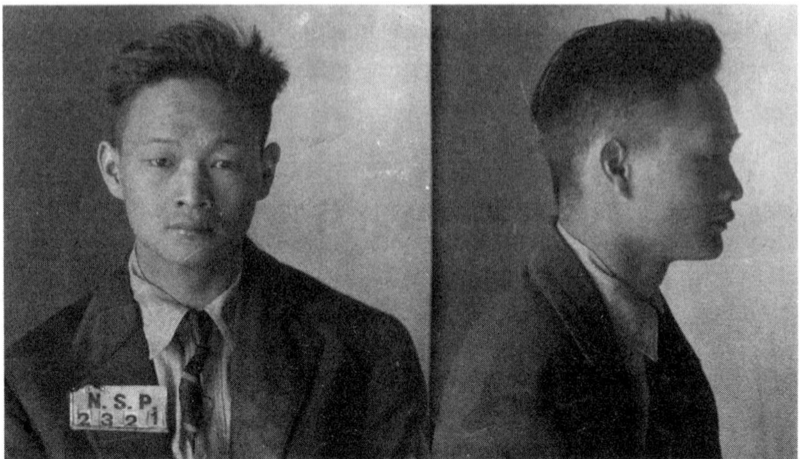

Figure 7 Hughie Sing, NSP 2321, who was condemned to lethal gas execution but spared. Unknown photographer. Courtesy of the Nevada State Archives.

Professor Sanford C. Dinsmore, the Nevada food and drug commissioner and a former member of the U.S. surgeon general's staff who had overseen the federal Public Health Service, advised the prison board as to what specific type of poison gas and apparatus should be used. The PHS had been using hydrocyanic acid (HCN) for years. Dinsmore said he selected HCN because "it is the deadliest poison known," as noted by no less an eminent authority on poisons than Dr. Taylor, the author of a leading treatise on the subject, who had said that, if respired, even the vapors of HCN would prove almost instantly fatal. Dinsmore said he had personally conducted "dozens of fumigating operations in this state for the extermination of bed-bugs in houses, weevils in warehouses, and the Mediterranean flour moth in flour mills," so he professed to be well acquainted with the cyanide gas.

At that time, the chemical companies were continuing to explore other applications of HCN. During 1923 and 1924, for example, the American Cyanamid Company conducted a series of experiments to test the use of liquefied hydrocyanic acid for the fumigation of grain elevators.[34] As of January 1924, the only company west of the Mississippi that sold hydrocyanic acid gas was the California Cyanide Company in Los Angeles, which had just started manufacturing quantities of the liquid for killing parasites in the California citrus groves. Dinsmore said that the gas, which was piped into heavy steel

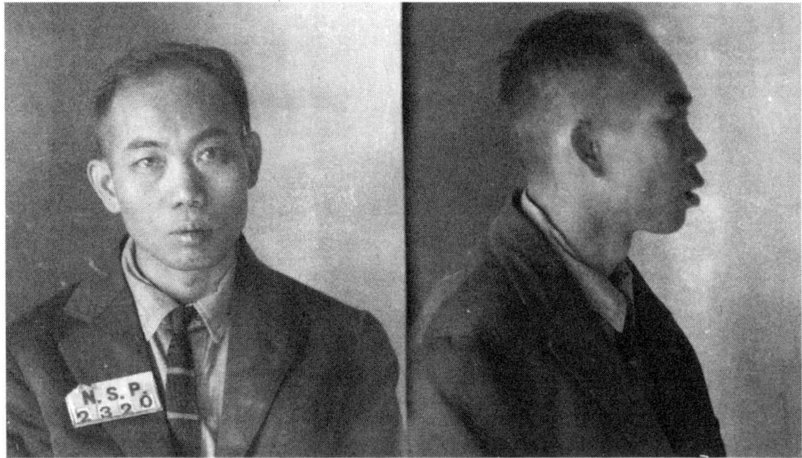

Figure 8 Gee Jon, NSP 2320. First person in the world to be legally executed by lethal gas, 1924. Unknown photographer. Courtesy of the Nevada State Archives.

cylinders about thirty inches high and eleven inches in diameter at a temperature low enough to liquefy it, had to be transported in the cylinders under high pressure. However, due to the cylinders' susceptibility to temperature changes, the company refused to transport them to Nevada, and no railroad or delivery service would bring the cylinders to Carson City. This meant the state would have to handle the transport itself.[35]

Dinsmore arranged with the company to purchase a quantity of the substance sufficient for multiple executions, and Warden Dickerson announced that a vehicle would be dispatched to Los Angeles to haul the death-dealing equipment. The cyanide cost one dollar per pound, and twenty pounds were purchased, although only about one and a half pounds would be used for the initial execution.

Authorities described the "agent of death" as a $700 mobile fumigating unit known as an "autofumer," which was equipped with tanks of liquid hydrocyanic acid. Officials at the California Cyanide Company of Los Angeles were quoted as saying the sprayer could kill somebody within thirty seconds, or in two to three minutes if the gas were dispensed directly from the tanks (the extra time would be necessary because of the time it would take for the spray to vaporize).[36] The company promised to send a truck driver's assistant with the electrically powered machine as well as a gas expert who would be available on site to ensure that the equipment was properly installed and in good working order for the execution.[37]

Warden Dickerson dispatched one of his most trusted staff members, Tom Pickett, on the dangerous mission to transport the gas from Los Angeles to Carson City. For company Pickett took along his wife, loaded the truck with several tanks of extremely deadly and partially gaseous liquid HCN, and carried them over rough and icy mountainous roads to the prison. It must have been a treacherous ride, but luckily for them the tanks did not explode or leak.[38]

State authorities reported that the War Department, on behalf of the Chemical Warfare Service, had requested that a competent observer prepare a report on the mode, materials, and effects, psychological and other, of the execution.[39]

Once the cyanide arrived at the prison, a chemical expert from the private sector, E.B. Walker, took charge of the poison. His orders were to ensure that the necessary precautions were taken to safeguard the executioners, attendants, physicians, and spectators.[40] Walker inspected the death house and checked its newly installed vents and exhaust system. He explained that the gas had been reduced to a liquid form that would be used during the execution. Once it was pumped through the death chamber and turned into gas, it would rise up, kill the prisoner, and then float away harmlessly over the prison walls via an outlet pipe, he said. Therefore, there would be no need for anyone to wear a gas mask.[41]

But others were not so sure. As preparations for the execution entered their final phase, four prison guards resigned from their jobs rather than participate, saying they "didn't want to take a chance on being mixed up in it."[42] Undaunted, Walker went ahead and conducted a "dress rehearsal" of the death chamber using a stray white cat and two kittens. Warden Dickerson estimated that the cats died within fifteen seconds after the liquid was sprayed into the chamber through a hole in the floor.[43] The tests also revealed a small leak in the chamber, which was quickly patched to avert the possible poisoning of the witnesses or staff. Although he still had his doubts about the chamber's safety, Dickerson had no choice but to proceed.

Guards described the twenty-two-year-old Russell as calm and apparently untroubled by his approaching death. Attended by a Catholic priest, he continued to maintain his innocence. Accounts pictured Gee as "very nervous," solitary, and brooding. He reportedly hadn't eaten for nine days and weighed a gaunt ninety pounds. Although authorities sometimes used an interpreter to explain the latest developments in his case to him, he often seemed confused or resigned to his fate.[44] One reporter quoted him as saying, "Gas allesame lope or shootem gun—me no wolly."[45]

The day before the scheduled execution, prison authorities allowed a delegation of reporters into the prison to interview both of the condemned men. Gee had trouble understanding their questions and had little to say. He said he had emigrated from Canton, China, to San Francisco about eighteen years earlier and denied being a member of any tong. Russell, meanwhile, clung to his story that his girlfriend had been slain by her own mother after a quarrel over money, claiming that he had fled the scene out of fear he would be attacked by an Indian mob.[46] Reporters described the other prisoners and guards as exhibiting horror and terror over the approaching execution, averting their eyes from the small stone barber shop that had been turned into a "death sepulchre."[47]

The night before the execution, Warden Dickerson received a last-minute commutation order from Governor Scrugham, saving Russell from death. But Gee was still doomed to face the lethal chamber.[48] Now his execution was scheduled for only thirteen hours later. Two Chinese friends from Reno and a cousin from Garnersville visited Gee in his cell and talked with him in low tones for about half an hour. Nearby Hughie Sing and Thomas Russell counted their blessings.[49]

At dawn on Friday, February 8, slate-colored clouds hung low over Carson City. The weather was humid and cold, with temperatures in the forties. In addition to the usual sounds of the prison awakening, the chilly air reverberated with the noises of approaching automobiles, shouted instructions, and clanging gates as waves of camera-toting newsmen and other participants converged on the scene with their engraved invitations. The excitement was growing. Finally the warden appeared at the door and said, "Come inside, gentlemen," directing the group of about thirty men to file into the hard-baked prison yard.[50]

The official physicians included Dr. Anthony Huffaker, the prison doctor; Dr. Joseph B. Hardy of Reno; Major Delos A. Turner of the Army Medical Reserve Corps; and others. Turner was an associate of Governors Boyle and Scrugham in the American Legion and acting as General Fries's official representative on the scene.[51] He already had caused a sensation before the execution by telling some members of the press that he wanted to revive the Chinese prisoner after the gas had been expelled from the room. Warden Dickerson, however, refused to comment publicly on such a plan, which he must have considered out of the question and bizarre.[52]

Clusters of visitors gathered around as prison officials imparted to the reporters a few precious bits of information: After acting extremely nervous and restless for weeks, they said, Gee seemed to have braced himself last night, his last night on earth. For breakfast he had eaten ham and eggs, toast, and coffee. The warden also warned his guests that the cold temperature might slow the gas inside the room, and they would have to be especially careful not to break the glass separating them from the poison gas.

Accompanied by two beefy guards clad in bulky overcoats, Captain Joe Muller headed over to Gee's cell to fetch the condemned man. Finding the prisoner lying on his bunk, Muller unlocked the steel door and stepped inside. Gee was dressed in prison overalls and an old green sweater over a faded yellow shirt open at the throat. The captain wasted no time with pleasantries. "Get up, Gee; it's time to go," he said gruffly. When the prisoner stirred but didn't rise, Muller tersely said, "Come, Gee; it's time."

Gee stood up and gulped, appearing unsteady. But when Muller said, not very sympathetically, "Take it like a man," Gee seemed to steel himself. He stepped into the corridor where Lieutenant Ducker and Officer Sheehan promptly buckled leather straps around his thighs and hands.

Then, with Muller leading the way and one guard grasping Gee by each arm, they proceeded outside toward the death house.[53] Soon they confronted the crowd gathered by the window. Upon seeing Gee, several witnesses shuddered at his small and vulnerable form, escorted by men twice his size. They noted the doomed man was bareheaded and rather shabbily dressed. A thin patch of jet-black hair swept back from his forehead, and his red lips and black eyes accentuated his prison pallor. Stubble covered his expressionless face. His eyes flickered over the crowd before he passed by. At 9:35 A.M. two guards escorted Gee through the open door and into the death chamber.

The witnesses grew more agitated. Although the warden had warned all of the visitors to stay behind a black line that had been painted on the stone floor outside the building, some of the correspondents kept pressing forward, scribbling onto sheets of paper that from time to time they would hand back to messengers, who would rush off to waiting telephones or telegraph.[54]

Gee gazed at the plain, unpainted pine chair and quickly sat down.

The guards immediately strapped him in, and he started to weep as they hurried out and sealed the doors.[55] The seconds had ticked into minutes. As the witnesses crowded closer to the glass, they spied him seated in the death chair facing the observation window. Everyone fell silent.

At 9:40 A.M. the silence was pierced by the terrifying hiss of the hydrocyanic acid that was being introduced into the chamber. Out of view from the witnesses, a technician had begun to spray a solution of the deadly liquid into the chamber from a small pressurized tank.

"The gas is turned on," said the warden, stopwatch in hand.

Hydrocyanic acid becomes volatile at 75 degrees Fahrenheit, but the air temperature inside the execution chamber was only 49 degrees, prompting Walker to bring in an erratic electric heater that had raised the temperature to only about 52 degrees. As a result, most of the HCN had not vaporized but was instead accumulating in a widening pool of liquid on the floor beneath the chair.[56] The witnesses' eyes flared wide to see what would happen next. Everyone's attention was focused on Gee.

"A startled expression appeared on his hitherto calm face," one reporter observed, "and he threw his head back, [filling] his lungs with the first of the gas to reach him." The faces at the window grew tense, as the witnesses could hear his labored breathing. Then his chin dropped to his chest. After a suspenseful moment passed he threw his head back and took another breath. Again, his chin dropped to his chest. The reporters were recording every movement they could detect.

Some spectators thought they began to smell the deadly gas, with its fragrance like almond blossoms, and a few of them lurched back from the window in terror, but the warden and the newspapermen and most of the physicians steadfastly remained at their posts. This time, two long minutes passed. "He's unconscious," someone finally whispered. But Gee's head pulled back and his mouth opened, showing his crooked teeth. His eyes rolled back until his pupils disappeared and his head jerked forward.

"He's dead now," one physician said, leaving the spectators to scour Gee's body for any movement, any sign of life. For an entire minute they saw none, but just when it appeared over, Gee suddenly raised his head again and extended it all the way back, causing many of the onlookers to gasp in horror. His chin dropped again and rested on his chest. The witnesses craned their necks to look, but nobody saw any stirring. The gas clouding the window made it difficult to see inside with perfect clarity, but it appeared that Gee had not ceased to move until 9:46 A.M. After that he remained motionless.

Dickerson cleared his throat and abruptly said, "The execution was a success, but the method of application is dangerous. . . . You will leave the prison yard, gentlemen."

Once the spectators had been removed from the area, at 10 A.M., the warden ordered the ventilator gate opened and the suction fan was turned on, while inside the guardroom the men talked excitedly about what they had just witnessed.[57] Under advice from his experts, however, Dickerson decided to wait until the liquid pool on the floor had evaporated before allowing anyone to enter. The chamber door was not opened until noon, more than two hours after the gassing had started, and the visitors were allowed back into the prison yard to witness the final act.

At long last, at 12:20 P.M., Captain Muller, clutching a jar of ammonia salts to his nostrils but not wearing a mask or any other protective gear, stepped into the death cell. He and Dan Ranean, an inspector for the state police, gingerly unfastened the straps, removed Gee's inert body from the chair, and lugged it to the prison hospital. At 12:30 P.M. they deposited the body faceup on a table, where it was perfunctorily examined by a ring of excited physicians including Dr. Huffaker, Dr. Hardy, Dr. Turner, and Dr. Edward E. Hamer of Ormsby County.[58]

Nobody wanted to get too close. Huffaker held his stethoscope to Gee's heart and listened as best he could. Although he and the others agreed that Gee was dead, Turner continued to insist he was still alive enough to be resuscitated and he wanted to inject the body with camphor to bring him back to life, "in the interests of science." But Warden Dickerson refused to allow it.[59]

Gee Jon was officially pronounced dead at 12:25 P.M. Seven doctors—M.H. Gray, Leo C. Owen, Harry C. Lang, Dr. Hamer, Dr. Hardy, Dr. Turner, and Dr. Huffaker—signed the death certificate.[60] No autopsy was performed because cutting open the body was deemed too dangerous due to the poison gas that might have accumulated within. This would make gas chamber executions different from electrocutions, for which an autopsy was legally required. Nobody saved his brain as a souvenir. Instead, the intact body was simply slipped into a plain pine box, and after a quick Christian ceremony it was buried in the cemetery behind the prison.[61]

Turner later startled some reporters by saying lethal gas represented "an extremely dangerous method" of execution because the victim might come to consciousness or be brought to consciousness, and also because a witness or observer could be accidentally killed (which he characterized as "an idiosyncrasy"). He also considered it "dangerous because the amount of HCN used would kill or suspend animation to the entire community, and as accidents will happen, any or all persons present are liable to an overdose."

Nevertheless, he pronounced it "a wonderful and humane way of execution."[62] "Even under the handicaps of improper equipment," he later said, the lethal gas method was the "quickest and most humane method of putting a human to death." Compared to hanging, where the doomed victim might suffer for seven to fifteen minutes after the trap was sprung, or electrocution, which was so shocking to watch, particularly if it took three or four jolts to finish the job, and even shooting, which sometimes didn't cause instantaneous death, lethal gas produced instantaneous unconsciousness and practically instantaneous death, so there was no chance of suffering.

Still, he acknowledged, there had been some problems in carrying out the world's first gas execution. First, the heater had failed to warm the stone execution chamber to the required 70 or 80 degrees Fahrenheit. As a result, "the lethal gas was liquefied instead of vaporized into fine particles. It also took a full minute and a half to pump the death chamber full of gas. With proper equipment and a specially constructed glass-lined chamber, death could be made both instantaneous and painless."[63] Turner also claimed that when Gee's body was removed from the death cell two and a half hours after his execution, it was still warm and lacking any signs of rigor mortis, which led him to believe it would have been possible to resuscitate Gee using a little electric shock, some warm blankets, and a pulmonator.[64] Turner later startled an audience at the Reno Lions Club by suggesting that Gee probably "died of cold and exposure."[65] He also suggested in his report to General Fries that all bodies removed from gas chambers in the future should be shot or hanged to ensure they were dead.[66] Many regarded his comments as bizarre.

Warden Dickerson commented as little as possible in public. "I am in favor of the lethal gas execution if spectators are not subjected to the death dealing fumes," he said.[67] However, Dr. Huffaker, the prison physician, conceded that future gas executions at the prison probably would require the addition of a specially constructed glass canopy to prevent any gas from seeping out and endangering the witnesses—in other words, a lethal chamber to be encapsulated within the death house.[68]

A correspondent for the Consolidated Press Association reported, "Those who witnessed the first lethal gas execution here Friday were unanimous in declaring that if they had to suffer capital punishment they would prefer to die that way."[69] The state's biggest newspaper, the *Nevada State Journal,* began its extensive coverage by pronouncing, "Nevada's novel death law is upheld by the highest court—humanity."[70]

But others took a dim view. Some critics complained that the new execution method "robs capital punishment of its horror."[71] The *San Jose Mercury Herald* warned, "One hundred years from now Nevada will be referred to as a heathen commonwealth controlled by savages with only the outward symbols of civilization."[72] An editorial in the *New York Times* noted that a white man had been spared at the last moment, "and the new method was tested on a Chinaman," adding, "That will need a good deal of explaining." The editorial concluded, "The details of the execution are not such as to prove the superiority of this innovation, and it obviously involves the possibility of some terrifying accidents."[73] The *Philadelphia Record* called it the worst piece of official barbarity since the dark ages, and the New Haven *Journal-Courier* observed, "Nevada is the first state to take human life by this means, and we hope it will be the last." Said the Philadelphia *Public Ledger,* "Nevada sought a way to make executions more humane. In her seeking she stumbled into new refinements and depths of cruelty."[74] The Women's Peace Union, a disarmament group based in New York, condemned Governor Scrugham for the execution, saying, "As opponents of all capital punishment, because we believe that violence and the destruction of human life are never justified, we strongly denounce the execution of Gee Jon by lethal gas. We expressly protest against this experiment having been tried against a defenseless Chinese."[75]

Nevertheless, the *Los Angeles Times* reported that Gee's death might have proved an effective catalyst for convincing the tongs to end their violent infighting. Two hundred worried tong leaders from eighty-one cities throughout the United States and Canada were said to be hurriedly planning a "peace" conference to discuss the matter in the wake of the Nevada gassing.[76]

Notwithstanding all of the hoopla, Dickerson later coolly reported his views to Governor Scrugham:

> This method of execution, while no doubt painless, is not, in my judgment, practicable. The presence of an expert in handling this gas is necessary. Prison officials should be capable, at all times, of conducting an execution without outside help, as that help might fail at the critical

> moment. The gas is highly explosive and must be kept at a low temperature to prevent explosion. It must be carried by private conveyance, as express companies refuse to handle it. Los Angeles is the nearest, if not the only, point on the Pacific Coast, where it is manufactured, and it would be a hazardous undertaking to transport this gas from Los Angeles to Carson City by automobile during the summer months, and its rapid deterioration makes it impracticable to keep a supply on hand. . . .
>
> The real suffering of the condemned, regardless of the manner of inflicting the death penalty, is endured before the actual infliction of the death penalty. I have been a reluctant witness to executions by hanging, shooting and asphyxiation; and in each instance the condemned was unconscious, to all appearances, immediately after the trap was sprung, the rifle fired, or the gas released. Execution by shooting is the most humane, because death by this method is instantaneous, while life remains for some little time when the other methods are employed.[77]

Efforts to repeal Nevada's lethal gas execution law proved unsuccessful over the following year or so.[78] In 1926 a triple execution was scheduled, and the chamber's two pine chairs were freshly painted and a new electrical steam-heating apparatus was installed for the occasion. But once again, the governor commuted two of the death sentences.

Then, as Stanko Jukich, a strapping Croatian miner convicted of murdering his sixteen-year-old sweetheart, was set to become the second person sent to the gas chamber, officials from the War Department expressed particular interest. Gas experts from the army's Presidio base in San Francisco took part in the testing, leaving no doubt about the deadliness of the hydrocyanic vapor, particularly since there was no longer any winter cold to impede the gas. Jukich was put to death in May 1926. Once again, details of the execution were reported worldwide.[79] This time the condemned man was pronounced dead two and a half minutes after the gas was turned on.[80]

Word that Americans had become the first to use the gas chamber to execute a human being flashed across the world. In Russia, the nation that had sustained the largest number of chemical weapon casualties during World War I, Leon Trotsky, the Soviet war minister, expressed concern about where the United States was headed. "Americans are trying these new gases upon their criminals, discarding the use of electricity as a means of killing wrongdoers," he warned. "Picture yourself rich and satisfied America sending to famine-stricken, revolutionary Europe whole squadrons of airplanes which threaten to rain these noxious gases upon our heads! This is no fantastic romance." Trotsky continued, "Soviet Russia, however, will not resort to such inhuman methods to gain its ends. War cannot be eradicated entirely; but it cannot be done by these extreme measures. It can only be done by the annihilation of capitalist society."[81]

News of the Nevada gassing reached Germany, where modern chemical warfare had originated. German politicians and law enforcement professionals followed developments in the United States with keen interest, taking special notice of American ideas about law, policing, and prisons. German criminologists, eugenics researchers, and other scholars often visited the United States and vice versa, and the Germans closely monitored American publications. International wire services and professional association newsletters passed the latest news back and forth across the Atlantic. German scholars such as Hamburg law professor Moritz Liepmann, Berthold Freudenthal of Frankfurt, and the renowned criminologist Franz Exner as well as journalists such as Paul Schlesinger, popularly known as "Sling" (from the *Vossiche Zeitung*), often offered incisive reports on American criminal justice developments and racial laws. German media in the 1920s often ran stories criticizing the harshness of American penal practices, such as the heavy use of imprisonment and capital punishment. As one leading historian of this phenomenon has pointed out, "Both the liberal Weimar Republic and the oppressive Nazi régime were keenly interested in the American criminal justice system, although for very different and not always consistent reasons."[82] The poison-gas execution would have attracted special interest because of its implication for chemical warfare.

In early 1924, the right-wing Bavarian radical Adolf Hitler was awaiting trial at the People's Court in Munich for his role in the failed November 1923 Beer Hall Putsch. For the last year or so, American newspapers had reported on his extraordinary ability to sway crowds to his will, his hatred for Jews, Communists, Bolsheviks, and liberals, and his penchant for many of the trappings of fascism that had been introduced by Italy's Benito Mussolini starting in 1922.[83]

The new political ideology held widespread appeal. Historian Robert Paxton has defined fascism as "a form of political behavior marked by obsessive preoccupation with community decline, humiliation, or victim-hood and by compensatory cults of unity, energy, and purity, in which a mass-based party of committed nationalist militants, working in uneasy but effective collaboration with traditional elites, abandons democratic liberties and pursues with redemptive violence and without ethical or legal restraints goals of internal cleansing and external expansion."[84] Another historian, Roger Eatwell, has suggested, "Fascist ideology used primarily rational arguments to hold that people were largely swayed by irrational motives. . . . People were to be made whole again by bridging the more individualistic and collective aspects of modernity."[85]

The romance of fascism quickly enticed some elite Americans who were steeped in various ideologies of racial superiority, capitalist discipline, isolationism and protectionism, and ultranationalism. News reports came out of Germany that American money from German-American anti-Semites was helping to fund not only Mussolini, but also the Bavarian-based fascist movement. The automobile manufacturer Henry Ford was singled out as a major Hitler backer.[86] The ferment in Germany attracted attention from foreign racists, including the American Ku Klux Klan, which founded a chapter in Germany in 1921.[87]

One of Hitler's friends who visited him in jail and kept him abreast of recent developments in the United States was Ernst "Putzi" Hanfstaengl, a six-foot-seven-inch German-American patrician graduate of Harvard University who was descended from a Union army general who had helped to carry Abraham Lincoln's coffin. Hanfstaengl's family owned an art-publishing house in Munich and belonged to the German and American aristocracies.[88] When Hanfstaengl wasn't entertaining his friend with his piano playing, he stimulated Hitler's imagination with stirring accounts about American skyscrapers, gangsters, and college football chants. Hitler had been gassed and temporarily blinded while serving as a dispatch runner at the front during the war, so he already knew that gas was an ugly, painful, and unpredictable weapon, and he disdained its use on the battlefield. He would have been keenly interested to hear about what the Americans had done in Nevada.

Hitler's trial began on February 26, 1924, only eighteen days after Gee Jon's execution. Convicted and sentenced to five years in prison on April 1, 1924, he was taken to cell number seven at Landsberg Am Lech Fortress Prison, where he proceeded to read everything he could lay his hands on, including piles of publications that his friends supplied.[89] "Landsberg was my college education at state expense," he would later say. Hanfstaengl often came by to translate and read to him from British and American newspapers. During his confinement Hitler also read several books about eugenics and racial supremacy, including the two-volume *Menschliche Erblichkeitslehre und Rassenhygiene* (The Principles of Human Heredity and Race Hygiene) by E. Baur,

E. Fischer, and F. Lenz, which collected references to Dugdale's *The Jukes*, Popenoe's *Applied Eugenics*, and work by New York blueblood Madison Grant. A number of works he read had been written by Americans, including Henry Ford's *The International Jew*, as well as Grant's *Der Untergang der grossen Rasse: Die Rassen als Grundlage der Geschichte Europas* (The Passing of the Great Race, or the Racial Basis of European History).[90] Hitler called Grant's book "my Bible."[91]

During his imprisonment Hitler commenced composing his own political creed, which he at first titled *Eine Abrechnung* (Settling Accounts) but later would call *Mein Kampf* (My Struggle). In it he calls upon Germans to restore their nation to greatness by overthrowing the Weimar Republic, removing the Jews from Germany, and defying the Versailles Treaty. From time to time Hitler would dictate some of these thoughts to one of his fellow prisoners; to Emil Maurice, his chauffeur and bodyguard; or to another close follower, Rudolf Hess.

On December 20, 1924, Hitler was released from confinement after serving only nine months, and a *New York Times* correspondent described him as "a sadder and wiser man" due to his imprisonment.[92] At first he stayed briefly with Hanfstaengl, who gave him a copy of Ford's autobiography, *Mein Leben und Werk* (My Life and Work), and then he headed up to Berchtesgaden for an Alpine holiday.[93] A friend made available a one-room cottage with a deck overlooking the Obersalzberg for Hitler to continue his dictation. A visitor approaching on the dirt path could hear a series of sharp verbal cracks like gunshots that sometimes continued in a long volley like bursts from a machine gun, coming from inside the cottage. On one of the walls inside Hitler had hung up a picture of his idol, Ford.[94] He paced the floor in a white shirt and lederhosen, barking out orders and sometimes swinging a dog whip to punctuate his phrases.[95] Hess hunched over a Remington typewriter, taking down Hitler's words.

"The spider was slowly beginning to suck the blood out of the people's pores," Hitler said. "The Jewish doctrine of Marxism" rejects the "aristocratic principle of Nature. . . . It is Jews who govern the stock exchange forces of the American Union. . . . [O]nly a single great man, Ford, to their fury, still maintains full independence." In another key passage, Hitler said, "If at the beginning of the War and during the War, twelve or fifteen thousand of these Hebrew corrupters of the people had been held under poison gas, as happened to hundreds of thousands of our very best German workers in the field, the sacrifice of millions at the front would not have been in vain." Decades later, a historian of the Holocaust, Lucy S. Dawidowicz, would wonder about this statement: "Did the idea of the Final Solution originate in this passage, germinating in Hitler's subconscious for some fifteen years before it was to sprout into practical reality?" she asked.[96]

Another biographer would write, "Hitler's concept of concentration camps as well as the practicality of genocide owed, so he claimed, to his studies of English and United States history. He admired the camps for Boer prisoners in South Africa and for the Indians in the Wild West, and often praised to his inner circle the efficiency of America's extermination—by starvation and uneven combat—of the red savages who could not be tamed by captivity."[97] Hitler learned about the American enslavement of blacks and Jim Crow laws enforcing racial segregation, about the shipment of Native Americans to faraway prisons via boxcars, and recent court rulings upholding the involuntary sterilization of the unfit. *Mein Kampf* also displayed Hitler's "keen familiarity with the recently passed U.S. National Origins Act, which called for eugenic quotas," another historian has noted.[98]

Historians have not yet turned up any evidence that Hitler's thinking was influenced by the first gas execution, which would have been in the news during his life-changing trial, imprisonment, and writing of *Mein Kampf*. But it was then, during the crucial period of 1924 and 1925, that the seeds of some of Hitler's most genocidal ideas took root.

During the same period, in the years immediately following the Nevada gassing, several delegations of German officials, criminologists, and legal scholars toured the American penal system, closely inspecting its prison conditions and methods of punishment and exchanging information with their American counterparts. Those results, too, were widely circulated in Germany. So it is likely that some Germans may have brought back news about the Nevada gassing. Executives of certain German chemical companies must have also noted the news from Nevada. After all, cyanide was their business.

CHAPTER 5

"LIKE WATERING FLOWERS"

In the few years following Gee's and Jukich's executions, Nevada officials were in no hurry to gas another prisoner. Doing it right would require extensive improvements.

In 1929 prison officials tore down the original death house and built a more elaborate structure using convict labor. The new stone and cement death house contained two cells, each facing a nine-foot corridor and meant to hold a condemned prisoner who was awaiting execution. Each cell was equipped with a toilet, washstand, and steel bed. The building also had a space for guards. The building was steam-heated and equipped with a shower and hot- and cold-water faucets. A separate room housed the execution equipment.

In response to the safety concerns posed by the first lethal gassing, the designers had devised a sealed compartment to fit inside the building, as Dr. Huffaker had recommended. It measured seven by eight by nine feet and had a double-paned window looking into the chamber on the east that measured ninety inches; a window on the south extended for forty-nine inches. Movement to and from the chamber was through a great wooden door that resembled a refrigerator door and was made to be airtight, like all of the chamber's apertures. Inside the chamber, two large wooden chairs resembling electric chairs without the wires were bolted to the floor, with space for a third chair if necessary, indicating that Nevada was prepared to carry out multiple executions.[1]

The double-paned windows of the sealed gas chamber represented a radical departure from an open-air public gallows or hanging tree. It also meant the witnesses would occupy a closer vantage point than they did in their pewlike benches at Sing Sing and other electrocution sites. The glass would serve several important functions. First, it would encapsulate the condemned prisoner and seal in the poison gas so that it could better work its lethal magic. Second, it would keep the deadly gas safely away from the staff and witnesses. Third, it would permit the witnesses and staff to observe the condemned as he or she succumbed to death. Fourth, it would eliminate or reduce the witnesses' experience of any unpleasant smells or sounds associated with the killing—no sizzling, excremental stench, gasps, gurgles, or sighs. The glass established distance between the doomed and the audience while at the same time providing the illusion of transparency that would satisfy the demands of democracy and the standards of modern civilization, decency, and humane killing. It served to contain the pain of dying and block the pain of execution. All that was left was the visual impression.

Given all of the problems with employing liquid cyanide and the crude gas-delivery system used in the first execution, Nevada authorities tried to be more careful in selecting the type of lethal gas they would employ in future executions. In this respect the federal government proved helpful. Under Surgeon General Cumming, the United States Public Health Service—a branch of the U.S. uniformed services, organized on a military model and closely tied to the armed forces—conducted extensive field tests to investigate different types of cyanide gas. There were several options.

The newest and most potent form of cyanide gas in the United States came from Germany. In 1922 the German firm Deutsche Gold und Silber Scheideanstalt (DEGUSSA) had perfected a process for packing volatile hydrogen cyanide into tins filled with absorbent pellets, for use as a fumigant. An ingredient such as sulfuric acid or oxalic acid could be added to the hydrocyanic acid in order to prevent the latter from decomposing. This agent stabilized the chemical until the airtight tins were opened, at which point the contents vaporized upon exposure to the atmosphere and in a short time blocked the transfer of oxygen to any organism in the vicinity. The empty tin could later be thrown away without further precautions. The product was called Zyklon. It amounted to a major breakthrough in insecticides and enjoyed immediate success as a fumigant, though DEGUSSA earned more through licensing the technology than through direct sales revenue, given the limited demand for it within Germany at the time.[2] Walter Heerdt of

Frankfurt am Main, who before the war had worked for Roessler & Hasslacher in the California fumigation tents, had applied for a patent with the U.S. Patent Office on June 9, 1923, and the patent was received on July 22, 1924, shortly after Gee's execution.[3]

A version of this product known as Zyklon-B, consisting of a carrier of kieselguhr impregnated with liquid hydrocyanic acid and a volatile irritant, was sold through Deutsche Gesselschaft für Schädlingsbekämpfung, or the German Pest Control Company (DEGESCH), the firm that had emerged in 1919 out of an earlier unit in the War Ministry and which Haber had used to conduct insecticide research. DEGESCH, which was part of DEGUSSA and a subsidiary of IG Farben, licensed two German companies for the manufacture and distribution of Zyklon. Prior to 1931, Zyklon was sold in the United States by Roessler & Hasslacher, but the company may have been reluctant to make it available for U.S. executions.[4]

In 1931 American Cyanamid would reach an agreement with DEGESCH to divide the world market for Zyklon-B.[5] Americans would use a lot of it—so much so that during the 1920s and '30s the Germans derived most of their profits from Zyklon-B's licensing fees in the United States.[6] The Americans found all sorts of uses for Zyklon. Under Surgeon General Cumming's leadership, the federal Public Health Service (PHS) had spearheaded the use of potent pesticides to "delouse" ships and prisons. (A few years later the PHS would commence its infamous forty-year-long Tuskegee syphilis experiment on black sharecroppers under Cumming's successor, Surgeon General Taliaferro Clark.) Starting in the late 1920s, American public health officials initiated one of their most shocking uses of Zyklon insecticide. A PHS officer in El Paso, Texas, J.R. Hurley, ordered Zyklon to be administered to cleanse tens of thousands of Mexicans who were arriving in the United States from Juárez.[7] Officials and the news media seemed oblivious to the attendant public health consequences of spraying the clothes of incoming Mexicans with the deadly gas at the Santa Fe Bridge. At the time, the *El Paso Herald* noted approvingly, "Hydrocyanic acid gas, the most poisonous known, more deadly even than that used on the battlefields of Europe, is employed in the fumigation process."[8]

Chemical company executives in Germany followed these developments very closely, since it had obvious commercial ramifications. Dr. Gerhard Peters of DEGESCH of Dessau, considered the world authority on Zyklon and its biggest promoter, authored numerous articles in scientific and trade journals about the virtues of Zyklon for preventing disease, especially typhus. Peters happily cited the Americans' use of the poison on immigrants and circulated photographs showing what the Americans were doing with his pet product.[9] (After World War II, Peters would be convicted in war crimes trials; in 1949 he was sentenced to five years for complicity in the extermination of the Jews.)

From August 1929 to February 1930, officers of the Public Health Service carried out experiments at the San Francisco Quarantine Station, Angel Island, California, a facility that processed many Asian immigrants. These experiments were conducted in a tightly sealed and unheated room measuring approximately five hundred cubic feet. The room adjoined a laboratory, and apertures were arranged so that live subjects or chemicals could be placed in the room without opening the door. Through a window in the door the researchers could observe the effect of the gas upon the subjects, which in these experiments were roaches. The roaches were kept in tiny wooden cages with screened sides, measuring six by four by four inches, with anywhere from two to two hundred roaches in each cage.

Different chemicals used for fumigation were administered to the imprisoned creatures. One combination consisted of straight hydrocyanic acid gas, generated from sodium cyanide, sulfuric acid, and water; another was hydrocyanic acid and cyanogen chloride gas generated from a mixture of sodium cyanide, sodium chlorate, hydrochloric acid, and water; a third involved liquid hydrocyanic acid with 10 percent chloropicrin; another was liquid hydrocyanic acid with 20 percent cyanogen chloride, or liquid hydrocyanic acid with 5 percent chloropicrin as a warning agent; and the last was Zyklon-B, which consisted of "an earthy substance impregnated with liquid hydrocyanic acid and marketed at present with five per cent chloropicrin as a warning gas." In thirteen tests Zyklon-B in the proportion of sixty grams per one thousand cubic feet for one hour of exposure was found to be the most effective in killing all of the subjects. The researchers also reported that Zyklon was effective at both warmer temperatures and temperatures close to freezing.[10]

Federal officials went to some lengths to extol the virtues of Zyklon. "The past 20 years has seen both a tremendous increase in the use of fumigation for the destruction of vermin on ships and great improvements in fumigation methods," a publicly released Public Health Service report of July 24, 1931, announced. "In both cases the advances are due to the introduction of hydrocyanic acid as a fumigant. Leaving the cumbersome, laborious, and time-consuming sulphur fumigation, we have passed through the method of generating HCN, with its still cumbersome apparatus and paraphernalia, through the period of liquid HCN, complicated by the difficulty of transporting so dangerous a material, and have arrived at the exceedingly simple procedure of knocking a hole in a can of Zyklon, pouring the contents down the hold, and throwing the can overboard."[11] Zyklon could simply be dumped through an opening into an enclosed space to effectively kill the vermin inside.

Another PHS report of the period noted:

> For some time the American Cyanamid Co., of New York, has been endeavoring to develop a practical means of measuring small doses of "solid type" cyanide products for use in fumigating super-structure compartments on ships. The New York Quarantine Station has cooperated with representatives of this company by suggesting possible lines of development and by testing containers and material. The selection of a porous material seems undoubtedly influenced by the growing popularity of Zyklon, and with the HCN discoids the difficulty of measuring small doses required for use in fumigating small compartments has apparently been overcome. This has been done by developing a product, representing HCN in a solid form, in units, each unit carrying a definite and relatively small amount of fumigant.[12]

Although the PHS reports referred only to bugs, researchers realized that the findings had other implications—particularly ramifications for human beings who might be exposed to the poison. Scientists had become increasingly aware that cyanide was actually *more effective* on warm-blooded animals such as human beings than on insects, because vertebrates carry oxygen in their blood via hemoglobin, whereas insects do not. In humans, cyanide was also absorbed through the lungs, gastrointestinal tract, skin, and especially the mucous membranes and the eyes. Unprotected exposure and breathing of the hydrogen cyanide gas in an enclosed space therefore appeared especially deadly to people. However, gathering proof of that fact would have to be left to prison authorities.

The government reports about the killing power of Zyklon and other forms of hydrocyanic acid were widely distributed, with some copies going to its officers who were posted in Germany and other foreign countries, and others going to foreign and domestic company executives. PHS officials and their foreign counterparts also traveled back and forth between Europe and the United States, and the military and commercial implications of the tests guaranteed that there was no doubt that German chemical executives knew about the American tests involving Zyklon and other poisons. Every public health official in charge of American prison operations also received a copy of the reports.

Zyklon contained a lacrimatory warning agent of chloropicrin or cyanogen chloride, which acted as an irritant to cause tears and other discomfort to prevent unwanted death from the lethal gas. This use of chloropicrin as a warning agent was invented by Hans Lehrecke of Frankfurt am Main in 1925 and assigned to Roessler & Hasslacher of New York by U.S. Patent 1,786,623 on December 30, 1930. But such warning agents would be considered counterproductive for executions, both because the irritants caused unwanted discomfort and suffering and because they did not lend themselves as neatly to the execution ritual. One of the chief selling points of cyanide gas as an execution tool was that it was supposed to kill quickly, without warning or pain. Its planners did not want witnesses to report otherwise. Hence Zyklon did not appear well suited as an execution gas. (In Nazi Germany, DEGESCH would later manufacture Zyklon without the troublesome warning agent, thereby overcoming this obstacle and making the deadly agent less detectible to humans.)

Fritz Haber had established a rule in inhalation toxicology that stated: $C \div T = \text{constant}$, meaning that identical products of concentration of an agent in air (C) and duration of exposure (T)—the $C \div T$ product—will yield an identical biological response. Based on his research under Haber during World War I, his assistant Ferdinand Flury determined that the value of $C \div T$ for hydrogen cyanide depended upon its concentration. As an outgrowth of Haber's law, Flury in 1921 had published the equation:

$$g/G = Z$$

with g denoting the amount of poison taken up, G the body weight of the experimental animal, and Z the number where a certain effect (for example, death) occurred. As far as the inhaled poison was concerned, wrote Flury, "It is possible to define g as a product of three factors: the number of milligrams of the poison present in one cubic meter of inspired air (C), the number of minutes (T) during which air with the concentration C of the poison is inhaled, and finally A, expressed in cubic meters, the volume inhaled by the animal per minute."

According to Flury's experiments, it was possible to use the equations he and Haber had developed to compare with reasonable accuracy the effects of different toxic inhalants. Based on their varying concentrations and breathing times, not all toxic war gases had constant effects, with the exception of hydrocyanic acid. But HCN did, and this made it particularly suitable for executions as far as the American prison authorities were concerned.

Flury described an experiment he conducted involving hydrocyanic acid. As explained by a scientist writing in 1999:

> Originally, paper bags filled with sodium or potassium cyanide were placed beside vats filled with dilute sulfuric acid. A technician then emptied the contents of the bags into the sulfuric acid while working his way towards the exit of the room. The procedure was obviously hazardous, and so better methods had to be developed. In such an improved process, hydrocyanic acid and a strong irritant, for example xylilbromide, were bound to an inert carrier (infusorian earth) and kept within tin cans. When the cans were opened and the material dispersed onto the floor of a room, both the cyanide and the irritant evaporated, the irritant serving as a warning sign for the presence of the lethal gas. The process was called the "Zyklon system." It was later commercialized and several companies were licensed to manufacture it.[13]

Thus it was evident in the chemical field that although Zyklon may not have been ideal for use as an execution gas in American prisons due to its irritating warning agent, other forms of hydrocyanic acid could be better suited. Dipped by string into a mixture of sulfuric acid and water, as part of the established "bucket" or "pot" method, a gauze-wrapped pouch of sodium cyanide or potassium cyanide could produce the lethal agent with manageable and predictable results.

So far, no records have turned up to document why prison authorities opted against the more commonly available sodium cyanide. However, given the widespread use of that material in fumigation, the companies involved may not have wanted to have their product identified in the public mind as being highly lethal to humans. Instead, the decision makers may have preferred to utilize a form of cyanide that was already known to be lethal; indeed, the newspapers had long reported it had figured in many suicides and murders. And besides, potassium cyanide was not presently manufactured in the United States.

As it would turn out, potassium cyanide eggs would prove to be the type of cyanide used exclusively in American executions from 1930 onward.

The late 1920s and early '30s witnessed some intense jockeying among the major chemical firms for more control over the world cyanide market, sometimes pitting German interests against American and British ones. William Bell, whom *Fortune* magazine described as "the precise, unobtrusively autocratic gentleman" who had guided American Cyanamid through its most prosperous period of growth to become America's fourth-largest chemical company, was one of industry's leading opponents of the New Deal and a staunch supporter of the economic policies of Mussolini and Hitler. He further expanded the firm's business into other cyanide-related products, including cyanogas calcium cyanide for use as a rodenticide and insecticide.[14] Bell also entered into agreements with the international cartel, doing business with the German dye trust controlled by IG Farben. Indeed, during World War II American Cyanamid would face federal prosecution for allegedly conspiring with the Germans to suppress competition and monopolize the manufacture of dyestuffs, including cyanide.[15]

In 1930 DuPont, the immensely powerful American corporation, purchased Roessler & Hasslacher. DuPont had dominated U.S. gunpowder sales for more than a century, earning the moniker "merchant of death"; it was also America's leading chemical company and a major producer of synthetic rubber and cars. Prior to 1926 DuPont was run by the U.S. industrialist Irénée du Pont, a strong supporter of eugenics, right-wing political groups, and IG Farben. In 1934 he would help lead an attempted coup d'etat against President Franklin Roosevelt—a plot that was exposed and short-circuited, but never prosecuted, even though it amounted to high treason and involved plans to kidnap and murder the president and subvert the Constitution. His equally conservative brother, Lammot du Pont Jr., succeeded him as president in 1926 and guided the company through the turbulent 1930s. The du Ponts were not the only leading capitalists involved in the coup conspiracy; they were joined by representatives from J.P. Morgan, General Motors (which they controlled), and other oil, chemical, and pharmaceutical interests, as well as such well-known politicians as National Democratic Party chairman John Raskob and former New York governor Al Smith.[16] But as happened with so many other investigations into the company's misdeeds, the du Ponts managed to evade criminal accountability.

DuPont said it had purchased Roessler & Hasslacher "primarily to ensure a steady supply of raw materials for the manufacture of dyes and tetraethyl lead." The acquisition also provided the company with high-grade cyanide for insecticides and other uses.[17] One of its products was "cyanegg," briquettes or egg-shaped pellets of high-grade (96–98 percent) sodium cyanide the size of pigeon eggs that were used to generate hydrocyanic acid gas for the fumigation of flour mills.[18]

Roessler & Hasslacher had long produced cyanide eggs for DEGUSSA, using the Castner-Kellner process, during which high-test sodium cyanide was produced by reacting sodium, glowed charcoal, and dry ammonia gas to form sodamide, which was converted to cyanamide before then being converted to cyanide with charcoal. (Cyanamide or cyanamid is an amide of cyanogen, a white, caustic, acidic crystalline compound.) In 1926, however, the American chemist James Cloyd Downs invented for DuPont a new process for the commercial preparation of sodium directly from salt, which proved a less expensive way to manufacture cyanide. Shortly after DuPont became a major producer of high-grade cyanide, which held all kinds of industrial applications, it would bolster its position by coming out in 1932 with a new synthetic process for making hydrogen cyanide.

Starting in the early 1930s, the giant chemical firms—DuPont, American Cyanamid, IG Farben, DEGUSSA, and Britain's Imperial Chemical Industries (ICI) and the German-controlled London Fumigation Company—would begin to play the cyanide cartel game for several years, enmeshed so tightly that it was difficult to tell them apart.[19] In 1934 they reached a patent and processes accord (amended in March 1935) concerning research in cyanides, formaldehyde, and derivatives. The 1935 Farben project involved ICI, DEGUSSA, London Fumigation Company, and others for the "manufacture and sale of [the] fumigation product known as Zyklon."[20] After 1935 the DuPont Company increased its holdings in Nazi Germany, purchasing 3.5 percent of DEGUSSA, among other investments.[21] American Cyanamid was also a big player. In 1936 Harry J. Langhorst of Larchmont, New York, assignor to American Cyanamid, applied for a U.S. patent for an improved fumigant carrier combination related to the Zyklon discoids product, reflecting some of the collaboration that was going on between American and German chemical interests at that time.[22]

American Cyanamid would continue to manufacture Zyklon-B discoids under license from DEGESCH through 1943, selling large quantities to the U.S. Army for fumigation.[23] In short, the Germans, British, and Americans were in business together, at least as far as cyanide was concerned.

Nevada's shiny new gas chamber was inaugurated on June 2, 1930, on Bob White, a sturdy two-hundred-pound man who had been condemned for killing a fellow gambler at Elko. Instead of the unwieldy liquid cyanide that had posed so many problems in Gee's execution, the state had prepared ten one-ounce "eggs" of cyanide of potassium in a screen container, to be dropped into a jar of sulfuric acid and water to form lethal HCN. Government officials insisted that their new system was superior to the old one in many key respects, and now they were ready to try it out.

Fifty-three spectators crowded close to witness the execution. Two were women: Mae E. Kenney of Carson City and Margaret Skeeter of Reno, both of them trained nurses. Warden Matt Penrose escorted White into the chamber. The condemned man seemed composed, and he smiled at the faces gaping at him through the thick glass. After the guards had strapped him into the straight-backed chair, he gave each of them a firm handshake. Off to the other side and out of view of the spectators, Dr. Edward E. Hamer, the uniformed state health officer, stood at his station, monitoring the sounds of White's beating heart from a specially built stethoscope that was connected to the condemned man's chest—another innovation that was designed to avert some of the problems encountered in the first gas execution, when the prison officials were unable to pronounce death or remove the body from the chamber for hours.

This time the executioners expected to be able to proceed much more quickly. When all of the guards had left the cell, Warden Penrose glanced at the two-gallon jar of acid. Then he turned to the condemned man, grasped his hand, and said, "Good-bye, Bob."

"Good-bye, Matt," said White with a broad grin.

Penrose then stepped out of the cell and shut the heavily insulated door. His next nod signaled a hidden staff member to cut the string holding the cyanide container, and ten eggs plopped into the acid, giving off their warning like a cobra hissing before it delivers its deadly venom.

"As the first cloud of gas arose from the jar," the correspondent for the Associated Press wrote, "White looked at the crowd. With his head held high he took a deep breath. Then his eyes closed, his head fell back, the muscles of his arms and legs moved and a convulsive movement shook his entire body. This movement ended after three more breaths and his head dropped forward."

Everyone waited for White to die. At first it seemed that the end had come very quickly, but it was several more minutes before the doctor declared White dead and unfastened his stethoscope. Afterward, Warden Penrose told the assembled reporters that they had just witnessed "by far the simplest and most humane method yet devised.... The prisoner is subject to no torture or violation of any kind. The prisoner's body is not disturbed or distorted in any way, and there is absolutely no chance for any slip up. Death by gas is quick, sure and painless."[24] His official report would later claim that the execution had gone off without a hitch and been a perfect success. Hamer later published a brief article about the execution that appeared in the widely circulated *Journal of the American Medical Association*.[25]

News reporters, however, learned that there was more to the story. In fact, Dr. Hamer's stethoscope had indicated that White's heart had stopped beating shortly after he first inhaled the gas, but it had resumed beating ten seconds later and not stopped for more than seven minutes.[26] As a result, some lingering questions hung over the new process, and the warden's credibility had become somewhat suspect.

Throughout the 1920s and early '30s newspaper syndicates and newsreels circulated graphic accounts of American crime and punishment throughout the country and across the globe. By virtue of the nation's long track record of lynching, legally sanctioned hangings, and modern electrocutions, the United States was known as a world leader in capital punishment. The postwar invention of the gas chamber further cemented its reputation and added some new dimensions. Coming on the heels of rampant chemical warfare in Europe that had helped revolutionize the nature of warfare itself, and amid continued calls by the eugenicists for governments to initiate the lethal chamber for euthanasia, the selection of lethal gas to intentionally kill civilians in peacetime must have struck some people as a harbinger of more deadly things to come—a signal, perhaps, of future state-sanctioned mass killing, and even extermination.

At first many Americans viewed the adoption of the new method as a sign of progress, since it helped to replace distasteful images of gruesome hangings or electrocutions with a modern scientific procedure that was called "humane."[27] In the face of new refinements in gas-chamber design and fumigation, other states also began to consider switching to gas.

Arizona was one of them. In February of 1930 Arizona had legally hung a fifty-two-year-old woman, Eva Dugan, for the slaying of a Tucson rancher. But when Dugan's body dropped from the gallows and plunged through the trapdoor, her head snapped off and rolled away, to the horror of those who saw it and others who later heard the grisly accounts. George W.P. Hunt, a liberal Democrat who said he personally opposed the death penalty, used the ghoulish incident in his campaign to win back the governor's post, then upon his election he called for the state to institute a means of capital punishment that was "more humane than the rope." A fellow Democrat, Bridgie M. Porter, introduced legislation to substitute lethal gas, and the senate approved it. With input from the biology department at the University of Arizona, state officials settled upon hydrogen cyanide as the poison of choice, saying the gas had often been used as a fumigator and was known to have caused plenty of accidental deaths. (One of the most common causes involved victims who employed it to clean their mattress but failed to allow the mattress to dry sufficiently before sleeping on it, after which their body heat would release a fatal dose of poison gas.)[28] Its killing power had also been demonstrated in the first four Nevada executions.

Arizona amended its constitution to provide for the death penalty to be inflicted by administering lethal gas, effective on October 28, 1933.[29] But from the time of the last hanging until the new change could be legally tested and administered, from August 21, 1931, until July 6, 1934, Arizona didn't conduct any official executions.[30]

This hiatus gave Colorado the chance to become the next state to make history. A mining state, like Nevada and Arizona, Colorado also had an ugly history of frontier justice and vigilantism. During the 1920s the Ku Klux Klan had dominated the state Republican Party, resulting in a governor, a U.S. senator, the Denver mayor, and a majority of judges who were pro-KKK, prompting the *Denver Post* to observe, "Beyond any doubt the KKK is the largest and most cohesive, most efficiently organized political force in the state."[31] The Klan had an especially strong chapter (Klan No. 21) in Cañon City, where the prison was located, and many of its prison employees were klansmen.[32]

Colorado had been the scene of at least 175 recorded lynchings from 1859 to 1919 alone. By 1930 there had been fewer than half that number of legal hangings, though many of the government's productions had proved ugly spectacles as well.[33] As in Arizona, official hangings prompted some revulsion. During an official execution on January 10, 1930, the authorities had set out to dispatch a black convict, Edward Ives, who had been convicted of killing a policeman during a raid on a Denver brothel. Instead of using a conventional trap door, however, the state had relied on its "Do It Yourself Hanging Machine," a complicated contraption involving weights and pulleys that often went awry. But when it came time to jerk Ives, who weighed only eighty-two pounds, the system functioned more like a catapult, causing his body to sail through the air and land in the prison yard without breaking his neck. Ives survived well enough to argue, "You can't hang a man twice," but his captors strung him up again anyway, leaving him to slowly strangle to death after a protracted struggle.[34]

Colorado had briefly abolished the death penalty around the turn of the century, but it had been brought back to prevent mobs from taking the law into their own hands. Too many residents feared a return to "necktie parties." But now, like Arizona's embarrassing decapitation of Eva Dugan, the Ives execution would provide the impetus for some citizens to finally change their state's capital punishment policy.

In 1933 Colorado's new governor, anti–New Deal Democrat Edwin C. ("Big Ed") Johnson, came out for a new approach—one that would overcome abolitionists' claims about cruelty by making executions "humane" and efficient. The legislature went along with it. On March 31, 1933, Johnson signed legislation making Colorado the third state in the nation and the world to adopt lethal gas as its official method of legal execution.[35] With Arizona and Colorado both preparing to start gassing prisoners, the question of which state would move first took on a competitive spirit.

Roy Best recently had become the warden of the Colorado State Penitentiary at Cañon City, the place where all of the state's executions would have to be carried out. A former rodeo cowboy who had once performed at Madison Square Garden, Best had been in the state police and served as the governor's driver. The warden's vacancy occurred when Best's father was killed in a train accident, and the governor, William H. Adams, had appointed the thirty-two-year-old former broncobuster to run the hard-rock institution that only three years earlier had been the scene of one of the worst riots in American prison history.[36] Roy Best set about making all kinds of high-profile changes. The assignment to modernize the prison's execution machinery was just one more challenge, and he took to it with aplomb.

In March of 1933 Best drove out to Carson City to inspect Nevada's death house in order to learn as much as he could about gas executions. Despite the improvements that had been made since 1924, some of the staff there told him privately that they still considered executions dangerous for the executioners and bystanders alike.[37] Based on his study of the situation, Best supported the idea of a specially constructed, leakproof apparatus resembling a diving bell, which would eliminate the risks to staff and witnesses while ensuring the chamber's maximum effectiveness. It would be housed in a separate building designed to blend in with the prison decor (critics would later dub the building

"Roy's Penthouse"). Like Nevada's new model, Best's design contained enough room for three seats.

At Governor Edwin Johnson's request, Warden Best hired a Denver firm for $2,500 to design and build a state-of-the-art gas chamber that would improve on Nevada's model.[38] The move would prove to have national ramifications. Founded in 1919, Eaton Metal Products was a leading steel plate fabricator that manufactured gasoline tanks, grain bins, and other industrial items. It also had experience in working with cyanide, by virtue of its metal-processing work. Best worked closely with Eaton's Denver plant superintendent, Earl C. Liston, to design a suitable apparatus.[39]

The Colorado gas chamber prototype would turn out to be a signature specialty item that would enable Eaton to enjoy worldwide dominance in that line of products for several years. Although later generations of Eaton managers might come to wish that their employer had never gotten into the business of building death devices, during the 1930s the company's bosses seemed pleased to be associated with such a cutting-edge product.[40] Eaton took to the task with unbridled enthusiasm.

The result was a wonder to behold, and when it was completed photographers were assembled at the prison to record its arrival for posterity. Through the Cañon City Penitentiary's gate and into the prison yard came a truck towing a long trailer on which sat a strange boxlike structure that looked like something straight out of a Jules Verne fantasy. Measuring eight feet in diameter and seven feet high, it had eight sides, with walls of painted corrosion-resisting steel that were half an inch thick, and oddly shaped vents on top. Its wheel-operated, oblong door appeared fit for a submarine, and its small, square windows contained bulletproof viewing glass that had been specially sealed and riveted to prevent leaks.[41] Against the side of the trailer somebody had placed a printed sign that proudly announced "MANUFACTURED BY EATON METAL PRODUCTS CO., DENVER, COLORADO," and the door also bore the company's stamp.

As curiosity seekers approached the object with its door flung open and peered in, they were surprised to see an attractive young woman (Margaret Fliedner) wearing an office dress. (She had been placed there for laughs.) Somebody pointed out that the very plain-looking metal chair she was sitting in would soon claim a murderer's life. Closer inspection revealed that Eaton's creation was a complicated apparatus, painstakingly made to perform all the necessary functions of a modern

Figure 9 Eaton's new gas chamber arrives at Colorado State Prison with a woman inside. Unknown photographer. Courtesy of Best Collection, Cañon City Public Library.

killing machine and carefully constructed to deliver and remove the most lethal type of gas that American ingenuity could manufacture.

To encapsulate this steel trap, Warden Best enlisted some of his convict laborers to construct a tidy edifice in a corner of the prison yard. The death house, jocularly known as "Best's Penthouse," resembled a spruced-up version of Nevada's converted prison barbershop. The small building was a one-story Mission-style stone structure with a slanted roof and long, low windows with brick parapet and sills that made it look almost like a hamburger stand, save for a series of curious pipes and wires that protruded from its roof. Best and some of his cohorts enjoyed posing for photographs beside it at various stages of its construction. Based on its outward appearance, an uninformed observer would never guess that its function was to snuff out human lives.

The keepers of Best's Penthouse didn't have to wait long to receive its first guest. William Cody Kelley and an accomplice had been convicted of murdering a pig rancher with a lead pipe, binding him with barbed wire, and torching him inside his looted house to try to cover up the crime. His accomplice's death sentence was commuted, but Kelley was

Figure 10 Warden Roy Best (left) and Dr. R. E. Holmes outside Colorado's newly constructed death house. Unknown photographer. Courtesy of Best Collection, Cañon City Public Library.

too poor to pay the $200 needed to prepare a trial transcript, and the court itself was not about to oblige, so his case stood to become Colorado's first death sentence not to receive a review by the state supreme court.[42] Although he continued to insist he was innocent and his young wife publicly begged for mercy, citing the welfare of the couple's four-month-old infant, nobody moved to stop his execution. Governor Johnson said, "I believe legal executions are barbaric and I am opposed to capital punishment, but I think that the prompt carrying out of sentences in cases such as this will do much to hold in check any possible outbreak of mob violence in Colorado."[43]

When word of the situation reached a passing tourist named Lorena A. Hickok, however, she prepared to donate the money—until a friend urged her not to do so, warning that her actions might embarrass President Franklin D. Roosevelt, since none of his supporters would want it revealed that Hickok was the intimate companion of Mrs.

Roosevelt. Consequently, Hickok didn't intervene, and she later wrote a private letter to Eleanor Roosevelt, confiding, "I feel as though we were living in the Dark Ages, and I loathe myself for not having more courage and trying to stop it, no matter what the consequences were." By the time the first lady indicated she would not have wanted her friend to compromise her principles in such a way, it was already too late for Kelley.[44]

With nothing to stop the state's first gas execution, Best prepared to try out his new apparatus. After consulting a list of scientific advisors, he had his team run through their execution protocol using a crated hog. During its execution the pig squealed and squirmed, but two minutes and twenty seconds after the cyanide gas was released, the animal was pronounced dead. The technicians also tested the gas on an old dog, a pigeon, and a bunch of canaries, all of which also died in rapid order.[45] Colorado was now ready to gas its first man.

On the night of June 22, 1934, Kelley was stripped down to his shorts and socks (to prevent his clothes from absorbing any of the gas or prolonging his life) and marched into the death house. The guards seated him in the middle wooden chair and strapped him down tightly, putting a black blindfold over his eyes.

Beneath the chair was a trough containing twelve potassium cyanide "eggs"—three more than Nevada had used. Under the trough was a pan of sulfuric acid. The guards quickly withdrew and sealed the door.

Peering through the windows were fifteen physicians and a contingent of other witnesses. Somebody out of their sight pulled a lever and the "eggs" dropped into the bucket. White fumes boiled up from beneath the chair. In ten seconds Kelley was unconscious. In thirty seconds he appeared to be dead.

"Warden Best," a newspaperman reported, "pronounced the execution the most successful and painless one ever conducted at the penitentiary," saying the materials for the execution had cost the state of Colorado only ninety cents.[46] Again, the latest developments were reported worldwide.

With the horse already out of the gate, some American state courts were pressed to decide if the new method was unconstitutional as a violation of the Eighth Amendment's ban against cruel and unusual punishment. "The fact that it is less painful and more humane than hanging is all that is required to refute completely the charge that it constitutes cruel and unusual punishment," the Arizona Supreme Court declared.[47]

Shortly after the court's ruling and only two weeks after Colorado's execution of Kelley, on July 6, 1934, Arizona moved to execute two Chicano brothers, Manuel and Fred Hernandez, aged eighteen and nineteen years old, who had been convicted of killing an elderly prospector. The pair went to their deaths at the new prison at Florence, their eyes covered with gauze. But as Fred Hernandez was being strapped into the double-sided chair, he continued to insist, "I am innocent. You are killing an innocent man."[48]

After the procedure was underway, some of the witnesses noticed a strange smell and the taste of metal in their mouths. "Stand back!" a prison official shouted. "It isn't working—it isn't safe!" The witnesses fled in panic, only to be told later that the smell had simply been from the ammonia they had stored to help neutralize the lethal vapors after the deed was done.[49]

A week later Arizona went ahead with the gassing of nineteen-year-old George J. Shaughnessy. Six weeks after that, Louis Sprague Douglas, aged forty-seven, went to his death as well.[50]

Like other states, however, Arizona soon found that each gas execution presented some new problems. For example, after Frank Rascon was successfully put to death at Florence and his corpse was about to be buried three hours later, his grieving widow opened the coffin lid to give him a parting kiss—and she quickly fell ill from inhaling too much cyanide, according to a Maricopa County physician.[51] Prison officials did their best to meet each of these unexpected challenges.

In Arizona, as elsewhere in those days, the process of condemning a prisoner to death moved at a brisk pace compared to today's standards: executions were generally carried out within several months of the crime and only a few months after the verdict. For example, Burt Anderson, a white man in his fifties, was arrested for allegedly shooting to death Cecil Kuykendall outside the Antlers Pool Hall in Prescott on December 23, 1936. On February 4, 1937, he was convicted; on June 7, 1937, the Arizona Supreme Court affirmed his judgment and sentence; and he was put to death on August 13, 1937—less than eight months after the murder and six months after being found guilty. Usually the public could expect that a gassing would occur less than a year and a half after the capital crime had taken place.[52]

Meanwhile, back in Colorado, the second execution in Best's Penthouse did not take place until June 1935. It involved two Mexican-American brothers, Louis and John Pacheco, who had allegedly invaded a rancher's home, killed two men, and sexually assaulted and shot the rancher's wife before lighting the place on fire. A reporter at their execution described them as sitting in their adjoining chairs "as stolid as a pair of Aztec dolls."[53]

Three weeks after that, Leonard Lee Belongia went to his death in the same gas chamber after his conviction for killing a rancher and injuring the rancher's wife and child. Witnesses testified that Belongia possessed the mental capabilities of a ten-year-old. After his arrest he had put up little defense and willed his body to a medical school for scientific study.[54] The following February, Otis McDaniels was gassed to death there for allegedly robbing and murdering a rancher and later killing a deputy sheriff who was transporting him to jail.[55]

With the Great Depression still going on and fear of crime running high, other states also jumped on the gas chamber bandwagon. North Carolina had never been known to be squeamish about punishing criminals, often resorting to brutal chain gangs and other harsh penal methods. But some of its attitudes appeared to be softening. In 1935 North Carolina enacted a new law changing its official method of execution to lethal gas, making it the first state east of the Mississippi and the first southern state to authorize the use of the gas chamber. Dr. Charles A. Peterson of Mitchell County, a physician and popular Republican house member, wrote the legislation for what the *Raleigh News & Observer* said had "largely been his . . . pet project" for some time—starting after he had witnessed a gruesome and messy electrocution.[56] Like many of the gas chamber's early adherents, Peterson claimed to oppose capital punishment but favored a humane method of execution over lynching and other painful means of death. He convinced the Joint Committee on Penal Institutions to hold public hearings so that he and six others, including other physicians, two dentists, and a newspaper reporter, could attest to the advantages of lethal gas over electrocution and hangings.[57]

One legislator, Representative U.S. Page, offered an amendment calling for "mobile executions" by means of a portable gas chamber that would be carried around by truck, in order to facilitate the process for local officials and residents and allow for public executions. But lawmakers rejected the approach as undignified, settling instead on Peterson's original version of the bill. The state senate approved the bill and the governor signed it into law. The new measure left North Carolina with two legal methods of execution: electrocution and lethal gas.[58] (In 1941 the Nazis would begin using gassing vans—hermetically sealed trucks with the engine exhaust diverted to the interior compartment—to kill thousands of prisoners who were being transported to the crematoria at Chelmno in German-occupied Poland.)

Supporters claimed the new stationary gas chamber method would result in quick, painless, odorless, and bloodless executions in North Carolina. One senator said he expected the gassing of two or three persons would take less time than a single electrocution, thereby saving time and expense. But building the new Eaton death device ended up costing taxpayers $2,800 instead of the $500 that was originally estimated.[59]

Getting it right in North Carolina would not prove easy, however. After hydrocyanic gas was first tested on two dogs at Central Prison, Warden H.H. Honeycutt complained that he had witnessed all 160 electrocutions carried out at the prison since 1910 but the gas had caused the poor animals to howl piteously. He said he didn't like it. Nevertheless, officials of the United States Public Health Service and the State Health Department pronounced the gassing equipment in order, and North Carolina went ahead with its first chemical execution.[60]

Like Colorado's gas chamber, the new North Carolina model was intended to incorporate technological improvements over previous versions. Eaton said that its latest changes would ensure that Honeycutt would not have to wait for more than an hour to clear the chamber of lethal gas in order to verify that death had occurred. And North Carolina's physician in charge would have a closer vantage point than ever before, observing the execution from an inner window that would be in the last of a series of air-sealed doors leading into the death chamber, thereby permitting him to do his job more effectively. Special protective plate windows would better allow witnesses to observe the execution through a window that was nine feet long and three feet high, and this better view would enable more of them to follow the movements of the condemned, who would be sitting only a few feet away. The new gas chamber was sixteen feet long, seven feet high, and nine feet wide and conformed to the general contours of the existing death house structure. Its interior largely consisted of bolted and welded steel plates that were three-sixteenths of an inch thick. The exterior was covered with masonry of terra-cotta tile, with the exception of openings for the windows.

Witnesses didn't have to be exposed to the prisoner as he approached the gas chamber, for there was a special walkway connecting death row to the gas chamber. This connection point was sealed by heavy refrigerator-like doors that could be closed airtight to prevent any gas—or person—from escaping or entering. The condemned prisoner would be strapped to the chair. A jar containing hydrochloric acid (rather than sulfuric acid) would be placed beneath the chair, just below a rack containing five pellets or "eggs" of potassium cyanide. At the chosen moment, an electric button would release these eggs into the acid, and the chemical reaction would immediately cause deadly hydrocyanic gas to quickly fill the chamber in the area closest to the condemned. The first whiffs of the Prussic acid would cause unconsciousness and almost immediate death. Safety locks would prevent the doors from being opened until all of the gas had been exhausted by means of a fan and flue through the roof.[61]

But North Carolina's first use of its new machinery did not go well. On January 24, 1936, the tarheel state proceeded to kill Allen Foster, a mentally impaired black youth from Alabama who had been convicted of raping a white woman after straying from a Civilian Conservation Corps camp. Foster's distraught mother had done all she could to save him, slipping desperate notes to Governor J.C.B. Ehringhaus. "I hate to worrie you so much but I just can't help it Gov.," she wrote in one of them. "If it is just some way [he] could get life sentence and not be killed. I want to him to live that all I got to live for in this world. Please save him from that Gas please. I taught him all I could and all I knowed about the white people law."[62] But Ehringhaus was unmoved.

On the day of the scheduled execution, the bold headline in the Raleigh newspaper read: "TERRIFIED NEGRO FACES FIRST GAS DEATH HERE." Foster was quoted as saying, "The soul can be ready, but the flesh ain't, and I'm worried." The story by reporter John Parris, who was allowed to spend the eve of the execution on death row with Foster and his fellow condemned inmates, recounted:

> Foster had a last word too, before he "catches the train to heb'n." . . .
> "You all shore bin good to me," he began. His voice was clear.
> "I certainly does appreciate everything you all's done for me. You've been tellin' me to find God. I've found God, and I'll always keep him dere in my heart."[63]

Two dozen white newspapermen and other witnesses watched as the twenty-year-old prisoner—whom one reporter described as a "husky dusky Negro"—entered the freezing white chamber in cotton boxer shorts and was strapped, shivering, into the high-backed oak chair, as someone taped the cold stethoscope to his bare chest. The temperature in the death cell hovered at 32 degrees. His "kinky hair" had been shaved and his clothes removed to hasten his death and prevent any deadly cyanide from lingering after the execution. As everyone left the room, Foster said something that was inaudible to most of the witnesses, and he also appeared to raise a clenched fist in an uppercut. Then he said goodbye to his mother and shouted his innocence.

The executioner, R.L. Bridges, pulled his string, releasing the eggs into the bath of sulfuric acid and discharging the gas. As fumes swirled around him, the youth drew in what one reporter called a mouthful of "concentrated hell" as if it were cigarette smoke. For the next ten minutes his head dropped, his eyes rolled, his body convulsed, and he continued to keep trying to speak. Halfway through the process, a horrified witness, Dr. Ransom L. Carr of Duplin County, exclaimed, "We've got to shorten it or get rid of it entirely."

Authorities later acknowledged it had taken more than eleven agonizing minutes to kill him. Foster's heartbeats were monitored by Dr. George S. Coleman, the dean of Duke University's School of Medicine. The physician later said Foster had been fully conscious for at least three minutes, thereby contributing to many of the witnesses' anger and revulsion.[64] One witness, the Raleigh newsman W.T. Bost, who in his day had observed 160 executions and five lynchings, said, "It was the most barbarous thing I have ever seen." The coroner said, "Never again for me. It's slow torture—that's what it is."

In the end, what would be most remembered about the execution were the words the dying prisoner had called out. According to the most celebrated version of the story, he had pleaded, "Save me, Joe Louis! Save me, Joe Louis! Save me, Joe Louis!" as if begging for the great African-American boxing champion to intervene. Decades later, Reverend Martin Luther King Jr. would cite the episode in one of his books.[65]

After death was pronounced, the witnesses were made to wait for another twenty-four minutes until the gas was removed from the chamber and the body was removed. A reporter said witnesses were so shocked and repulsed that "they forgot that the Negro in the chair was paying the penalty for raping a white woman." But Dr. Charles Peterson, the father of the gas chamber law, stoically pronounced, "I am satisfied that Foster's death was painless. I am positive that the new method is more humane than electrocution."[66]

In the wake of the botched Foster execution, the *Raleigh News & Observer* commissioned an organization known as Science Services to make a scientific report regarding the effects of execution by lethal gas on a human being. The resulting study reported:

> Internal asphyxia, or suffocation of the tissues, is what occurs in death by hydrocyanic acid gas. . . . The body, however, is not deprived of air as in ordinary suffocation, say by strangling. There is plenty of oxygen in the blood of a person poisoned by hydrocyanic acid. But the protoplasm—the essential of living cells—cannot absorb the oxygen that is available. . . . Cyanide poisons the central nervous system, first stimulating it and producing convulsions and then causing paralysis. Paralysis of the breathing center in the nervous system is the immediate cause of death. So persons poisoned by hydrocyanic acid stop breathing several minutes before their hearts stop beating.

According to the expert report, electrocution was by far the more humane method of execution than hanging or lethal gas, for unconsciousness was immediate and death almost certainly followed very soon thereafter.[67]

In preparing for their second gas execution, North Carolina officials consulted with chemists in Colorado in a frantic effort to avoid a repeat disaster. One of the chief recommendations was for them to raise the death chamber temperature in order to achieve more vigorous vaporization and thereby reduce the amount of suffering. Another was to alter the mixture of the hydrocyanic solution to the "Colorado formula"—fifteen one-ounce pellets of potassium cyanide, three pints of sulfuric acid, and three quarts of water (in effect, a lot more cyanide, less acid and more water).[68]

North Carolina's second gassing, of Ed Jenkins, a forty-year-old white man convicted of murder, took seven and a half minutes from the springing of the trap until death was pronounced, thus amounting to a significant improvement, but still not an ideal standard. Nevertheless, most physicians and prison officials were later quoted as saying that Jenkins hadn't suffered; his death was painless and humane. Oscar Pitts, the state's acting director of the State Penal Division, announced, "Lethal gas has come to stay in North Carolina."[69]

Thus the state appeared ready to repair its tainted image and poised to proceed efficiently with smooth and rapid executions. Barely a week after the second gassing, three black men were scheduled to be put to death in the chamber, one by electrocution and the other two (J.T. Sanford and Thomas Watson) by lethal gas, thereby affording citizens some basis of comparison between the two methods and against the record of the previous two gassings.[70] After the first subject, William Long, was dispatched in the electric chair, the electrical equipment was removed and the sulfuric acid and white cyanide pellets were readied.

Sanford was brought into the chamber in his boxer shorts and strapped into the chair as stethoscopes were taped to his chest.

But when the executioner pulled the lever to release the pellets, a mechanical malfunction delayed the drop and the ensuing vaporization for four minutes, during which time the puzzled inmate kept straining to detect the fumes. Twenty seconds later he appeared unconscious and his breathing "was rapid and violent, accompanied by groans and grunts so loud that they could be heard through the concrete-covered steel walls of the chamber." Although his breathing stopped after two more minutes, his body continued to undergo spasms, until, finally, a witness wrote, "The Negro's lips drew back over his teeth in a ghastly grin of death"—something one medical expert later called a "sardonic smile" that signified an involuntary reflex of the muscles around the mouth.[71]

After the gas was cleared and Sanford's lifeless body was removed from the chamber, the last prisoner was brought in. Watson was described as "one of the most intelligent looking Negroes ever executed at the prison here." After the lever was pulled, he appeared unconscious within thirty seconds of taking his first breath, but his attempts to breathe and strains against the straps persisted violently for more than a minute until the same ghastly grin came over his face as well.[72] Afterward, with four gassings on his record, Dr. Peterson defended his new method against any and all criticism, blaming the media for being uninformed laymen who had no background or training in executions of criminals.[73]

Six weeks later North Carolina executed two more men.[74] Then two more blacks, one of them seventy-three years old, were gassed on August 21.[75] In December, Martin Moore, a twenty-two-year-old African-American who continued to repudiate his "confession" was pronounced dead twelve and a half minutes after entering the gas chamber, making him the twenty-third person executed and the nineteenth person gassed to death in North Carolina in 1936.[76] At that pace, North Carolina was carrying out almost as many executions as New York, a much more populous state, did in its Sing Sing electric chair.

North Carolina's reliance on the gas chamber was unmatched among all the states in the 1930s. By the end of 1941 the gas chamber had claimed eighty-two lives, at least sixty-eight of them African-American—many of them for crimes other than murder. Several classic criminological studies would find North Carolina punished least severely whites who had killed, raped, or burglarized blacks and penalized most severely blacks who killed, raped, or burglarized whites.[77] Its use of capital punishment also disproportionately targeted persons of low intelligence—a class of citizens the state also sought to curb through its strong eugenics program of compulsory sterilization and institutionalization.[78]

By the late 1930s, however, many key players in North Carolina had grown uneasy with the gas chamber. Another horrible spectacle surrounded the double execution in February 1938 of Edgar Smoak and Milford Exum, both of which dragged on for interminable spans—thirteen and seventeen minutes, respectively.[79] Former warden H.H. Honeycutt publicly favored returning to electrocution, saying, "The gas chamber is horrible. Gas is so long and drawn out. . . . I believe most of the men on death row would rather die by electricity than gas."[80]

In late 1938 Governor Clyde Roarke Hoey expressed concern that lethal gas asphyxiation was slower and consequently "far less humane" than electrocution.[81] Clergymen, editors, physicians, and members of the general public also voiced their disdain for the painful and protracted nature of gas executions. Gruesome accounts of the gassings at Central Prison continued into the 1940s, leaving many North Carolinians ashamed of their state, particularly as they became more aware of what was happening in Europe.

North Carolina was not alone in gassing mentally retarded persons. In 1936 Colorado experienced a case that would come back to haunt the state for many years; as late as 2007 groups were demanding a posthumous pardon and other remedies. The story began when Frank Aguilar, a thirty-four-year-old Mexican laborer, was arrested for the brutal rape and murder of a fifteen-year-old girl in Pueblo on August 15, 1936. He confessed after police found the murder weapon in his home, admitting that he had a grudge against the girl's father. There was no mention or other evidence of an accomplice. Aguilar was quickly tried, convicted, and sentenced to death. But police in Cheyenne, Wyoming, later arrested a twenty-year-old vagrant, Joe Arridy, who obviously was severely retarded but who claimed that he had participated in the crime in Pueblo with "Frank." Arridy, a child of Syrian immigrants, had run away from the Colorado State Home and Training School for Mental Defectives and was picked up by Wyoming police sixteen days after the murder. The *Wyoming State Tribune* labeled Arridy a "feeble-minded moron," noting that his story changed every time he told it, but

Cheyenne's police chief insisted he was guilty. Despite doubts about his guilt, Arridy was charged with capital murder, and a trial was held to determine if he was sane. Although his IQ was measured at 46, authorities said he knew the difference between right and wrong, and therefore he was ultimately convicted and sentenced to death.

Arridy's appellate attorney, Gail Ireland, pleaded for Arridy's life to be spared, saying, "Believe me when I say that if he is gassed, it will take a long time for the state of Colorado to live down the disgrace." But the conviction was narrowly affirmed, and Aguilar went to his death without being called upon to testify about Arridy's innocence or guilt.[82] As the gas was being pumped into the chamber around Aguilar, one of the witnesses, Ed Hamilton, fifty-seven, of Pueblo, suffered a heart attack and died a short time later.[83]

Meanwhile, on death row Warden Best and many of the convicts took a liking to the "simple-minded" youth, buying him toy trains and picture books, which led to a stream of heart-wrenching newspaper stories and pictures. One account included a transcript from this exchange that was tape-recorded on December 1, 1938.

> "Don't you [Arridy] want to be killed?" somebody asked.
>
> "No, I want to live," Arridy replied, "I want to live here with Warden Best."
>
> "Don't you want to go back to the home in Grand Junction [an institution he ran away from six years earlier]?"
>
> "No, I want to get a life sentence and stay here with Warden Best. At the home the kids used to beat me."
>
> "Would you rather be here Joe?"
>
> "Yes I want to stay here, I can't get in trouble here . . . "
>
> "Do you remember after the little girls were killed, you ran to the train, and they arrested you in Cheyenne, Wyoming?"
>
> "No, I don't remember that. But I remember the judge wanted to kill me."
>
> "You know what it means to go to the gas house, don't you Joe?"
>
> "Yes, they kill you there. But I don't want to be killed. I want a life sentence and stay here all the time."

In the end, on January 6, 1939, Best and Father Albert Schaller accompanied Arridy to the gas chamber. Best asked the grinning youth if he still planned to raise chickens in heaven. "No," Arridy replied, "I would like to play the harp like Father Schaller told me I could."[84] Then Best put him to death.

Best continued to fine-tune his executions in an effort to show that they minimized suffering. On September 30, 1939, he personally put to death two convicted murderers by releasing the gas into the acid containers beneath their chairs. One of them—Pete Catalina, forty-one, a Salida pool hall operator who had supposedly shot a patron to death during an argument over a fifty-cent bag of poker chips—was hooked up to a cardiogram that recorded each of his heartbeats before and during the action. I.D. Price, the electrical expert who operated the cardiac instruments for the occasion, reported that Catalina's heartbeat had appeared strong and even for one minute and ten seconds, then stopped abruptly when he inhaled the deadly fumes, supposedly showing that he had died quickly and without fear. The other executed man, Angelo Agnes, a thirty-one-year-old African-American from Denver who had been condemned for slaying his estranged wife, was pronounced dead exactly two minutes after the warden pulled his string.[85] By the end of 1941, eleven men, at least six of them nonwhite, had died in Colorado's lethal chamber.

But Colorado's death house stories became lost in the blur as more states joined in the movement to adopt lethal gas. At the start of 1935 Wyoming adopted legislation prescribing lethal gas as its official execution method. The editor of the *Rawlins Republican*, W.L. Alcorn, commended his local state representative, Senator I.W. Dinsmore, for introducing the bill following the newspaper's revulsion over a hanging that had nearly decapitated George Brownfield in 1930.[86] Their opponents put up a stiff fight, but the pro-gassing forces ultimately won.[87] Wyoming officials sought guidance from Nevada and Colorado and from Eaton Metal Products in establishing their new system. A Cheyenne architect, William Dubois, oversaw the design and construction in collaboration with Eaton.

In mid-November 1936, the Associated Press reported that Eaton had completed a "glistening, all-steel lethal gas chamber, guaranteed by the makers to 'bring almost instant death.'" Earl Liston said his "tank" was completely airtight and should be "just as efficient" as the larger one in use in Colorado. "The gas swirls upward like smoke from a cigarette," he said, "and the prisoner is unconscious at almost the first whiff."[88]

In August 1937 Wyoming inaugurated its new Eaton-built gas chamber by executing Paul H. ("Perry") Carroll, a thirty-six-year-old white man who allegedly had murdered his boss, the superintendent of the Wyoming division of the Union Pacific Railroad, at Rawlins (seventy miles from the Colorado border), on October 27, 1935. A small black blindfold was placed over Carroll's eyes and the guards shook hands with him before exiting the chamber. Warden Alex McPherson pulled a control lever dropping a cheesecloth sack containing thirty-two cyanide eggs weighing half an ounce each into a bucket containing a mixture of three quarts of water and three pints of sulfuric acid beneath the chair, sending deadly fumes swirling through the cell. After a few deep breaths, his head pulled back and he gasped, then his head fell to his chest; his body made further reflex spasms for about six minutes. As soon as death was pronounced, another switch was thrown to open a vent at the top of the chamber, and an electric fan helped evacuate gas from the room. Valves on four ammonia tanks were then opened to neutralize the lethal fumes. Finally, after fourteen minutes of the ammonia treatment, guards wearing gas masks unbolted the door and removed Carroll's body.[89]

In 1940 a thirty-eight-year-old Jewish rail worker, Stanley Lantzer, met the same end for allegedly murdering his wife. Lantzer's executioner later said he preferred hanging to the gas chamber because the victim lost consciousness as soon as the trap fell, whereas lethal gas took several minutes to kill its victim. But Dinsmore, the author of the 1935 legislation that replaced hanging, was quoted as saying, "Lethal gas execution probably can be improved upon . . . but I'm sure now that it's the most humane way of taking a life currently known to man."[90]

In April 1937, Missouri also voted in lethal gas. Missouri was a state rooted in both the Midwest and the South, reflecting yet another expansion of lethal-gas executions—several legislators expressed concern that local capital cases were "too dangerous" because they often resulted in "Roman holiday" lynchings. Like three of its predecessors who had moved to gas (Colorado, Oregon, and Arizona), it, too, had previously abolished capital punishment for a time, but then reinstated it.[91] Defense attorneys complained the new method would make juries more likely to hand out death sentences in the belief that death was "painless" and "humane."[92] But their arguments fell flat, and lethal gas became the official method of execution. Missouri's Eaton model, almost an exact duplicate of Wyoming's, claimed its first victim, William Wright, a thirty-three-year-old black man, in September 1937.[93] By the end of 1941, of the first thirteen persons executed, at least eight were black.

Discussions about lethal gas went on in California for more than a decade. In 1930 Governor James Rolph vetoed a bill to substitute gas for hanging. But after members of the legislature continued to agitate for the new method, in 1932 the Republican Rolph ordered the wardens of the state's two largest prisons to witness a gas chamber execution in Nevada and report back their impressions. James B. ("Big Jim") Holohan of San Quentin and Court Smith of Folsom visited Carson City for the gassing of Everett T. Mull, and they brought back two sharply contrasting views.

Warden Holohan, a former sheriff who had witnessed several botched hangings, said he preferred the Nevada system for being painless and less prone to mistakes. "Nevada authorities inform me that never in a lethal gas execution has there been the slightest slip up, the least error," he claimed. "Every execution has gone off smoothly." Smith, on the other hand, concluded the noose was more merciful than complicated and drawn-out gassing procedures.[94]

The chemical companies dreamed up all sorts of publicity gimmicks to sell the image of the gas chamber in California. At the beginning of 1933 Wide World Photos distributed a photograph of a librarian at Pasadena's famed Huntington Library poring over $50 million worth of rare books and manuscripts that were being processed through a specially built gas chamber designed to rid the paper treasures of the *Sitodrepa panicea* menace. The headline in the *New York Times* read "Lethal Gas Chamber for Book Worms."[95]

While Rolph was mulling over his wardens' reports, he found himself the object of disdain as a result of his response to a November 1933 lynching of two alleged kidnappers in San Jose. The day after a mob broke into the jail and hanged the two suspects, Rolph responded, "If anyone is arrested for this good job, I'll pardon them all. The aroused people of that fine city of San Jose were so enraged . . . it was only natural that peaceful and law abiding as they are, they should rise and mete out swift justice to these two murderers and kidnappers." Governor Rolph added that he would like to release all the kidnappers and murderers in San Quentin and Folsom prisons and deliver them to the "patriotic San Jose citizens who know how to handle such a situation."

His comments created a firestorm of criticism. Editorial writers had a field day. In New York City, Protestant, Catholic, and Jewish leaders, including the president of the American Jewish Congress, launched an antilynching campaign. Some Jewish leaders complained that their efforts to protest Nazi persecutions in Germany had been weakened by the ability of Europeans to point to lynchings of African-Americans in America, and Reverend Adam Clayton Powell of Harlem warned, "If lynching is not stopped the mobs will lynch not only Negroes, but white men, and not only white men, but Governors and newspaper reporters and photographers. If we don't put a stop to the situation we will have mob rule right here in our city."[96] Such warnings struck a chord, as newspapers had recently pointed out that more than one thousand members of Hitler's Swastika organization had recently immigrated to the United States and organized themselves into an American division of the Nationalsozialistische Deutsche Arbeiterpartei (Nazi Party), based in New York.[97]

Saddled with the new nickname "Governor Lynch," Rolph died in office a few months later. But the California lynching situation continued to take on national and international implications. The San Jose lynching and its aftermath caused more embarrassment throughout the United States after a prominent Nazi magazine published photographs of the California necktie party to illustrate the decadence of American life, and Metro-Goldwyn-Mayer also released a feature movie, *Fury* (1936), which was based on the vigilante hanging.[98]

Rolph's successor, Frank F. Merriam, assumed office at the height of the Depression, and he immediately faced intense labor unrest that saw the police use tear gas and army troops from the Presidio to regain control. Such actions involving chemical agents and civil unrest were duly noted by agents reporting to the Nazi regime. German lieutenant general Friedrich von Boetticher, for example, served as Hitler's military attaché in Washington from 1933 to 1941, and he often traveled around the country performing inspections at the Presidio and other sites and sharing his anti-Semitic views with sympathetic members of the U.S. Army Corps, Charles Lindbergh, prominent authors, and other key players.[99]

During Governor Merriam's third year in office, in May of 1937, he received a bill to switch the method of execution to lethal gas. The bill's sponsor was Senator Holohan, the former San Quentin warden, who urged that California model its gas chamber on Wyoming's and carry on the best in state-of-the-art technology. Merriam signed the bill into law, making California the eighth and the most populous state thus far to embrace lethal gas.[100] The gas chamber had achieved a new level of acceptance. The latest developments were reported around the world.

Attention focused on Eaton Metal Products, which was now supplying its fifth gas chamber under contract. A reporter for the United Press began his account by pointing out that "Denver—nationally famous as a health center—ironically has become the nation's leading producer of lethal gas chambers." He described one of the company's designers, Earl C. Liston, as a "quiet, self-styled steel architect," and wrote that Liston and his fellow workers were putting the finishing touches on the new gas chamber that was bound for San Quentin in California. "We seem to have a monopoly on the gas chamber business," the mild-mannered designer happily noted. "We've built five of them—and that's exactly five more than any other company ever made." He pointed out that California's version incorporated the latest innovations in death cell manufacture.

In the past, acid was placed in an ordinary crock under the death chair, and the cyanide eggs were dropped into the acid by pulling a lever. But under the new system, the acid, which generated deadly gas when it came into contact with the balls of cyanide, would be piped into the chamber through special tubes. "This new system will make it easier for the executioner," Liston explained. "Pulling a lever to kill a man is hard work. Pouring acid down a tube is easier on the nerves, more like watering flowers. But it gets results."[101]

Liston's patent was filed with the U.S. Patent Office on October 16, 1937, and patent number 2,172,768 was issued on September 12, 1939. A copy is included in Appendix 1. (A few years after Liston's design was completed, Nazi death camps would utilize a similar method, assigning a soldier to pour Zyklon-B pellets down a chute. The shafts at Auschwitz would become a focus of intense study for many years, mistakenly assumed by most scholars to have been invented completely from scratch by the Nazis.) As far as Eaton was concerned, a company spokesman later explained, the hardest design problems were fitting the chamber with enough windows to accommodate all the spectators and making it airtight so that the fumes would kill only the prisoner or prisoners being executed.[102]

Shipped from Denver by rail and barge, the strange contraption finally arrived at San Quentin, where a team of workers was assembled to help Liston install it. One of them was a hunchbacked convict, Alfred Wells, who was serving time for burglary. Wells later explained its workings to some of his fellow inmates, saying, "That's the closest I ever want to come to the gas chamber." (Five years after he helped to put the gas chamber together, however, Wells was sentenced to death for a triple murder and he was executed in it, a victim of his own handiwork.)[103] Once he had his unit properly put together and inspected, Liston prepared his chemicals and tried out his new death device on a small red pig that was cheerfully selected from the prison farm. "Our calculations show that this new chamber should snuff out life in about fifteen seconds, much faster than any of the others we have built," he said. The *Denver Post* proudly proclaimed, "Denver has become the capital city of the country, possibly the world, in the manufacturing of lethal gas chambers."[104]

By December 1937 national discussion about the pros and cons of lethal gas had become so widespread that *Reader's Digest* published a comparison of the arguments. "Gas is practically foolproof," the spokesman for the pro–lethal gas side contended. "No black hood to hide a hanged man's fantastic grimaces. No sickening among witnesses as an electrocuted man's hair stands straight on end, burning smokily. No chance of some horrible miscue to make the headlines scream." In rebuttal, the spokesman for the "anti-gas side" argued that the new method was neither painless nor easy to watch. Some victims, he said, could take up to thirty seconds of agonizing struggle to fall unconscious, and any witness could see that "his tortured body suddenly protests with clutching, writhing convulsions."[105]

The California gas chamber received its first victims on December 2, 1938, when two hardened convicts, Albert Kessell, twenty-nine, and Robert Lee Cannon, thirty, were put to death in succession for murdering the warden of Folsom. Thirty-nine spectators looked on as each convict acted rebelliously, shouted, and then suffered convulsions. Dr. L. L. Stanley, the prison physician who was one of four medical participants to listen to the men's heartbeats during the executions, emerged shaken by his experience to tell the ravenous reporters, "Hanging is simpler, quicker, and far more humane." Another attending physician, Dr. J. C. Geiger, agreed with Stanley, saying, "The idea that cyanide kills immediately is hooey. These men suffered as their lungs no longer absorbed oxygen and they struggled to breathe. They died of an internal suffocation against which they had to fight and from which they must have suffered." Even Warden Smith went on record to complain, "Hanging is a damned sight quicker and better." But others endorsed the new method. "These men went easy," said Sheriff Dan Cox of Sacramento. "They didn't appear to suffer at all."

Completion of the double execution was delayed for more than two hours when the exhaust system failed, requiring staff to use a suction device to clear the chamber of deadly gas. A guard wearing a gas mask entered the gas chamber to make sure the two men were dead. Some spectators were sickened by their exposure to the gas. In the fiasco's wake the *San Francisco Chronicle* reported, "Their execution . . . precipitated an immediate controversy over the relative merits of cyanide and the scaffold as humane agents of death and may be the signal for a new drive to abolish capital punishment."[106] The *San Francisco Examiner* referred to "California's new robot executioner," calling the gleaming new unit "a chamber of horrors."[107]

During the same period California was known for its cutting-edge eugenics program, for leading the nation in forced sterilizations, and for providing scientific and educational support for Hitler's regime. In 1934 Sacramento's rabidly racist real estate developer Charles M. Goethe, a founder of the Eugenics Society of Northern California and Pasadena's influential Human Betterment Foundation, returned from a trip to Germany to report to a fellow eugenicist, "You will be interested to know that your work has played a powerful part in shaping the opinions of the group of intellectuals who are behind Hitler in this epoch-making program. Everywhere I sensed that their opinions have been tremendously stimulated by American thought. . . . I want you, my dear friend, to carry this thought with you for the rest of your life, that you have really jolted into action a great government of 60 million people."[108] In 1935 Goethe hailed Germany and the United States for "two stupendous forward movements" but complained that "even California's quarter century record [in eugenics] has, in two years, been outdistanced by Germany." Some Californians endorsed the chilling words of Dr. John Randolph Haynes, the Los Angeles philanthropist who said, "How long will it be before society will see the criminality of using its efforts to keep alive these idiots, hopelessly insane and murderous degenerates. . . . They should go to sleep at night without any intimation of what is coming and never awake."[109]

But others, including Berkeley's German-born police chief August Vollmer, an internationally known figure in law enforcement and a member of the advisory councils of both the American Euthanasia Society and the American Eugenics Society, firmly opposed capital punishment and disdained theories of racial superiority.[110] Some of Hollywood's movie moguls, who had grown concerned about anti-Semitism, also tried to tone down the public discourse. But most Californians weren't ready to give up their death penalty—at least, not yet.

Meanwhile, Eaton's workers were keeping busy. Immediately after Wyoming and California's first gassings the company had also installed a chamber in Oregon's state penitentiary at Salem.[111] Like California and North Carolina, sparsely settled Oregon also conducted involuntary sterilizations. Signing the authorizing legislation was Governor Charles H. ("Iron Pants") Martin, a West Point graduate and former army commander who had served with Pershing and Fries in the Philippine Insurrection and World War I and had formed a secret Red Squad in the Oregon State Police that had operated up and down the West Coast. The conservative Democrat staunchly opposed the New Deal and favored German rearmament for Hitler's regime as a cudgel against Communism.[112] But Martin didn't get to carry out any gas chamber executions while he was in office. Oregon's first gassing occurred on January 20, 1939, during the new administration of Governor Charles A. Sprague, a progressive Democrat, when LeRoy Hershel McCarthy, aged twenty-seven, was executed for a robbery and murder. By the end of 1941 Oregon's lethal chamber had taken the lives of three convicts, all of them white.[113]

By November of 1939 Missouri's gas chamber had claimed the lives of eight men, five of them African-American and five from Jackson County. The sixth victim, Adam Richetti, a criminal associate of "Pretty Boy" Floyd, had been convicted on highly circumstantial evidence of participating in the Kansas City Union Station Massacre of five policemen. During his four-year stay in jail before his execution some of his keepers had tortured him with lighted cigarettes, and his sanity had become an open question. To the end Richetti protested that this was one crime of which he was innocent. Even after the gangster was strapped into the chair, he kept asking, "What have I done to deserve this?" and he struggled and let out a piercing scream before he finally expired.

Dr. W. W. Rembo, the prison physician, recorded the following timetable on a scorecard:

Prisoner entered chamber	12:06–30/60 AM
Doors locked	12:10 AM
Eggs enter solution	12:10–15/60 AM
Gas strikes prisoner's face	12:10–30/60 AM
Prisoner apparently unconscious	12:11 AM
Certainly unconscious	12:12 AM
Head falls forward	12:11–30/60 AM
Head falls backward	—
Heart stopped	—
Respiration stopped	—
Blower started	12:28 AM
Chamber doors opened	12:46 AM
Prisoner removed from chamber	12:50 AM
Pronounced dead	12:14 AM

After the gas was removed a federal agent took a fingerprint from Richetti's limp hand to verify the positive identification, and the FBI trumpeted the gangster's demise. But one witness, the popular writer Courtney Riley Cooper, later went public to say he favored hanging or electrocution, because in those cases the "victims apparently don't suffer so long."[114]

CHAPTER 6

PILLAR OF RESPECTABILITY

An indication of how powerful and respectable the German-dominated cyanide cartel had become in the 1930s can be found by examining the career of John J. McCloy, a pillar of the East Coast establishment who is considered by many to be one of the most influential yet overlooked American figures of the twentieth century.

A top U.S. assistant secretary of war during World War II, McCloy was a key player behind the internment of the Japanese, the dropping of the atomic bomb, and the strategic victories over Nazi Germany and Imperial Japan. He later served as the first high commissioner of Germany, president of the Chase Manhattan Bank and the World Bank, trustee of the Rockefeller Foundation, member of the Warren Commission, and advisor to nine U.S. presidents, all of which gained him the appellation as the "most influential private citizen in America." McCloy spent much of his career in service to some of America's wealthiest families, especially the Rockefellers. Most of the criticism leveled against him has been as a result of his decision not to bomb rail lines leading to Auschwitz, his opposition to Jewish emigration from Europe, and his lenient postwar treatment of Nazi war criminals.[1] Missing from the discussion, however, has been sufficient recognition of some of McCloy's other lawyerly activities, particularly his connections to German interests in the periods before and after World War II.

McCloy was born in Philadelphia in 1895 to a family of humble means. His Irish-American father died when he was six, leaving him to be raised by his Pennsylvania-Dutch mother, who worked as a hairdresser. Excelling as a student, he graduated from Amherst College in 1916 and subsequently entered Harvard Law School, but he suspended his education in May 1917 to serve in the U.S. Army when America entered the war. He was a field artillery officer in France, where he saw limited combat and rose to the rank of captain, before he returned to Harvard, where he received his law degree in 1921. He then began a prosperous career in law and banking, starting at the prestigious New York firm of Cadwalader, Wickersham and Taft.

In December 1924 he joined the high-powered Wall Street firm of Cravath, Henderson & de Gersdorff (later Cravath, Swaine & Moore), where he quickly made a name for himself. Soon after he joined Cravath, the firm participated with J.P. Morgan in a huge $110 million loan to the German government. This work in investment banking often took him to France, Italy, and Germany, all of which had been ravaged by the war. "Practically every merchant bank and Wall Street firm, from J.P. Morgan and Brown Brothers on down, was over there picking up loans," McCloy later said. "We were all very European in our outlook and our goal was to see it rebuilt."[2]

In 1929, while traveling west on a train, McCloy ran into a friend from his days at Amherst and in the army, Representative Lewis Williams Douglas, scion of one of the most powerful families in Arizona and sole heir of the Phelps Dodge copper mining fortune. After a brief stint as a state representative in Arizona, Douglas had worked in his family's mining operation and gotten himself elected to Congress in 1926. Douglas and McCloy had several friends in common, including Trubee Davison, whose father was a partner in the J.P. Morgan Company, and they moved in some of the same social circles. Douglas was married to Margaret "Peggy" Zinsser from back in New York, and the young congressman introduced McCloy to his wife's elder sister, Ellen Zinsser, as a possible beau.

The Zinsser girls had grown up in Hastings-on-Hudson, New York, in a well-to-do German-speaking household, and they were sent to Germany to complete their education. Their father, Frederick G. Zinsser, ran Zinsser & Company, a successful chemical manufacturing firm founded by his grandfather that was one of the establishments contracted to produce mustard gas for Uncle Sam in 1918. At the same time Zinsser had also served as assistant to the commander of Edgewood Arsenal, Colonel William Walker, during the Great War. Frederick Zinsser's wife (and the girls' mother), Emma Sharmann

Zinsser, was also descended from German immigrants. Both Ellen and Peggy had attended elite preparatory schools and Smith College. McCloy married Ellen Zinsser in 1930, and from the time of their honeymoon they often traveled in Europe together as he pursued his career, operating from Cravath's Paris office.

One of McCloy's most demanding legal projects in those days was pursuing a high-stakes lawsuit against Germany in which he sought major civil damages in the infamous "Black Tom" case, stemming from a deadly blast at a munitions depot in Jersey City that had shaken Ellis Island and lower Manhattan on July 30, 1916. McCloy's client, Bethlehem Steel, had suffered the biggest damage, losing fifty-two railcars full of shells and fuses. Many investigators attributed the explosion to German sabotage intended to disrupt the flow of ammunition to the front for America's embattled allies, but the Germans had always denied any involvement. After the war, Black Tom was brought before the Mixed Claims Commission to enforce German government liability for the alleged sabotage. After several years of relentless investigation, McCloy uncovered evidence about the involvement of two prominent Germans in the conspiracy: Franz von Papen, a German army captain who would later become vice-chancellor to Hitler, and Ernst Hanfstaengl, the former classmate of Franklin Delano Roosevelt at Harvard who had been a close friend of Hitler from his *Mein Kampf* days and would later rise to become his foreign-press chief. McCloy's intrigue-filled work took him deep into German and American industrial and military espionage. In one bizarre episode, he was interviewing a czarist Russian adventurer, Count Alexander Nelidoff, who said he had proof linking the German government to the Black Tom explosion. McCloy lifted a pencil from Nelidoff's vest to take some notes, leading the anxious Russian to warn that the pencil was actually a tiny pistol loaded with poison gas. McCloy's investigation took him and the twenty lawyers under his supervision to many exotic locations, where he got to know many top spies, including Franz von Rintelen, the former German espionage chief.[3]

Throughout the 1930s, as a member of the well-connected Cravath law firm, McCloy represented the financier Paul Warburg and the Rockefellers, among other clients.[4] He also continued his work for J.P. Morgan. (One of his brothers-in-law, John Zinsser, would become a director of Morgan.) McCloy lived in Italy for almost a year, where he helped to raise money for Mussolini's regime.[5] Much of this work entailed huge loans to the German and Italian governments, which brought him into close connection with many fascist leaders.[6]

In addition to Morgan and Rockefeller, some other big American financial backers of the fascist regimes included DuPont, Ford, IBM, and General Motors. Many of these German investments involved financing for IG Farben, the all-powerful German oil, drug, and chemical concern. McCloy's law firm represented the Farben affiliates in America, and McCloy was often their point man in Europe.[7] Farben had spearheaded the development of insecticides and chemical weapons during World War I, and in the 1930s it was playing a central role in Germany's quest for world domination. It was Hitler's biggest source of political contributions and the biggest recipient of German defense spending, as well as the world's most important developer and supplier of poison gases. Some of its customers included fascist Italy and Imperial Japan, both of which used chemical weapons in the 1930s. (Farben was also the principal sponsor of Japan's chemical industry.) By 1934 Farben was closely associated with the Gestapo; many of its executives stationed abroad served as spies. Nevertheless, despite its shady background, Farben remained closely allied with several of America's most powerful corporations and banks, at least well into the 1930s, and in some instances even during the war.[8]

The Rockefellers were closely tied to Farben through Standard Oil and other holdings. As a result, from 1929 onward, as the German combine came under increased criticism for its defense profiteering and fascist involvement, John D. Rockefeller assigned his public relations counsel, Ivy Ledbetter Lee, to help Farben clean up its image in America. In 1934 Lee testified to the House Un-American Activities Committee regarding his work for Farben. The congressional investigation revealed that the directors of American IG Chemical Corporation included some of the leading names in American finance and industry, such as Charles E. Mitchell, the director of the Federal Reserve Bank of New York and National City Bank, Paul M. Warburg, the first member of the Federal Reserve Bank of New York and the Bank of Manhattan, and Edsel B. Ford of Ford Motor Company, as well as at least three German executives who later would be convicted of war crimes at Nuremberg.[9] McCloy had close ties to all of them.

Throughout the Nazi era, Farben and its American subsidiary were extensively involved in spying—so much so that many U.S. government investigators considered it an intelligence operation—and some of Farben's competitors probably spied on them as well. By the late

1930s, McCloy's legal work inside the shadowy world of espionage and fascist politics culminated when he conducted direct negotiations in the Black Tom munitions case with top leaders of the newly installed Third Reich, including Hermann Göring. (At the time, Göring, among various other positions, served as commissioner for raw materials and foreign exchange, and he also headed the Gestapo.) During the negotiations, in August 1936 McCloy attended the Berlin Olympics with Göring and Rudolf Hess as a guest in Hitler's private box; McCloy and his wife also socialized with leading Nazis. McCloy later said that the connections had provided him "a window on the center of the Nazi régime."[10] His $50 million settlement with the German government, at the time one of the greatest civil awards in legal history, also represented a huge triumph that made McCloy a courthouse and boardroom celebrity, which would later lead to his appointment with the U.S. government.[11]

Meanwhile, McCloy's old college friend, fishing partner, and brother-in-law, Lewis W. Douglas, also occupied several noteworthy positions during the 1930s. After leaving Congress in 1933, Douglas—a conservative Democrat—briefly served as President Franklin Roosevelt's federal budget director. But Douglas quickly turned against the New Deal for its liberal economic policies. He said privately that FDR had come under too much "Hebraic influence," adding that, "most of the bad things which it [the administration] has done can be traced to it. As a race [the Jews] seem to lack the quality of facing an issue squarely."[12] Douglas made little effort to conceal his anti-Semitism and became an outspoken opponent of the New Deal. Upon quitting the Roosevelt administration, he received several offers from like-minded organizations, including the bankers who controlled Paramount Pictures and James B. Conant, the former army gas-warfare officer who had gone on to become president of Harvard University.[13]

After weighing his options with McCloy and others, Douglas decided to go into the chemical industry. From 1934 to 1938 he was vice president and board member of American Cyanamid, America's fourth-largest chemical company, which was secretly allied with Farben through a web of trade agreements. American Cyanamid's president, the ultraconservative Quaker lawyer William B. Bell, served as chairman of the Republican National Finance Committee. A harsh critic of Roosevelt's policies, Bell was also a stickler for formality. Peggy Zinsser privately referred to Bell as "Buttonshoes," but her husband and his new boss never reached a first-name basis. After relocating to the corporation's headquarters in New York's Rockefeller Center, Douglas also became affiliated with several organizations, including the American Museum of Natural History and the Rockefeller Foundation, both of which were major players in the eugenics movement and other causes.[14]

During Douglas's tenure at American Cyanamid, while McCloy was serving as a lawyer for investment banking interests involving Nazi Germany and other clients, and as states throughout America were adopting lethal gas as their official means of execution and building gas chambers to carry out the death penalty, American Cyanamid was making cyanide. It manufactured Zyklon under license from the patent holders, DEGUSSA, and secretly made business pacts with IG Farben. Until 1938 the bulk of the Germans' profits from distributing Zyklon came from abroad, particularly from the United States, and American Cyanamid was one of the fastest growing chemical concerns that thrived during the Great Depression.[15]

Douglas served mainly as a troubleshooter and economic analyst for American Cyanamid, frequently traveling to inspect the company's various operations and meeting with stockholders. In Great Britain he obtained audiences with Neville Chamberlain (the chancellor of the exchequer) and often met with his friend Winston Churchill. In the course of his professional and social activities Douglas also maintained close relations with many Nazi businessmen, some of whom were doubtless agents of the Gestapo. He traveled extensively in Germany and also widened his social and political connections at home, hoping someday to win national political office. An advocate for laissez-faire policies, he also continued to lash out against FDR's programs, claiming they had unleashed forces that could lead to socialism.[16] After one such speech that Douglas made at the Wharton School of Finance and Commerce, President Roosevelt drafted a response calling Douglas's comments "reprehensible," saying they came "very close to the kind of lack of patriotism which tends to the destruction of government. In time of war, that kind of lack of patriotism goes under the word 'treason.'" Roosevelt opted not to make his comments public, however, and left it to Harold Ickes to assail the speech. Douglas also supported the radical American Liberty League, which had been organized by the du Ponts and other FDR adversaries, but he declined membership as the group was plotting a coup to overthrow the administration.[17] Although Douglas was a contender for the 1936 U.S. vice presidential nomination under Alfred M. Landon, a bout of poor health hindered his campaign, and he failed to win the nomination.

In the mid-1930s neither McCloy nor Douglas was as famous as their wives' uncle, Dr. Hans Zinsser, a celebrated bacteriologist at Columbia and Harvard who was best known for authoring the best-selling book *Rats, Lice and History,* in 1935.[18] In it the popular professor presented information about his study of typhus, still regarded as one of the world's deadliest diseases, particularly in places where there were high concentrations of people, such as in army barracks and prison camps. Zinsser's fascinating account explained that typhus was spread by rodent-borne lice.[19]

A focal point of Zinsser's study of typhus involved its outbreak among immigrants, especially Mexicans. Other observers were also following the subject very closely. The German military had begun using Prussic acid for delousing during the Great War. In Poland and other parts of Europe during the war's immediate aftermath, efforts to thwart further typhus epidemics had increasingly involved the use of HCN gas to disinfect trains and other places where refugees had congregated, along with their clothes and other personal effects.[20] The use of Zyklon-B on the United States–Mexico border was already a matter of intense interest to DEGESCH, the subsidiary of IG Farben's DEGUSSA that controlled the licensing for Zyklon-B. In 1938 Dr. Gerhard Peters, DEGESCH's general manager and the leading proponent of Zyklon-B, wrote an article in a German pest science journal, *Anzeiger für Schädlingskunde,* in which he called for its use in German *Desinfektionskammern* (disinfection chambers), citing its extensive use in the United States and featuring photos of El Paso's delousing chambers. In Germany on June 7, 1938, and in the United States on May 26, 1939, Peters applied for a patent for a new "exterminating agent for vermin," explaining, "My invention relates to the extermination of animal pest-life of the most varied kinds, for instance, warm-blooded obnoxious animals and insects." He also made a German-language film extolling the benefits of using Zyklon-B for pest extermination. In 1940–41 he also wrote an article recommending its use to kill typhus-bearing insects. (Peters went on to supply much of the Zyklon-B to Nazi death camps. As a result, he was subsequently tried and convicted at Nuremberg, but later retried and found not guilty.)[21]

The Nazis seized upon the typhus-related work by scientists such as Charles Nicolle and Zinsser to use in their argument equating Jews with vermin that needed to be exterminated. In August of 1935 thousands of Germans gathered at a Nazi rally in Berlin to hear anti-Semitic speeches calling for a future Germany "cleansed" of Jews. Such rhetoric was becoming more commonplace among Hitler's followers.

This notion of *disinfection* was demonstrated most graphically in the famous 1940 Nazi propaganda film *Der ewige Jude* (The Eternal Jew), directed by Fritz Hippler, who worked under propaganda minister Joseph Goebbels. Amplifying on a book and an exhibit of the same name, their presentation marshaled the persuasive emotional force of film to spread hysterical anti-Semitic ideas. A Nazi reviewer said the movie showed Jews as filthy, lazy, ugly, corrupt, vicious, and perverse subhuman creatures that lived like vile parasites.[22] Shot partly in the squalid Lódź ghetto the Nazis had created, using some scenes of actual squalor and filthy living conditions (which, again, the Nazis had helped to construct), the film purported to show the Jews in their "natural habitat" without the "mask of civilization." Images of repulsive-looking Jews were juxtaposed with footage of swarms of rats, said to be vectors of typhus and other diseases, suggesting that both pests needed to be eliminated from civilized society. The Jewish race was depicted as a sanitation problem, not a social or political problem, and thus requiring a hygienic solution. The film culminated in Hitler's chilling warning to the Reichstag in 1939: "If the international finance-Jewry inside and outside Europe should succeed in plunging the nations into a world war yet again," he raged, "then the outcome will not be the victory of Jewry, but rather the annihilation of the Jewish race in Europe!" The "documentary" helped turn ordinary Germans into Hitler's willing executioners.

The Jews were not the Nazis' only target. Fed by the crackpot social science of Dr. Robert Ritter, the German psychiatrist and "race" expert, the Nazis also stereotyped European Gypsies (Roma) as biologically inferior, antisocial, and criminal. Starting in 1935 they incorporated Gypsies of mixed ancestry *(Zigeunermischlinge)* into Germany's racial laws and decrees. As far as the Nazis were concerned, any classification of Gypsy had to be "scientific"—the catchall label of "nomadism" used by some American eugenicists such as Charles Benedict Davenport wasn't sufficient—but once that determination was made, the subject was considered subhuman.[23]

Even in parts of polite society in the United States in the early to mid-1930s, talk about gas-chamber "euthanasia" was becoming quite casual and respectable. Around the same time that Zinsser's book about rats and lice appeared, the best-selling nonfiction book in the world was *Man, the Unknown* (1935, written in 1933), by Dr. Alexis Carrel, a French-American Nobel Prize–winning medical researcher from the Rockefeller Institute for Medical Research and "father of human vessel and organ transplantation." Carrel was strongly profascist. So was his laboratory assistant at the time, Charles A. Lindbergh, the aviator whose first crossing of the Atlantic had made him one of the world's most famous men (and who, in 1936, like McCloy, had also visited Hitler's box at the Olympics). A fervent eugenicist, Carrel in his book championed an expanded use of the gas chamber for executions. "Those who have murdered, robbed while armed with automatic pistol or machine gun, kidnapped children, despoiled the poor of their savings, [or] misled the public in important matters," he wrote, "should be humanely and economically disposed of in small euthanasia institutions supplied with proper gases." Echoing a long line of distinguished writers going back to W. D. McKim, the esteemed surgeon and author added, "A similar treatment could be advantageously applied to the insane, guilty of criminal acts."[24]

In 1939 Carrel left the United States to return to his native France, where he subsequently joined the profascist Vichy government, but he died before he could be brought to trial as a Nazi collaborator. Lindbergh also remained supportive of the Nazis; his wife, Anne Morrow Lindbergh, also published a controversial book, *Wave of the Future* (1940), in which she argued that democracy was dead and fascism was the "wave of the future." But by 1941 the couple's profascist activities suddenly caused them problems in the United States.

From the time that Hitler assumed power as German chancellor on January 30, 1933, he never left much doubt about his repressive intentions. He instituted laws to exclude Jews and Gypsies from German life and utilized the most brutal measures to destroy his opponents. He smashed dissent, initiated sweeping compulsory sterilization and prohibitions against racial mixing, began building concentration camps, and ruled by terror. The only question was, how far would he go?

The Germans had been closely following developments in the U.S. criminal justice system for years. In Weimar days, many leading German jurists had expressed shock over such high-profile cases as Sacco and Vanzetti, in part because of the protracted delay between the time of their trial and their execution, which many saw as an inexplicable flaw in American judicial methods.[25] Under Nazi influence, the Germans had also closely examined such American criminal justice issues as the "third degree" (the use of police brutality and torture to extract confessions), corruption, the "war on crime," intelligence-gathering and crime-fighting approaches by the Federal Bureau of Investigation, criminal identification techniques, centralized police operations, sentencing policies, and racial laws. American policies of racial exclusion, for example, were approvingly detailed in Heinrich Krieger's book *Das Rassenrecht in den Vereinigten Staaten,* published in Berlin in 1936.[26]

Immediately prior to the rise of the Nazis, Germany had not been considered a highly punitive state; during the Weimar Republic, for example, the number of executions had dropped to only two or three a year between 1928 and 1932. Austria and Germany had virtually abolished capital punishment and rejected calls for a euthanasia law.[27] But the National Socialists brought back the death penalty with a vengeance. Before 1933 the only capital crimes were murder and high treason, punishable in Berlin by beheading with the axe; other German states used the axe or the guillotine. But Hitler changed all that. In 1932, when President Paul von Hindenburg's administration adopted new antiterrorist decrees that resulted in five Nazi storm troopers being sentenced to death for murdering a Communist worker near the Polish border, the Nazis rioted in protest.[28] But upon taking power in 1933 they reinstituted capital punishment in Austria and Germany for "treason" and other offenses, seeking the death penalty in the prosecution of two American Communist organizers.[29] Spurred by the Lindbergh baby kidnapping in America, they also adopted the death penalty for kidnapping. In April 1935 the Nazis declared they would expand executions in time of war or danger of war to exterminate pacifism and antimilitary organizations. The German Board of Jurisdiction announced that persons arranging such meetings as well as those attending them would be punished accordingly. At first, the number of known executions amounted to only sixty-four in 1933, seventy-nine in 1934, ninety-four in 1935, and sixty-eight in 1936. It would not be until the war started that the German nation would carry out capital punishment on such a massive scale. And it was not until the war that Hitler would order his aides to begin seriously pursuing various gassing options.[30]

When Hitler's regime began persecuting Jews, Rabbi Stephen Wise of New York and other prominent Jewish Americans responded by pleading for the United States to relax its tight immigration restrictions to allow more endangered German Jews into the country. One of their harshest opponents was retired general Fries, former head of the Chemical Warfare Service, who insisted the Nazis were merely persecuting known Communists and Communist sympathizers. Instead of backing loosened immigration quotas to admit more refugees, Fries urged that countless undesirable immigrants already residing in the country should be deported, in order to return America "to that homogeneity that we had in 1860, in 1776." Once again, Fries rallied veterans groups to his banner.[31] And in large measure, they prevailed. Aiding the Jews was not a priority for Roosevelt or the Congress.

Prior to the late 1930s, many prominent American eugenicists, rather than being ignorant of the Nazis' increasingly radical racist actions, were keenly interested in and wholly supportive of what the Nazis were doing. Some of the Americans had been in frequent communication with their German counterparts for decades. The Germans were credited with achieving preeminence in the fields of genetic research and racial biology, and they cultivated especially close ties with the American foundations and researchers, who often reciprocated. German racial science, meanwhile, was said to have originated in the United States.[32] In August 1932 the Third International Congress on Eugenics, held at New York's fabled American Museum of Natural History, rammed home the theme that progress made by eugenicists was ushering in the "era of Supermen."[33] Racist themes dominated many of the exhibits and discussions.

In August and September 1935, several German organizations held the World Population Congress in Berlin, showcasing recent moves by the "Führer and Reichschancellor Adolf Hitler, whose far-seeing population policy based on racial hygiene and principles of heredity," its hosts proclaimed, "will secure the future of the German *Volk*." Several top Americans were among the honored attendees. They included Dr. Harry H. Laughlin of Long Island, the leading authority on eugenic sterilization, and Dr. Clarence G. Campbell of New York, honorary president of the Eugenics Research Institute. Campbell stood up and hailed "that great leader, Adolf Hitler," and his racial policies. Afterward Laughlin returned to the United States to distribute Nazi propaganda films and received an honorary degree from the University of Heidelberg.[34]

The Nazis also honored America's leading euthanasia advocate, Foster Kennedy (a psychiatrist who was professor of neurology at Cornell Medical College and director of neurology at New York City's Bellevue Hospital), as well as Henry Fairfield Osborn (the famed paleontologist and director of the American Museum of Natural History), among others. The famous Harvard legal scholar Roscoe Pound also received an honorary degree from the Nazis.

In turn, some American government officials lauded radical eugenics. In 1934 William W. Peter of the U.S. Public Health Service praised the German sterilization program in the pages of the *American Journal of Public Health*.[35] A bill to legalize voluntary euthanasia (referred to as "the granting of peaceful death to incurable sufferers") in New York was proposed by the treasurer of the American Euthanasia Society, State Assemblyman Charles F. Nixdorff, on January 26, 1939, shortly before Hitler enacted his own euthanasia measure. But the New York bill fell short of being introduced. A few weeks later, Foster Kennedy urged that "mercy killing" be expanded to include infants who were born "defective" and were doomed to remain so.[36] (In May 1941, Kennedy addressed the American Psychiatric Association, saying, "We have too many feebleminded people among us. . . ." He advocated the formation of a competent medical board that was legally authorized to "relieve the defective . . . of the agony of living." In 1942 he set off a bigger controversy when his arguments were published in the *American Journal of Psychiatry*.)[37]

A number of leading American bankers and industrialists continued to finance and applaud Mussolini's and Hitler's fascist approaches. "As the Hitler régime took each step in its war against the Jews and all of Europe," historian Edwin Black has written, "IBM custom-designed the punch cards and other data processing solutions to streamline those campaigns into what the company described as '*blitzkrieg* efficiency.'" At the company's inauguration of its new Hollerith machine–manufacturing facility in Berlin, the manager of IBM's German subsidiary proclaimed, amid swirling swastika flags and storm trooper guards, "Hail to our German people and *der Führer*!"[38] Such backing and involvement by many American investors, corporations, and foundations continued even after Italy and Germany had begun to display their bellicose tendencies—and well after they had laid out their racial agendas.

The willingness of the fascist powers to use poison gas against populations they considered racially inferior was demonstrated in 1936, when Italy's air force (propelled by German know-how) dropped German mustard gas bombs on soldiers and civilians in Ethiopia—and international protests by Emperor Haile Selassie fell on deaf ears.[39] Such actions didn't faze Germany's American business partners. A few months after the bombings, Nazi propagandists at the Olympic Games in Berlin informed McCloy and other guests that German race policy was based on "internationally accepted science," which they said had been developed in the United States and elsewhere.[40] And McCloy continued to hobnob with Göring, Hess, and other leading Nazis.

Starting in 1937, however, as the Nazis began to put into effect their racial laws and as war with militaristic Germany loomed, American corporate support for the Third Reich began to become more problematic. One of the more intriguing developments involved the sudden apparent suicide of the world's top organic chemist, Wallace Hume Carothers, the young genius who had briefly taught in Conant's chemistry department at Harvard before going on to invent nylon and neoprene at DuPont. Shortly after returning from an extended trip to Germany, Carothers apparently committed suicide by swallowing a cyanide pill with lemon juice.[41] Shortly after Carothers's death amid a congressional investigation linking American Cyanamid to secret German interests, Lewis Douglas abruptly resigned from the firm and left the country to become president of McGill University in Canada.[42] Germany's annexation of Austria in March 1938 apparently convinced him that another global conflict was inevitable, and out of concern that Great Britain and the United States would ultimately become involved, he began to soften his stance on isolation and strongly supported U.S. military assistance for France and Britain. (Both Douglas and McCloy strongly supported the Lend-Lease bill.) Douglas would remain in Canada until late 1939, when he returned to New York as president of the Mutual of New York Life Insurance Company.

On September 1, 1939, the day that Hitler launched the blitzkrieg attack against Poland that started World War II, eleven corporations (including DuPont and Allied Chemical and Dye Corporation and its subsidiaries) that sold a large percentage of the nitrate products used in commercial fertilizer and explosives in the United States were secretly indicted by a federal grand jury in New York, charged with conspiracy to control the supply and prices of those products in violation of antitrust laws. The indictments weren't announced until more than a year later, leaving the firms to repair their standing with the government.[43]

Starting in December 1940 German imports of potassium cyanide were no longer allowed in the United States. The Roessler & Hasslacher chemicals division of E.I. DuPont de Nemours and Company subsequently announced that it would begin manufacturing the chemical, spurred by "current U.S. needs and the urgency of national self-sufficiency."[44]

In April 1941, one hundred corporations (including American Cyanamid, DuPont, and Dow Chemical Company) were subpoenaed to provide records regarding the extent to which Germany's IG Farben had gained control over vital sections of America's drug and chemical trade.[45] In May 1942 it was revealed that executives of DuPont,

American Cyanamid, Allied Chemical, and twenty of their officers and directors had been indicted by a federal grand jury in Trenton, accused of a worldwide conspiracy with IG Farben to monopolize the manufacture of dyestuffs.[46] It came out that DuPont had first sought its alliance with Farben in 1919, and in 1926 the corporations had contracted to divide the world market for military powder and cross-licensed patents and exchanged technical information. DuPont had also agreed to serve as the sales agent for the German companies so they could overcome the restrictions of the Versailles Treaty.[47] Even after such disclosures, Justice Department officials continued to report that "German firms masquerading in this country as American" were still continuing to operate without interference, just as they had begun to do at the end of World War I.[48]

McCloy had been among those who believed that Germany had been unfairly penalized by Versailles; he had worked on behalf of several major financial institutions, helping to rebuild the German state into a formidable industrial and military power. He had never condemned the fascists. But the world was changing. In the 1940 American presidential election, Douglas supported Wendell Willkie, the Republican candidate, but McCloy, who was a Republican, said he didn't support either Willkie or FDR, adding, "People take for granted that such things must be the democratic process. If they are, I say a plague on it—let's invent something different."[49]

Roosevelt won the 1940 election, however, and with America's entry into the conflict appearing much more imminent, McCloy left his Wall Street law firm in December 1940 to become special assistant to Secretary of War Harry L. Stimson in the Roosevelt administration. In September 1941 Douglas spoke up against Hitler, saying, "Anti-Semitism is one of the characteristics of Nazism wherever it has stuck up its ugly head."[50]

It turned out that McCloy was the ranking person on duty in the War Department on December 7, 1941, when word was received that the Japanese had bombed Pearl Harbor. One of his early actions working with Stimson was to push for the roundup and internment of 120,000 Japanese Americans (but not German Americans) in concentration camps based on their ancestry—an action that one historian later called "the greatest deprivation of civil liberties by government in this country since slavery."[51] Overnight, McCloy became one of the lead officials charged with prosecuting the war against Germany, Italy, and Japan—a war against enemies he had helped to arm and equip.

CHAPTER 7

THE RISING STORM

In 1940 and '41 Americans remained mired in the Great Depression and deeply worried about their future. The country was about to become entangled in another world war, this one waged on an even broader scale and under more desperate conditions than the last. Freedom, democracy, and prosperity were very much in peril. In addition to fearing they might become dominated by foreign powers, many Americans wondered if some sinister inner forces would engulf their society and change their way of life, as had happened abroad. The Lindberghs were not alone in regarding fascism as the wave of the future. It already had swept Italy, Germany, Spain and other parts of the globe, and many of the seeds required for fascism to flower in the United States, some warned, were already planted. From the other end of the political spectrum, capitalist defenders warned that Communism was threatening to impose another sort of dictatorship, against which only the harshest measures could prevail.

European social scientists had followed the Nazis' rise to power with awe. At least one close observer took from it fresh insights about the fascists' focus on punishment. In his study *Moral Indignation and Middle Class Psychology* (1938), the distinguished Danish sociologist Svend Ranulf explored some of the dynamics that shape the attitudes of different social classes toward transgressors, offering a classic discussion of social structure in punitive moralizing—what Nietzsche called *ressentiment*. Ranulf pointed out that the urge to assist in the punishment of criminals, as awful and primal as it might be, was nevertheless a "disinterested disposition," since "no direct personal advantage is achieved by the act of punishing another person who has injured a third party." He noted that it was furthermore a disposition "not equally strong in all human societies and indeed seems to be entirely lacking in some." He suggested, consistent with the writings of Max Weber, the American V.F. Calverton, and others, that "the disinterested tendency to inflict punishment is a distinctive characteristic of the lower middle class, that is, of the class living under conditions which force its members to an extraordinary degree of self-restraint, and subject them to much frustration of natural desires." "Moral indignation (which is the emotion behind the disinterested tendency to inflict punishment)," Ranulf explained, was "a kind of disguised envy, if 'envy' is understood not in a pejorative but in an ethically neutral sense, such as it is used by Herodotus."[1]

According to Ranulf's reasoning, Americans, with their Calvinist roots, were especially susceptible to showing their strong desire to see other people punished for their immorality. The colonial legacy of slavery, indentured servitude, and convict transportation, as well as the subjugation of the Native Americans, had established a strong foundation for penal severity. There was also a long tradition of lynching and vigilantism. More recently, the eugenics movement had enhanced some of this eliminationist tendency by injecting into American discourse a "scientifically based" desire to create a master race. This eugenic fervor was couched in seemingly noble but practical visions of weeding out the unfit to better the cause of humanity, reduce taxes, and improve the gene pool. It appealed to nativist and nationalistic sentiments that sought to curb immigration and advance white Anglo-Saxon supremacy, and it softened its surgical thrusts with plenty of anesthesia—sedative for body and conscience alike—to make killing as quick and painless as possible in order to minimize suffering for everyone concerned. The economic hardships caused by the Great Depression had further threatened the lower middle class, feeding their sense of persecution, their feelings of economic and social insecurity, their disillusionment with democratic institutions, and their need to find scapegoats. As events in Germany had demonstrated, this could make for a particularly dangerous situation, possibly making them susceptible to demagogic manipulation by a "strongman" leader who would use his position to target one minority or another for the most severe kind of punishment.

It was true that as the United States prepared to enter the war, Americans had good reason to be worried about their future. Yet there was also reason for encouragement. Roosevelt's New Deal programs had saved the lower middle class and others from total economic destruction and staved off mob rule. American society was also surprisingly peaceful given all of the pressures it was under. Despite the FBI's highly publicized gun battles with public enemies such as John Dillinger and Pretty Boy Floyd, the newspapers' obsessions with crime waves, and politicians' urgent calls about the "war on crime," homicide in the United States actually had dropped by nearly 50 percent from 1933 to the early 1940s, and other reported serious crime (rape, robbery, assault, and burglary) had declined by one-third.[2] As most Americans saw it, J. Edgar Hoover's crackerjack G-men commanded respect throughout the world as a professional law enforcement agency that had virtually invented crime control, and the federal government had established one of the world's toughest prisons, Alcatraz Federal Penitentiary, in San Francisco Bay, matching several states in "strict but fair" prison discipline.

As well, lynching—which one black writer characterized as "much more of an expression of Southern fear of Negro progress than of Negro crime"—had finally gone into steep decline.[3] In terms of the most severe punishment, the United States hadn't joined the distinct international trend away from the death penalty that criminologists said had been increasing during the course of the last century—and the number of executions had increased during the Depression. But American executions hadn't skyrocketed. (The national tally of persons put to death by the state had gone from 140 in 1932 to 194 in 1936.) Six states (all in the North) didn't have capital punishment on their statute books at all, and other states had reduced the number of crimes considered capital crimes.

Many Americans figured they had "modernized" the death penalty by having the state take over executions, moving them inside prisons instead of making them such a mob spectacle, and changing the method of execution from grisly hangings to mechanical, clinical, and scientific procedures. Citizens prided themselves on the fact that their government went to considerable lengths to reduce the pain and suffering of those it put to death. By 1940, twenty-one of the forty-two states that had the death penalty used electrocution and eight employed lethal gas; the rest still clung to the noose or the firing squad. "In any case," America's leading criminologist, Edwin H. Sutherland, commented, whatever the method, "the principal distress is due to the anticipation of death rather than to the actual execution of the penalty."[4]

Most penal experts contended that a gassing was not as bad as a lynching, a hanging, or even an electrocution, calling the gas chamber the "most humane" form of capital punishment. They also said it compared favorably to how the death penalty was meted out in other countries. After all, it could be argued, everyone asphyxiated by lethal gas had been tried in a court of law, convicted of a capital crime, legally sentenced to death, allowed to appeal, and put to death in front of witnesses that included members of the press. There were no secret executions, no mass executions. Nearly every one of those condemned to die had been sentenced for murder (except that North Carolina's capital offenses included rape, or burglary with attempted rape). And although eugenicists in several states had tried to introduce euthanasia laws, as late as the early 1940s there still were no such statutes on the books in the United States, and hence there were no executions drawn from mental hospitals or institutions for the retarded. The only "unfit" persons gassed to death in the United States were dangerous criminals, went the argument.

In 1940 twenty-two men in eight American states were gassed to death by hydrogen cyanide, and in 1941 six states registered twenty-four such capital punishments—not much of an upsurge. These were not huge numbers, and, at the time, so far as most Americans knew, they were the only lethal gas executions carried out in the world. But that was about to change.

The American criminal justice system in 1940 remained riddled with defects and deficiencies. A decade earlier, the blue-ribbon Wickersham Commission had documented the scandalous way that justice was being administered throughout the United States. Its report had devoted an entire volume to "Lawlessness in Law Enforcement," detailing such abuses as police corruption and the "third degree" (torture), which it defined as "the inflicting of pain, physical or mental, to extract confessions or statements." The panel characterized police brutality as "extensively practiced" throughout the United States and described suspects whom the police subjected to beatings or sexual indignities in order to get what they wanted. When Buffalo's police chief was brought to testify, he openly expressed his contempt for the guarantees of individual rights in the U.S. Constitution.[5] The commission's voluminous findings shook up the legal system, but they did not bring an end to all of the abuses and shortcomings highlighted in its reports.

By current standards, the courts of the period granted fewer rights to criminal defendants than they do today: police routinely used beatings and torture to extract their confessions; poor defendants weren't constitutionally entitled to a lawyer; police could question a suspect without an attorney present; forensic techniques were shockingly primitive; illegally obtained evidence could later be used to send someone to the gas chamber; and so on. Mental patients, hospital patients, and other wards of the state also enjoyed fewer protections than they would later obtain.

Blacks during the Depression suffered disproportionately from poverty, discrimination, and harsh criminal penalties. In one of the era's most infamous cases, nine young black men in Scottsboro, Alabama, had been arrested for allegedly raping two white women on a freight train. The "Scottsboro Boys" were later convicted in a kangaroo court and sentenced to death, but the Communist Party seized on the case and fought their cause all the way to the Supreme Court, which sent the case back to state court in 1932. But the case dragged on for more than a decade, and by the time the defendants went free, they had served in the aggregate more than one hundred years for a crime they had not committed.[6] Nevertheless, the conditions that produced the injustice still existed in 1940, just as they had in 1900.

Also during the Depression, the U.S. Supreme Court took on a case in which white deputy sheriffs in Mississippi used leather straps to repeatedly beat black defendants suspected of murder until they confessed. Asked how much he had whipped one defendant, a deputy replied, "Not too much for a Negro."[7] In that instance the court reversed the convictions, but the ruling didn't end such brutal practices in the South or elsewhere.

Racial problems weren't confined to Alabama or Mississippi; they existed in one form or another in every region of the country. Throughout the United States race often helped determine who was labeled a dangerous criminal and how severely they were punished. National studies found that racial minorities—namely, blacks, Native Americans, and Asians—were several times more likely than whites to be arrested, convicted, and imprisoned or executed.[8] A report of the era from North Carolina noted that although blacks comprised only 27.5 percent of the state's population, they accounted for more than 56 percent of the state prisoners. The most common offense was burglary, but blacks were also convicted of homicide at a rate more than three times that of whites.[9] Although some whites cited such statistics to bolster their argument that the "black race was more criminal than the white race," the fact was that blacks in North Carolina (and in other parts of the nation, especially the South) were subjected to Jim Crow discrimination, excluded from juries, denied the right to vote, and sharply restricted in their educational and economic opportunities, so it was by no means clear that blacks were inherently any more criminal than whites would have been if subjected to the same treatment. This, however, didn't stop whites from labeling them as such. By the 1940s scholars were increasingly producing studies suggesting that blacks were more likely to be condemned to death, wrongfully and otherwise, than whites, due to the power of racial discrimination.[10] Yet the problem of the color line remained one of America's most deep-seated and vexing problems.

William Wellman's ordeal was illustrative of what was going on in North Carolina at the time. In 1941 Wellman, a black ex-convict, was accused of raping an elderly white woman in Statesville, North Carolina. Police showed Wellman's mug shot to the victim and a witness and officers put the suspect in a police lineup, but the pair failed to identify him. When the police made him stand in a second lineup, the victim declared, "He looks like the man, but if he is the man, he has changed somewhat from the time I saw him." Although Wellman claimed to have been at his job in Virginia on the day in question, and there was no other evidence against him, he was charged with capital rape, and his alibi was ignored.

Even at that late date, someone in Wellman's situation might have been lynched in some parts of the South. In North Carolina, however, authorities had been discouraging that kind of action for more than a generation. In 1906, after a mob in the backcountry strung up and mutilated five African-Americans, the governor had called out the National Guard, and the ringleader was prosecuted and sent to state prison. There was also a state antilynching law in effect. So, although Wellman was accused of raping a white woman, he wasn't lynched. An all-white jury quickly convicted him soon enough, however, based on very little evidence.

The day after the verdict, the local newspaper reported on its front page that Nazi forces had invaded Russia and an African-American in town had been sentenced to die in the gas chamber. After Wellman's court appeal was quickly denied, his appellate lawyer enlisted several prominent scholars (including Guy B. Johnson, the sociologist, and Paul Green, a Chapel Hill playwright and activist) to help him seek clemency. They finally succeeded in finding a dated pay receipt and other documentary evidence proving that Wellman was telling the truth. Although the North Carolina prosecutor, E. M. Land, continued to press for his execution, on April 15, 1943, Governor J. Melville Boughton ultimately issued a full and unconditional pardon. What made Wellman's case so unusual was simply that he was one of the lucky few blacks to cheat his executioner after proving his innocence.[11]

While Wellman was struggling to save his own life, another black North Carolina man, George Peele, was convicted of murder and sentenced to death despite his stubborn pleas of innocence and the shaky evidence against him. Peele insisted that the police had extracted a false confession from him when he was drunk, but his attorney failed to file a brief on his behalf. At the time, some capital appeals were dismissed because the court had failed to prepare a trial transcript, and this sealed his fate. And so, on October 10, Peele "appeared thoroughly unnerved as he was led into the gas chamber." He died still insisting he hadn't committed the crime.[12]

Ideas based on eugenics continued to exert a significant influence on the administration of American justice, as reflected in the race, ethnicity, and mental status of the accused, as well as the eugenic approaches of segregation, exclusion, and execution by lethal gas. Besides skin color, "feeblemindedness" was another factor that sometimes contributed to suspects being executed. Although North Carolina and other states had laws on their books prohibiting the punishment of the "insane," the U.S. Supreme Court hadn't held that executing a mentally incompetent person violated the Eighth Amendment prohibition against cruel and unusual punishment. Mental incompetence was not considered a mitigating factor. In fact, in 1927 the U.S. Supreme Court, in *Buck v. Bell,* had upheld forcible sterilization of the feebleminded, with Justice Oliver W. Holmes declaring in his famous opinion, "It is better for all the world, if instead of waiting to execute degenerate offspring for crime, or to let them starve for their imbecility, society can prevent those who are manifestly unfit from continuing their kind."[13] Being labeled "feebleminded" had implications beyond just involuntary sterilization. Neither legislators nor the courts exempted persons of low intelligence from the death penalty. On the contrary, instead of disqualifying such persons from receiving a capital sentence, many Americans still believed that "feebleminded" criminals *should* be put to death. John Sullivan, another severely mentally retarded prisoner whom Colorado put to death, was just one example.[14] Police found it much easier to extract a confession from mentally handicapped persons, and prosecutors noticed that they also were far less likely to defend themselves.

By the early 1940s gender was also becoming less of a disqualifying factor for execution in the United States. Until that point, women had rarely been put to death, and no female had ever been gassed. But in November of 1941 a new milestone was established in California when an American gas chamber received its first woman—Mrs. Ethel Leta Juanita Spinelli, a fifty-two-year-old grandmother known as "The Duchess," said to be the leader of a robbery gang, who had been convicted of murder. Police depicted her as a professional criminal, saying she could throw a knife to pin a poker chip at fifteen paces, and prosecutors demanded her execution. Yet convicts at San Quentin were repulsed by the notion of a woman being put to death; many of them signed a petition protesting her execution, and they even offered to draw straws among themselves to select a replacement. But after the state and federal courts swiftly denied Spinelli's attorneys' applications for a writ of habeas corpus, and the governor refused to grant her clemency, the state went ahead with her execution the day after Thanksgiving. A news photographer snapped a picture of the smiling Italian-American woman holding a crucifix, and it went out on the international wire. When her time came, the authorities strapped the woman into the death chair with her back to the crowd of more than one hundred witnesses. Under her green prison smock she carried faded snapshots of her daughter, "Gypsy," her two young sons, and her infant grandson. A week later, two of Spinelli's alleged associates were also put to death. The chief witness against them remained in an insane asylum.[15]

By the end of 1941, San Quentin's chamber had claimed twenty-four lives, twenty-two of them whites, which at the time put it second in the nation behind North Carolina in total gassings. Before the year was over, North Carolina followed California by executing its first woman, Rosanna Phillips, who was black. During the early 1940s the age range of those sent to the gas chamber was also stretched. In June 1941 Colorado executed someone who was seventy-six years old, and in 1942 and 1944 Oregon and Nevada tied the record for youngest person executed by dispatching a seventeen-year-old.[16] In 1942, Arizona matched an earlier North Carolina milestone from 1938 when it executed three persons (all of them black) on the same day. In 1944, the first lethal gas execution of a federal prisoner took place when Wyoming put to death Henry Ruhl at Rawlins Penitentiary for the crime of murder on a federal reservation. (The federal government lacked its own lethal gas execution apparatus.)

The demise of Hungarian immigrant Leslie Gireth at San Quentin on January 22, 1943, in some ways exemplified the ideal in American gas chamber executions of that era. Convicted of murdering his former jewelry store employee during an adulterous affair, Gireth later expressed remorse, pleaded guilty, refused to appeal his sentence, and left Warden Clinton T. Duffy (Holohan's former assistant) a warm letter saying, "Thank you so much for everything," as he settled comfortably into the death chair.[17] There was no resistance and no outcry.

In summary, the technology of gas chamber executions had been fairly well established in the United States by 1940, and the following decade saw some new milestones to America's gas chamber history. By and large, however, the nation's lethal gas executions went on as before, documented in news accounts but not viewed as a pressing social issue. But that was about to change because of what was happening in Europe.

For one thing, America's entry into the war renewed many citizens' fears about chemical warfare. Accounts circulated that Japanese and Italian military commanders had used poison gases on the battlefield and against civilians, and there was no doubt that the Germans would resort to doing so again if it suited their interests; everyone was sure the enemy had worked in their secret laboratories to devise even more diabolical gases and had probably stockpiled massive quantities of deadly chemicals for use when the time was right. The Americans' greatest consolation was that geography would likely protect them from possible gas assault at home.

"Why have the Germans not used it?" Winston Churchill growled in a secret memorandum. "Not certainly out of moral scruples or affection for us. . . . [T]he only reason they have not used it against us is that they fear the retaliation. What is to their detriment is to our advantage."[18]

Like the British, the U.S. Army secretly revived its chemical warfare program during the war, making gas masks, training soldiers and civilians, and preparing response plans. The government also conducted extensive research that included large-scale experimentation on human subjects, mostly U.S. military personnel and convicts. Some of the tests exposed about sixty thousand members of the U.S. armed forces to lewisite and mustard gas. Decades later a congressional inquiry would report: "Most of these subjects were not informed of the nature of the experiments and never received medical follow-up after their participation in the research . . . [and] some of these human subjects were threatened with imprisonment at Fort Leavenworth if they discussed these experiments with anyone, including their wives, parents, and family doctors."

One seventeen-year-old sailor, Nathan Schnurman, participated in the testing of gas masks and clothing while he was locked in a gas chamber and exposed to mustard gas and lewisite. Schnurman was not allowed to leave the chamber even after he became violently ill and passed out. "What happened after that, I don't know," he later recalled. "I may only assume, when I was removed from the chamber, it was presumed I was already dead." At least four thousand of the army's guinea pigs were Seventh-day Adventists, conscientious objectors who were especially prized as research subjects because they didn't drink, smoke, or engage in other harmful behaviors.[19] The army also continued to utilize gas-chamber drills as part of its required basic training for new recruits.

Soon, however, the notion of the gas chamber would change radically forever.

CHAPTER 8

ADAPTED FOR GENOCIDE

As Hitler prepared his plans for world conquest, his henchmen explored options for chemical warfare. A major program was initiated to develop all kinds of lethal gases. Some advisors expressed interest in Prussic acid, which IG Farben manufactured in large quantities as a pesticide.[1] Hitler did not favor using gas on the battlefield. But as he invaded Poland, he used the press of war to secretly authorize a euthanasia program that at first was ostensibly limited to eliminating an incurably sick patient who could be killed "by medical measures of which he remains unaware."[2] In fact, it was just a first step. To make it happen, on October 1, 1939, the Führer placed the program under the supervision of Philipp Bouhler, chief of his chancellery (personal office), and Dr. Karl Brandt, his personal physician.

In keeping with the medical nature of this approach, Hitler's SS Criminal Police used psychiatrists to provide legal authorization and help them explore different methods to secretly carry out the "mercy killings."[3] Nazi physicians experimented with lethal injection but found using a needle on one patient after another too cumbersome and intimate. As a result, they also began to test various gases. A psychiatrist, Dr. Werner Heyde, suggested they try carbon monoxide.

The "mercy killing" program was code-named Aktion T4 because its main office was at 4 Tiergartenstrasse, the address of the chancellery. In 1939 *SS-Obersturmführer* Christian Wirth, a former Stuttgart police officer then with the SS Criminal Police and assigned to the

T4 staff, supervised the construction of the first Nazi gas chamber at Brandenburg State Hospital and Nursing Home, which had become a killing center. (Police officers would prove to be among the most zealous agents of genocide.) The unit was housed in a former brick barn. The initial arrangement included a fake shower room with benches, designed to accommodate about eighteen to twenty persons. A physician examined each patient and assigned him or her a number. Each one was then photographed and ordered to assemble with the others to prepare for their group shower. The inmates were told to take off their clothes. Some who expressed anxiety were given a sedative; others who resisted were simply beaten or shot.[4]

Two SS chemists with doctoral degrees, Dr. Albert Widmann and Dr. August Becker, operated the gas chamber from behind the scenes, watching through a tiny peephole. Becker observed how quickly "people toppled over, or lay on benches"—all without making any "scenes or commotions." But he also noticed that one of the physicians (Dr. Irmfried Eberl) had opened the gas container too quickly, causing the escaping gas to make a hissing sound. Worried that this noise "would make the victims uneasy," Becker demonstrated how to open the valve slowly and quietly, and "thereafter the killing of the mental patients progressed without further incidents." Once the gas had done its work, the gas chamber was quickly ventilated, and SS men used special stretchers to push the naked corpses into the specially constructed crematory ovens.

A delegation of Nazi officials and physicians also witnessed the demonstration, and those in charge pronounced the gassings a success.[5] One of the witnesses, Dr. Brandt, who served as Hitler's physician and plenipotentiary for the euthanasia program, later met with the Führer and discussed various killing methods, whereupon Hitler is said to have asked him, "Which is the more humane way?" Brandt told him it was gas.[6] And so, gas it was.

History does not record whether the subject of American gas chamber executions ever came up, nor has anyone found documents indicating that the Nazis closely studied the American experience. Yet it is not hard to believe that at least some Nazis, particularly chemists, psychiatrists, and perhaps some police officials, were aware that gassings had been carried out in the United States.

With Hitler's approval, a gas chamber was built at each of six mental institutions in different parts of Germany to carry out the "mercy killings." The initial models resembled the first makeshift chamber built in Nevada fifteen years earlier, but they had a few new twists. One of the euthanasia administrators, Viktor Brack, described the setup: "No special gas chambers were built. A room suitable in the planning of the hospital was used, a room attached to the reception ward. . . . That was made into a gas chamber. It was sealed, it was given special doors and windows, and then a few meters of gas pipe was laid, some kind of pipe with holes in it. Outside of this room there was a bottle, a compressed bottle, with the necessary apparatus, necessary instruments, a pressure gauge, etc."[7]

Within a period of just nine months, Brandenburg alone "disinfected" (killed) at least 9,772 individuals, more than four hundred of them Jews. After the corpses were cremated, the patients' next of kin or guardians received notices through the mail that their loved ones had passed away due to some sort of natural cause.[8] Between January 1940 and August 1941 the euthanasia killing centers gassed to death seventy thousand patients and killed an estimated twenty thousand more with drugs.

One of the centers, Grafeneck, was located in a sixteenth-century castle near Stuttgart that had been converted to a hospice for invalids. Its old coach house had been converted to accommodate the gas chamber in a room disguised as a shower room. It could "shower" up to seventy-five persons at a time. It too had a crematorium and was surrounded by a heavily patrolled barbed-wire fence. Some of those gassed included disabled veterans of the German army who had fought in World War I. But in November 1940, after their relatives received sanitized death notices and rumors flared about comings and goings at the institution, local residents complained to a Nazi judge and a controversy arose.

Word of the incidents soon reached local priests and circulated up the church hierarchy. On August 4, Catholic archbishop Count Clemens August von Galen delivered a stern public sermon at Münster warning that German mental hospitals were gassing to death thousands of severely wounded German soldiers; he urged an end to the killings as well as less Nazi interference with the Church.[9] The scandal spread from there. After British intelligence dropped propaganda leaflets reporting the archbishop's charges, on August 24, 1941, Hitler suspended the euthanasia program and the Nazis scurried to cover their tracks.

But Hitler didn't end the T4 program; instead, his killers simply slowed the pace of the killing and shifted the action to concentration camps, using traveling physicians to determine who among the inmates was unfit to work. Under this arrangement, between mid-1941 and mid-1943 nearly 4,500 inmates were taken from Mauthausen, Gusen, and Dachau camps to Hartheim killing center near Linz for gassing. Another 830 inmates from Buchenwald concentration camp were gassed at the Sonnenstein killing center in Saxony. Many more victims were later selected from other camps to suffer the same "mercy death."[10] As German forces swept over Europe, they rounded up prisoners of war, Jews, Gypsies, typhus victims, insane persons, and other targets. The Nazis constructed a steel web of prison labor facilities and death camps throughout Poland. The Polish killing centers included Chelmno (Kulmhof), Bełżec, Sobibór, Treblinka, Majdanek, and Auschwitz-Birkenau, with Auschwitz being the largest and, as one writer has called it, "their eugenic apocalypse."[11]

Like the other killing centers, Auschwitz at first used carbon monoxide. But on or about September 3, 1941, its killers began to try out another gas. An SS officer took cans of Zyklon-B from the camp's supply room and ordered staff to use it against 600 Soviet prisoners of war and 250 or so other prisoners—mostly Poles—who had been selected from the camp's infirmary. The victims were crammed into basement cells of Building 11 ("The Bunker"), which served as the camp's punishment block. Soldiers dumped Zyklon into the cells and closed the windows and sealed them with sand to prevent leakage. Then they waited to see what would happen. After the gas had cleared, they discovered that some had survived, so they repeated the procedure. This time they found everyone dead.

The SS had begun to divert large quantities of the insecticide, planning to murder millions of prisoners. Medical imperatives and the involvement of physicians in the "euthanasia" process had been replaced by sheer brutality, trickery, and the treatment of human beings as vermin in an attempt to exterminate masses of people.

The Zyklon-B used in the gas chambers consisted of hydrogen cyanide and a warning agent impregnated into a solid support.[12] Instructions for its use, published by one of its German manufacturers, DEGESCH, mentioned three possible solid supports, claiming, "Wood fibre discs (discoids), a reddish brown granular mass (diagriess—Dia gravel) or small blue cubes (Erko) are used as carriers."[13] The most common solid carrier of Zyklon-B used at Auschwitz-Birkenau consisted of the small, chalky, grayish-blue cubes or pellets (Erko).[14]

In selecting Prussic acid, the Nazis chose one of their own German

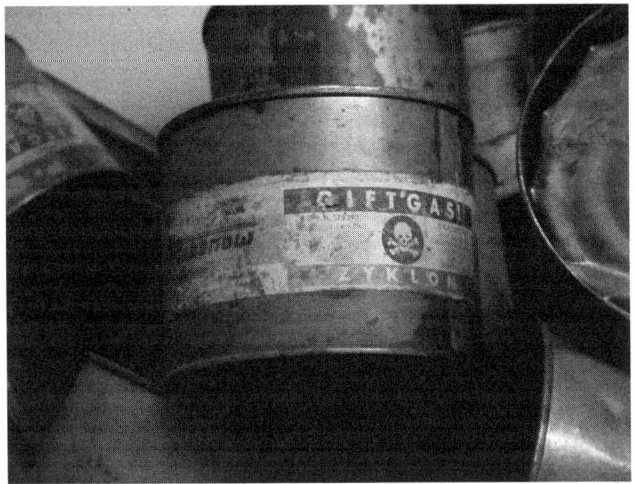

Figure 11 Zyklon-B container, KL Auschwitz, Birkenau. Photo by Michael Hanke.

creations. Hydrocyanic acid had a long history of being used for delousing and fumigation in Germany and around the world, and the German military was already using it to fumigate barracks in the concentration camps, just as American Cyanamid was using it to fumigate American military barracks. The United States Public Health Service had utilized large quantities of Zyklon for pest removal. For fifteen years hydrocyanic acid had also been used throughout America in legal executions, which had been written up in countless journals and apparently widely accepted as causing a quick and painless death.[15] But never before had it been used for mass murder.

For years Holocaust researchers wondered about the particular form of Zyklon-B that was used in the death camps, and particularly about what kind of solid support was used. In July 2000 a sample of Zyklon-B pellets from Auschwitz was obtained from Director Jerzy Wróblewski of the Panstwowe Museum Auschwitz-Birkenau in Oświęcim, Poland. Harry W. Mazal of the Holocaust History Project conducted physical and chemical analysis in an effort to identify the substrate employed for Zyklon-B that was designated for murdering prisoners there. The sample Wróblewski provided and samples of two other materials—diatomaceous earth and Drierite (anhydrous calcium sulfate)—were examined using a scanning electron microscope, and they produced dramatic results. The sample containing a Zyklon-B pellet showed a microcrystalline structure with orthorhombic crystals that were approximately 1.5 micrometers wide and 7 to 15 micrometers long. The pore size was several micrometers in diameter.

Further analysis was conducted using an energy dispersive X-ray analysis (EDX) accessory mounted on the scanning electron microscope. This method would permit accurate qualitative and semi-quantitative elemental analysis of inorganic materials in the sample. The Zyklon-B sample showed clear peaks for calcium, oxygen, and sulfur, as well as some very minor traces of barium and aluminum. It was calcium sulfate, but not soluble anhydride.

A comparison between the EDX analysis of the Zyklon-B pellet and a sample of calcium sulfate clearly showed they were identical in composition. The analyst concluded that the Zyklon-B sample was "either the natural form of anhydrous calcium sulfate, also known as the mineral anhydrite, or, equally likely, the insoluble anhydrite resulting from heating gypsum at temperatures above 650 degrees centigrade."[16] Anhydrite is a colorless, white, gray, blue, or lilac mineral of anhydrous calcium sulfate, $CaSO_4$, occurring as layers in gypsum deposits.

It is unclear who manufactured the anhydrite and whether they knew the use to which it was being put in the camps. DEGESCH had licensed two German companies—Tesch und Stabenow (Testa) of Hamburg and Heerdt-Lingler (Heli)—along with American Cyanamid of the United States to manufacture and distribute Zyklon-B. The Zyklon-B crystals that killed prisoners at Auschwitz-Birkenau were allegedly furnished by Tesch und Stabenow and DEGESCH. Tesch und Stabenow supplied two tons of the cyanide crystals a month and DEGESCH provided three quarters of a ton, according to the bills of lading that were presented into evidence at the war crimes trials.

Hydrogen cyanide had been absorbed into the substrate and placed in sealed steel cans. At the time of packaging the substrate and the gas had been combined with a stabilizing chemical that made it considerably more manageable and less volatile than other forms of hydrocyanic acid. Unlike the potassium cyanide used in American gassings, the Zyklon-B did not require immersion in sulfuric acid and water to vaporize. When the Zyklon tins were unsealed and their contents dumped into an enclosed and heated chamber crowded with naked human beings, the pellets simply released deadly hydrocyanic acid gas into the atmosphere, thereby killing those in the gas chamber.

The Nazis' first use of Zyklon-B at Auschwitz appeared to have worked so well that it became the gas of choice for mass extermination. Systematic gassing of Jews began shortly thereafter.

A former Auschwitz gas chamber officer coldly described how the poison was used. "The *disinfectors* were at work," he said. "One of them was *SS-Unterscharführer* Teuer, decorated with the Cross of War Merit. With a chisel and a hammer they opened a few innocuous-looking tins which bore the inscription 'Cyclon, to be used against vermin. Attention, poison! to be opened by trained personnel only!'. The tins were filled to the brim with blue granules the size of peas. Immediately after opening the tins, their contents was thrown into the holes which were then quickly covered."[17] Rudolf Höss, *SS-Kommandant* of Auschwitz, later testified, "The gassing was carried out in the detention cells of Block 11. Protected by a gas mask, I watched the killing myself. In the crowded cells, death came *instantaneously* the moment Zyklon-B was thrown in. A short, almost smothered cry, and it was all over."[18]

At another gassing, in autumn 1941, an officer ordered the institution's registrar of new arrivals (Hans Stark) to pour Zyklon-B into the roof opening because only one medical orderly had shown up. "During a gassing Zyklon-B had to be poured through both openings of the gas-chamber room at the same time." Stark later recalled:

> This gassing was also a transport of 200–250 Jews, once again men, women and children. As the Zyklon-B . . . was in granular form, it trickled down over the people as it was being poured in. They then started to cry out terribly for they now knew what was happening to them. I did not look through the opening because it had to be closed as soon as the Zyklon-B had been poured in. After a few minutes there was silence. After some time had passed—it may have been ten to fifteen minutes—the gas chamber was opened. The dead lay higgledy-piggledy all over the place. It was a dreadful sight.[19]

By war's end, Auschwitz-Birkenau's gas chambers would claim an estimated 1,100,000 men, women, and children.[20]

Bełżec was another forced labor camp that in 1941–42 was expanded into an extermination center as part of Aktion Reinhard, the program for the liquidation of the Jews living in Poland that was named after the assassinated Nazi leader Reinhard Heydrich. Wirth served as the camp's first commandant, supervising the construction of six gas chambers with a huge capacity of 1,200 people. As the commencement of Bełżec's large-scale extermination program approached, a flood of prisoners arrived via rail. Then, on August 1, 1942, Wirth and his colleagues conducted a demonstration in one of Bełżec's new gas chambers using Zyklon-B.[21]

Most historians assert that Hitler's order for the Final Solution, or the destruction of European Jewry, which he had publicly vowed for years would happen and which his henchmen had been carrying out piecemeal for years, was formally put into action sometime in the latter part of 1941, after failures in the Russian campaign and the entry of the United States into the war. Although pains were taken to keep written proof of Nazi actions to a minimum, Propaganda Minister Joseph Goebbels wrote in his diary on December 12, 1941, "With respect to the Jewish question, the Führer has decided to make a clean sweep. He prophesied to the Jews that if they again brought about a world war, they would live to see their annihilation in it. That wasn't just a catchword. The world war is here, and the annihilation of the Jews must be the necessary consequence."[22]

One of the enduring controversies of the Holocaust has been whether the Allies could and should have done something to try to disrupt the gassings. Within a few months after the first gassings, detailed reports about the Nazis' use of gas-chamber executions had begun to leak out to Allied countries. In *The Holocaust in American Life* (1999), Peter Novick claims "few Americans" during the war "were aware of the scale of the European Jewish catastrophe." Even many of the most informed, such as longtime foreign correspondent William L. Shirer, who later would write *The Rise and Fall of the Third Reich,* didn't grasp "for sure" what the Nazis had done until 1945.[23] But that doesn't mean that the Americans weren't told. They were informed, just as millions of Germans knew of the mass slaughters, despite the regime's halfhearted attempts to keep the genocide out of sight.[24] (How could the Germans living near the camps not have known given the "unmistakable odor of death hanging in the air for miles"?)[25]

American government officials had innumerable sources of reliable intelligence that kept them apprised of the Nazis' plans and actions almost as soon as they happened. News organizations also reported on many atrocities shortly after they occurred. From the early months of America's involvement in the war, dispatches from Europe warned about the Nazis' escalating atrocities, including their gassing of helpless civilians, although many readers may have dismissed them as exaggerated war propaganda. On December 7, 1941, the *New York Times* reported that Thomas Mann, the famous German author, had broadcast a radio appeal to his countrymen, urging them to "make the break while there is still time before the 'ever-growing gigantic hatred engulfs you.'" Mann was quoted as saying, "In German hospitals the severely wounded, the old and feeble are killed with poison gas—in one single institution two or three thousand, a German doctor said."[26]

In June 1942 the British Broadcasting Corporation announced that Germans had slain seven hundred thousand Jews in Poland. "To accomplish this," a Polish communiqué stated, "probably the greatest mass slaughter in history, every death-dealing method was employed—machine-gun bullets, hand grenades, gas chambers, concentration camps, whipping, torture instruments and starvation."[27] According to some early reports, the Germans' killing methods included a "mobile gas chamber for wholesale executions."[28]

In response, members of the Polish government in exile and the Polish resistance made frenzied efforts to convince Allied forces to threaten retribution against the "Nazi terrorists" for the "systematic campaign of extermination being carried out in German-occupied Poland." But the Allies demurred, believing they did not yet possess the strength to coerce the German war machine, and many Americans discounted the reports of atrocities. "A Jew," one old world saying went, "did not 'make *rishis*'" (did not stir up a fuss) for fear of waking a sleeping giant.[29]

Around Thanksgiving in 1942, in an effort to refute German propaganda claiming that the Polish people were "grateful" to have their country cleansed of Jews, Polish exiles stepped up their outcries. Refugees confirmed the existence of "human slaughter houses" where Germans used "technical means" to liquidate masses of hapless civilians, including women and children. Smuggled reports increasingly described the Germans' use of gas chambers in "death camps."[30] By July of 1943, official estimates by the Polish resistance placed the number of Poles executed at an astonishing 3.2 million, including 1.8 million Jews. Władysław Banaczyk, the Polish minister of home affairs, asserted to a reporter in London that one death camp alone, established at Majdanek in the Lublin district of his homeland, was executing more than three thousand persons a day in gas chambers.[31] (Final estimates set the number of Polish Jews gassed from March 1942 to November 1943 at around two million.)[32]

In the wake of such dire intelligence, Allied officials were divided over how to respond. Britain's Victor Cavendish-Bentinck, chairman of the Joint Intelligence Committee, played down the reports. "It is true that there have been references to the use of gas chambers in other reports," he acknowledged in the summer of 1943, "but these references have usually, if not always, been equally vague, and since they have concerned the extermination of Jews, have usually emanated from Jewish sources." He added, "Personally, I have never really understood the advantage of the gas chamber over the simple machine gun, or the equally simple starvation method. These stories may or may not be true, but in any event I submit we are putting out a statement on evidence which is far from conclusive, and which we have no means of assessing."[33] Representative Emanuel Celler of New York, who was Jewish, publicly criticized the United States government for its continued silence regarding the Nazis' treatment of European Jews. Similarly, the American Women's International League for Peace and Freedom (Fries's former nemesis and the first critic of the American gas chamber) reiterated that Germans already had murdered millions of Jews in Poland, and it bitterly concluded that Americans must share the guilt—because, the activists said, Americans were "complacent cowards" covered "with a thick layer of prejudice."[34]

The political climate became so agitated in some quarters that even politicians who were not considered friendly to Jewish interests began to voice their concern. At a ceremony held at the Hotel Roosevelt on March 28, 1944, New York governor Thomas Dewey condemned the Nazi campaign to wipe out Polish Jewry—this only a few days after he had refused to stop the high-profile electrocution of Louis "Lepke" Buchalter, the Jewish gangster. "We as a people are spending the blood of our soldiers, our toil and our substance in the fight against the beasts in human form who seek to exterminate a race," Dewey said. "But what is going on daily in the gas chambers of Poland and what impends because of the Nazi occupation of Hungary and Rumania requires even more." Americans, he urged, needed to rouse themselves against anti-Semitism and extend to the victims every kind of assistance.[35]

Fears intensified in May 1944, when reports from Budapest noted the construction of "special baths" for Jews that were in reality disguised gas chambers arranged for mass murder. Hungary's Jews were said to be living in fear of imminent annihilation.[36] In June 1944 the Czechoslovak state council disclosed it had received reports from Nazi-occupied Europe of at least seven thousand Czechoslovak Jews being dragged to gas chambers in the notorious German concentration camp of Auschwitz.[37]

Grim reports of Nazi gassing galvanized more representatives of world Jewry to intensify their campaign to stop the genocide. On June

21, 1944, John W. Pehle, executive secretary of the War Refugee Board, urgently pleaded with the U.S. War Department to "bomb the railroad line . . . used for deportation of Jews from Hungary to Poland," and on November 8 he urged the bombing of Auschwitz itself.

On behalf of the War Department, however, Assistant Secretary of War John J. McCloy rejected both of Pehle's requests, saying such an operation would divert "air support essential . . . to decisive operations elsewhere" and would "be of doubtful efficacy." Besides, said McCloy, "such an effort, even if practicable, might provoke even more vindictive action by the Germans."[38]

The American failure to bomb Auschwitz is a topic hotly debated among historians, but McCloy's role in making that decision has come in for persistent criticism from a variety of perspectives.[39] Some of McCloy's arguments to Pehle in retrospect seem to ring hollow. According to McCloy's biographer, Kai Bird, writing in 1992, at least as early as 1943 McCloy was one of the few Washington officials who had both detailed intelligence information about Hitler's proposed Final Solution and the power to do something about it. It is possible he could have saved as many as 100,000 Jews from the gas chamber, yet he refused to intervene. The question of whether to bomb Auschwitz was never brought to President Roosevelt. As a result, says Bird, McCloy "bears substantial responsibility for this misjudgment."[40]

Jan Karski, a Polish resistance fighter who escaped from Nazi imprisonment to warn Western leaders about the extermination camps, without success, later got to view several American aerial reconnaissance photos showing Auschwitz. "It was the saddest thing," he later bitterly recalled. "With a magnifying glass we could actually read the names and numbers of the Hungarian Jews standing on line waiting to be gassed. Yet McCloy claimed the target was too far away."[41]

Others have argued that the Allies did not have the ability to conduct precision bombing, and even if they had struck Auschwitz, the damage could have been quickly repaired or replaced. According to Peter Novick, "Though Allied intelligence knew about some of the gas chambers at Auschwitz, they had no knowledge of two cottages converted to killing facilities in the woods west of Birkenau, one no longer used and the other used on a standby basis."[42]

Eventually the world began to receive independent confirmation that the alarmists' worst assessments were true. On August 30, 1944, the *New York Times* published a stunning firsthand account by one of its correspondents, W.H. Lawrence, from Lublin, Poland, where he had toured the just-liberated Nazi death camp at Majdanek, where as many as 1.5 million persons had been killed in the last three years according to Soviet and Polish authorities.[43] Lawrence acknowledged he had been skeptical of the veracity of the stories of the atrocities, and particularly of the accounts of Hitler's systematic extermination campaign against the Jews. After witnessing the scene with his own eyes, however, he admitted, "I have just seen the most terrible place on the face of the earth, inspecting its hermetically sealed gas chambers, in which the victims were asphyxiated, and five furnaces in which the bodies were cremated, and I have talked with German officers attached to the camp, who admitted quite frankly that it was a highly systematized place for annihilation, although they, of course, denied any personal participation in the murders." Calling it "a place that must be seen to be believed," he added, "I have been present at numerous atrocity investigations in the Soviet Union, but never have I been confronted with such complete evidence, clearly establishing every allegation made by those investigating German crimes."

Lawrence noted that a twelve-foot-high barbed-wire fence that was charged with death-dealing electricity encircled the death camp, cutting off escape. "Inside you see group after group of trim green buildings, not unlike the barracks in an Army camp in the United States," he wrote. "Outside the fence there were fourteen high machine-gun turrets and at one edge were kennels for more than 200 especially trained, savage man-tracking dogs used to pursue escaped prisoners." Lawrence's story described scenes of hastily buried bodies, tens of thousands of shoes piled high, huge crematoria, and other searing images. Some newly arrived prisoners, he noted, had been taken directly to a room that was "hermetically sealed with apertures in the roof, down which the Germans threw opened cans of 'Zyklon-B,' a poison gas consisting of prussic acid crystals, which were a light blue chalky substance. This produced death quickly." Near the shower house were two other death chambers fitted to use Zyklon gas or carbon monoxide, one of them measuring seventeen meters square. Lawrence's report didn't mention where or how the Germans had gotten their ideas for the execution gas chamber. Nor did he point out where the chemicals had come from, except to say, "We saw opened and unopened cans of Zyklon gas that bore German labels. We were told the victims always received a bath in advance of execution because the hot water opened the pores and generally improved the speed with which the poison gas took effect," added Lawrence, who also wrote, "There were glass-covered openings in these death chambers so the Germans could watch the effect on their victims and determine when the time had come to remove their bodies." Based on his personal inspection, he concluded, "I am now prepared to believe any story of German atrocities, no matter how savage, cruel and depraved." He also stated that German war criminals should be hunted down and severely punished.

Lawrence's account was not an isolated one. By November 1944 the Jewish underground had clandestinely printed a booklet from Nazi-occupied Poland that described the gas-chamber killings in the German death camp at Treblinka.[44] Increasingly, oral reports as well circulated about the network of gas chambers and crematoria the Nazis had constructed—so much so that the Allied commander, General Dwight D. Eisenhower, a German American, felt duty-bound to demonstrate to the world that such reports of Nazi brutality were not mere propaganda, and he ordered all available units to tour a captured concentration camp. "We are told the American soldier does not know what he is fighting for," Eisenhower said. "Now, at least, he will know what he is fighting against."[45] Eisenhower also encouraged his forces to document what they found when they liberated the camps. William Casey, the head of secret intelligence for the European theater for the Office of Strategic Services, later observed, "The most devastating experience of the war for most of us was the first visit to a concentration camp. . . . We knew in a general way that Jews were being persecuted, that they were being rounded up . . . and that brutality and murder took place at these camps. But few if any comprehended the appalling magnitude of it. It wasn't sufficiently real to stand out from the general brutality and slaughter which is war."[46]

Future discoveries proved to be even more ghastly. On April 18, 1945, the *New York Times* published a front-page story by Gene Currivan, who reported that twelve hundred German civilians were brought from the city of Weimar (long celebrated as a fount of high German culture) to see for themselves the horrors their countrymen had perpetrated at the infamous Buchenwald death camp. (One of the emaciated inmates photographed there was Elie Wiesel.) Currivan and the others saw lampshades made from human skin, shelves lined with jars containing shrunken human heads, and "human skeletons who had lost their likeness to anything human."[47] The evidence pointed to unspeakable depravity—crimes against humanity.

With Russian and American troops rapidly closing in, executives of the chemical giant IG Farben at their immense headquarters in

Frankfurt frantically assembled and burned as many incriminating documents as they could, hoping to destroy the paper trail that might seal their fate. Farben officials would later say that they had destroyed tons of documents upon orders of the counterintelligence officers of the German army and the German police. But the industrialists were also motivated to remove evidence of their own crimes. Some of the important records and files that were destroyed on March 21, 1945, included the following:

> Reports about visits to the United States and South America . . . all correspondence dealing with payments and deliveries of war materials to occupied, neutral, or allied countries . . . secret files containing information about certain individuals and visits of foreign guests to Farben plants . . . records, invoices, and information concerning sodium cyanide . . . all secret correspondence with Wehrmacht departments and government offices . . . records and plans for new chlorine cartel agreements to be made after the war . . . and circular letters from Reich Office Chemistry concerning supply and prices of chemicals in occupied countries.[48]

In short, some of the cartel's most incriminating records were gone, although shards of other evidence kept turning up. In April 1945, a few days before Germany's surrender, a Russian news film of the "Nazi death factory" at Majdanek was shown to horrified audiences at the packed Embassy Newsreel Theatre at Broadway and Forty-sixth Street in New York. Released through Artkino Pictures, the Soviet film distributors, the footage showed the gas chambers and furnaces in grim detail, leaving the moviegoers stunned and silent. Nobody had ever seen anything like it.[49]

Two days later, members of the American press captured additional graphic images of yet another death camp. The concentration camp Dachau, outside Munich, had officially opened on March 22, 1933, as a model prison for Communists and other political enemies. When American troops liberated it on April 29, 1945, they were shocked to find emaciated survivors as well as withered corpses stacked helter-skelter near the ovens. Mountains of shoes and other clothing attested to those who had perished in the institution's four gas chambers. Some visitors couldn't smell the faint odor of bitter almonds that pervaded the cavernous, empty chambers, but the telltale piles of discarded canisters emblazoned with yellow-and-red "ZYKLON B . . . Giftgas! . . . DEGESCH" and "FARBEN INDUSTRIE" stickers suggested how the Germans had murdered millions of defenseless prisoners, using deadly cyanide gas that was purportedly manufactured as pesticide. The gas chamber was only one of the Nazis' countless atrocities, but it furnished some of the most graphic proof of their commitment to carrying out mass murder and extermination.

The word went out—by wire, telephone, radio, newsreel, and print—about the immense scope of the genocide. Yet nobody noted that it had been the United States Army and American scientists, industrialists, and politicians who had invented the gas chamber in the first place. No American commentators acknowledged how close their own country may have come to realizing the dream of using the lethal chamber to "rid society of the unfit." Writers seemed to have forgotten that philosophers, authors, and do-gooders on both sides of the Atlantic had been yearning for the lethal chamber for decades. Nobody stated the lamentable fact that the radical eugenicists and racial supremacists seemed to have gotten what they had wished for.

References to the American version of the gas chamber made people uneasy, as a piece of motion picture history illustrates. In 1944 the Hollywood director Billy Wilder, a German-born Jew, filmed one of the great noir movies of all time, *Double Indemnity,* starring Fred MacMurray. However, in adapting Raymond Chandler's story for the screen, Wilder decided at the last moment to leave out a final dramatic scene he had shot showing his star being executed in San Quentin's gas chamber—perhaps because it struck too closely to a nerve and could have reminded viewers of matters too sensitive to ponder.

Immediately after the discovery of the German death camps, many American officers and GIs initially expressed outrage toward the Germans and sympathy for the survivors they had liberated. It didn't take long, however, for some latent prejudices against Jews and Eastern Europeans to resurface. "About June of 1945, I began to feel and see a change in attitudes in the American military towards refugees and displaced persons, especially towards Jews," one Jewish-American officer assigned to the occupation confided. Among the arriving Americans, many of whom came from the hinterlands of the South and Midwest, where white-supremacist views remained strong, Jews were sometimes viewed as "scum, dirty, filthy people, undisciplined, dangerous, troublesome scavengers," whereas Germans were seen as "salt of the earth." In the words of one United Nations truck driver, "Hitler should have killed all the Jews." As historian Joseph W. Bendersky has pointed out, many U.S. military commanders of the period were also anti-Semitic.[50]

In fact, the concentration camps had been "liberated," but their prisoners had not. Jewish former inmates of Dachau were kept confined to their barracks and sprayed with DDT to rid them of vermin.[51] "We appear to be treating the Jews as the Nazis treated them except we do not exterminate them," Earl G. Harrison, the U.S. representative on the Inter-Governmental Committee on Refugees, complained in a report to President Harry S. Truman in August 1945. "They are in concentration camps in large numbers under our military guard instead of S.S. troops. One is led to wonder whether the German people . . . are not supposing that we are following or at least condoning Nazi policy."[52] Truman received Harrison's report shortly after authorizing the plan that Harry Stimson, McCloy, and others had put forward for the dropping of the atomic bomb on Japanese cities.

Exposure of the genocide in Europe raised concerns about race to a new level in the United States. Racism—particularly against Native Americans, blacks, Mexicans, Asians, and other people of color—was far from alien to the American ethos, but talk about racial problems was still relatively muted. And while American anti-Semitism had never been as virulent as the German strain, nor had America's treatment of Jews been as vicious as its treatment of Indians and blacks, the reports from Europe nevertheless highlighted the fact that Jews were still discriminated against in certain spheres of American society. They were often excluded from membership in elite clubs and educational institutions, for example, and barred from living in certain neighborhoods.

In 1947 Hollywood released two major motion pictures dealing with American anti-Jewish prejudice, *Crossfire,* directed by Edward Dmytryk, and *Gentleman's Agreement,* starring Gregory Peck, which won the Academy Award for Best Picture. A few months later the journalist Carey McWilliams noted in *A Mask for Privilege* (1948), his classic study of American anti-Semitism, "The Jewish stereotype is to be sharply distinguished from the Negro stereotype in two respects. In the first place, the Jew is universally damned, not because he is lazy, but because he is *too* industrious; not because he is incapable of learning, but because he is *too* intelligent—that is, too knowing and cunning."[53]

Passions ran high in some quarters to hold the Nazi leaders to account for their barbarous behavior. In anticipation of the Allied victory over Nazi Germany, Churchill, Stalin, and Roosevelt had agreed at Yalta in February 1945 that Axis leaders should be prosecuted after the war, and shortly before he died, in April of that year, President Roosevelt appointed Associate Justice Robert H. Jackson of the U.S. Supreme Court to serve as chief U.S. counsel for the prosecution of

Nazi war criminals. Jackson and his counterparts met to discuss ground rules for the tribunals, and the victorious nations later signed a formal agreement establishing the basis for the proceedings. After the judges and lawyers were selected and indictments were issued against the major figures, the International Military Tribunal opened its trials at Nuremberg on November 20, 1945. "Not only are they in peril of the death sentence," wrote Rebecca West in *The New Yorker,* "but there is constant talk about millions of dead and arguments whether they died because of these men or not, and there now emanates from them a sense of corruption hardly less tangible than the smell which, as one walks through the old town of Nuremberg, sometimes rises from the rubble where one of the thirty thousand missing Nurembergers has not fully reacted to time and the disinfectant spray."[54]

On October 1, 1946, people around the world were riveted as verdicts were handed down at Nuremberg, resulting in death sentences for eleven of the twenty-one major defendants. Announcements of *"Tode durch den Strang!"* (Death by the rope!) reverberated in the courtroom. And yet, although more trials continued through April 1949, resulting in additional sentences for Nazi doctors, military and government officials, and Nazi party leaders, the American public seemed far less concerned about the outcome of the trials than the Europeans were.

One of the Nuremberg trials prosecuted the least energetically was the IG Farben case, conducted from August 27, 1947, to July 30, 1948.[55] One of the charges outlined in the complicated case was that DEGESCH, in which Farben had a 42.5 percent interest, had supplied Zyklon-B for the extermination of enslaved persons in concentration camps throughout Europe.

According to the prosecutors, the proprietary rights to Zyklon-B belonged to DEGUSSA, which had developed the process by which Zyklon-B was manufactured using absorbent pellets. DEGUSSA had for a long time sold Zyklon-B through DEGESCH, which it and Farben controlled. DEGESCH did not physically produce Zyklon-B itself, but because it owned the patent and the manufacturing license, it was therefore considered the producer of the substance.

Dessauer Werke für Zucker und Chemische Werke (located about fifty kilometers north of Leipzig) manufactured the lethal product. Dessauer had acquired the stabilizer from IG Farben, the warning agent from Schering AG, and the Prussic acid from Dessauer Schlempe, and then assembled them into the final Zyklon-B. Starting in 1943 it was manufactured with the warning agent, so that it could better serve its purpose as an execution gas. Once it produced Zyklon-B, DEGESCH sold the product to DEGUSSA. To cut costs, DEGUSSA sold the marketing rights of the gas to two intermediaries: Heerdt-Lingler (Heli) and Tesch und Stabenow (Testa), who split their territory along the Elbe River, with Heli handling the clients to the west and Testa handling those in the east. According to the prosecutors, Testa supplied most of the Zyklon-B to Auschwitz, and Testa's owner, Dr. Tesch, personally conducted experiments on the feasibility of using Zyklon-B not only as a pesticide but also as a means of mass murder.[56]

The owner of DEGESCH, the German chemist Dr. Gerhard Peters, was fully aware of everything the Nazis had done with his product, although he denied responsibility. With the support of IG Farben, Peters and Tesch had initiated research that had circumvented many of the problems associated with hydrogen cyanide's use as a fumigating agent in order to adapt it for use in the gas chambers. Some of this had involved adding an irritant tear gas to the odorless hydrogen cyanide that would warn anyone of the lethal gas's presence. They had also added a chemical stabilizer that was soaked into some porous, highly absorbent material in order to produce a mixture that was not a liquid, but solid, free-flowing granules that were different from the discoids.

As the patent holder for Zyklon-B and the leading authority on its uses for fumigation, Peters had also closely followed its use in the United States and often publicized how U.S. immigration officials and others employed it to remove pests. In the 1930s and '40s Peters produced articles, advertisements, and at least one film to extol the virtues of Zyklon-B.

DEGUSSA's business manager, Dr. Walter Heerdt, the individual credited as the inventor of Zyklon-B, was among those who testified at Nuremberg. Twenty-four Farben executives were charged with plunder and spoliation of private property in German-occupied territories and other war crimes, and thirteen were convicted and sentenced to prison. But given what they had done, they got off lightly.

At Nuremberg the victors amassed voluminous reports and shocking testimony about the Germans' atrocities: their "waging of aggressive war"; their war crimes (violations of the laws or customs of war), such as the murder or ill-treatment of prisoners of war or persons on the seas, killing of hostages, plunder of public or private property, wanton destruction of cities, towns, or villages, or devastation not justified by military necessity; and "crimes against humanity"—namely, murder, extermination, enslavement, deportation, and other inhumane acts committed against any civilian population, before or during the war, as well as persecution based on racial, religious, or political grounds. But although the Nazis' use of the gas chamber against the Jews figured prominently in the war crimes trials, it was not the main focus. When the war criminal defendants attempted to argue that some of the acts they were accused of perpetrating were not so different from acts their accusers may have committed, the court's president, Lord Justice Sir Geoffrey Lawrence, simply responded, "We are not interested in what the Allies may have done."[57]

In addition to the Nuremberg tribunal, numerous trials of Nazi war criminals were held in the British, French, American, and Soviet sectors of Germany, in Austria, at Bergen-Belsen and Auschwitz, and in many other places where the crimes took place. Most of the later proceedings involved physicians, *SS-Einsatzgruppen* officers, or camp guards.[58] The British Military Tribunal in Hamburg tried three executives of the firm that had the exclusive agency for the supply of Zyklon-B gas east of the River Elbe.[59] The defendants included Tesch; Tesch's *prokurist,* or second-in-command, Karl Weinbacher; and Dr. Joachim Drosihn, a zoologist who was employed as the firm's first gassing technician. All three were accused of having supplied poison gas used for killing Allied nationals in concentration camps, knowing how it was to be used. Tesch and Stabenow had also supplied heating elements to vaporize Zyklon-B gas, as well as pipes for the gas-chamber circulation system, which they claimed had been standard issue for fumigation chambers. The defendants claimed they had no knowledge about the gas being used for anything other than fumigation purposes.[60]

Prosecutors contended that from 1941 to 1945 the company accepted orders for vast quantities of Zyklon-B (two tons per month to Auschwitz-Birkenau alone), knowing that it was being used to exterminate human beings. They also presented testimony to support their charges. The judge advocate agreed that "among those unfortunate creatures [who were gassed to death in the camps,] undoubtedly there were many Allied nationals." Tesch and Weinbacher were convicted, sentenced to death, and hanged, although Drosihn was acquitted. Known as the "Zyklon-B Case," it included no references to America's invention and use of the gas chamber, American Cyanamid's and DuPont's manufacture with IG Farben of Zyklon-B, or the collaboration of American and German officials and executives in gas-chamber technology.[61]

Dr. Peters, the former general manager of DEGESCH, got off more lightly. The German insecticide expert and chief promoter of Zyklon-B had been the executive in charge of its manufacture. His defense included the claim that in producing Zyklon-B he acted in good faith, thinking that he was "bringing relief to people sentenced to death in any case." The Frankfurt Court of Assizes sentenced him to five years imprisonment in 1949 for having "contributed to manslaughter." His treatment prompted an outcry among German democrats, prompting the superior court to upgrade the crime from manslaughter to murder. But after much legal wrangling, his sentence was only increased to six years. His case would continue to spark controversy throughout the 1950s, as the Frankfurt district attorney brought him up on trial again based on newly discovered evidence. This time he was charged with being "an accessory to murder in 300,000 cases." He ended up being acquitted, allowing him to return to his position as a management executive at a chemical plant near Cologne.[62]

During the war crimes era it would have been problematic for the U.S. to delve too deeply into the Zyklon-B can of worms. For one thing, since 1924 several states in the United States had been using hydrogen cyanide in gas chambers to legally execute prisoners, and all of those states and the federal courts accepted that such lethal gas executions resulted in a quick and painless death that did not violate the Eighth Amendment ban on cruel and usual punishment.

Farben and DuPont had a close relationship going back to 1919. Farben had owned $838,412 in DuPont stock, and DuPont owned more than $2 million worth of Farben shares. American Cyanamid had also been part of the same cartel. Their communications and linkages continued well into the war. As a result of their close business relationship, some German chemical executives and Nazi officials must have known a great deal about America's development and use of gas-chamber executions, just as some American chemical executives and government officials must have been informed through corporate channels about what the Nazis were doing with their gas chambers against the Jews.

Throughout the war and during its aftermath, for instance, American intelligence agents were alerted to the longstanding commercial relationship and information exchange between DuPont and IG Farben by means of a secure route through Basel, Switzerland, involving IG Chemie. According to a secret agent (code-named "Ralph") for the Office of Strategic Services (OSS), the forerunner of the Central Intelligence Agency, top-secret correspondence between the German and

American chemical interests were kept "locked in a special safe, to which no one in the company had access other than three or four special directors." Sources reported that this exchange had continued even through the war.[63]

"Ralph" was Erwin Respondek.[64] Respondek (1894–1971) was a German economist, politician, and secret resistance fighter against the Nazis who spied for the United States. He originally came from Upper Silesia, the region in which Auschwitz and other death camps were located. Respondek had a son-in-law—Friedrich W. "Fritz" Hoffmann—who was a Frankfurt chemist working in the Germans' chemical warfare laboratories near Berlin.[65] Hoffmann and others passed information about the Germans' poison gases to Respondek, who passed it on to Sam E. Woods, who served from 1937 to 1941 as the junior U.S. commercial attaché in Berlin and from 1942 served as consul general in Zurich and Vaduz.

According to Respondek, a prominent German industrialist spoke with him in December 1945 to urge him to intervene with former U.S. secretary of state Cordell Hull to try to squelch the war crimes prosecution of IG Farben's directors for having knowingly supplied the SS with poison gas to murder Jewish prisoners. At the time the industrialist reminded Respondek of Farben's connections to DuPont and other powerful American interests.[66]

Respondek said he would relay the information to Ambassador Robert D. Murphy, who was a key American intelligence agent and diplomatic go-between, then stationed in Berlin. Shortly after Christmas 1945, Murphy sent a report to the U.S. State Department. Respondek later learned that when the U.S. State Department confronted DuPont executives about the allegations, they confirmed the industrialist's statements. Afterward the criminal charges against IG Farben executives for shipping the poison gas to Auschwitz could not be conclusively proven.[67]

One reason American prosecutors were pressured to avoid digging too deeply into the cartel was that since late 1942 E.I. DuPont de Nemours and Company had been the leading private contractor in the all-powerful Manhattan Project, building and operating all of the project's installations, including the Clinton Engineer Works in Oak Ridge, Tennessee, and elsewhere. Many U.S. military insiders thought that DuPont *was* the War Department, and vice versa. There were also many personal and political ties. For example, FDR's son, Franklin D. Roosevelt Jr., had married Ethel du Pont, a daughter of Eugene du Pont Jr.[68]

McCloy must have been particularly relieved that further disclosures were avoided. In March 1945, President Roosevelt greeted him one day with a mock Hitler salute, saying, "Heil, McCloy, Hochkommisar für Deutschland!" (Hail McCloy, High Commissioner for Germany!).[69] But FDR's close advisor, Secretary of the Treasury Henry Morgenthau Jr., privately objected that McCloy's "clients are people like General Electric, Westinghouse, General Motors," noting just some of the corporations his nemesis had done battle with over the years.[70] McCloy himself recommended that FDR select a military man, General Lucius D. Clay, to become the first high commissioner. Clay was duly appointed.

In late 1945, after working on the Germany peace plan, participating in the decision to drop the atomic bomb, and drafting the articles of surrender for Japan, McCloy left government service to return to private practice. Nelson Rockefeller had invited him to join the family firm, which then became known as Milbank, Tweed, Hadley & McCloy. His main task involved lobbying for the gas and oil industry. In 1947 he became the first president of the World Bank.[71]

In 1949 President Truman appointed McCloy as the second high commissioner of West Germany (over another candidate, his brother-in-law Lewis Douglas). At the same time, an obscure figure in Germany, Konrad Adenauer, the former mayor of Cologne, was selected to be West Germany's first postwar chancellor. Adenauer, seventy-three, had been married to Gussy Zinsser, a cousin of McCloy's wife (and Douglas's wife), who had died in 1945 after her release from a German concentration camp.[72] "There is some destiny about all this business," McCloy said. "Germany seems to dog my footsteps."[73]

In his supremely powerful post as high commissioner, a post he held until 1952, with offices housed in IG Farben's former corporate headquarters, McCloy shaped the course of postwar Germany. He also unilaterally granted clemency to dozens of convicted Nazi war criminals (including Alfred Krupp, Klaus Barbie, Friedrich Flick, and the organizer of the Berlin Olympics) and suspended the hunt for others still on the loose. Eleanor Roosevelt wrote to McCloy to ask, "Why are we freeing so many Nazis?"[74]

Whether it was because of a "soft spot" McCloy had for German fascists or realpolitik (the pressures of the cold war and the onset of the Korean War had "made more important than ever a pro-American West Germany, rearmed and thus a bulwark against the Russians"), his failure to hold the Nazis and American interests to full account for their crimes put a disturbing twist on both the judgment at Nuremberg and his own legacy as far as some historians are concerned. Telford Taylor, who took part in the prosecution of the Nazi war criminals, wrote, "Wittingly or not, Mr. McCloy has dealt a blow to the principles of international law and concepts of humanity for which we fought the war."[75] But McCloy's posture toward Nazi Germany also needs to be reexamined with closer scrutiny of his deep ties to Nazi interests and American corporations that were linked to IG Farben.

Regardless of to what extent any of the Nazis were held accountable for their war crimes, by the early 1950s the gas chamber had acquired an extremely bad reputation as a result of what the Nazis had done. Nevertheless, it remained to be seen how Americans would view their own gas chambers. The nation's leading anti–death penalty organization, the American League to Abolish Capital Punishment, had "barely survived the 1940s," and up until that point gas executions had generally been regarded as "humane."[76] Lethal gas was still the law of the land in several American states, and the death penalty itself did not seem to be in much danger of ending.

PART TWO

THE FALL OF THE GAS CHAMBER

CHAPTER 9

CLOUDS OF ABOLITION

In the wake of two world wars that had occurred in the span of less than thirty years and cost more than ninety million lives (more than a million of those by the gassing of innocent civilians in prison camps), and with growing fears of annihilation from nuclear bombs or other mass destruction, not to mention rising concerns about the "enemy within," Americans had much to reflect upon. Among other things, the traumas of World War II had sensitized many nations to the need for international standards of human rights and treatment of prisoners. Millions of POWs and civilians had died or been murdered in captivity, both during the war and after.[1]

Britain's Royal Commission on Capital Punishment, appointed in May of 1949, undertook what was to that point the most exhaustive study of capital punishment. Although its five-hundred-page public report, issued in 1953, did not directly argue for abolition of the death penalty, it did question its underlying rationales, including the principle of deterrence, which was becoming so crucial in the nuclear arms race. Based on scientific review, the panel further concluded that executions by lethal gas, electrocution, or lethal injection were no more "humane" than killing by hanging. The commission's conclusions prompted intense debate in England, Canada, and elsewhere about the appropriateness of capital punishment by any method. By 1954 many nations, including Belgium, Portugal, Switzerland, Norway, Sweden, Denmark, most countries in Latin America, and New Zealand, had already abandoned the death penalty.[2]

In the United States, however, serious consideration of abolition was slower in coming, for political reasons. On the one hand, capital punishment had been used since the earliest days of exploration and colonization; it was still legal in all but a few states. On the other hand, America was entering the early stages of the black civil rights movement, with its calls for desegregation, racial equality, and an end to lynching. Moreover, the period 1951–53 witnessed one of the greatest waves of prison revolts in American history, including disturbances in some of the gas-chamber states, such as Arizona, California, Colorado, New Mexico, and Oregon. Prisoners' rights and the abolition of the death penalty were suddenly on many reformers' agenda, and capital punishment was emerging as a key civil rights issue.

The memory of World War II cast a painful shadow over American society, but like the aftermath of so many catastrophes, the postwar period often prompted deep-seated desires to suppress, forget and overcome the traumatic past. "By the late 1940s and throughout the 1950s," one historian later wrote, "talk of the Holocaust was something of an embarrassment in American life." Deeper recognition of Germany's crimes against humanity, including its use of the gas chamber, was hampered in part by cold war considerations that suddenly had transformed America's former ally, the Soviet Union, into a new apotheosis of evil, and its former archenemy, Germany, into a "gallant" outpost against Communist domination.[3] As a result, some of the revulsion previously expressed toward Nazism was now converted into disdain for "totalitarianism," which included Communism as well as National Socialism. American cold warriors framed the Soviets' ruthless persecution of political opponents, curtailment of civil liberties, and resort to extensive use of labor camps and executions as something like what the Nazis had done, conflating Stalin's crimes with Hitler's. At the same time, any effort to confront America's shortcomings and complicity was swept aside as unpatriotic.

Because the Soviets hadn't used lethal gas for execution purposes, and the Americans had, litanies involving gas chamber executions were not so readily invoked in cold war America; and such particulars as the manufacture of Zyklon-B and American complicity in the international cyanide cartel were scrupulously avoided.

Also, with many assessments of the Communist threat in the United States numbering Jews as the most numerous supporters of Communist organizations and ideas, anti-Communist zealots such as Fries and Senator Joseph McCarthy still tended to depict Jews as the most dangerous group. This paranoia about Jews reached its zenith in the case of Julius and Ethel Rosenberg, a married couple of New York Jewish Communists who in 1950 were charged with stealing "the secret of the atomic bomb" and passing it on to the Soviets.[4] When the United States government found the pair guilty and sentenced them to death, a Rosenberg supporter from the Communist-dominated Civil Rights Congress told a rally, "Every Jew knows in his heart that the Rosenbergs have been convicted because of anti-Semitism."[5] The Rosenbergs and their supporters also cited Hitler's persecution of the Jews and use of the gas chambers. Hours before they were to be executed, while thousands of supporters gathered at Seventeenth Street in New York to protest the executions, Julius Rosenberg wrote, "Ethel writes it is made known we are the first victims of American-Fascism."[6] President Eisenhower had the power to stop the Rosenbergs' execution, but he did not. Originally scheduled to take place on the Jewish sabbath, the event was moved up a few hours to avoid giving offense. Many Jews, however, were still incensed. "We were only eight or so years past the discovery of the mounds of dead in Dachau, Bergen-Belsen, Auschwitz, and other marks of Cain on the forehead of our century," wrote the playwright Arthur Miller. "They could not merely be two spies being executed but two Jews."[7] The couple went to their deaths in Sing Sing's electric chair on June 19, 1953, delivering a brutal warning to American dissidents, especially Jewish ones.

Even in the wake of the controversial Rosenberg execution, a Gallup poll of November 1953 found that 68 percent of the American public still supported capital punishment for murder, with only 25 percent opposing it. Public support in the East actually stood at 73 percent. As the method to carry it out, most (55 percent) favored electrocution, and 22 percent favored lethal gas, compared to only 4 percent for hanging and 3 percent for shooting.

At the time, most makers of American public opinion also backed the country's continued use of the gas chamber. In one ruling of 1953, the California Supreme Court claimed, after examining fifteen years of San Quentin's death house medical records, that the gas chamber met "contemporary scientific standards," adding, "For many years, animals have been put to death painlessly by the administration of poison gas."[8] In addition, many prominent writers in American law and criminology still endorsed lethal gas as the most humane execution option. In a typical statement from that period, the liberal professors Harry Elmer Barnes and Negley K. Teeters proclaimed in their popular textbook *New Horizons in Criminology* (1954):

> Lethal gas is certainly painless. It is a physically pleasant form of meeting death, and humanitarian sentiment would recommend it as a universal method of execution (until capital punishment is abolished). But even this method is revolting to many who are by profession somewhat inured to seeing men die at the hands of the state. The argument is not that gas is painful to the condemned men but that the spectacle of gradual expiration is "torture to the spectators."[9]

Such support remained so strong that for a decade or so after the end of World War II the states using lethal gas continued to put prisoners to death with it, albeit usually at a slower pace than before the war. At first, things seemed to go on as before. Indeed, on October 3, 1947, North Carolina carried out its first quintuple gas-chamber execution, putting to death three blacks and two whites (one of them for first-degree burglary) after one of the condemned had tried to prevent his execution by jamming his cell door lock with an ice cream spoon. A few weeks later, on Halloween, the state carried out a quadruple gassing of four black men.

But the pace of executions was slowing. North Carolina's tally of 111 gassings in the 1940s dropped to only eighteen in the 1950s, signaling a radical turnaround. Colorado's total plummeted from twenty-two to three, Missouri went from fourteen to nine, and California dropped from eighty-one to seventy-three.

The fact that the number of states employing lethal gas continued to expand struck many observers as a sign of progress, not a cause for alarm. Oklahoma passed a law in 1951 providing for electrocution as the official method of execution until a gas chamber was built, but no gas unit was ever constructed.[10]

Developments in Mississippi were more complicated. When Mississippi abandoned its portable electric chair for gas in 1954, many progressives initially viewed it as a major step forward, provided that the move did not encourage a return to lynching. There was good reason to worry that it might. Faced with the start of the civil rights movement, white supremacists had gone on the warpath. Both the Ku Klux Klan and many local government officials vowed to defy that year's landmark decision of *Brown v. Board of Education,* as well as any other slights to white status. That summer the battered body of a fourteen-year-old black boy from Chicago, Emmett Till, was found in the Tallahatchie River with a heavy fan tied to his neck, a victim of racial hatred. And Till was just the beginning.

It was in this tempestuous climate that Mississippi's new gas chamber sprang forth. The state's main prison was Parchman Penitentiary, a sprawling former slave plantation. In one of its cotton fields, convicts had been forced to build a bunker surrounded by guard towers and a razor-wire fence. Inside was a solitary confinement wing where troublesome convicts could be isolated and at times beaten, and next to that stood the small redbrick death house that resembled a gas station.[11]

Designed for Eaton Metal Products Company in Denver by Thomas Clyde Williams, Mississippi's shiny new hexagonal execution chamber was equipped with one chair and made to kill one person per hour. As set forth in the patent, the inventor had endeavored "to provide a neat, compact mechanism which will humanely execute the criminal or criminals with the least possible delay and confusion, [and] which will allow quick entry after the execution without danger to the attendants." There were separate rooms for the witnesses, warden, doctor, and executioner. One executioner controlled the whole operation, including the injection of the gas and the quick clearing of the chemicals and gas from the chamber afterward. According to the designer's description, "While a specific form of the improvement has been described and illustrated herein," the new version did not depart "from the spirit of the [original] invention."[12] Controls outside the chamber released cyanide pellets into a four-gallon stainless-steel container holding sulfuric acid. Two men were required to operate the chamber—one to serve as official executioner, tripping the controls to start the release of gas, and the other (his assistant) to manipulate the ventilating and neutralizing systems. Eaton's production manager Gene Clark tested the new unit on site in January 1955. According to the company's established routine, he made sure the unit was properly installed and later worked with the would-be executioner to test the chamber's killing power on a pig.[13]

Three months later Mississippi began carrying out its first human gas-chamber executions at Parchman. Its first occupant, Gerald Gallego, was a white bank robber from Biloxi who had allegedly killed a constable trying to arrest him. Later he had slain a jailer by slitting his throat. Shortly before his death Gallego was described as a blasphemous killer, but at his execution he credited a local Baptist minister for bringing him "back to God." Reverend Kermit Canterbury called the condemned man's spiritual resurrection the "greatest conversion

I've ever seen." As Gallego went to meet his maker, a chorus of condemned men in C Tier could be heard singing, "Up Above There's Heaven Bright."

But when the executioner pulled his fatal lever, nothing happened: the pellets were stuck. The doomed man had to wait in his chair while his killer entered the chamber, fixed the problem, returned to his station, and pulled the lever again. This time the situation was even worse, for only a few of the pellets dropped into the acid, so that Gallego was only sickened, not killed. The executioner had to start from scratch, evacuating the chamber and allowing the gas to disperse and detoxify before he delivered a full load of enough fresh cyanide to ensure Gallego's demise. Afterward the executioner donned vinyl gloves, a leather apron, and an oxygen mask, and he entered the chamber to dust down the corpse, running his gloved hands through the dead man's hair and the folds of his clothes to ensure that no cyanide gas remained trapped to later cause problems at the funeral home.[14]

Mississippi continued its gassings at a brisk pace. The next day, a black man from Louisiana was put to death for mugging a white woman. In five years alone, from 1955 to 1959, Mississippi's deadly chamber was the site of twenty executions, seventeen of them of black men. One of the rare white men executed, William Alvin Wetzel, was characterized as a "New York mobster" who had been trying to free his imprisoned brother. (Wetzel's brother had recently been convicted of first-degree murder after killing a North Carolina policeman while he was at large after fleeing a New York mental hospital.)[15] Unlike hangings and electrocutions, the new method seemed kind but potent as far as many Mississippians were concerned.

Maryland didn't adopt lethal gas until 1955, and it carried out its first two gassings in that decade. Both involved black youths convicted of the robbery, rape, and murder of a white woman, giving the case a strong racial flavor.[16] New Mexico decided in 1955 to substitute lethal gas for electrocution but did not in fact gas anyone until 1960.

America's gassings of the 1950s reflected the times. A week before Christmas in 1953, Missouri followed the Rosenbergs' example when Carl Austin Hall and Bonnie Brown Headley (known as the Greenlease Kidnap Killers) were gassed together at Jefferson City. Like the Rosenbergs, they went to their death without revealing their secret—in this case, the whereabouts of the $600,000 ransom they had received after allegedly snatching and killing a six-year-old boy. Justice for them proved swift, and there was no appeal. Before the pair died they chatted together and shared a cigarette while manacled in a detention cell and shadowed by an anxious federal marshal. When it came time for them to be strapped down, however, Hall seemed to be cracking under the pressure while Headley shouted obscenities at their executioners. "Shut the fuck up and take it like a man," she told her partner.[17] After they were bound into their chairs, Bonnie asked her lover if he had enough room.

"Are you doing all right?" she asked.

"Yes, Mama," he replied.

The guards who had watched over them on death row came by and shook their hands, and then left them alone. They were still talking with each other after the door was shut and the fumes were swirling around them. The woman took ten long minutes to die. "Death of the dissolute playboy and his drunken paramour climaxed the nation's most horrible kidnapping in twenty years," wrote one national reporter, trying to milk the sex scandal nature of the case for all it was worth.[18]

But in the 1950s it was California's gas chamber that attracted the most attention. Leandress Riley was a thirty-two-year-old one-eyed black man who weighed less than one hundred pounds. One of eleven children of an abusive father and a mentally ill mother who believed her children were possessed by demons, he had run away at age fourteen to fend for himself. On July 18, 1949, Riley allegedly shot an innocent bystander who got in his way, for which he was later convicted of robbery and murder. After he was sentenced to die, however, six psychiatrists couldn't agree if he was sane. Therefore, he had to undergo a special trial. Upon the jury's nine-to-three vote that he was sane, state law didn't allow any appeal, and he went to the gas chamber on February 20, 1953.

To everyone's horror, however, Riley didn't cooperate, and he even tried to hold onto his cell bars while making "a long shrieking cry." One prison official who was there later said, "The poor devil [had] slashed his wrists. They couldn't keep his handcuffs on because his arms were slippery with blood, and we had to almost literally carry him in there, set him in the chair while he was screeching and yelling." Once inside the chamber Riley became the first inmate in California gas chamber history to wrest himself free from the restraining straps. Guards had to reenter the room to subdue him, after which he held his breath for several minutes before finally expiring. His execution was a nightmare for staff and witnesses alike.[19]

Gas chamber guards rehearsed their roles in dread of making a mistake. Their supervisors sometimes assigned them to walk selected members of the press through the procedures in advance as well, both to minimize confusion and to try to make the procedures seem more clinical and bureaucratic.[20] But errors and the unexpected invariably happened. San Quentin's prison personnel became accustomed to two or three witnesses fainting during each execution, and others vomiting or otherwise breaking down under the stress.

For one San Quentin staff member the prospect of having to participate in a lethal gassing was especially distressing. John M. Steiner was a survivor of Auschwitz and Dachau who had taken a position at the prison as a psychiatric counselor. However, he refused to witness an execution and, reminded of the horror of the death camps, he ultimately decided he could not work in an institution that executed people by the use of lethal gas.[21]

Throughout the United States appeals lawyers were becoming more involved in trying to prevent executions, and California received some of the highest-profile media attention into the agonizing delays and suspense that the lawyers' maneuvering produced. In one San Quentin incident the condemned man nodded off from the fumes just as Governor Goodwin J. Knight's secretary telephoned in a frantic effort to relay a last-minute stay. Asked if he could halt the execution, the warden could only reply, "No." He had already released the cyanide pellets.[22]

Sometimes an execution came back to haunt the executioners long after the gassing was done. For example, the public's views about the San Quentin execution of Barbara Graham, a thirty-two-year-old white woman, changed dramatically over time as attitudes toward capital punishment evolved. Described as a former B-girl and petty criminal, Graham, who had been married four times and had three young children, got hooked on drugs and was convicted with two male accomplices of suffocating an elderly widow during a robbery. After gaining several stays, she finally entered the gas chamber on June 3, 1955. A hard-boiled wire service reporter who covered her death described her as "deceptively demure" and characterized her demise as "one of the most confused executions in California history" due to all the last-minute machinations.[23]

Three years after Graham's gassing United Artists released the movie *I Want to Live!* directed by Robert Wise. The black-and-white film classic re-created her execution with clinical precision. The film featured an Oscar-nominated performance by Susan Hayward and a background score of cool jazz, but the main subject seemed to be

Figure 12 Scene from *I Want to Live!* (1958). United Artists.

the gas chamber itself. Wise had his production designer, Victor A. Gangelin, photograph the holding cells and gas chamber in complete detail so that his crew would be able to reproduce every aspect back in the studio. Wise's team also interviewed the prison nurse who had been with Graham that night. The result was extraordinarily powerful. Cleansed of sap, the film's documentary-like quality contributes to its sense of authenticity. "As the minutes tick off and the tension of last-gasp appeals is sustained through the pacing of death-house formalities against the image of the near-by telephone," one critic wrote, "attendants go through the grisly business of preparing the gas chamber for its lethal role. Anyone who can sit through this ordeal without shivering and shuddering is made of stone." It was, he said, "a picture to shake you—and give you pause," which is exactly what the film did for the image of the gas chamber.[24]

By 1955 American attitudes toward capital punishment seemed to be changing. Some historians would later attribute this to the early rumblings of the American civil rights movement. From a historical peak in legal executions of 199 in 1935, the nation's total fell to eighty-two in 1954, and twenty-seven states had no execution at all. Six states—Michigan, Rhode Island, Maine, North Dakota, Minnesota, and Wisconsin—didn't have a death penalty law in force. And while no state had abolished capital punishment since 1918, leaders of America's anti–death penalty coalition that year had managed to get abolitionist legislation introduced in thirteen states. None was successful.

But that September Sara R. Ehrmann, executive director of the American League to Abolish Capital Punishment and wife of a prominent Boston attorney, Herbert R. Ehrmann (formerly an associate counsel to Sacco and Vanzetti), announced she had detected a "change of attitude" toward the death penalty in the United States. As a result, she decided to step up the campaign against capital punishment by taking her case before the annual meeting of the American Correctional Association held in Des Moines. At the time, twenty-four states used the electric chair, and seven still used the gallows or firing squad, but eleven—more than ever before—had opted for the gas chamber. Interviewed at her tiny office above a print shop, Ehrmann said, "More public officials are speaking out against it. There aren't as many executions. Juries seem more inclined to recommend leniency. The gas chamber is being substituted for hanging in some states because people think it's more humane." She added that whenever a shocking or brutal crime was committed, efforts were made to increase the severity of punishment. "But this brings only a temporary emotional satisfaction," she concluded. "The fact remains that killing criminals has never succeeded in lessening crimes."[25]

One of the corrections leaders Ehrmann knew to oppose capital punishment was Clinton T. Duffy. He had served as San Quentin's warden from 1940 to 1952, although he had since moved to a post with the parole board. Duffy was a West Coast version of Sing Sing's famous Warden Lewis Lawes, who had published several best-selling books, hosted a radio show, and inspired several Hollywood movies, even spearheading the nation's leading anti–capital punishment organization at the same time he was required to carry out more executions than any other warden in American history.[26] Like Lawes, Duffy was a professional penologist who believed in rehabilitation as much as he disdained executions. The author of a best-selling book about San Quentin that was made into a major motion picture, he displayed his views about the death penalty in *88 Men and 2 Women*, published in 1962.[27] "Each of the 150 executions I watched was a separate and distinct ordeal," he explained, "unsavory, nauseating, and infuriating. I faced them all with dread and look back on them with revulsion."[28]

Duffy claimed to hate the death penalty due to its inhumanity and its inequality. "Doomed men rot in a private hell while their cases are being appealed," he said, "and they continue to rot after a death date is set." He called executions the "privilege of the poor."[29] Lionized by progressives and Hollywood, Duffy brought enormous stature to the anti–death penalty cause and shifted attention from Sing Sing's infamous electric chair to San Quentin's gas chamber.

One individual case in the postwar era exerted a particularly profound effect on American public opinion about the gas chamber and the death penalty in general. Caryl Whittier Chessman was a career petty criminal and convict in California who waged a legendary twelve-year struggle to save his own life, becoming in the process one of the most famous prisoners in history. He spent much of his life in San Quentin under Warden Duffy and Duffy's successors.

Although Chessman looked as if he might be Jewish, and prison authorities constantly complained he possessed "superior intelligence" along with an "anti-social personality," he had been born in rural Michigan in 1921 to Baptist parents and was a direct descendant of the poet John Greenleaf Whittier. He was raised in difficult family circumstances during the Great Depression. His first institutionalization occurred at age sixteen, when he entered reform school for stealing a car. For the rest of his life, over the next twenty-three years, he would spend all but three in state custody for various infractions. Because he was so smart and unruly, many prison officials considered him a "dangerous individual."[30] After spending all of World War II behind bars, he was paroled in December 1947, but he soon reverted to crime.

In early 1948, at age twenty-six, he allegedly carried out armed robberies and other jobs with some of his ex-convict friends. On the night of January 23 the police spotted him and another parolee in a Ford that appeared to match the description they had just received in an all-points bulletin. Chessman was driving the stolen car without a driver's license, and he tried to flee. The police fired shots through his rear window during a high-speed chase, and he was eventually cornered and taken into custody. He landed in jail with swollen cheekbones, a dislocated thumb, and extensive scrapes and bruises suffered during his arrest and interrogation, although the police medical report claimed, "inspection reveals no marks, scars or bruises."[31]

At that moment the political and social climate of Los Angeles was nothing short of hysterical. The police were waging war against unidentified sexual predators and murderers whom the tabloids dubbed with such monikers as the "Black Dahlia" and the "Red Lipstick Murderer." Coverage of sex scandals dominated many of the papers. Although Chessman's guilt or innocence would be debated for decades to come, he was charged with being the notorious "Red Light Bandit" and committing sexual assaults on two young women on local lovers' lanes.[32]

Under California's "Little Lindbergh Law," a defendant who moved a victim even a few feet, or from one car to another, could be found guilty of kidnapping, and "sodomy" (in these instances, forced fellatio) was considered an unspeakable perversion, so Chessman found himself in very serious trouble. His trial, which took place from April 29 to May 21, 1948, received lurid media coverage. When it was over he was convicted of "kidnapping and sexual assault," and the judge, Charles Fricke, who had sent more defendants to the gas chamber than any other judge in state history, sentenced him to death.[33]

Arriving at San Quentin's death row on July 3, Chessman was searched, photographed, fingerprinted, and issued the prison identification number 66565. Consigned to North Block, fifth floor, he ended up in Cell 2455, a clammy and lifeless concrete tomb that was 10.5 feet long, 4.5 feet wide, and 7.5 feet high, with a solid steel door. The only furnishings were a hard metal cot, a tiny wooden table with an overhanging shelf, a steel commode and sink that were bolted to the wall, and a stool. There was no window to the outside world. The only thing he could glimpse through the bars was a government-issue clock that relentlessly ticked away his remaining time. It was there that he would spend the rest of his life.

One of the most momentous events in his new life occurred a month after his arrival, when he received a typewriter. He used it to tap out his first diary entry. "A fool, incontrovertibly, is a fool is a fool," he wrote.[34] The typewriter proved to be the instrument of Chessman's salvation. He banged out letters, legal briefs, petitions for writs of certiorari, and, ultimately, a book-length manuscript about the profound personal transformation he was undergoing on death row.

A previous convict on San Quentin's death row, David Lamson, had successfully challenged his conviction in the Supreme Court and published a popular book, *We Who Are About to Die* (1935), describing his thirteen-month ordeal on the condemned block. Lamson had not only avoided the hangman's noose, but he had also cleared his name, his book was made into a classic movie in 1937, and he became a celebrity.[35]

Although Chessman lacked Lamson's privileged background, his writing soon attracted the interest of his lawyer, Rosalie Asher, and a literary agent, Joseph E. Longstreth, and others such as the courtroom mystery writer Erle Stanley Gardner, the creator of Perry Mason. Somehow he managed to avoid execution for six long years, and he was still fighting. In 1954 his memoir was published as *Cell 2455, Death Row: A Condemned Man's Own Story.* It became a national best seller, selling more than half a million copies and translated into eighteen languages. A year later it appeared in movie theaters as *Cell 2455 Death Row,* directed by Fred F. Sears and starring William Campbell.[36]

His autobiography, told in the third person and filled with intimate details about his family and sexuality, received rave reviews and struck a chord with the American public. "No condemned criminal," one critic wrote, "has ever produced so literate and lucid a piece of self-analysis."[37] In the meantime, he evaded execution, sometimes by as narrow a margin as a few hours, by invoking scores of hair-splitting but life-saving legal technicalities, which added to his fame as a genius jailhouse lawyer. And somehow he managed to maintain his calmness and grace in the face of the most intense personal, legal, and literary pressures.

Over the next several years Chessman followed up his initial triumph by writing more best-selling books and magazine articles.[38] He also was portrayed in movies, news broadcasts, documentary films, and countless articles circulated throughout the world. Accounts depicted him as a psychopath, sex fiend, rebel, wily jailhouse lawyer, con man, fall guy, poster boy for rehabilitation, and literary genius. On March 21, 1960, his likeness appeared on the cover of *Time* magazine with the gas chamber in the background—an iconic mark of distinction for both him and the chamber at that critical time. His apotheosis from three-time loser to worldwide celebrity amounted to one of the great personal transformations in American history. Chessman's case, through his writings and all the coverage about him, shined a spotlight on many festering issues in crime and punishment. Foremost was the death penalty, and to a lesser extent the gas chamber in particular.

Like other famous cases before his—Tom Mooney, Sacco and Vanzetti, the Rosenbergs—Chessman's struggle became a political cause célèbre, even though, unlike the others, he was not overtly political. Instead, much of the fight on his behalf was waged on "humanitarian" grounds, although, as one commentator observed, the "cat-and-mouse game" also "provided an outlet for incipient anti-Americanism, as well as the expression of honest doubts about law and justice in the United States." Some of his supporters included the actors Marlon Brando and Shirley MacLaine, television host Steve Allen, writers Norman Mailer, Aldous Huxley, and Dorothy Parker, and throngs of demonstrators from Rio de Janeiro to London and New York to Sacramento. Every day newspapers throughout the world reported new developments in his drama. The Vatican, through its newspaper *L'Osservatore Romano,* appealed to the courts and the governor to spare his life. University students in Montevideo threatened to picket President Eisenhower during his visit there unless the execution was stopped. In the face of such pressure, Governor Edmund G. Brown of California, a Democrat, issued a sixty-day reprieve, causing many abolitionists to think they had won.[39]

But the reprieve set off a political firestorm in the United States. When it was revealed that Brown said his decision had been influenced by the State Department, out of concern for potential embarrassment to Eisenhower during his trip to South America, many American conservatives cried federal interference. Senator Barry Goldwater of Arizona, a Republican candidate for president, accused the State Department of being "weak-kneed," and the pro-segregationist Senator Strom Thurmond of South Carolina complained that federal officials had become "less and less able to discern" what was a "domestic" question. When Brown tried to defuse the crisis by proposing legislation to abolish the death penalty in California, his approach triggered more attacks from the political right. Comments by Vice President Richard Nixon in favor of capital punishment were assailed by leaders of Reform Judaism organizations, who said Nixon's statement "demonstrates an ignorance of the scientific studies which prove that the death penalty is not a deterrent to crime."[40]

By then, thirty-five nations and nine U.S. states had abolished capital punishment, and the trend throughout the Western world seemed to be running against the death penalty.[41] An April 1960 poll found that sitting governors outside the South opposed capital punishment by a six-to-one ratio.[42] But both houses of the California legislature refused to pass Brown's abolitionist legislation.

Chessman, meanwhile, continued his barrage of legal appeals, raising one argument after another. The courts rejected them all. On April 30, 1960, he and his attorneys were allowed to hold a long morning news conference at San Quentin. In it the condemned convict steadfastly reasserted his innocence and held out hope for gubernatorial clemency that would save his life.[43]

But after receiving eight stays of execution, on May 1, 1960, Chessman's legal luck appeared to have finally run out. Media from around the world rushed to San Quentin, where hundreds of protesters, many of them Catholic, camped out alongside the road with signs saying, "CAPITAL PUNISHMENT IS MURDER" and "EACH MAN'S DEATH DIMINISHES ME," and banners bearing such messages as "THE WORLD IS WATCHING US." Through that night they continued their vigil.

Chessman's ninth scheduled appointment in the gas chamber proved to be his last. Sixty witnesses, about two-thirds of them reporters, crammed into the first-floor room adjacent to the execution room. Five guards sat on a bench outside, one for every observation window. Just after 10 A.M. on May 2, Chessman was escorted into the small octagonal steel chamber with its dark green walls and strapped into one of its two sturdy chairs. Wearing a white shirt, new blue jeans, and socks, he showed no emotion. After two guards strapped him in and walked out, he glanced over at two reporters he knew and mouthed out the words, "Tell Rosalie [Asher, his attorney] I said good-bye. It's all right." Then he half-smiled. Reporter Harold V. Streeter noted, "He grimaces but managed a deep breath. His face with its hawk-nose and protruding lower lip goes back as though he was looking at the ceiling."

At 10:03:15, a click was heard and potassium cyanide pellets dropped from a container under the chair into a basin of sulfuric acid solution. Fumes began their ascent. "Now Chessman's mouth falls wide open," the AP reporter wrote, in a dispatch sent round the world. "His fingers which once typed out four books and numerous court appeals on his death row typewriter twitch nervously. The head darts involuntarily forward but falls back again. The mouth makes convulsive movements. It almost seemed like it was trying to form a shouted word." Nearby, the telephone rang and witnesses winced when they heard the mumbled words. Once again, the call had come too late. This time, the notice of a judge's one-hour reprieve had failed to prevent the execution.[44]

Another reporter, John R. Babcock, who witnessed Chessman's execution from only two feet away, later recalled, "The thrashing and gasping continued for five to eight minutes of excruciating agony and pain as he slowly suffocated. After a total of approximately nine minutes, the prison doctor evidently had pronounced Mr. Chessman dead. Next, a metallic voice came over the loudspeaker. . . . The voice referred to Mr. Chessman by his inmate number rather than his name and gave the details of the exact times at which Mr. Chessman was prepared for execution, brought to the gas chamber, when the pellets were dropped and when he was pronounced dead. Then I distinctly recall the voice saying, 'that's all, gentlemen.'"[45]

Caryl Chessman was thirty-eight years old.

His gassing unleashed a wave of revulsion across the globe and contributed to scores of anti-American outbursts. Students in Uruguay shouted, "Assassins!" Police in Stockholm mobilized to head off vandalism at the U.S. embassy. A headline in Italy read, "Chessman Killed in the Gas Chamber; Cruel America." Demonstrations also occurred in Brazil, Spain, Germany, Portugal, Italy, France, and other countries.

As one historian later put it, "The fight to save Caryl Chessman [had been] the most important attack on capital punishment in American history."[46] Much of the most heated opposition had occurred abroad, in nations considered friendly to the United States, yet somehow it seemed not to have engendered such an enormous outcry at home. Foreigners seemed to be more agitated about American capital punishment than Americans were. Most Americans remained uneasy or oblivious. The greatest domestic response occurred in the San Francisco Bay Area. Over the weeks and months that followed, Chessman's execution became a rallying cry in Berkeley's burgeoning Free Speech Movement, and a touchstone for Beatniks' poems and folksingers' laments. Author Paul Goodman cited the killing as "violently, sickeningly, sadistic, pornographic, and vindictive." Prison reformers questioned the wisdom of executing someone who not only hadn't taken another life but who also had proved such a model of rehabilitation. Young lawyers and activists contemplated what they could do to attack the death penalty itself. And American diplomats worried about how their country's death-penalty policies might injure America's standing in the cold war.[47]

At the precise moment this was happening, another global event that would have an impact on the gas chamber began to unfold. It started after Israeli intelligence agents located a murderer they had been pursuing for years. The suspect, who was living in Buenos Aires, Argentina, under the name Ricardo Klement, was actually the fugitive Nazi war criminal *SS-Obersturmbannführer* Karl Adolf Eichmann, fifty-four, who had been head of the Department for Jewish Affairs in the Gestapo from 1941 to 1945 and chief of operations in the deportation of three million Jews to extermination camps. A key figure in implementing Hitler's Final Solution, Eichmann, known to the Jews as the "Angel of Death," had supervised the creation and operation of the death camps. After the war Eichmann had managed to escape and eventually made his way to South America. He had destroyed all evidence of his former identity as best as he could, even cutting away the SS tattoo he carried under his left armpit. But once the Mossad obtained proof of his true identity, on May 11, 1960, they kidnapped him and took him to Jerusalem for extensive interrogation and trial. Word of Eichmann's arrest was announced to the world on May 23.

An Israeli tribunal heard extensive testimony about his slaughter of Jews in Nazi death camps, and Eichmann himself acknowledged his moral guilt but maintained that his role was minor.[48] The evidence against him included extensive testimony by survivors and a Russian film from Auschwitz showing a gas chamber that looked from the outside like an ordinary brick warehouse.[49] The trial, which received worldwide news coverage, was controversial in some quarters, primarily because Eichmann had been illegally seized in violation of international law years after the last of the Nuremberg criminals had been pardoned. On December 13, 1961, the former Nazi was sentenced to death, and following the rejection of an appeal to the Supreme Court for clemency, he was executed by hanging close to midnight on May 31, 1962.

The Eichmann case revived attention on the Nazis' use of the gas chamber against the Jews. It also raised haunting questions about the nature of culpability for crimes against humanity and how to punish such crimes. In anticipation of the verdict, the noted British historian, H.R. Trevor-Roper published an essay entitled "Eichmann Is Not Unique," in which he argued that the human capacity to commit horrible crimes, including genocide, was much more widespread than generally acknowledged. "Seen historically and in perspective," he wrote, "anti-Semitism is only the most obvious expression of a more general social and psychological phenomenon. That is why it may easily be stirred into life again." In Europe the Final Solution had applied to Jews and Gypsies, but members of other groups and classes had also been targeted for elimination. For Americans, warnings such as Trevor-Roper's carried other implications, especially given the nation's historical treatment of blacks and Native Americans as well.[50]

Writer Hannah Arendt covered the trial for *The New Yorker* and later expanded her articles into a best-selling book, *Eichmann in Jerusalem* (1963), in which she explored "the banality of evil." In it she argued that rather than representing evil incarnate, as many sought to depict him, Eichmann was actually just an average man, a petty bureaucrat interested only in advancing his career. His evil actions stemmed from the seductive power of the totalitarian state and an unthinking adherence to the Nazi cause. His only defense during the trial was, "I was just following orders."[51]

Interestingly, some social commentators of the period who were arguing for capital punishment took to invoking the image of Eichmann as a criminal, which he certainly was. Yet abolitionists attacking the gas chamber might just as readily have cited him as an example of *an executioner,* for he was that, too.

For intellectuals, perhaps the most influential statement of the period about the death penalty was the essay "Reflections on the Guillotine," written by Nobel Prize–winning author Albert Camus in 1957. Camus was a leading voice against totalitarianism and a critic of capital punishment on philosophical grounds.[52]

At the same time as the Chessman execution and Eichmann's arrest, Americans were also flocking to read or watch, among other works, *Anne Frank: The Diary of a Young Girl* (1947 book, 1955 play, 1959 movie), depicting the life of a Jewish teenager in hiding from the Nazis before she was ultimately caught and sent to her death; *Exodus,* by Leon Uris (1958 book, 1960 movie), about the founding of Israel; *Judgment at Nuremberg* (1959 television play, 1961 movie), about ethical issues raised by the war crimes trials; and William L. Shirer's best seller *The Rise and Fall of the Third Reich* (1960), regarding the history of the Nazi regime.

The image of the gas chamber hung over all of them: humanizing and ennobling the victims, exposing the executioners and holding them accountable, and detailing the rise and fall of fascism that had engulfed the world. While the American gas chamber and cyanide executions of Chessman and others were not mentioned in any of them, and Chessman's works specifically avoided mentioning the Nazis, they all inhabited the same arena and raised many of the same issues. Thoughts about one infected thinking about the other.

Historian Peter Novick has argued in *The Holocaust in American Life* (1999) that the American concept of "the Holocaust" gradually gained ground in the public awareness during the 1960s. Until then, many American Jews did not tend to stress the special quality of Jewish suffering. This was because it might have drawn attention to the fact that many Eastern Jews were sympathetic to Communism when International Communism was such a bogeyman to most Americans. What caused the situation to change, in Novick's view, was the television coverage of Eichmann's show trial in 1961. He suggests that to meet the need for an English word to translate the Hebrew "Shoah" (catastrophe, destruction), the word *holocaust* emerged as the preferred term, and it has been used ever since. The Holocaust did not become capitalized, he says, until after the Six Day War of 1967, when Jews again presented themselves as being threatened with extinction.[53]

The powerful image of the Holocaust affected not only Jews. It also intensified the guilt experienced by prison staff who participated in the executions. As one San Quentin veteran of the period later explained, "You know, in Hitler's Germany, the Nazis killed people who were simply nuisances: the mental defectives, the Gypsies, and mentally ill people. They were killed not because they committed a crime, but because they were inconvenient for a society to have around. Now *we* have a lot of people in this society who are nuisances, who are inconvenient, and I would be afraid that a society that became too comfortable with killing people would extend that charter, so to speak, to dispose of other groups."[54]

Even Earl Liston, the once-proud designer of Eaton gas chambers, who had since retired from the company, seemed to have changed his tune with regard to the appeal of gas executions. After Oregon voters turned out against the death penalty in a November 1964 referendum, a Portland bar owner was seeking to acquire the old gas chamber as a novelty attraction. Liston professed his disdain. "I'd put that thing on a ship and dump it five hundred miles at sea," he said. "I don't believe in capital punishment and I never have."[55]

CHAPTER 10

THE BATTLE OVER CAPITAL PUNISHMENT

By the early 1960s American capital punishment was being attacked on several fronts. The stream of books, movies, and news reports against the death penalty continued, and some churches and other religious organizations also voiced their opposition. Numerous Western nations continued to pressure the United States to end its executions, and America's cold war adversaries and their proxies had a field day harping on inequities and excesses in American criminal justice. These factors contributed to changing public attitudes. After 1953, Gallup polls began to show a continuing decline in public support for capital punishment, from 70 percent in 1953 to a low of 42 percent in 1966.[1]

The change in attitudes was also reflected in an expanding multipronged campaign to abolish the death penalty. Although Governor Brown's legislative attempt had failed in California, other lawmaking efforts of the era were more successful. Delaware ended hanging in 1958 but restored it in 1961. Kansas observed a moratorium in the late 1950s and early 1960s, when its Republican governor said, "I just don't like killing people." In 1964 Oregon voters strongly supported a referendum ending capital punishment in that state. New York's lawmakers moved to establish a moratorium in 1965, and some other states followed suit. A legislative campaign to abolish the death penalty in New Mexico was also successful. From 1964 to 1966, five states either totally abolished capital punishment or severely limited its use, bringing to thirteen the number of states that had effectively repealed the death penalty, and several more followed closely. In 1966 a constitutional amendment abolishing capital punishment was rejected in Colorado. The federal government had carried out only one execution in ten years, and Senator Philip A. Hart of Michigan had a bill pending to abolish it for all federal crimes.

Many judges, prosecutors, and juries had become more reluctant to impose the death penalty than they had been in the past. Compared to a total of 158 persons received on American death rows in 1935, the number had dropped to 75 each year in 1944 and 1945, during World War II, and to 79 in 1950, at the start of the Korean conflict. In the wake of the Chessman execution, the number dropped from 140 to 103 from 1961 to 1962, and in 1965 it fell to 86 as 62 prisoners were reprieved from their death sentences. At the end of 1965 there were 331 prisoners awaiting execution in the United States, and the average length of time they were spending on death row was rapidly increasing.[2] American executions plummeted dramatically, from 56 in 1960 to 42 in 1961, 47 in 1962, 21 in 1963, 15 in 1964, 7 in 1965, and only 1 in 1966.[3] Lynching had also become almost extinct. For the first time in American history it seemed likely that the death penalty was about to become a thing of the past.

On April 12, 1967, however, these hopes appeared to be in jeopardy as California prepared to carry out its first gassing in four years. Protesters completed an all-night vigil outside the home and office of Brown's conservative Republican replacement, Governor Ronald Reagan, trying to get him to grant executive clemency to Aaron Mitchell, a thirty-seven-year-old black man convicted of slaying a Sacramento policeman during a robbery in 1963. Reagan staunchly refused. "Here was a case in which every legal avenue had been tried—the U.S. Supreme Court twice, the California Supreme Court twice," he said. "The law is the law, and it must be upheld."[4]

Five hundred demonstrators gathered outside San Quentin, some of them fastening flowers to the gate and singing mournful folk songs. George Lincoln Rockwell, the American Nazi leader, caused a fracas when he appeared with a sign supporting the execution. Amid the furor, the fifty-eight official witnesses were let in to assume their posts. California's Episcopal bishop, C. Kilmer Myers, had requested churches throughout the state toll their bells at the scheduled hour of Mitchell's execution. Media organizations rushed to prepare background features.

Meanwhile, in the holding cell, Mitchell's behavior had turned bizarre. The guards found him stark naked, and his left arm was covered with blood where he had cut himself. His eyes were wild, and his hair, which had always been neatly combed, stood up at odd angles. "The state never executes the person who committed the crime," the prison chaplain who was with him later observed. "The one who finally steps into the gas chamber is by no means the same person who entered death row years earlier. To believe so is to ignore the terrible forces that mold, strengthen, shatter a man in the surrealistic world of the condemned."

When Chaplain Byron Eshelman entered Mitchell's cell and inquired about his condition, the doomed prisoner replied, "You're not Jesus Christ," and he later kept saying, "I am Jesus Christ, this is the blood of Jesus Christ. I am Jesus Christ, this is the blood of Jesus Christ." The doctor and three psychiatrists examined him in the cell and held up his bloody arm to test for catatonic tension. When they left him, he asked, "Can I put my arm down?" to which one doctor simply replied, "Put your arm any way you want." Later guards came in, wrestled him down, and pulled on his clothes. When they tried to cover his wound, he resisted, saying, "You don't want to help me, you just wanna kill me." As they dragged him to the gas chamber he let out a piercing shriek that chilled the witnesses gathering in the nearby room. The guards thrust him into the chair and slapped on the eight thick straps, binding him tight. Then the escorts stepped out and the heavy Eaton door was clamped shut, leaving him to twist and squirm. "I am Jesus Christ!" Mitchell said.

Moments later, the lever clicked, releasing the poison pellets into the acid, and blowers began sucking the lethal gas upward all around him. Outside the prison some demonstrators wailed or cheered as smoke curled from the chimney above the death chamber that some called "the smokehouse."[5]

Howard Brodie, a veteran news artist, had received permission from Warden Lawrence Wilson to attend the execution. Now he found himself just across the glass from Mitchell's struggling body. Working as fast as he could, Brodie summoned all his skill and composure to hurriedly sketch the sight just four feet away. "I did not want to believe what was happening in front of me," Brodie later declared. "His mouth was constantly moving. Bubbles of saliva formed on his lips. His chest was heaving. . . . His clenched hands showed the extraordinary duress that he suffered. Aaron sat tense, heart pounding, and mouth opening and closing, for many minutes, long enough to burn into my memory

lips
moved
slowly
dying
He sat upright
for many minutes
Brodie
67
Execution
San Quentin

Figure 13 Gas chamber execution of Aaron Mitchell, San Quentin, April 12, 1967. Eyewitness drawing by Howard Brodie. Courtesy of Howard Brodie.

the images that I used for my drawing, images which have remained with me for 25 years."[6] Another witness, who had been told by prison authorities that the proof of a painless death could be spotted in a person's hands, was shocked to note that Mitchell died "with clenched fists, the skin taut over his knuckles," adding, "I don't believe those hands ever relaxed."[7]

California's gas chamber had become an agonizing crucible for prison staff as well. James W. L. Park, a clinical psychologist, was one of those who participated in Mitchell's execution. "I find that people who function fairly calmly in tight situations have a little tape recorder in their heads that records all this stuff," he said, "then they have to work through it later." After the Mitchell ordeal, Park's first reaction was that once the lever went forward and the gas was released, nobody could stop an execution, underscoring the fact that the whole action was "irrevocable . . . and whatever potential that person may have had was never realized. Any possibility of redemption is gone." Park said his second observation was how "task-oriented" he and the other participants became. "I wasn't concerned with taking Mitchell's life," he told an interviewer, "I was concerned with, 'Was that phone on the wall going to ring? Was I going to have to answer some judge's or governor's question?' And so I was totally focused on the task—not on the fact that a man was being killed."[8]

Mitchell's execution set off waves of revulsion and exultation among death penalty opponents and supporters. Details were reported worldwide. A month and a half after Mitchell's execution, Colorado carried out a gassing of its own. Republican governor John Arthur Love, a former navy pilot and federal prosecutor, refused to grant clemency. A forty-eight-year-old Puerto Rican car salesman, Luis J. Monge, was about to enter the history books. He stood convicted of killing his pregnant wife and three of the couple's ten children after his wife had discovered he'd had an incestuous relationship with one of their daughters. In Denver, demonstrators wearing black armbands paraded in front of the statehouse, while outside the prison in Cañon City an encampment of picketers protested the impending execution.

Unlike Mitchell, Monge, who had fired his attorneys, seemed calm and cooperative. After learning that he would not receive a third stay of execution, he handed over his possessions, including a painting of the crucifixion and his pet parakeet, to two of his sons, and he signed papers giving his corneas to a blind boy in Buena Vista. Then, after a short walk to the changing room on the third floor, he stripped to his shorts as directed and walked into the gas chamber.[9]

A Denver reporter who witnessed what happened next later wrote, "The public likes to believe that unconsciousness is almost instantaneous, but the facts belie this." Journalist Gary Stiff noted that the official execution log concluded that unconsciousness came more than five minutes after the cyanide splashed down into the sulfuric acid. "And to those of us who watched," he said, "this five-minute interlude seemed interminable. Even after unconsciousness is declared officially, the prisoner's body continues to fight for life. He coughs and groans. The lips make little pouting motions resembling the motions made by a goldfish in his bowl. The head strains backward and then slowly sinks down to the chest. And, in Monge's case, the arms, although tightly bound to the chair, strained at the straps, and the hands clawed tortuously, as if the prisoner were struggling for air. Any account that leads readers to believe that death comes quickly, painlessly, almost pleasantly, is less than accurate."[10]

Colorado's execution of Luis Monge in June of 1967 would turn out to be the last execution in the United States for a decade, and the last gas-chamber execution for twelve years. This gassing, and the others preceding it, as well as the thousands of capital punishments carried out by hanging and electrocution, were about to become a legal relic, at least for a while. Now increased attention was being focused on what the U.S. Supreme Court would rule about the constitutionality of the death penalty.

Until recently, the constitutionality of the death penalty had not been in serious doubt, nor had any of the legal execution methods, including hanging, electrocution, firing squad, and lethal gas. No court had ever found any method to violate the ban against cruel and unusual punishment that the framers of the Constitution had added to the Bill of Rights, and the U.S. Supreme Court had never reviewed evidence concerning whether any method of execution violated the Eighth Amendment.[11] As early as 1910 the Court had recognized that the Eighth Amendment's prohibitions weren't limited to only those punishments that had been in effect at the time the Bill of Rights was adopted.[12] What was or was not "cruel and unusual" remained legally vague.[13] In 1958, however, the Supreme Court decided in *Trop v. Dulles* (356 U.S. 86) that the Eighth Amendment contained an "evolving standard of decency that marked the progress of a maturing society."[14] Although *Trop* was not a death penalty case, abolitionists argued that the United States had progressed to the point at which its "standard of decency" should no longer tolerate the death penalty. Then, in 1963, Justice Arthur Goldberg, joined by Justices William O. Douglas and William J. Brennan Jr., indicated a willingness to consider the legality of the death penalty on several grounds, at least for rape.[15] This signal had contributed to the de facto moratorium on capital punishment that had generally held at the time of the Mitchell and Monge executions and their aftermath.

Under the Warren Court revolution of the 1960s, the Supreme Court radically transformed the rights of criminal defendants. Virtually all of the prisoners sitting on death row at that time, who had been convicted under the old rules, suddenly found themselves with a legal leg to stand on. Their capital convictions were open to attack because the evidence against them had been illegally obtained, because they had been subjected to the "third degree" or questioned without a lawyer; because nobody had advised them of their legal rights; or because their access to the courts had been obstructed or they had been denied counsel because they were poor—matters that hadn't troubled the courts before, but which now were suddenly deemed unconstitutional.[16] Even if the death penalty itself was not found unconstitutional, the criminal justice practices that had resulted in the convictions were themselves subject to constitutional challenge. Looking back on his more than twenty years as death row chaplain at San Quentin, Reverend Eshelman sadly exclaimed, "It is numbing to realize that all of the 501 persons executed to this point in history by the state of California would have grounds for retrial in light of new decisions brought forth by the courts."[17] In other words, the Court had not only "handcuffed the police," but it had also detained the executioner.

The filing of a large number of lawsuits in the late 1960s contributed to a voluntary moratorium on executions from June 2, 1967, to 1972, as the Supreme Court wrestled with the issues. No state attempted to conduct an execution during this period. The legal moratorium was largely the work of the NAACP Legal Defense Fund (LDF), led by Stanford University law professor Anthony Amsterdam, who mounted a full-scale attack on the death penalty that succeeded in blocking all executions for five years, creating a death-row logjam. The LDF, founded in 1940, had handled a number of landmark racial discrimination cases and worked closely with the Reverend Martin Luther King Jr. and other civil rights activists.[18] Amsterdam, a descendant of a long line of rabbis and former law clerk to Associate Justice Felix

Frankfurter, had drafted briefs in several important criminal cases, including *Miranda v. Arizona,* and soon established himself as the most brilliant legal strategist in capital punishment. In the fall of 1967 he successfully argued the case of *Maxwell v. Bishop* before the Eighth Circuit, leading the Supreme Court to strike down the Arkansas death penalty and require a separate postconviction hearing on sentencing.[19] In that case, the LDF utilized America's most respected criminologist, Marvin E. Wolfgang of the University of Pennsylvania, to present data showing the impact of racial discrimination.

During the 1968 presidential campaign, the Republican candidate Richard M. Nixon made crime one of his benchmark issues and the Supreme Court his whipping boys. Upon his election in 1969, Nixon appointed Warren E. Burger to replace Earl Warren as chief justice and the Court became increasingly conservative. By early 1972 the liberal bloc was down to three justices, and some observers wondered if they would adopt an abolitionist position, even though world opinion seemed to have turned against capital punishment. But Amsterdam devised webs of intricate arguments designed to tie up the Court on several fronts for years to come. In January 1972 he returned to the Court to argue a major death penalty case, *Furman v. Georgia.* William Furman was a burglar whose pistol accidentally went off when he was fleeing a home, the bullet tearing through a screen and killing the owner. "If a penalty is generally, fairly and uniformly enforced," Amsterdam argued, "then it will be thrown off the statute books as soon as the public can no longer accept it. But when the penalty is enforced for a discriminatorily selected few, then all the pressures which normally exist to strike an indecent penalty off the books no longer exist. The short of the matter is that when a penalty is so barbaric that it can gain public acceptance only by being rarely, arbitrarily and discriminatorily enforced, it plainly affronts the general standards of decency of the society."[20]

A month after oral arguments had been heard in *Furman,* but before the final outcome of the case was announced, the California Supreme Court ruled 6–1 that the state's capital punishment statute violated the state constitution's ban on "cruel and unusual punishment," and it vacated 107 death sentences.[21] Some activists at the time concluded that there would never again be an execution in the United States. Soon they seemed to be proven right. The U.S. Supreme Court announced its decision in *Furman* on June 29, 1972, stunning many legal observers. It struck down the death penalty for the first time in U.S. history, invalidating all death penalty laws that existed at the time throughout the country. The nation's entire capital punishment system was found unconstitutional. For the first time, the Court held that the death penalty laws as written violated the "cruel and unusual punishment" provision of the Eighth Amendment and the due process guarantees of the Fourteenth Amendment. The Court found the death penalty had been administered in such a discriminatory, capricious, and arbitrary manner as to violate the Constitution, and two members of the majority held that the death penalty itself was unconstitutional regardless of how it was administered. Georgia was an electric chair state, and Justice Byron ("Whizzer") White observed that Furman's sentence seemed so freakishly arbitrary and capricious that he likened it to being struck by lightning.

The Supreme Court's decision in *Furman* was the longest and most complex pronouncement in high court history, with each of the nine justices penning his own opinion. Finding points of agreement required the services of legal experts with a lot of time on their hands. By a 5–4 margin the Court did not rule the death penalty itself to be unconstitutional for all crimes and all circumstances, only under the specific laws by which it was applied.[22] One justice, Brennan, who went the farthest in rejecting capital punishment per se, held that "death is an unusually severe and degrading punishment; there is a strong probability that it is inflicted arbitrarily; its rejection by contemporary society is virtually total; and there is no reason to believe that it serves any penal purpose more effectively than the less severe punishment of imprisonment."[23] Nixon's appointees formed a solid bloc in defense of the death penalty. In his lead dissent Chief Justice Burger referred to the "worldwide trend toward limiting the use of capital punishment, a phenomenon to which we have been urged to give great weight," but he said the Court had to rely on its "written Constitution."[24]

As a result of the decision, more than six hundred prisoners who had been sentenced to death between 1967 and 1972 had their death sentences lifted—the greatest mass reprieve in U.S. history.[25] But *Furman* had left the door open to more contentious debate, making capital punishment what some scholars later called "the central doctrinal conflict of the 1970s."[26]

Conservatives rallied to make the death penalty a hot-button political issue. Governor Ronald Reagan, who wanted to run for president, said he was "deeply shocked and disappointed" by the California court's action, calling it "one more step toward totally disarming society in its fight against violence and crime." Other Republicans teamed with law enforcement groups to restore the death penalty in the state by public referendum.[27] Then the reaction to *Furman* added more fuel to the fire. All over the country, tough-on-crime politicians attacked "lenient" judges, and Democrats and Republicans alike scrambled to outdo themselves in supporting severe punitive penalties. In the wake of *Furman,* legislators in many states soon began to write new death penalty laws that would comply with the ruling. Within four years, thirty-four states responded by passing new capital punishment laws, and death rows around the country swelled to more than six hundred condemned prisoners—back to where it had been before. During the backlash to the *Furman* decision, only one state—Rhode Island—drafted its new death penalty statute with the gas chamber as its new method of execution. (Nobody was executed in it, and Rhode Island eventually abolished its death penalty in 1979.)[28]

But lethal gas, electrocution, hanging, and the firing squad all had a significant history in the United States. Their methods of administration were more than a line in the statute books—they had actually been carried out, and each method left its own paper trail. Some of the evidence showing exactly how executions had been performed could be found in the states' own archival files. Like the Watergate tapes, such records had been compiled and kept by the government itself, and the evidence had never left state custody. Because of this unbroken chain, the evidence could prove particularly incriminating for the state. Evidence of botched, cruel, or torturous executions might make a specific method of execution susceptible to constitutional challenge on Eighth Amendment grounds.

California's Governor Reagan was well aware of the realities of capital punishment, having experienced both the legal and political turmoil over the death penalty issue, and the messiness of an actual lethal gas execution. He had not forgotten about Aaron Mitchell. And as an experienced image maker he recognized the public's distaste for the gas chamber in particular. But Reagan wanted to champion the death penalty, so he devised a smart political move.

Just as Vice President Spiro Agnew was about to resign on corruption charges and before President Nixon selected Representative Gerald Ford as his replacement, Reagan slyly suggested an alternative execution method that might overcome a variety of problems. "Being a former farmer and horse raiser," he said, "I know what it's like to try to eliminate an injured horse by shooting him. Now you call the veterinarian and the vet gives him a shot and the horse goes to sleep—that's it." (In addition to avoiding any explicit reference to lethal gas, Reagan's example about killing a horse instead of a small animal such as a cat or dog avoided an obvious link to the gas chamber, since the usual method vets used to euthanize them was to put them in a portable gas chamber, not to give them a shot. A horse, however, was too big to fit in a veterinarian's gas chamber.) Reagan continued, "I myself have wondered if maybe this isn't part of our problem [with capital punishment], and maybe we should review and see if there aren't even more humane methods now—the simple shot or tranquilizer." In closing, he left another clue that he had not forgotten about the gas chamber and its eugenic ideals, saying, "I think maybe there should be more study of this to find out, if there's a *more humane* way, can we still *improve our humanity*."

Reagan's remarks were picked up by *Time* magazine in October 1973 and widely circulated among conservatives.[29] They not only buttressed his credentials as a conservative supporter of capital punishment, thereby possibly aiding his political ambitions, but they also offered the pro–death penalty movement a useful suggestion for a new stratagem to employ in their revised death penalty statutes. His comments appeared just as Israel was responding to being attacked in the Yom Kippur War.

After *Furman,* the pro–death penalty campaign continued to turn public opinion back in favor of executions. In 1976, in considering *Gregg v. Georgia,* the U.S. Supreme Court revisited the death penalty, upholding Georgia's new capital-sentencing procedures when it concluded that Georgia officials had sufficiently reduced the problem of arbitrary and capricious imposition of death associated with earlier statutes. The plurality opinion specifically addressed "the basic contention that the punishment of death for the crime of murder is, under all circumstances, 'cruel and unusual' in violation of the Eighth and Fourteen Amendments," and concluded "the punishment of death does not invariably violate the Constitution."[30] In its plurality opinion, the Court held, "Considerations of federalism, as well as respect for the ability of a legislature to evaluate, in terms of its particular State, the moral consensus concerning the death penalty and its social utility as a sanction, require us to conclude, in the absence of more convincing evidence, that the infliction of death as a punishment for murder is not without justification and thus is not unconstitutionally severe."[31]

Given the rising tide of political agitation in favor of the death penalty, the decision left no doubt that executions would be resumed. Soon after the new *Gregg* ruling, what had been a nearly ten-year national voluntary moratorium on executions ended with the firing-squad killing of Gary Gilmore in Utah on January 17, 1977. To call Gilmore a "volunteer" for execution was an understatement: he had waged a vocal campaign demanding to be put to death.[32] Like the breaking of a taboo, the moratorium was smashed. The huge backlog of prisoners facing execution on death row quickly overwhelmed the resources of the LDF, the American Civil Liberties Union, and other capital defenders, prompting fears of a "blood bath."[33]

Amid the ensuing turmoil, several states contemplated whether to retain their existing method of execution or to switch from the electric chair or lethal gas to the latest alternative: lethal injection.[34] Texas and Oklahoma legislators vied to become the first to adopt the new method. Oklahoma's governor David Boren signed it into law on May 11, 1977, with Texas following the very next day. "I would like to see this [legal execution] carried out in a nice clean room, something that doesn't look like a prison," the Texas Department of Corrections Protestant chaplain was quoted as saying in June 1977. "I hesitate to use the word pleasant, but it would be just like going in, laying down and going to sleep."[35]

As legal analysts debated how to craft or challenge new death-penalty statutes to meet constitutional muster, the realities of death by lethal gas would finally begin to come into sharper focus.

CHAPTER 11

"CRUEL AND UNUSUAL PUNISHMENT"?

By the late 1970s American public opinion was swinging ever more strongly in favor of the death penalty. Although the public's appetite for gas chambers had diminished, eleven states—Arizona, California, Colorado, Maryland, Mississippi, Missouri, Nevada, New Mexico (until 1978), North Carolina, Rhode Island, and Wyoming—still clung to that method of capital punishment. But the legal battle over the constitutionality of lethal gas executions, and the rise of the new method of lethal injection, were just beginning to take hold.

Henry Schwarzschild, the director of the American Civil Liberties Union Capital Punishment Project—and a German émigré who had worked both in U.S. counterintelligence during World War II and the antiwar movement during the Vietnam War—served as one of the key national players in the anti–death penalty movement in the late '70s. Schwarzschild, like the NAACP Legal Defense Fund (LDF), was based in New York and familiar with all the latest developments involving the death penalty throughout the nation and beyond. He was a keen political observer and shrewd strategist who spent much of his time dealing with lawyers, scholars, and members of the news media.

Schwarzschild once told an interviewer, "American self-esteem rode high from the end of World War II to the Vietnam War. It was the century of America. We were the richest, most powerful, most industrialized, most sophisticated, most effective country in the world. That was very much the sense that America had of itself." But the long

Vietnam War proved extremely divisive and resulted in a tremendous blow to American self-esteem. As the war ended, and Watergate further shook many Americans' faith in their political institutions, the culture became "dominated by a kind of macho reaction," according to Schwarzschild. Toughness became the "universal solvent to every problem that America face[d] abroad or at home," and Americans exhibited an overwhelming desire to demonstrate to themselves and everyone else that they were a tough people. They wanted to show that they were hard on crime. They wanted long sentences and harsh prisons. Even though it had been shown that the death penalty did not deter crime or make citizens safer, and although other nations increasingly regarded executions as barbaric, Americans increasingly supported capital punishment.[1] In retrospect, Schwarzschild's analysis appears to have been very astute.

Once legislatures had passed new death penalty measures that were upheld by the courts, and the nation's ten-year "voluntary moratorium" on executions had ended, the only remaining question was how the resumption of killings would unfold. At first, the most vulnerable targets for execution appeared to be prisoners who refused to fight for their lives and rejected legal efforts on their behalf.

John Spenkelink of Florida, however, fiercely contested his electrocution, with urgent assistance from the LDF and others. Beginning in 1977 his case became a cause célèbre, and his portrait was published on the cover of the *New York Times Magazine* with the headline "Will He Be the First?" He actually became the second person executed in the United States since *Gregg* when on May 25, 1979, he was put to death in the electric chair. His gruesome execution required three separate jolts of electricity, until death was finally pronounced after five excruciating minutes.[2]

After Spenkelink's execution, attention shifted to Jesse Walter Bishop, who was facing execution by lethal gas in Nevada. Bishop, a white, forty-six-year-old drug addict, was awaiting his execution on Carson City's death row for fatally shooting a newlywed while robbing a Las Vegas casino two years earlier. Bishop had pleaded guilty and scorned appeals, preferring instead to accept his fate. As his execution date approached, Bishop took refuge in psychiatric treatment, as blond nurses in white dresses brought him plenty of tranquilizers. The Maryland man whose son Bishop had murdered said, "I don't think killing him will help my son or my feelings. . . . I just can't see where it's going to do any good." But Bishop was determined to die.[3] Bishop got his wish on October 22, 1979, becoming the first person to be executed by lethal gas since Luis Monge in Colorado in 1967.[4]

Nevada hadn't used its gas chamber for eighteen years, and those assigned to carry out the execution weren't entirely confident about their ability to pull it off without a problem. Some of them warned the witnesses that if they smelled anything "funny," they should hold their breath and exit the chamber quickly. In the end, the chamber did not leak, but one eyewitness, the TV reporter Tad Dunbar, later said, "I was surprised to see that death did not appear to come quickly or painlessly under that method of execution."[5] Such wrinkles didn't stop other states from going forward with executions by whatever means they had on their statute books, including lethal gas. But the gas chamber was no longer touted as a "humane" method of execution.

The tiny platoon of anti–death penalty lawyers kept fighting an unrelenting battle against overwhelming odds, and it wasn't until September 1983 that the next gas execution became imminent. It happened in Mississippi, a state notorious for its impoverished capital defense.

Jimmy Lee Gray, a thirty-four-year-old former computer operator who had been on parole for killing his childhood sweetheart, stood convicted of abducting a three-year-old girl, carrying her to a remote area, sexually molesting her, suffocating her in a muddy ditch, and throwing her body into a stream. Gray, not surprisingly, did not engender much public sympathy. In the seven years before his execution, judicial review of the case had been undertaken eighty-two times by twenty-six different state and federal judges. One of his latest arguments was to try to convince the courts that execution by lethal gas amounted to cruel and unusual punishment, in violation of the Eighth Amendment.

On September 1 the U.S. Supreme Court denied Gray's request for a stay by a 5–3 vote. "This case illustrates a recent pattern of calculated efforts to frustrate valid judgments after painstaking judicial review over a number of years," Chief Justice Warren Burger declared. "At some point, there must be finality."[6] However, Justice Thurgood Marshall, with whom Justice Brennan concurred, noted in his dissent that "Petitioner argues that the method by which the state of Mississippi plans to execute him—exposure to cyanide gas—constitutes cruel and unusual punishment. In support of that claim, he submitted to the United States District Court for the Southern District of Mississippi numerous affidavits that described in graphic and horrifying detail the manner in which death is induced through this procedure." In one of these declarations, Dr. Richard Traystman, director of the Anesthesiology and Critical Care Medicine Research Laboratories at Johns Hopkins Medical School, had described the gassing process as follows:

> Very simply, cyanide gas blocks the utilization of the oxygen in the body's cells. . . . Gradually, depending on the rate and volume of inspiration, and on the concentration of the cyanide that is inhaled, the person exposed to cyanide gas will become anoxic. This is a condition defined by no oxygen. Death will follow through asphyxiation, when the heart and brain cease to receive oxygen.
>
> The hypoxic state can continue for several minutes after the cyanide gas is released in the execution chamber. The person exposed to this gas remains conscious for a period of time, in some cases for several minutes, again depending on the rate and volume of the gas that is inhaled. During this time, the person is unquestionably experiencing pain and extreme anxiety. The pain begins immediately, and is felt in the arms, shoulders, back, and chest. The sensation is similar to the pain felt by a person during a heart attack, where essentially, the heart is being deprived of oxygen. The severity of the pain varies directly with the diminishing oxygen reaching the tissues.
>
> The agitation and anxiety a person experiences in the hypoxic state will stimulate the autonomic nervous system. . . . [The person] . . . may begin to drool, urinate, defecate, or vomit. There will be muscular contractions. These responses can occur both while the person is conscious, or when he becomes unconscious.
>
> When the anoxia sets in, the brain remains alive for from two to five minutes. The heart will continue to beat for a period of time after that, perhaps five to seven minutes, or longer, though at a very low cardiac output. Death can occur ten to twelve minutes after the gas is released in the chamber.

Dr. Traystman further testified that the execution by lethal gas is sufficiently painful that it is disfavored in the scientific community as a method of putting animals to sleep. "We would not use asphyxiation, by cyanide gas or by any other substance, in our laboratory to kill animals that have been used in experiments—nor would most medical research laboratories in this country use it." He continued:

> In my view, if the lethal-gas method operates in the manner described by petitioner, the Court of Appeals clearly erred in ruling that the method is not "cruel" under "present jurisprudential standards." The Eighth Amendment proscribes "punishments which are incompatible with 'the evolving standards of decency that mark the progress of a maturing society.'"[7]

Gray was known to have become a born-again Christian and taken up writing poetry while on death row. The night before his scheduled execution, he had a final meal of Mexican food, strawberries, and milk. About thirty-five minutes before his final appointment, he was taken from his cell in a maximum-security unit to the "last night room," a windowless cubicle that adjoins the death chamber, where he received services from several ministers and prepared to meet his maker. Outside the prison, several dozen members of the Mississippi Coalition Against the Death Penalty continued to chant for the governor to grant clemency while the mosquitoes drank their blood. "I'm glad it's happening," said Richard A. Scales Jr., the father of the slain girl, Deressa Jean. "It should have happened years ago."[8]

Ivan Solotaroff, the journalist who published *The Last Face You'll Ever See* (2001), a vivid account of recent executions in Mississippi, described the six-sided death chamber as "smaller than one would think, roughly four feet square and ten feet high. Almost beautiful, if one is mechanically inclined, it's also extremely alien looking, like an antique, six-sided diving bell someone painted gray, slathered with petroleum jelly, and jammed into a metal wall that divides two of the three rooms that form the death house." (The heavy coating of Vaseline on the doorway's rubber gaskets was intended to prevent any cracking that might allow gas to escape from the seal once the door was shut.) The chamber's waist-high, wire-reinforced, tinted green windows were embedded on five of the hexagon's sides, offering a close view of the proceedings. Three windows were for the witnesses, one was for the two physicians who would monitor Gray's heartbeat with an EKG machine and a stethoscope, and the last, located to the left of the chamber's heavy door, was for the executioner.[9]

At 12:01 A.M. the condemned, dressed in a red jump suit, was brought into the death chamber. Jimmy Lee Gray's face was ashen. Guards strapped his arms and legs to the chair and bound his head to a metal pole behind him. The place was muggy, hot, and reeked of bug spray. Mississippi's official executioner, T. Berry Bruce, was a school custodian who had handled every one of the state's thirty-two gassings at the prison since Parchman's chamber was built in 1954, and he made it his practice never to communicate with the condemned. Bruce received a go-ahead knock on his door, indicating there would be no further reprieve. A voice quickly read the death warrant, and the sheriff announced, "Let us begin."

Soon after that, Bruce remained in full view of Gray as he pulled the lever, which made a creaking metallic sound as it released the pellets into the sulfuric acid bath beneath the wire-mesh chair. The cyanide landed with a plop and the gas started to rise in an eerie cloud. Once he was certain that the poison had been unleashed, the executioner turned his back and lit up a Lucky Strike.[10]

Witnesses noticed that Gray appeared to inhale deeply and then moaned. His body jerked violently at the black leather straps binding his arms, chest, and legs. His head slumped forward and then pitched backward several times, causing him to bang his head against the pole so violently that the chamber seemed to shake from the impact. According to one witness, United Press International reporter Daniel Lohwasser, four minutes into the execution, "It was obvious that Mr. Gray was in excruciating pain."[11]

Eight minutes into the execution, when Gray was still smashing his head on the metal pole behind him, a prison official sternly ordered all the witnesses to leave the area. "Gentlemen of the press," the deputy warden commanded, "that was the pre-agreed-upon signal for witnesses to leave the room."

"He hasn't been pronounced dead, has he?" one journalist asked.

"No questions," said the official.[12]

Gray's lawyer also protested, but he, too, was ordered to leave. Thirteen years later, Lohwasser, a former Vietnam combat veteran, would state, "The images of Jimmy Lee Gray searching the room with his eyes, straining to escape the gas, and smashing his head against the pole, are permanently burned into my memory. These images are far more cruel, barbaric, and demoralizing than any other violent and gruesome acts that I have witnessed."[13]

Few Americans took note of Mississippi's resumption of executions, or if they did, they cared little about the child killer Jimmy Lee Gray. In December 1984 a Gallup poll found that 72 percent of all Americans supported the death penalty for murder, but 56 percent favored lethal injection as the preferred method of execution, compared to 16 percent for the gas chamber and only 6 percent for the electric chair.

One by one, states had backed away from the continued use of the gas chamber, usually substituting lethal injection instead. New Mexico switched to lethal injection in 1979, and in 1983 Nevada, the pioneer in lethal gas, also moved to the needle. After a state court had declared Oregon's capital punishment statute unconstitutional in 1981, the state was without any execution law for three years. In the wake of Gray's botched execution, Mississippi turned away from the gas chamber, adopting lethal injection in 1984 for cases after the act's effective date, as did Wyoming—although such an approach meant that the gas chamber was still in force for older cases.

In early 1984 North Carolina, which had used the gas chamber more times than any other state except for California, debated whether to keep it. Representative John W. Varner, a physician, said on the house floor, "There's no doubt about it. Death in a gas chamber is a horrible death. You're strapped in a little room. For many minutes, not a few, he's struggling, trying to breathe and all he can breathe is gas." Although Varner's comments about asphyxiation were accurate, he then added a plug for lethal injection that would later become much more controversial: "With lethal injection, he feels no pain. It's like going into an operating room and going to sleep. He passes away with no struggle."

In the end, North Carolina authorized the use of lethal gas or lethal injection at the condemned's election, with lethal gas used if the condemned failed to choose a method. Rhode Island abandoned not only its gas chamber but abolished the death penalty in 1984. Colorado abandoned lethal gas in 1987. Missouri in 1988 began to offer a choice: lethal gas or lethal injection.[14]

At about the same time that the Supreme Court denied Jimmy Lee Gray's final stay of execution, in September 1983, the *Journal of Historical Review,* a neo-Nazi Holocaust-denial journal published by the Institute for Historical Review (IHR) in Newport Beach, California, published a noteworthy article. In 1979 the IHR had begun offering a reward of $50,000 for verifiable "proof that gas chambers for the purpose of killing human beings existed at or in Auschwitz." In 1983 the journal published "Zyklon B, Auschwitz, and the Trial of Dr. Bruno Tesch," written by William B. Lindsey. Although Lindsey did not publicize the fact at the time, he was a chemist with a Ph.D. from Indiana University who worked as a research chemist for DuPont. (He worked there from 1952 to 1985.) Not only was Lindsey a Holocaust denier who disclaimed that Zyklon-B had ever been used to carry out executions at Auschwitz, but he also contended that convicted German war criminal Dr. Bruno Tesch and his *prokurist* Karl Weinbacher were unfairly convicted and hanged after the Allies had dissolved Germany's "legitimate" (Nazi) government. His detailed study of Zyklon-B also failed to mention that his longtime employer, DuPont, had also furnished chemicals used in U.S. gassings.[15]

The IHR's $50,000 reward (and an additional $40,000) was eventually paid in 1985 to Auschwitz survivor Mel Mermelstein of Huntington Beach, California, who had sued the IHR for breach of contract for initially ignoring his evidence (a signed testimony of his experiences in Auschwitz). As a result of Mermelstein's case, on August 5, 1985, Judge Robert A. Wenke of the Superior Court of California for the County of Los Angeles declared the Holocaust an indisputable legal fact and ordered the defendants to apologize, which they did.[16] The IHR, however, has continued to espouse pro-Nazi, Holocaust-denying positions.

In February of 1985 Dr. Lindsey testified in the first "false news" trial of Ernst Zündel in Canada, where he rejected the claim that masses of prisoners had been gassed to death at Auschwitz. "I have come to the conclusion that no one was willfully or purposefully killed with Zyklon-B [hydrogen cyanide] in this manner," he testified. "I consider it absolutely impossible." The trial ended with Zündel's conviction and sentencing to fifteen months in prison. It also ended Dr. Lindsey's tenure at DuPont.[17]

The legal struggles over America's use of lethal gas for executions continued in states that had not completely abandoned the gas chamber. Mississippi was one of the fiercest battlegrounds. In 1979 Edward Earl Johnson, a poor black youngster from Leake County, had been charged with killing a white police officer and assaulting an elderly white woman. Prior to his arrest the eighteen-year-old had never been in trouble with the police. His lawyers put up scant defense before he was convicted, after which he spent eight years in a windowless cell on death row. Although the Catholic Church and others advocated on his behalf, Johnson still faced execution by gas due to the pre-1984 date of his conviction. With only three weeks to go until Johnson's scheduled gassing, a new appeals attorney finally joined the case. Clive Stafford Smith was a twenty-eight-year-old Englishman who had come to Atlanta to work for the Southern Prisoners' Defense Committee with such famous capital defenders as Millard Farmer and Stephen Bright, and he was determined to try to stop the youth's execution.

At the time, Mississippi prisons had a relatively open media policy, and the filmmaker Paul Hamann had decided to focus a television documentary on Johnson because his was the next scheduled execution. Hamann received permission to film Johnson, his family, and his lawyer as the case reached its conclusion. The resulting ninety-minute documentary, *Fourteen Days in May,* produced for the BBC, would be shown in the United States on HBO, becoming the only documentary film released to the public showing the last-minute machinations surrounding a lethal gas execution. Smith kept fighting for his client until the end—and Johnson continued to deny that he had killed the policeman—but he was executed on May 26, 1987.[18]

Seven weeks later, on July 8, 1987, Mississippi executed another black man after the U.S. Supreme Court refused to block the event. Connie Ray Evans, twenty-seven, the self-confessed killer of a convenience store clerk, had admitted the killing, saying, "I wasn't thinking; I wasn't feeling. . . . I was there. I did it. But it wasn't me."[19] He appeared to have become a changed man in prison. Before Evans died, Warden Donald Cabana asked the condemned man if he had any final words. Evans requested to tell him something privately. He then told the warden, "From one Christian to another, I love you," to which Cabana replied, shortly before releasing the gas into the chamber, "I love you too."[20] A prison spokesman said Evans would probably be dead within a minute or two, but a healthy young male like him could live for several minutes before becoming brain dead, and in fact it took thirteen painful minutes for him to die. Five years later his lawyer, who had witnessed the execution, was still haunted by recurring images and nightmares.[21] Shortly afterward, the warden had a heart attack.

On June 21, 1989, it was time for another Mississippi gassing under the old death penalty law. Leo Edwards Jr. was a thirty-six-year-old black man who stood convicted of murdering three people during a five-day robbery spree, although he claimed to have been unjustly convicted by the all-white jury. He and his alleged accomplice had escaped from the Louisiana State Penitentiary at Angola, but now he had reached the end of the line. When it came time for Edwards to go to the gas chamber he was groggy from the Valium he had received at his own request. The guards had to drag and carry him to the chamber. As the cyanide gas swirled around him, he gasped for breath and shrugged his shoulders several times. Five minutes into the gassing he opened his eyes and began crying out before going into involuntary spasms. The doctors had to wait a full fourteen minutes before pronouncing death. Edwards became the fourth person executed at Parchman, and the 113th prisoner put to death in the nation since the United States resumed executions.[22]

At the end of the 1980s, since *Gregg*, about 120 persons had been executed in the United States, eighty-six of them in four southern states: Texas, Florida, Louisiana, and Georgia. Blacks continued to be disproportionately represented on death row, and serious questions remained about the death penalty, especially who received it and who did not.[23]

In 1987 the abolitionist cause received another blow when the U.S. Supreme Court under Chief Justice William Rehnquist, in *McCleskey v. Kemp*, rejected by a 5–4 vote that the death penalty in Georgia discriminated against individual black defendants in violation of the Eighth and Fourteenth amendments.[24] Using state execution records, David C. Baldus of the University of Iowa had produced the most exhaustive statistical analysis of racial discrimination in capital sentencing ever conducted. The study showed that the odds that the killer of a white victim would receive the death penalty was 4.3 times greater than the odds that the killer of a black victim would receive that penalty.[25] But the majority of justices held that establishing a statistical likelihood of that nature was not sufficient to establish a violation of equal protection. In order to prevail, they said, the defendant would have to demonstrate that "the decisionmakers in his case acted with discriminatory purpose." In the end, the Court acknowledged that *McCleskey* was challenging "decisions at the heart of the State's criminal justice system," but the justices were reluctant to infer that the state had abused its discretion.[26]

By 1992, the center of the legal action over the gas chamber had moved to Arizona, California, and Maryland. In California, the state's mandatory death penalty statute was judicially abolished in 1991. In 1992 a new law provided for lethal gas or lethal injection at the condemned's election, and lethal gas if the condemned person failed to choose a method. In Arizona, a defendant who was sentenced to death for an offense committed before November 23, 1992, had to choose either lethal gas or lethal injection; those convicted for an offense after that date as well as those convicted before who failed to choose got lethal injection. Maryland still retained lethal gas as its official method, but it seldom resorted to execution.[27]

On April 6, 1992, just three weeks before California was scheduled to reactivate its gas chamber, Arizona prepared to use its apparatus for the first time in twenty-nine years. Donald Harding, forty-three, was convicted of killing three businessmen in 1980. As the end approached, the condemned man had thoroughly studied all he could about death by gas and done everything in his power to prepare himself for it. News media and lawyers from around the country followed every step in Arizona with keen interest, seeing it as a possible preview of what might follow in high-profile California. The suspense reached its peak as Arizona's execution ritual began to unfold. The warden stood with his left hand raised and looked Harding, barely six feet away, straight in the face. Then he glanced at his watch for a long moment, dropped his left arm, and said, "Now!" There was a loud clunking sound, followed by a hiss and the sight of white gas rising under the black chair.

As was the state's requirement, Harding was dressed only in white undershorts that resembled a diaper. When strapped to the chair, Harding saw in the witness gallery Attorney General Grant Woods, the official most responsible for bringing back the death penalty, and he gave Woods the finger as his final gesture. He breathed deeply. There were groans and gasps, heaves and shudders, followed by convulsions.[28] As Harding was thrashing against the restraints in obvious agony, his spiritual advisor glanced around at the other witnesses and saw "disbelief and shock in their faces." The expression of a normally composed TV reporter turned beet red and his face contorted with emotion. One witness, a woman, rushed over and grabbed the minister's hand, shaking and shivering. "It was extraordinarily difficult," the clergyman later declared, "the most testing situation my commitment to God and humanity has ever asked of me . . . how macabre and barbaric it all was. I could feel evil and humanity like a wet mist encircling all of us who witnessed it and all those monitoring his demise."[29]

Harding wasn't pronounced dead until eleven agonizing minutes later. At first his body had been red, but now it had turned ashen gray and beige, the color of the gas chamber itself.[30] Afterward, a shaken newsman who had witnessed the event said, "We put animals to death more humanely than this guy."[31]

The messy execution increased the pressure on other states to substitute lethal injection for the gas chamber.[32] It also lent more credence to the statements of lawyers who contended that execution by lethal gas was neither quick nor painless, and that it was a form of cruel and unusual punishment.

The drama increased as California was poised to conduct its first legal execution in twenty-five years. For more than a decade, its corrections officials had engaged in technology transfer with other death-penalty states to try to prepare for the likely resumption of executions. California staff communicated with their counterparts in North Carolina, Oklahoma, Utah, Texas, Arizona, and Mississippi.[33] In an era of growing awareness about the impact of post-traumatic stress, one of their biggest concerns was how killings would affect the prison's personnel. In 1989 California started stress-management sessions for managers and staff who were likely to participate in executions. Their purpose, as described by San Quentin warden Daniel B. Vasquez, was to "achieve a sort of 'stress inoculation.'" San Quentin's "execution team" also underwent special training. Extensive post-trauma procedures were put into effect to ease the psychological burden on the executioners.[34]

But as the state rushed to make ready for the scheduled execution of Robert Alton Harris, all their planning could not fully prepare them for the trials to come, not the least of which were unprecedented challenges to the constitutionality of their famous gas chamber. A coalition of abolitionist lawyers began planning a major class action lawsuit in 1990. On April 12, 1992, three California prisoners sentenced to death—David Fierro, Robert Harris, and Alejandro Gilbert Ruiz—filed a complaint in federal district court in San Francisco alleging violation of their federal civil rights. They were represented by a legal team led by Michael Laurence of the American Civil Liberties Union of Northern California and Warren George and Carolyn L. Reid of McCutchen, Doyle, Brown & Enersen of Los Angeles. The plaintiffs sought to have the method of execution by lethal gas declared unconstitutional and requested a temporary restraining order to prevent the next scheduled execution, involving Robert Alton Harris. On April 18, district court Judge Marilyn Hall Patel granted a temporary restraining order and enjoined the state of California from executing Harris in the gas chamber.

On April 21, however, the U.S. Supreme Court subsequently vacated three stays of Harris's execution. Justice John Paul Stevens, with whom Justice Harry Blackmun joined, dissented, saying, "In light of all that we know today about the extreme and unnecessary pain inflicted by execution by cyanide gas, and in light of the availability of more humane and less violent methods of execution, Harris' claim has merit. . . . To my mind, the gas chamber is nothing more than a chemical garrotte."[35] However, the U.S. Supreme Court had barred judges of the Ninth Circuit Court of Appeals from entering any more stays of execution for Harris.[36]

The facts of the case seemed damning. In 1978 Robert and Daniel Harris allegedly kidnapped two sixteen-year-old boys, took them to an isolated area near San Diego, and shot them to death in cold blood. After he murdered the teens, Robert Harris ate the hamburgers they had left behind, then took their car to use in robbing a bank. The pair was arrested, and when Robert Harris confessed to the shootings he was sentenced to death. By 1992 he had been on death row for more than thirteen years.[37] His execution was set to proceed as planned on April 21.

During the lead-up to the execution, a nationally known psychologist and lawyer, Craig W. Haney, conducted an intensive psychological study of Robert Harris while he was on death row. Haney documented his subject's history of abuse, beginning with Harris's birth three months prematurely after his father kicked his pregnant mother in the stomach during a drunken rage; he also suffered from fetal alcohol syndrome and cognitive disabilities. Haney discovered that Harris's fears had greatly increased as a result of the news of the horrific execution in Arizona, and he was afraid of how much he would suffer. Harris came to form a bond with the psychologist, and he asked Haney to witness his execution. When the time finally arrived, Haney reluctantly appeared as requested. He found himself in "a ghastly display case, a huge aquarium-like structure, brightly lit with windows in front and around the sides. Because the chamber is painted green," he wrote, "the reflected light gave a faint green color to the room where the witnesses stood."[38] Somebody said it was the same color as a dollar bill.

To everyone's horror, Harris's executioners went through the whole ritual, until the moment when the gas was about to be released, when suddenly the procedure was stopped due to a judge's stay. The process was resumed two hours later. Witnesses noted that in that time Harris had aged ten years.[39] By order of Judge Patel the execution was videotaped for the lawsuit—the only known film made documenting an American execution. It was never shown in court, however, and the tape was destroyed in January 1994 after lawyers for the state agreed not to offer new testimony of witnesses to executions in the gas chamber if the suit was retried.[40]

Based on his experience as a witness to the Harris execution, Haney declared:

> Lethal gas draws out the process of suffering and it does so in the course of a calculated, deliberate spectacle. The public invasiveness of this horrible process is made all the more unbearable by the prolonged view of a human being struggling in agony and in terror. . . . I cannot shake free from my memory of this spectacle, an organized violation of human nature's most basic prohibition—a prohibition more profound than the one against killing: to stand by and wait and watch and do nothing while another person writhes and shudders in deadly pain. Execution by lethal gas requires both victim and witnesses to experience not just death but dying.[41]

Other legal commentators also condemned the suffering Harris had been forced to endure and the courts' contribution to it.[42]

Meanwhile, investigators working for the plaintiffs in *Fierro v. Gomez* had obtained affidavits from persons like Haney who had witnessed gas executions, participated as staff, or studied cyanide and related issues. They found a neighbor who lived five houses away from San Quentin who declared he was "deeply offended and outraged" that the state continued to carry out gas chamber executions in his community. The researchers also took statements from several Holocaust survivors who recounted their personal experiences with gas-chamber executions during World War II.

Paul V. Benko, Ph.D., was a death camp survivor who witnessed its horrors up close. He later moved to the United States and tried to move on with his life. While studying at the University of California at Berkeley for his Ph.D. in plant pathology, Benko was assigned to kill insects in a jar full of cyanide gas. He said the sight of the insects struggling in pain reminded him of the millions of Jews, Gypsies, and political and social prisoners gassed by the Nazis. Benko became a biology professor at Sonoma State University, where he helped found its Center for the Study of the Holocaust. When he learned about Robert Harris's scheduled gas execution, he said, "it immediately rekindled my memories of the death camps. There is no way to compare the millions of innocent Holocaust victims with the convicted men and women on death row, but the . . . use of the gas chamber by the State of California is an atrocity."[43] (Benko died in 1998.)

Another Holocaust survivor, Gloria H. Lyon, declared, "As a person who saw the daily horror of mass extermination by gas, I know that execution by gas is torture and it can never be anything less. The torture begins with one's awareness of the way in which his or her life would be taken, and intensifies with one's knowledge of how low and painful a method of execution gas is."[44]

Deputy Attorney General Gerald Engler, on the other hand, argued that using such evidence in this case "demeans the memory of those who died" in the Holocaust "and the spirit of those who survived, through comparison of the unforgivable slaughter of innocent victims with the lawful execution of convicted murderers." He also said the similarities of the execution methods had not been established. But the statements provided by the Holocaust survivors proved extremely pertinent and powerful.[45]

As the lawyers in *Fierro* continued their lawsuit to try to get the federal courts to find execution by lethal gas unconstitutional, the district court allowed the next condemned inmate, David Mason, to be excluded from the class pursuant to his withdrawing any further challenges to his death sentence. California had recently enacted legislation giving inmates a choice between lethal gas and lethal injection. On August 24, 1993, Mason, accused of the murder of five persons, refused to select a method of execution and thus went to the gas chamber pursuant to Penal Code §3604. Right until the end, when he was strapped into the gas chamber, prison officials pressured him to choose—did he want lethal injection instead? Warden Vasquez told Mason he would likely be conscious for two to three seconds, but as it turned out, he remained conscious for three agonizing minutes after the cyanide was released, and his prolonged death struggle shocked many of the witnesses present.[46]

Shortly after Mason's gassing, a trial on the plaintiffs' motion for a preliminary and permanent injunction in *Fierro* was conducted in San Francisco. It lasted from October 25 to November 5, 1993. The court heard several days of testimony from eight experts and forty-six lay witnesses.[47] It also reviewed many scientific articles addressing the effects of lethal gas on the human body and viewed the death house facilities at San Quentin. Some of the evidence used included the state's own execution records that recorded the nature and duration of each phase of the lethal gas executions, and which, like the eyewitness testimony, indicated that substantial periods of time elapsed before inmates exposed to cyanide gas lost consciousness.

One of the defense experts, Professor John M. Friedberg, M.D., of the University of California at Berkeley, used 113 San Quentin "Lethal Gas Chamber—Execution Records" to estimate the duration of consciousness and awareness of pain experienced by prisoners executed by hydrogen cyanide gas over the past fifty years. The estimates were based on notations completed by the chief prison medical officer attending the executions. Entries made by thirty-one different prison physicians included times for "gas strikes face," "apparent unconsciousness," "certain unconsciousness," and "dead." There were also lines for "remarks." One EKG rhythm strip (that of David Mason, who was executed at San Quentin in August 1993) was also available for examination. Friedberg found that the state's own prison records indicated that average survival time was 9.3 minutes, including 1.6 minutes during which the prisoner was reported to be conscious. In addition, his estimates, which were derived from the records coupled with the extensive medical literature on cyanide, indicated that a typical gassing victim continued to remain conscious for almost five minutes.

Friedberg concluded, "Prison estimates of time to certain unconsciousness did not correlate with times to death. Additional comparisons show that physiologically based estimates of minimum consciousness are not correlated with the original estimates from the prison forms. The persistence of consciousness and the pain of myocardial and skeletal muscle ischemia and tetany, induction of autonomic reflexes (e.g., drooling, defecating, emesis), and the terror of slow asphyxiation qualifies this form of execution as cruel and unusual."[48]

The state of California relied on only one scientific expert, an army pharmacologist and toxicologist who claimed that cyanide gas caused rapid, virtually painless death. Under questioning, however, he came off as unreliable, and he also seemed to place stock in embarrassing information that had been spouted by discredited Holocaust deniers. The lack of credible scientific witnesses proved to be a major blunder, particularly since the plaintiffs had presented a compelling battery of diverse and credible witnesses and scientific data to support their arguments. As a result, the plaintiffs appeared to have made an exceptionally strong case before Judge Patel.

At that time, connections between the Holocaust deniers and the American execution industry were being hotly exposed. One name that came up in the *Fierro* trial served as a bombshell against the state of California. Fred A. Leuchter Jr. was a Massachusetts-based consultant who had advised twenty-seven states on execution methods, equipment, and procedures from 1979 to 1990. His self-proclaimed specialties were the electric chair, the gas chamber, and lethal injection. States he advised about lethal gas included Arizona, California, Mississippi, Missouri, and North Carolina. Leuchter received extensive news coverage due to his invention of a lethal injection machine and his authorship of reports denying that gas chambers had been used to kill Jews in the Holocaust. In late 1990 he was exposed as a fraud when it was revealed that he was not a licensed engineer, contrary to his claims, and he became engulfed in an avalanche of negative publicity. At the time it was revealed that some of his work had included refurbishing California's gas chamber.[49]

Leuchter's most controversial activities involved his denial of the Holocaust. In 1988 he had received an advance payment of $37,000 in connection with the defense of Ernst Zündel, a German-born Canadian neo-Nazi who was on trial for violating Canada's "spreading false news" statute, based on his publication of Holocaust denial pamphlets such as Richard Verrall's *Did Six Million Really Die?* and his own screed, *The Hitler We Loved.* Zündel's writings had challenged the notion that the Nazis had used hydrocyanic gas to exterminate more than a million persons in gas chambers during World War II, and he claimed that claims about gassing had been fabricated for propaganda purposes.[50]

Leuchter was best known for having published several reports, widely circulated internationally, in which he purported to have uncovered forensic proof supporting the Holocaust revisionists' claims.[51] Accompanied by a video crew, he had visited several former Nazi death camps and taken scrapings from the walls, ceilings, and floors and collected soil from around the remains of suspected gas chambers. He then took his "forensic evidence" back to Boston for laboratory tests. Then, based on his own analysis, Leuchter prepared technical reports in which he offered numerous conclusions, such as the claim that a lack of Prussian blue coating on the gas chamber walls proved that they had not been subjected to Zyklon-B.[52]

In 1990 the first of several reputable scholars, Professor Jan Markiewicz, director of the Forensic Institute of Krakow, Poland, conducted his own analysis and reached different conclusions. In fact, his findings refuted Leuchter's, and he noted that the chemical analysis proved that the gas chambers had remnants of high levels of cyanide whereas the living quarters did not. Leuchter had claimed that the traces of cyanide found in the camps were due to low levels of cyanide exposure from delousing, but his claims did not hold up to serious scrutiny.

For death penalty opponents, one interesting fact about Leuchter is that he was originally referred to Zündel by Bill Armantrout, warden for the Missouri State Penitentiary in Jefferson City, Missouri, and the official responsible for that state's gas chamber executions. When the state's sole expert witness regarding cyanide acknowledged knowing Leuchter but failed to dismiss his work and that of other discredited Holocaust deniers, it did not help the state's case with Judge Patel. After the trial and before the judge's decision was announced, Leuchter's bizarre activities received even more embarrassing publicity.

While these events were taking place, another death penalty case reached a head in North Carolina. David Lawson, a white thirty-eight-year-old, had been convicted in 1981 on charges of murder, assault, and breaking and entering (he had allegedly shot two helpless victims in the back of the head during a burglary). Death row inmates in North Carolina had the option of lethal injection, but Lawson refused to choose, saying that doing so would amount to sanctioning his execution, so state law required him to be executed in the gas chamber. His lawyers tried to get the federal courts to find his execution by lethal gas declared unconstitutional. The *Phil Donahue Show* had sought to obtain permission to have the execution videotaped, and Lawson himself had said that having his execution filmed would give his life meaning. But in June 1994 the U.S. Supreme Court denied Lawson's petition for a stay of his execution, clearing the way for Lawson's execution by lethal gas. The Court also denied requests to videotape Lawson's execution.

At 2 A.M. on June 15, 1994, David Lawson was brought into the gas chamber wearing only white boxer shorts, a diaper, and socks. The hair on his legs and head had been shorn. When he was strapped into the large wooden chair, the guards proceeded to bind his face with a leather mask that covered his eyes. It had a large hole for his nose and small holes over his mouth, but it left his forehead bare. The mask also attached his head to the chair. Lawson began yelling as his executioners covered his face. His words weren't clear through the double-paned windows of the death chamber, but he seemed to be shouting, "I'm human, I'm human!" as the airtight door to the room was clamped shut. He continued screaming as the fog of gas rose about him. Many of the witnesses were horrified.

"After about three or four minutes," one witness said, "he was unable to say the full sentence, 'I am human,' but was still crying out the word 'Human!' about every twenty seconds. He did this for another two to three minutes. Finally, he couldn't say even part of the word, but he continued to grunt about every twenty seconds for another minute or minute and a half. His body continued to quiver for another minute or so, then he was still." It took twelve minutes for Lawson to die, but it seemed much longer. For many of those who saw and heard it, the experience would last a lifetime.[53]

At last, on October 4, 1994, the district court in San Francisco issued its long-awaited order in *Fierro*. The result amounted to one of the greatest victories in capital punishment law, for the judge declared execution by lethal gas under California Penal Code §3604 violated the Eighth Amendment ban against cruel and unusual punishment.[54] For the first time a federal court had found a specific method of legal execution to be unconstitutional. The ruling was particularly noteworthy because it occurred as the death penalty enjoyed its highest level of public support, a record 80 percent in favor according to a Gallup poll in 1994.

The district court noted that the abandonment of the gas chamber by several states stood in sharp contrast to the relatively slow movement away from other methods of execution, and it made clear that the gas chamber had become an outmoded method of execution. Based on the evidence presented, Judge Patel had agreed that cyanide kills by bonding with an enzyme called cytochrome oxydase. When pressed, each expert in the case had claimed that this cytochrome oxydase had something to do with "suffocation," or what the court quoted as "the transfer of oxygen to the cells," and that it was experienced much like a massive heart attack. Simply put, the district court found that cyanide blocks the transfer of oxygen to the cells, resulting in histotoxic hypoxia, or cellular suffocation. The district court's decision also noted that the primary point of disagreement was "whether unconsciousness occurs within at most thirty seconds of inhalation, as defendants maintain, or whether, as plaintiffs contend, unconsciousness occurs much later, after the inmate has endured the painful effects of cyanide gas for several minutes." Judge Patel found an inmate likely to be conscious for fifteen to sixty seconds from the time the gas first hit his or her face, and possibly conscious, or partly conscious, for up to two minutes.[55]

In reaching its determination, the federal district court in *Fierro* offered three major doctrinal expansions: 1) a more comprehensive Eighth Amendment framework than *Campbell v. Wood* by emphasizing an evolving standards of decency test (dependent upon legislative trends); 2) a broader process for challenging an execution method by allowing an inmate to bring a section 1983 action in lieu of a petition for a writ of habeas corpus; and 3) a more detailed measure of pain and unconsciousness.[56] The court held, "Objective evidence of pain must be the primary consideration, and evidence of legislative trends may also be considered where the evidence of pain is not dispositive."[57]

The *Fierro* ruling created a considerable stir in the world of capital punishment. It also appeared to influence a 1994 determination by the U.S. District Court of the District of Maryland, which allowed a Maryland inmate to videotape the lethal gas execution of another inmate. The purpose of the videotaping was to acquire evidence on the length of consciousness and level of pain an individual experiences when exposed to lethal gas.[58]

But the greatest shock waves from *Fierro* were yet to come. In 1996 the Ninth Circuit Court of Appeals unanimously endorsed the district court's suggested standards and held that an execution method may be unconstitutional if an inmate faces a "substantial risk" of suffering "extreme pain for several minutes."[59] The Ninth Circuit's action marked the first federal appeals court ruling holding unconstitutional any method of legal execution. No other court, state or federal, had ever sustained a general challenge to any method of execution. Prior to the court's ruling, several other courts had rejected the notion that eyewitness descriptions were valid indications of pain and suffering experienced by a prisoner undergoing execution. The Ninth Circuit Court's support for the finding that lethal gas violates the Eighth Amendment and enjoining the state of California from using that method to enforce its death judgments was also unprecedented.[60]

The U.S. Supreme Court later vacated the Ninth Circuit's decision in light of the California legislature's subsequent amendment of the state's death penalty statute allowing lethal injections to be used unless the capital defendant specifically requested to die by lethal gas.[61] But since the ruling by the District Court in *Fierro,* neither the federal Circuit Court of Appeals nor the U.S. Supreme Court had faulted the argument that death by lethal gas amounted to cruel and unusual punishment.

On January 30, 1998, after another North Carolina prisoner waived his appeals, the state prepared to execute him by lethal gas at Central Prison. Ricky Lee Sanderson had been on death row for ten years after he was sentenced for the rape and murder of a sixteen-year-old girl. Sanderson was a drug addict with a long criminal record, but his case was unusual in that he had come forward and confessed to the murder after the police had mistakenly charged another man in the case. A born-again Christian, Sanderson said he had come to believe he deserved to die for his crime and he didn't want to put the victim's family through any more grief by fighting his execution.

Martin Kady II was one of the reporters who appeared in Raleigh to witness the execution. When the guards pulled back the gas chamber curtains, Kady was surprised to see in the bright light a chubby, gray-haired man clad in a diaper and boxer shorts. Sanderson's eyes appeared to convey a sense of "eerie serenity." The murdered girl's father sat in front of Kady in the witness room. As the execution team prepared the death chamber, Sanderson called out from his chair, loudly thanking Jesus. As the white plume filled the chamber, Sanderson's skin turned beet red and he strained against the leather straps. "The executioners," Kady noted, "had placed a grim, medieval looking leather hood over his face. His eyes were covered so we couldn't look him in the eye as he died, but nostril holes ensured the deadly gas would be properly inhaled. As he squirmed, white fluid flowed from his nose. His chest heaved as the gas infiltrated his lungs and rendered them obsolete."

After ten minutes, the warden opened the door. "Ladies and gentlemen," he announced, "the judgment of the courts has been carried out. Time of death, 2:19 A.M."[62]

CHAPTER 12

THE LAST GASP

The last gasp of the American gas chamber came in 1999 in Florence, Arizona. Ironically, and fittingly some might think, the case involved the United States and Germany.

Two brothers, Walter LaGrand, born in 1962, and Karl LaGrand, born in 1963, were German nationals who had moved to the United States with their mother in 1965. In 1982 both were sentenced for stabbing to death a bank manager during a botched robbery.[1] After the case went all the way to the U.S. Supreme Court, which denied review, the LaGrands filed petitions for writs of habeas corpus. Arizona law gave the condemned the right to choose between lethal injection or lethal gas as their method of execution. Both brothers chose gas in the hope that the courts would find the method unconstitutional.

When this tactic failed, Karl accepted a last-minute offer of a lethal injection, and he was executed on February 24, 1999.[2] Walter, however, said he would prefer lethal gas as a means of protesting the death penalty, even though it was said to be more painful.

The possibility of executing a German in the gas chamber evoked potent images. One of the claims Walter LaGrand raised in his habeas petition was that execution by lethal gas constituted cruel and unusual punishment under the Eighth Amendment to the Constitution. But the U.S. District Court found the claim to be procedurally defaulted because LaGrand had failed to raise it either on direct appeal or in his petition for state postconviction relief.

Less than an hour before he was supposed to be put to death in the gas chamber, however, Walter's execution was delayed when the Ninth Circuit Court of Appeals found that death by lethal gas was "cruel and unusual punishment." As part of its order, the Ninth Circuit stayed his execution and enjoined Arizona from executing him "or anyone similarly situated, by means of lethal gas."[3]

Like his brother, Walter had filed a petition for writ of habeas corpus challenging lethal gas as a cruel and unusual form of execution. On March 3, 1999, the U.S. Supreme Court granted Arizona's application to lift the Ninth Circuit's order enjoining the use of lethal gas, granted certiorari, and summarily reversed the prior decision without oral argument.

In an 8–1 per curiam opinion, the Court rejected Walter LaGrand's argument of ineffective assistance of counsel and held that, by his actions, he had waived his claim that execution by lethal gas is unconstitutional. According to the Court, "On March 1, 1999, Governor Hull of Arizona offered Walter LaGrand an opportunity to rescind this decision and select lethal injection as his method of execution. Walter LaGrand, again, insisted that he desired to be executed by lethal gas. By declaring his method of execution, picking lethal gas over the state's default form of execution—lethal injection—Walter LaGrand has waived any objection he might have to it." The Court also found that his claims were procedurally defaulted because he hadn't challenged the unconstitutionality of lethal gas quickly enough. According to the Court's tortured legal logic:

> At the time of Walter LaGrand's direct appeal, there was sufficient debate about the constitutionality of lethal gas executions that Walter LaGrand cannot show cause for his failure to raise this claim. Arguments concerning the constitutionality of lethal gas have existed since its introduction as a method of execution in Nevada in 1921. See H. Bedau, The Death Penalty in America 16 (1982). In the period immediately prior to Walter LaGrand's direct appeal, a number of states were reconsidering the use of execution by lethal gas, see *Gray v. Lucas,* 710 F.2d 1048, 1059–61 (CA5 1983) (discussing evidence presented by the defendant and changes in Nevada's and North Carolina's methods of execution), and two United States Supreme Court Justices had expressed their views that this method of execution was unconstitutional, see *Gray v. Lucas,* 463 U. S 1237, 1240–44 (1983) (Marshall, J., joined by Brennan, J., dissenting from denial of certiorari). In addition, lethal gas executions have been documented since 1937, when San Quentin introduced it as an execution method, and studies of the effect of execution by lethal gas date back to the 1950s. See Bedau, *supra,* at 16.

Justice John Paul Stevens dissented, saying, "The answer to the question whether a capital defendant may consent to be executed by an unacceptably torturous method of execution is by no means clear. I would not decide such an important question without full briefing and argument."[4]

By then the Walter LaGrand case had become the subject of an international furor over American capital punishment. Germany, which did not have the death penalty, asked Arizona's Governor Jane Dee Hull to halt the execution, but she refused, saying the death penalty was popular in her state. She rejected appeals from German chancellor Gerhard Schröder and Foreign Minister Joschka Fischer. Germany asked the world court to intervene, and German officials contended that Arizona had failed to advise the LaGrand brothers of their right to consular assistance at their trials, as state officials were required to do under the Vienna Convention on Consular Relations.

Ultimately the case was heard by the International Court of Justice in The Hague as *Case Concerning the Vienna Convention on Consular Relations (Germany v. United States of America), General List No. 104 (March 3, 1999).* Although the international court had no enforcement powers, Judge Christopher Weeramantry of Sri Lanka urged the United States government to use "all the measures at its disposal" to prevent the executions.[5] President Bill Clinton turned a blind eye. The U.S. Department of State conveyed the wishes of the International Court of Justice to Governor Hull of Arizona without comment, and the Arizona clemency board recommended she grant a stay on the basis of the pending international case. But Governor Hull ignored the recommendation.

On March 3, 1999, Walter LaGrand, a prisoner who was both German and American, became the next person in history to be put to death in an American gas chamber. Minutes before he was killed, he apologized for his actions. He also said, "To all my loved ones, I hope they find peace. To all of you here today, I forgive you and I hope I can be forgiven in my next life."

Eighteen minutes after the cyanide pellets were dropped, he was pronounced dead.[6] LaGrand turned out to be the last person to be executed by lethal gas in the twentieth century. The lethal chamber had taken its final victim.

Afterward, many Germans accused the United States of "barbarism" and flouting international law, and ultimately the International Criminal Court ruled in favor of Germany and against the United

States.[7] The roles from Nuremberg had been reversed, and now it was the Americans who were found guilty.

Even after the end of the twentieth century, the U.S. Supreme Court of the United States still would not bring itself to address the question whether execution in the gas chamber amounted to cruel and unusual punishment in violation of the Constitution.[8] No amount of evidence could convince it otherwise.

But in the court of world opinion, the gas chamber represented one of modernity's worst crimes; it was an instrument of torture that first had been disguised as a humane alternative to pain and suffering. What originally had seemed to be such a noble and practical idea turned out to be something else entirely.

Dreamers, scientists, soldiers, merchants, lawmakers, lawyers, physicians, governors, journalists, wardens, keepers—and, of course, the condemned prisoners—all made their unique contribution to the rise and fall of the gas chamber. But the creation of a "painless and humane" method of killing proved elusive. Despite all of their utopian schemes, laboratory experiments and mathematical formulas, blind obedience, commercial arrangements, legislative clauses, legal briefs, stopwatches, stethoscopes, death warrants, witnesses peering into peepholes, execution protocols, and public relations pronouncements, America's use of lethal gas as a method of capital punishment ended with the close of the twentieth century. But its awful legacy will continue for a long time to come.

APPENDIX 1

EARL C. LISTON'S PATENT APPLICATION

Sept. 12, 1939. E. C. LISTON 2,172,768

LETHAL GAS CHAMBER

Filed Oct. 16, 1937 3 Sheets-Sheet 1

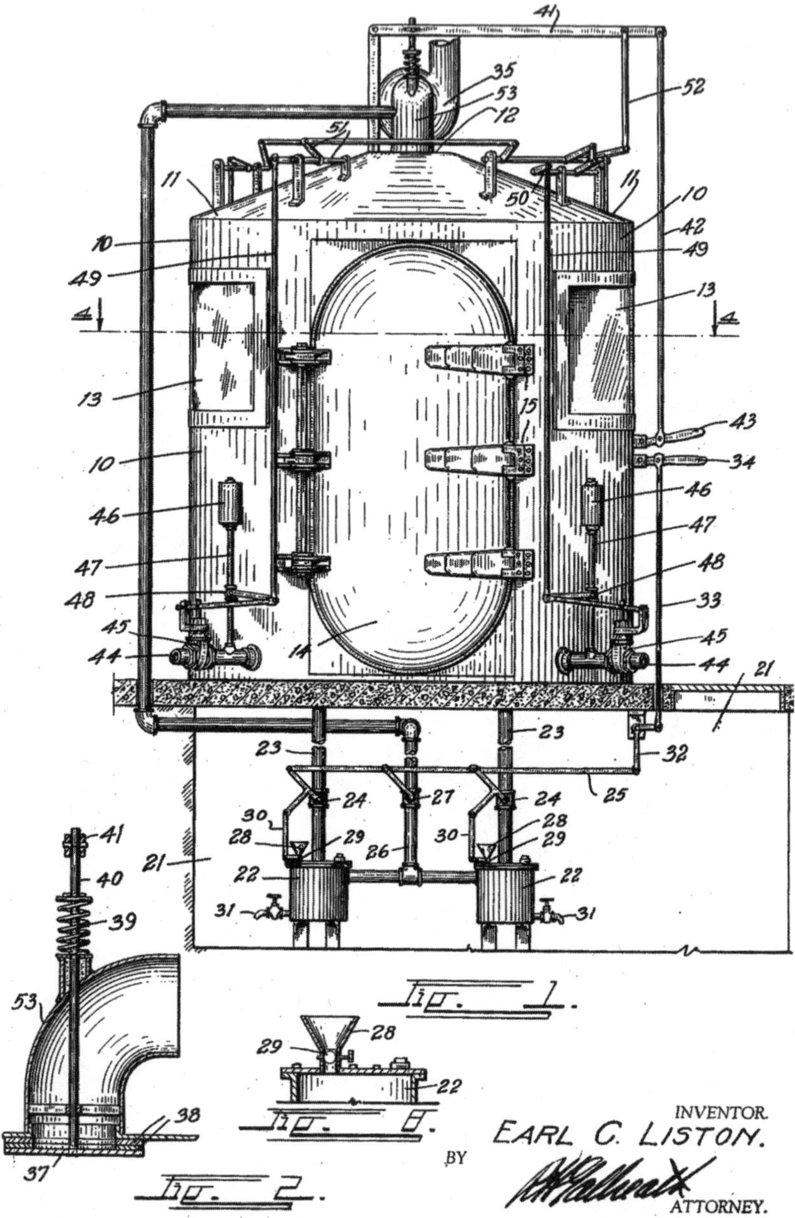

Sept. 12, 1939. E. C. LISTON 2,172,768

LETHAL GAS CHAMBER

Filed Oct. 16, 1937 3 Sheets-Sheet 2

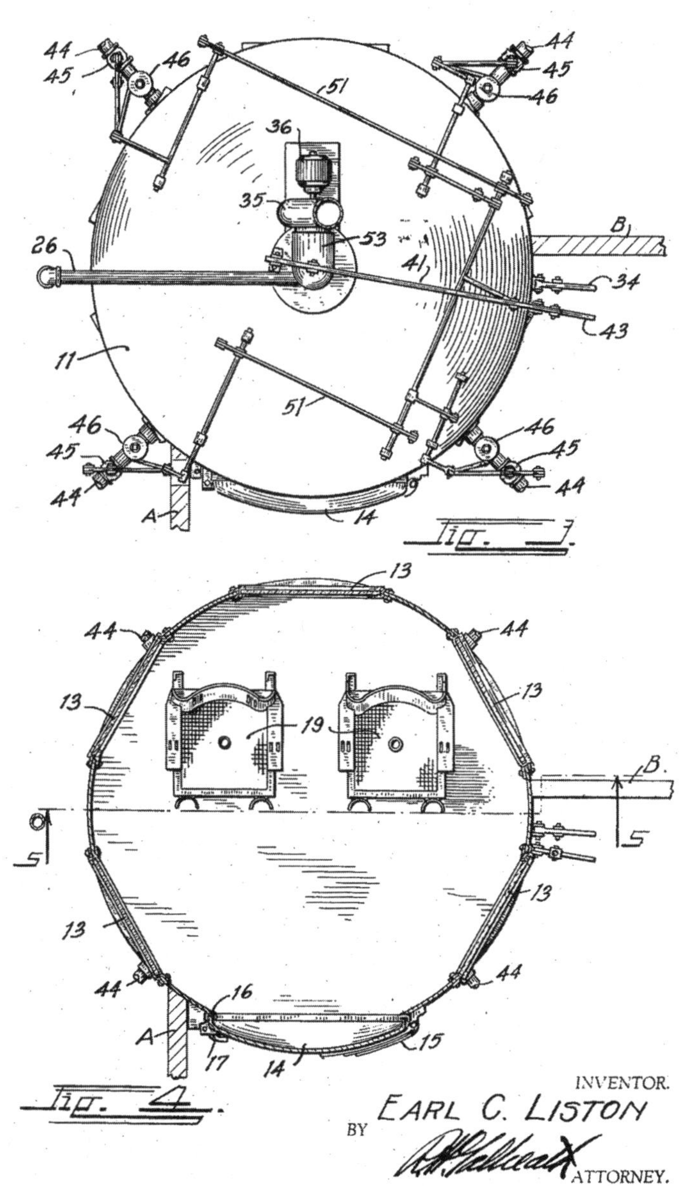

INVENTOR.

EARL C. LISTON

BY [signature] ATTORNEY.

Sept. 12, 1939. E. C. LISTON 2,172,768

LETHAL GAS CHAMBER

Filed Oct. 16, 1937 3 Sheets-Sheet 3

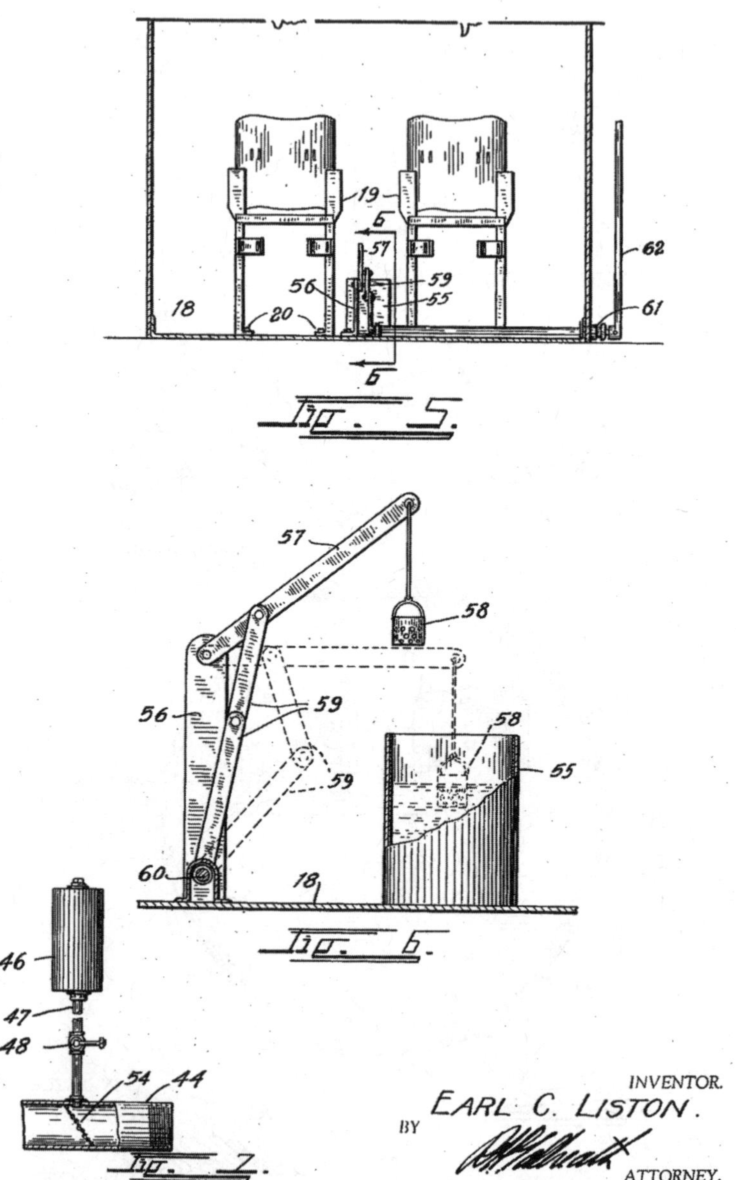

INVENTOR.

EARL C. LISTON.

BY

ATTORNEY.

Patented Sept. 12, 1939 **2,172,768**

UNITED STATES PATENT OFFICE

2,172,768

LETHAL GAS CHAMBER

Earl C. Liston, Denver, Colo.

Application October 16, 1937, Serial No. 169,359

2 Claims. (Cl. 128—303)

This invention relates to a lethal gas chamber for the execution of condemned criminals and has for its principal object the provision of a complete efficient assembly which will provide a gas tight chamber equipped with death chairs, gas generating equipment, gas exhaust equipment, and gas counteracting equipment, all under the control of one man located at one point so that a complete control can be had of the gas generation and the gas elimination from the executioner's position.

Another object of the invention is to so construct the above mechanism so that it will form a complete unit which can be efficiently built into a building structure to provide rooms for the witnesses, warden, doctor, and executioner, all grouped about the complete single unit.

Another object of the invention is to provide a neat, compact, mechanism which will humanely execute the criminal or criminals with the least possible delay and confusion, and which will allow quick entry after the execution without danger to the attendants.

Other objects and advantages reside in the detail construction of the invention, which is designed for simplicity, economy, and efficiency. These will become more apparent from the following description.

In the following detailed description of the invention reference is had to the accompanying drawings which form a part hereof. Like numerals refer to like parts in all views of the drawings and throughout the description.

In the drawings—

Fig. 1 illustrates a front elevation of the lethal gas chamber and gas generating pit.

Fig. 2 is a detail view of the gas exhaust valve.

Fig. 3 is a plan view of the chamber.

Fig. 4 is a horizontal section, taken on the line 4—4, Fig. 1.

Fig. 5 is a detailed section, taken on the line 5—5, Fig. 4.

Fig. 6 is a detail view illustrating an alternate form of gas generator.

Fig. 7 is a detail view of the cyanide crystal valve.

Fig. 8 is a detail view of the ammonia distributing screen.

The invention comprises a vertical cylindrical metallic cell 10 closed at its top with a conical roof 11, the central portion of which is flattened to provide a fan platform 12.

The cell is provided with a series, preferably five, of gas-tight glass windows 13 and with a door 14 swung from suitable hinges 15. The door, when closed, is clamped against a sealing gasket 16 through the medium of a clamping latch mechanism 17. The hinges and the latches are of the usual heavy duty refrigerator type.

The cell is sealed at its bottom with a metal floor 18. The floor, walls, and roof are all preferably welded together to form a hermetically sealed structure.

One or more death chairs 19 are secured to the floor 18 by means of suitable stud bolts 20. In the cell illustrated, two chairs are employed. These chairs are of metal throughout and are provided with wire screen seats through which the lethal gas may pass.

In the form illustrated in Figs. 1 and 4, a generating pit 21 is excavated below the cell 10. This pit contains two lead lined, gas generating pots 22 for containing hydrochloric acid. A gas pipe 23 leads upwardly from each of the generating pots 22 and opens through the floor 18 directly below each of the chairs. The flow of gas through these pipes is controlled by the means of gas valves 24 which are actuated in unison from a connecting rod 25. A gas waste pipe 26 leads from the upper portion of each pot through a control valve 27 which is also connected with the connecting rod 25. The relation of the valves 24 and 27 is such that when the former are opened the latter will be closed.

Each pot 22 carries a cyanide funnel 28 for holding cyanide crystals. The flow of the crystals to the pots is controlled by means of butterfly valves 29 which are actuated by connecting links 30 from the handles of the valves 24. The relation of the valves 24 and 29 is such that both will open simultaneously. Each pot is provided with an acid drain cock 31. The connecting rod 25 leads through a bell crank lever 32 and rod 33 to a gas control lever 34 which is hinged on the side of the cell 10.

An exhaust fan 35 is mounted on top of the cell and driven from a suitable electric motor 36. The exhaust fan communicates with the interior of the cell through an elbow 53, shown in detail in Fig. 2. The elbow has an exhaust plate valve 37 controlling its opening to the cell. When this valve moves upwardly, it seals against suitable sealing gaskets 38. The plate valve is continuously urged to the closed position by means of a compression spring 39 acting on a valve stem 40. It is moved to the open position by means of a lever 41 which is actuated by a rod 42 from a second control lever 43.

Four compressed air pipes 44 lead into the bottom of the cell 10 from any suitable air supply (not shown). The air pipes are controlled by gate valves **45**. Between each gate valve and the cell is an ammonia container **46** supported upon a drain pipe **47** which leads into the air pipe **44**. The flow of ammonia is controlled by an ammonia valve **48** at each air pipe. Within the latter immediately below the ammonia pipe is an inclined screen **54** which acts to disperse the ammonia in the incoming air. At each air pipe the handles of the valves **45** and **48** are both connected to a pull rod **49**, so that when the rod is pulled upwardly both valves will open simultaneously. The pull rods **49** are suspended from cranks **50** on a series of cranks and linkage **51** positioned on the roof of the cell, which is so arranged that, when operated in one direction, all of the valves **45** and **48** will be opened simultaneously, and when operated in the other direction all will be closed. The linkage is operated by means of a tie rod **52** connected to the valve lever **41**. Thus, it can be seen that when the second control lever **43** is moved downwardly it will simultaneously open the valves **37**, **45**, and **48**. The waste gas pipe **26** may be connected to the intake of the exhaust fan **35**.

The operation of the device is as follows: The prisoner (or prisoners) is placed in the chair **19** and strapped thereto. The door **14** is closed and clamped against its gaskets. The lever **34** is lifted, this opens the valves **29** allowing the cyanide to discharge into the hydrochloric acid to generate the lethal gas. The movement of the lever also opens the valves **24** to allow the gas to flow directly to the cell **10** and closes the waste valve **27** to prevent the escape of gas from the pots **22**.

When the prisoner has been pronounced dead, the control lever **34** is lowered to close the gas valves **24** and the cyanide valves **29** and to open the waste valve **27** allowing the surplus gas to escape through the pipe **26**. The second control lever **43** is now pushed downwardly to open all of the air valves **45** and all of the ammonia valves **48** causing ammonia vapor to be forced into the cell. The movement of the lever **43** also opens the exhaust valve **37** and the fan **34** operates to discharge the neutralized gas. When the lethal gas has been completely neutralized and removed, the lever **43** is raised to shut off the incoming air and ammonia and the cell is opened.

The particular cylindrical construction of the cell adapts it to a building of the type necessary for its purpose. For instance, a partition wall can be built up to the cell at the left side of the door, as indicated at "A," and a second wall built up to the right side of the cell, indicated by "B." This devides the building about the cell into two rooms, a small prisoner's room and a large witness room. The small room contains the door through which the prisoner enters the cell and the control apparatus for the executioner. Observation is possible from this small room through the single window at the right of the door. The remaining four windows open to the large witness room wherein the legally entitled witnesses are assembled to witness the execution.

In Figs. 5 and 6 an alternate form of gas generator is illustrated. This form consists of an acid pot **55** open at its top and positioned between the two chairs in the cell **10**.

A post **56** is secured to the floor adjacent the pot **55**. A lever **57** extends from the post to support a porous cyanide basket **58**. The lever **57** is raised and lowered through the medium of toggel levers **59**, which are secured on a shaft **60** extending through a gas tight packing **61** to the exterior of the cell. On the exterior an operating lever **62** is secured to the shaft, by means of which the basket **58** can be lowered and raised from the acid pot **55**. This mechanism may replace the generating mechanism of the previous form. The air intake and exhaust mechanism of the previous form are retained, however.

While a specific form of the improvement has been described and illustrated herein, it is desired to be understood that the same may be varied, within the scope of the appended claims, without departing from the spirit of the invention.

Having thus described the invention, what is claimed and desired secured by Letters Patent is:

1. A device for evacuating and neutralizing an execution chamber comprising: a suction fan for exhausting said gas from said chamber; an exhaust conduit adapted to connect said fan with said chamber; an exhaust valve for controlling the flow through said exhaust conduit; a fresh air conduit for supplying fresh air to said chamber; a second valve controlling the flow through said latter conduit; an ammonia container; a conduit for carrying ammonia from said container to said chamber; a third valve controlling the flow of ammonia through the latter conduit; and a single control lever operatively connected with all three valves for simultaneously opening them so that fresh air and ammonia will flow into said chamber simultaneously with the exhausting of the gas therefrom.

2. Means for evacuating and neutralizing the gas in an execution chamber comprising: a fresh air conduit adapted to communicate with said chamber; an air valve for controlling the flow through said conduit; a reservoir for containing a neutralizing agent; a neutralizing pipe leading from said reservoir and communicating with said conduit between said air valve and said chamber; a neutralizing valve controlling the flow through said neutralizing pipe; means for operating said air and neutralizing valve simultaneously so that the neutralizing agent will be applied to the air as it flows to said chamber; and means for causing the air to flow through said conduit to said chamber.

EARL C. LISTON.

APPENDIX 2

PERSONS EXECUTED BY LETHAL GAS IN THE UNITED STATES, BY STATE, 1924–1999

State	Name	Age	Race	Offense	Date of Execution
AZ	Manuel Hernandez	18	Hispanic	Robbery/murder	7/6/1934
AZ	Fred Hernandez	19	Hispanic	Robbery/murder	7/6/1934
AZ	George Shaughnessy	19	White	Robbery/murder	7/13/1934
AZ	Louis Douglas	46	White	Robbery/murder	8/31/1934
AZ	Jack Sullivan	23	White	Murder	5/15/1936
AZ	Frank Rascon	26	Hispanic	Murder	7/10/1936
AZ	Roland Cochrane	28	White	Robbery/murder	10/2/1936
AZ	Frank Duarte	22	Hispanic	Robbery/murder	1/8/1937
AZ	Ernest Patten	37	Black	Murder	8/13/1937
AZ	Burt Anderson	54	White	Murder	8/13/1937
AZ	David Knight	31	White	Murder	9/3/1937
AZ	Elvin Odom	27	White	Robbery/murder	1/14/1938
AZ	Archie Short	26	White	Murder	4/28/1938
AZ	Frank Conner	22	Black	Robbery/murder	9/22/1939
AZ	Robert Burgunder	22	White	Robbery/murder	9/8/1940
AZ	Gray B. Cole	28	Black	Murder	1/8/1943
AZ	Charles Sanders	20	Black	Murder	1/8/1943
AZ	J.C. Levice	21	Black	Murder	1/8/1943
AZ	James Rawlings	46	White	Rape/murder	2/19/1943
AZ	Elisandro Macias	19	Hispanic	Robbery/murder	4/27/1943
AZ	John Ransom	47	Black	Murder	1/5/1945

(continued)

State	Name	Age	Race	Offense	Date of Execution
AZ	Lee Smith	NA	White	Murder	4/6/1945
AZ	U.L. Holley	38	Black	Murder	4/13/1945
AZ	Angel Serna	25	Hispanic	Murder	7/29/1950
AZ	Harold Lantz	28	White	Murder	7/18/1951
AZ	Carl Folk	55	White	Rape/murder	3/4/1955
AZ	Lester Bartholomew	28	White	Murder	8/31/1955
AZ	Leonard Coey	56	White	Murder	5/22/1957
AZ	Arthur Thomas	27	Black	Murder	11/17/1958
AZ	Richard Jordan	26	White	Rape/murder	11/22/1958
AZ	Lonnie Craft	40	Black	Murder	3/7/1959
AZ	Robert Fenton	24	White	Murder	3/11/1960
AZ	Honor Robinson	42	Black	Murder	10/31/1961
AZ	Patrick McGee	52	White	Robbery/murder	3/8/1963
AZ	Manuel Silva	42	Hispanic	Murder	3/14/1963
AZ	Donald Harding	43	White	Murder	6/14/1992
AZ	Walter LeGrand	37	White	Murder	3/3/1999
CA	Robert Cannon	24	White	Murder	12/2/1938
CA	Albert Kessell	29	White	Murder	12/2/1938
CA	Wesley Eudy	34	White	Murder	12/9/1938
CA	Fred Barnes	40	White	Murder	12/9/1938
CA	Ed Davis	37	White	Murder	12/16/1938
CA	David Claud	25	White	Robbery/murder	7/21/1939
CA	Charles McLachlan	57	White	Rape/murder	9/15/1939
CA	William Green	39	Black	Robbery/murder	10/20/1939
CA	James Williams	33	White	Murder	2/16/1940
CA	Neil Anderson	23	White	Robbery/murder	3/15/1940
CA	Virgilio Spinelle	60	White	Murder	5/17/1940
CA	Robert Perry	71	White	Robbery/murder	7/19/1940
CA	Everett Parman	30	White	Murder	8/16/1940
CA	Rodney Greig	22	White	Murder	8/23/1940
CA	Dewitt Cook	21	White	Rape/murder	1/31/1941
CA	Thomas Smith	60	White	Murder	4/18/1941
CA	Don Kay Wong	57	Asian/ Pacific Islander	Murder	7/11/1941
CA	John Lininger	41	White	Murder	8/29/1941
CA	Eldon Hawk	27	White	Robbery/murder	8/29/1941
CA	William Johansen	36	White	Murder	9/5/1941
CA	John Reed	42	NA	Robbery/murder	9/26/1941
CA	Juanita Spinelli	52	White	Murder	11/21/1941
CA	Gordon Hawkins	21	White	Murder	11/28/1941

State	Name	Age	Race	Offense	Date of Execution
CA	Mike Simone	32	White	Murder	11/28/1941
CA	Henry Jones	50	Black	Murder	4/10/1942
CA	Clark Dewey	30	Black	Murder	4/10/1942
CA	Maurice Briggs	26	White	Murder	8/7/1942
CA	Steve Crimm	30	Black	Murder	8/21/1942
CA	Barzen Hoyt	22	NA	Robbery/murder	11/13/1942
CA	Delmar Arnold	24	NA	Robbery/murder	11/13/1942
CA	Arthur Frazier	22	NA	Robbery/murder	11/20/1942
CA	Alfred Wells	32	White	Murder	12/4/1942
CA	Leslie Gireth	38	White	Murder	1/22/1943
CA	Warren Cramer	25	White	Murder	5/14/1943
CA	John Coleman	43	White	Murder	8/13/1943
CA	Marcellino Bautista	32	Asian/ Pacific Islander	Robbery/murder	1/21/1944
CA	Farrington Hill	33	White	Robbery/murder	1/28/1944
CA	Glenard Brown	19	White	Murder	2/15/1944
CA	Dan Kolez	53	White	Murder	5/12/1944
CA	William Shaw	35	Black	Murder	6/16/1944
CA	Florencio Alcalde	30	Hispanic	Murder	8/18/1944
CA	Charles Baa	22	Black	Robbery/murder	11/3/1944
CA	Rollie Anderson	29	White	Murder	1/5/1945
CA	Theodore Gonzales	21	Hispanic	Murder	1/5/1945
CA	Djory Nagle	32	White	Murder	3/2/1945
CA	Hershell Glenn	23	White	Robbery/murder	3/2/1945
CA	Ernest Keeling	26	White	Robbery/murder	3/2/1945
CA	Silas Kelso	25	White	Murder	5/25/1945
CA	Emery Bolden	26	Black	Robbery/murder	6/22/1945
CA	McElwee Harper	35	Black	Robbery/murder	6/22/1945
CA	Camargo M. Diaz	22	Hispanic	Rape/murder	8/14/1945
CA	Thomas Brigance	30	White	Murder	9/14/1945
CA	Benjamin Whitson	27	White	Murder	9/14/1945
CA	Louie Jackson	53	Black	Rape/murder	10/5/1945
CA	Albert Simeone	53	White	Robbery/murder	11/30/1945
CA	Robert Lee Ming	26	White	Murder	4/12/1946
CA	Sam Williams	38	Black	Attempted murder	4/26/1946
CA	Otto Stephen Wilson	35	White	Rape/murder	9/20/1946
CA	Charlie Bernard	41	Black	Murder	9/27/1946
CA	DeLaRoi Wilson	28	White	Murder	10/25/1946
CA	Willie Crain	40	White	Robbery/murder	11/29/1946
CA	John Honeycutt	33	White	Murder	2/7/1947

(continued)

State	Name	Age	Race	Offense	Date of Execution
CA	Thomas Hilton	29	White	Murder	2/26/1947
CA	Alger Simmons	30	Black	Robbery/murder	3/21/1947
CA	Louise Peete	58	White	Murder	4/11/1947
CA	Ernest Dunn	38	White	Murder	6/6/1947
CA	Joe Caetano	30	White	Murder	8/29/1947
CA	Francis Barnes	21	White	Rape/robbery/ murder	11/14/1947
CA	Jose Sanchez	28	Hispanic	Murder	1/26/1948
CA	Thomas McMonigle	33	White	Rape/murder	2/20/1948
CA	John Peterson	42	White	Robbery/murder	4/9/1948
CA	George Isby	27	Black	Murder	4/16/1948
CA	Paul Winton	51	Hispanic	Murder	5/28/1948
CA	Joseph Trujillo	30	Hispanic	Murder	10/1/1948
CA	Arthur Eggers	54	White	Murder	10/15/1948
CA	Sam Shockley	39	White	(Prison) Rioting	12/3/1948*
CA	Miran Thompson	31	White	(Prison) Rioting	12/3/1948*
CA	Carlos Ochoa	29	Hispanic	Murder	12/10/1948
CA	Robert Mehaffey	38	White	Robbery/murder	12/31/1948
CA	Robert Shorts	21	Black	Murder	1/7/1949
CA	Marvin Tuthill	45	White	Murder	1/28/1949
CA	Maxwell Bowie	23	Black	Robbery/murder	2/18/1949
CA	Henry Williams	24	Black	Robbery/murder	2/18/1949
CA	Joel Harrison	23	Black	Murder	4/1/1949
CA	Clayburne Campbell	33	Black	Murder	4/1/1949
CA	Daniel Zatzke	23	White	Robbery/murder	7/1/1949
CA	William Sanford	21	White	Robbery/murder	7/15/1949
CA	Admiral Adamson	49	Black	Robbery/murder	12/9/1949
CA	Jesse Murphy	25	White	Robbery/murder	12/16/1949
CA	Albert Nixon	34	White	Robbery/murder	12/16/1949
CA	Victoriano Corrales	47	Hispanic	Murder	2/24/1950
CA	Armand Letourneau	40	White	Murder	3/31/1950
CA	Edward Huizenga	59	White	Robbery/murder	6/2/1950
CA	Henry Hooper	45	Black	Murder	8/4/1950
CA	Henry Guldbrandsen	36	White	Murder	10/6/1950
CA	Herman Avery	50	Black	Murder	10/6/1950
CA	Paul Gutierrez	26	Hispanic	Rape/murder	12/1/1950
CA	Monroe Jackson	34	White	Robbery/murder	3/2/1951
CA	Harold Sexton	23	White	Robbery/murder	3/16/1951
CA	John Odle	59	White	Murder	8/17/1951
CA	Claude Osborn	36	Black	Robbery/murder	9/14/1951
CA	Ray Cullen	65	White	Murder	11/2/1951

State	Name	Age	Race	Offense	Date of Execution
CA	Felix Chavez	26	Hispanic	Rape/murder	11/30/1951
CA	William Phyle	37	White	Burglary/murder	2/29/1952
CA	Doil Miller	31	Black	Robbery/murder	3/7/1952
CA	William Coefield	23	White	Robbery/murder	3/21/1952
CA	Lloyd Sampsell	52	White	Robbery/murder	4/25/1952
CA	Stanley Buckowsk	26	White	Burglary/murder	5/9/1952
CA	Aurelio Martinez	38	Hispanic	Murder	6/20/1952
CA	Fred Stroble	70	White	Rape/murder	7/25/1952
CA	Bernard Gilliam	38	White	Murder	10/31/1952
CA	William Cook	23	White	Murder	12/12/1952
CA	Robert Dessauer	30	White	Murder	2/2/1953
CA	Leandress Riley	32	Black	Robbery/murder	2/20/1953
CA	Diamond Reed	34	Black	Rape/murder	4/17/1953
CA	Lovell Barclay	37	Black	Robbery/murder	5/15/1953
CA	Dario Amaya	21	Hispanic	Robbery/murder	5/22/1953
CA	Lloyd Gomez	29	Hispanic	Robbery/murder	10/16/1953
CA	Johnnie Harrison	51	Black	Murder	10/23/1953
CA	John Lawrence	38	White	Rape/murder	10/30/1953
CA	Evan Thomas	30	White	Murder	1/29/1954
CA	Henry McCracken	36	White	Rape/murder	2/19/1954
CA	Joseph Daugherty	54	White	Murder	3/5/1954
CA	Florentino Ortega	25	Hispanic	Robbery/murder	3/5/1954
CA	Frank Decaillet	52	White	Murder	4/2/1954
CA	Charles McGarry	66	White	Murder	7/2/1954
CA	Joseph Johansen	26	White	Murder	7/30/1954
CA	James Wolfe	42	White	Murder	7/30/1954
CA	Alfred Dusseldorf	33	Black	Robbery/murder	9/10/1954
CA	Walter Byrd	43	White	Murder	2/4/1955
CA	Richard Jensen	28	White	Murder	2/11/1955
CA	Johnson Caldwell	33	White	Murder	5/6/1955
CA	Leonard Baldwin	32	White	Robbery/murder	5/13/1955
CA	Anthony Zilbauer	53	White	Robbery/murder	5/18/1955
CA	John A. Santo	NA	White	Robbery/murder	6/3/1955
CA	Barbara Graham	32	White	Robbery/murder	6/3/1955
CA	Emmet R. Perkins	NA	White	Robbery/murder	6/3/1955
CA	Harold Berry	28	White	Murder	9/20/1955
CA	Robert Pierce	27	Black	Robbery/murder	3/6/1956
CA	Smith Jordan	27	Black	Robbery/murder	3/6/1956
CA	Michael Cavanaugh	29	White	Robbery/murder	4/13/1956
CA	Eugene Morlock	25	Native American	Rape/murder	6/15/1956

(continued)

State	Name	Age	Race	Offense	Date of Execution
CA	Henry Thomas	28	Black	Robbery/murder	7/13/1956
CA	Louis Smith	38	White	Murder	2/8/1957
CA	John Allen	48	White	Murder	2/8/1957
CA	Burton Abbott	29	White	Rape/murder	3/15/1957
CA	Thomas Johnston	25	White	Murder	6/28/1957
CA	John Cheary	24	White	Murder	7/19/1957
CA	David Hardenbrook	22	White	Murder	8/16/1957
CA	Foster Dement	50	White	Murder	10/2/1957
CA	Henry Simpson	62	White	Murder	10/4/1957
CA	Donald Bashor	27	White	Burglary/murder	11/11/1957
CA	James Reese	27	Black	Rape/murder	2/14/1958
CA	James Rogers	22	White	Murder	4/15/1958
CA	Eugene Burwell	24	Black	Murder	4/15/1958
CA	John Tipton	20	White	Rape/murder	9/26/1958
CA	Bert Caritativo	52	Asian/ Pacific Islander	Murder	10/24/1958
CA	William Rupp	18	White	Rape/murder	11/7/1958
CA	James Feldkamp	25	White	Robbery/murder	2/27/1959
CA	Richard Riser	33	White	Robbery/murder	5/22/1959
CA	Vander Duncan	31	Black	Rape/murder	5/29/1959
CA	Cecil Ward	27	White	Murder	6/26/1959
CA	Stephan Nash	35	White	Murder	8/21/1959
CA	Harvey Glatman	31	White	Rape/murder	9/18/1959
CA	Phillip Hamilton	23	Black	Rape/murder	1/8/1960
CA	Jimmie Jones	20	Black	Rape/murder	1/8/1960
CA	Lawrence Wade	32	Black	Robbery/murder	4/22/1960
CA	Caryl Chessman	38	White	Kidnapping/sexual assault	5/2/1960
CA	James Hooton	27	White	Murder	5/13/1960
CA	Richard Cooper	37	Black	Rape/murder	7/8/1960
CA	Robert Harmon	27	White	Attempted murder	8/9/1960
CA	George Scott	36	White	Robbery/murder	9/7/1960
CA	Raymond Cartier	32	White	Murder	12/28/1960
CA	Alexander Robillard	19	White	Murder	4/26/1961
CA	Ronald Rittger	25	White	Murder	6/29/1961
CA	Marion Linden	47	White	Murder	7/12/1961
CA	David Combes	32	White	Murder	10/18/1961
CA	James Kendrick	30	White	Murder	11/3/1961
CA	Richard Lindsey	30	White	Rape/murder	11/21/1961
CA	Billy Monk	26	White	Kidnapping	11/21/1961

State	Name	Age	Race	Offense	Date of Execution
CA	Jose Gonzalez	27	Hispanic	Burglary/murder	11/29/1961
CA	Rudolph Wright	31	Black	Criminal assault	1/11/1962
CA	Elbert Carter	24	Black	Murder	1/17/1962
CA	Henry Lane Jr.	24	Asian/ Pacific Islander	Murder	3/7/1962
CA	Robert Hughes	27	Black	Robbery/murder	4/18/1962
CA	Henry Busch	30	White	Murder	6/6/1962
CA	Elizabeth Duncan	58	White	Conspiracy to murder	8/8/1962
CA	Augustine Baldonado	29	Hispanic	Murder	8/8/1962
CA	Luis E. Moya	23	Hispanic	Murder	8/8/1962
CA	Lawrence Garner	27	White	Murder	9/4/1962
CA	Melvin Darling	28	White	Robbery/murder	10/1/1962
CA	Allen Ditson	42	White	Murder	11/21/1962
CA	James Bentley	26	White	Robbery/murder	1/23/1963
CA	Aaron Mitchell	37	Black	Murder	4/12/1967
CA	Robert Alton Harris	39	White	Murder	6/14/1992
CA	David Mason	36	White	Murder	8/24/1993
CO	William Cody Kelley	30	White	Robbery/murder	6/22/1934
CO	Louis Pacheco	37	Hispanic	Murder	5/31/1935
CO	John Pacheco	24	Hispanic	Murder	5/31/1935
CO	Leonard Belongia	24	White	Murder	6/21/1935
CO	Otis McDaniels	31	White	Murder	2/14/1936
CO	Frank Aguilar	34	Hispanic	Rape/murder	8/13/1937
CO	Joe Arridy	23	Hispanic	Rape/murder	1/6/1939
CO	Angelo Agnes	31	Black	Murder	9/29/1939
CO	Pete Catalina	41	White	Murder	9/29/1939
CO	Harry Leopold	30	White	Robbery/murder	12/9/1939
CO	Joe Coates	NA	Native American	Murder	1/10/1941
CO	James Stephens	76	White	Murder	6/20/1941
CO	Martin Suckle	38	White	Murder	5/22/1942
CO	Donald H. Fearn	23	White	Rape/murder	10/23/1942
CO	John Sullivan	43	White	Rape/murder	9/20/1943
CO	George Masayoshi Honda	37	Asian/ Pacific Islander	Murder	10/8/1943
CO	Howard C. Potts	41	White	Murder	6/22/1945
CO	Charles F. Silliman	35	White	Murder	11/9/1945
CO	Frank Martz	35	White	Rape/murder	11/23/1945

(continued)

State	Name	Age	Race	Offense	Date of Execution
CO	John Brown	50	Black	Murder	5/23/1947
CO	Harold Gillette	31	White	Murder	6/20/1947
CO	Robert S. Battalino	39	White	Murder	1/7/1949
CO	Paul Schneider	24	White	Robbery/murder	12/16/1949
CO	John J. Berger Jr.	34	White	Murder	10/26/1951
CO	Besalirez Martinez	42	Hispanic	Murder	9/7/1956
CO	John Graham	23	White	Murder	1/11/1957
CO	Lee Roy Leick	30	White	Murder	1/22/1960
CO	David Early	28	White	Robbery/murder	8/11/1961
CO	David Wooley	36	White	Robbery/murder	3/9/1962
CO	Walter Hammill	31	White	Murder	5/25/1962
CO	John Bizup	26	White	Robbery/murder	8/14/1964
CO	Luis Monge	48	Hispanic	Murder	6/2/1967
MD	Leonard Shockey	17	Black	Rape/robbery/murder	4/10/1959
MD	Carl Kier	25	Black	Rape/robbery/murder	6/24/1959
MD	Nathaniel Lipsco	33	Black	Rape/murder	6/9/1961
MO	William Wright	33	Black	Murder	3/4/1938
MO	John Brown	34	Black	Murder	3/4/1938
MO	Raymond Boyer	33	White	Robbery/murder	3/5/1938
MO	Raymond Batson	33	Black	Murder	3/30/1938
MO	Johnny Jones	35	Black	Rape	7/15/1938
MO	Adam Richetti	28	White	Murder	10/7/1938*
MO	Granville Allen	28	Black	Murder	10/28/1938
MO	Byron King	28	White	Robbery/murder	11/4/1938
MO	John J. Williamson	63	White	Murder	2/15/1939
MO	Robert Kenyon	24	White	Kidnapping/murder	4/28/1940
MO	Chester Jackson	31	Black	Murder	9/20/1940
MO	Robert West	25	Black	Murder	9/20/1940
MO	Wilburn Johnson	40	Black	Murder	1/3/1941
MO	Ernest Tyler	37	Black	Murder	4/24/1942
MO	Allen Lambus	73	Black	Rape/murder	6/16/1944
MO	James Thomas	21	Black	Rape	10/19/1944
MO	Leo Lyles	22	Black	Murder	5/25/1945
MO	William E. Talbert	24	Black	Murder	11/16/1945
MO	Fred Ellis	23	Black	Murder	8/16/1946
MO	Jesse Sanford	37	Black	Murder	8/16/1946
MO	Van Ramsey	36	Black	Robbery/murder	1/9/1947
MO	Marshall Perkins	59	Black	Rape	1/24/1947

State	Name	Age	Race	Offense	Date of Execution
MO	Floyd Cochran	37	Black	Rape/murder	9/26/1947
MO	Afton Scott	49	White	Murder	11/4/1949
MO	George Bell	35	Black	Murder	12/2/1949
MO	Charles Tiedt	56	White	Murder	5/19/1950
MO	Claude McGee	39	White	Murder	1/5/1951
MO	Willie Porter	29	Black	Rape	10/28/1952
MO	Ulas Quilling	53	Black	Murder	5/29/1953
MO	Kenneth Boyd	23	Black	Robbery/murder	7/10/1953
MO	Carl Hall	34	White	Kidnapping/ murder	12/18/1953
MO	Bonnie Headley	41	White	Kidnapping/ murder	12/18/1953
MO	Dock Booker	46	Black	Murder	4/1/1955
MO	Arthur Brown	31	White	Kidnapping/ murder	2/24/1956
MO	Thomas Moore	42	White	Murder	9/13/1957
MO	Sammy Tucker	26	White	Murder	7/26/1963
MO	Charles Odom	32	White	Rape	3/6/1964
MO	Ronald Wolfe	34	White	Rape	4/8/1964
MO	Lloyd Anderson	22	Black	Robbery/murder	2/26/1965
MS	Gerald Gallego	26	White	Murder	3/3/1955
MS	Allen Donaldson	28	Black	Robbery	3/4/1955
MS	August LaFontain	24	White	Murder	4/28/1955
MS	John Wiggins	60	Black	Murder	6/20/1955
MS	Mack Lewis	21	Black	Robbery/murder	6/23/1955
MS	Walter Johnson	19	Black	Rape	8/19/1955
MS	Murray Gilmore	32	White	Robbery/murder	12/9/1955
MS	Mose Robinson	21	Black	Rape	12/18/1955
MS	Robert Buchanan	35	Black	Rape	1/3/1956
MS	Edgar Keeler	38	Black	Robbery/murder	1/27/1956
MS	O.C. McNair	24	Black	Murder	2/17/1956
MS	James Russell	32	Black	Murder	4/5/1956
MS	Dewey Townsell	26	Black	Murder	6/22/1956
MS	Willie Jones	38	Black	Robbery/murder	7/13/1956
MS	Mack Drake	35	Black	Rape/robbery	11/7/1956
MS	Henry Jackson	21	Black	Murder	11/8/1956
MS	Minor Sorber	39	White	Murder	2/8/1957
MS	Joe Thompson	21	Black	Robbery/murder	11/14/1957
MS	William Wetzel	32	White	Murder	1/17/1958
MS	J. Cameron	23	Black	Rape	5/28/1958
MS	Allen Dean Jr.	23	Black	Rape/murder	12/19/1958

(continued)

State	Name	Age	Race	Offense	Date of Execution
MS	Nathaniel Young	39	Black	Rape	11/10/1960
MS	William Stokes	27	Black	Murder	4/21/1961
MS	Robert Goldsby	35	Black	Murder	5/31/1961
MS	J. W. Simmons	28	Black	Burglary/murder	7/14/1961
MS	Howard Cook	33	Black	Rape	12/19/1961
MS	Ellie Lee	31	Black	Rape	12/20/1961
MS	Willie Wilson	22	Black	Rape	5/11/1962
MS	Kenneth Slyter	28	White	Rape/murder	3/29/1963
MS	Willie Anderson	21	Black	Murder/burglary	6/14/1963
MS	Tim Jackson	22	Black	Rape/murder	5/1/1964
MS	Jimmy Lee Gray	34	White	Rape/murder	9/2/1983
MS	Edward E. Johnson	26	Black	Murder	5/26/1987
MS	Connie Ray Evans	27	Black	Robbery/murder	7/8/1987
MS	Leo Edwards	36	Black	Robbery/murder	6/21/1989
NC	Allen Foster	20	Black	Rape	1/24/1936
NC	Ed Jenkins	40	White	Murder	1/31/1936
NC	J. T. Sanford	30	Black	Robbery/murder	2/7/1936
NC	Thomas Watson	32	Black	Robbery/murder	2/7/1936
NC	Jake Johnson	36	Black	Rape	3/19/1936
NC	Ed Hester	19	White	Murder	3/20/1936
NC	Bright Buffkin	43	White	Murder	3/27/1936
NC	Germie Williams	23	Black	Robbery/murder	5/8/1936
NC	Lawrence Williams	32	Black	Robbery/murder	5/8/1936
NC	Marvin Batten	29	White	Murder	5/29/1936
NC	John Horne	37	White	Murder	6/19/1936
NC	William Hodgin	36	Black	Murder	7/17/1936
NC	Willie Galman	21	Black	Murder	8/21/1936
NC	John Kinyon	75	Black	Rape	8/21/1936
NC	George Alston	21	Black	Murder	9/4/1936
NC	John Pressley	43	Black	Murder	11/13/1936
NC	Evans Macklin	20	Black	Murder	11/20/1936
NC	Willie Tate	29	Black	Murder	11/20/1936
NC	Martin Moore	23	Black	Murder/burglary	12/11/1936
NC	Robert Brown	18	Black	Murder	7/9/1937
NC	Sam Jones	21	Black	Robbery/murder	7/16/1937
NC	Fred Steele	22	Black	Robbery/murder	7/16/1937
NC	Hunter Winchester	24	Black	Murder	7/23/1937
NC	Fred Grey	26	Black	Murder	7/23/1937
NC	Thomas Perry	23	Black	Rape	7/30/1937
NC	George Exum	22	Black	Murder	8/6/1937

State	Name	Age	Race	Offense	Date of Execution
NC	Larry McNeill	17	Black	Murder	8/13/1937
NC	William Perry	18	Black	Rape/murder	12/10/1937
NC	Walter Caldwell	37	Black	Rape	12/10/1937
NC	James Sermons	29	Black	Murder	1/21/1938
NC	James Marshallo	30	Black	Housebreaking/ burglary	2/4/1938
NC	Edgar Smoak	40	White	Murder	2/18/1938
NC	Milford Exum	39	White	Robbery/murder	2/18/1938
NC	Sylvester Outlaw	32	Black	Rape	4/29/1938
NC	Empire Baldwin	25	Black	Rape	6/10/1938
NC	Apsom Outlaw	29	Black	Rape	6/17/1938
NC	Lonnie Gardner	27	Black	Rape	6/17/1938
NC	Bill Payne	41	White	Murder	7/1/1938
NC	Wash Turner	36	White	Murder	7/1/1938
NC	Wiley Brice	35	Black	Murder	7/1/1938
NC	L.J. Jefferson	17	Black	Robbery/murder	9/23/1938
NC	Tom Linney	32	Black	Robbery/murder	9/23/1938
NC	George Ford	20	Black	Murder	9/30/1938
NC	Ed Robinson	33	Black	Rape	11/18/1938
NC	John Howie	29	Black	Rape	12/2/1938
NC	Baxter Parnell	33	White	Murder	12/9/1938
NC	King S. Stovall	26	Black	Robbery/murder	1/20/1939
NC	Clarence Bracy	24	Black	Robbery/murder	4/7/1939
NC	Bat Dejouirnette	43	Black	Murder	4/7/1939
NC	James Dixon	38	Black	Murder	5/5/1939
NC	Edward Mattocks	21	Black	Murder	5/26/1939
NC	Dave Burney	47	Black	Murder	6/9/1939
NC	Ed Alston	NA	Black	Robbery/murder	6/16/1939
NC	Bricey Hammonds	24	Native American	Murder	7/7/1939
NC	Alfred Caper	23	Black	Murder	7/7/1939
NC	James Henderson	21	Black	Rape/murder	7/7/1939
NC	Arthur Morris	25	Black	Housebreaking/ burglary	9/1/1939
NC	James Godwin	20	White	Robbery/murder	9/22/1939
NC	Charles Fain	26	Black	Rape/robbery	10/6/1939
NC	Willie Richardson	19	Black	Housebreaking/ burglary	10/27/1939
NC	Claude Bowser Jr.	22	Black	Murder	10/28/1939
NC	Raymond Williams	20	Black	Robbery/murder	11/24/1939
NC	Clarence Rogers	26	Black	Murder	1/19/1940

(continued)

State	Name	Age	Race	Offense	Date of Execution
NC	Glenn Maxwell	50	Black	Murder	1/19/1940
NC	Nathaniel Bryant	17	Black	Burglary/murder	2/16/1940
NC	William Young	22	Black	Burglary/murder	2/16/1940
NC	Robert Williams	20	Black	Rape	3/15/1940
NC	Zeb Page	29	Black	Rape	4/5/1940
NC	Simon Gibson	23	Black	Rape	5/24/1940
NC	Charlie Hopkins	64	Black	Murder	6/14/1940
NC	Lee Flynn	44	White	Murder	6/28/1940
NC	Zedekiel Smith	29	Black	Robbery/murder	12/6/1940
NC	Dollie Hudson	27	Black	Murder	4/18/1941
NC	Sylvester Woodard	30	Black	Murder	5/2/1941
NC	James Shaw	NA	Black	Murder	5/23/1941
NC	Fleet Wall	33	Black	Murder	6/6/1941
NC	Noah Cureton	51	Black	Murder	6/13/1941
NC	Hubert Cash	40	White	Murder	8/22/1941
NC	Tom Melvin	42	Black	Murder	9/5/1941
NC	George Peele	NA	Black	Murder	10/10/1941
NC	Luther Morrow	26	Black	Murder	12/12/1941
NC	Roland Wescott	21	White	Murder	1/9/1942
NC	Roy Sturdivant	29	Black	Murder	2/13/1942
NC	Arthur Gibson	32	Black	Rape	8/7/1942
NC	Walter Smith	63	White	Murder	8/21/1942
NC	Allen Herman	35	White	Murder	10/30/1942
NC	Otis Harris	17	Black	Rape	10/30/1942
NC	William Long	31	Black	Murder	11/13/1942
NC	Rosanna Phillips	25	Black	Robbery/murder	1/1/1943
NC	Daniel Phillips	29	Black	Robbery/murder	1/1/1943
NC	Sam Hairston	22	Black	Rape	1/29/1943
NC	Palmer Meares	35	White	Murder	2/19/1943
NC	John Lee	19	Black	Burglary/ attempted rape	4/16/1943
NC	Lewis Moody	26	Black	Murder	5/21/1943
NC	Harvey Hunt	21	Native American	Rape	6/4/1943
NC	Purcell Smith	22	Native American	Rape	6/4/1943
NC	Bill Bryant	39	White	Robbery/murder	6/4/1943
NC	James Utley	24	Black	Murder	6/18/1943
NC	William Poole	29	Black	Murder	10/8/1943
NC	Willie Smith	47	Black	Robbery/murder	10/29/1943
NC	John Redfern	40	Black	Murder	11/26/1943

State	Name	Age	Race	Offense	Date of Execution
NC	Clyde Grass	31	White	Murder	12/10/1943
NC	Alex Harris	48	White	Murder	1/28/1944
NC	Andrew Farrell	25	White	Rape	2/18/1944
NC	Waymon Grainger	31	Black	Murder	2/25/1944
NC	James Taylor	48	Black	Murder	11/3/1944
NC	Charles Alexander	24	Black	Rape	11/17/1944
NC	James Buchanan	19	Black	Rape	11/24/1944
NC	George Brooks	20	Black	Rape	11/24/1944
NC	Ralph Thompson	18	Black	Robbery/murder	12/29/1944
NC	Melvin Wade	24	Black	Rape	12/29/1944
NC	Bessie Williams	19	Black	Robbery/murder	12/29/1944
NC	John Messer	21	White	Robbery/murder	3/9/1945
NC	Elmer Biggs	23	White	Robbery/murder	3/9/1945
NC	William Biggs	21	White	Robbery/murder	3/9/1945
NC	Horis Hill	23	White	Murder	5/25/1945
NC	Lacy McDaniel	34	Black	Rape	6/6/1945
NC	Henry French	35	Black	Murder	6/22/1945
NC	William Jones	NA	Black	Murder	6/22/1945
NC	Burnett Williams	NA	Black	Rape	10/26/1945
NC	Edward Mays	NA	Black	Rape/murder	11/2/1945
NC	Walter Hightower	32	Black	Murder	2/15/1946
NC	Alligood King	NA	Black	Rape/murder	4/26/1946
NC	Thomas Hart	NA	Black	Murder	5/4/1946
NC	Gurney Herring	NA	Black	Rape	5/24/1946
NC	George Walker	23	White	Rape	6/21/1946
NC	Fred Deaton	39	Black	Murder	6/28/1946
NC	Fab Stewart	NA	White	Murder	6/28/1946
NC	Robert Nash	NA	White	Murder	11/1/1946
NC	Charles Primus	22	Black	NA	11/22/1946
NC	Wilbert Johnson	NA	Black	Rape/robbery	11/22/1946
NC	Calvin Williams	18	Black	Robbery/murder	12/13/1946
NC	Herman Matthews	19	Black	Robbery/murder	12/13/1946
NC	Otis Ragland	NA	Black	Rape	3/14/1947
NC	Bennie Montgomery	NA	Black	Robbery/murder	3/28/1947
NC	Richard Horton	NA	Black	Robbery/murder	4/4/1947
NC	Eunice Martin	NA	Black	Murder	4/11/1947
NC	Ben McLeod	NA	Black	Murder	5/23/1947
NC	Albert Sanders	NA	Black	Murder	6/6/1947
NC	James Farmer	NA	Black	Murder	6/6/1947
NC	Roy Kirksey	NA	Black	Murder	6/27/1947
NC	Woodrow Brown	NA	Black	Rape	6/27/1947

(continued)

State	Name	Age	Race	Offense	Date of Execution
NC	Moses Artis	NA	Black	Murder	6/27/1947
NC	Richard McCain	NA	Black	Robbery/murder	10/3/1947
NC	Earl O'Dear	24	White	Robbery/murder	10/3/1947
NC	Willie Cherry	25	Black	Burglary/ attempted rape	10/3/1947
NC	Robert Messer	21	White	Robbery/murder	10/3/1947
NC	Jethro Lampkins	NA	Black	Robbery/murder	10/3/1947
NC	Oscar Douglas	40	Black	Rape	10/10/1947
NC	J.C. Brooks	NA	Black	Murder	10/31/1947
NC	Grady Brown	NA	Black	Murder	10/31/1947
NC	Lester Stanley	NA	Black	Murder	10/31/1947
NC	Thurman Munn	NA	Black	Murder	10/31/1947
NC	Marvin Bell	33	White	Rape	11/14/1947
NC	Ralph Letteral	35	White	Rape	11/14/1947
NC	Willie Little	NA	Black	Rape	11/14/1947
NC	Frank Black	NA	Black	Murder	1/2/1948
NC	John Breeze	NA	Black	Murder	1/16/1948
NC	Buster Hooks	NA	Black	Burglary/ attempted rape	4/22/1948
NC	Booker Anderson	NA	Black	Arson/murder	4/23/1948
NC	James Jackson	NA	Black	Burglary/murder	5/7/1948
NC	Henderson Wilson	NA	Black	Robbery/murder	6/4/1948
NC	George Hammonds	NA	Black	Robbery/murder	6/4/1948
NC	James West	NA	Black	Robbery/murder	11/19/1948
NC	James Creech	NA	White	Murder	1/28/1949
NC	Emmett Garner	NA	White	Murder	3/18/1949
NC	Roy Cockrel	NA	White	Murder	3/25/1949
NC	James Lewis	NA	Black	Murder	6/17/1949
NC	Monroe Medlin	NA	Black	Burglary/murder	12/9/1949
NC	Allen T. Reid	NA	Black	Burglary/ attempted rape	12/9/1949
NC	Audie Brown	NA	Black	Robbery/murder	12/9/1949
NC	Uzelle Jones	NA	Black	Murder	12/16/1949
NC	Leander Jacobs	NA	Native American	Robbery/murder	12/30/1949
NC	Hector Chavis	NA	Native American	Robbery/murder	12/30/1949
NC	Lee Heller	NA	Black	Murder	1/6/1950
NC	Jack Bridges	NA	White	Murder	5/19/1950
NC	Claude Shackleford	NA	White	Rape	7/21/1950
NC	Covey Lamm	NA	White	Murder	11/10/1950
NC	Ernest Lyles	33	White	Rape	11/24/1950

State	Name	Age	Race	Offense	Date of Execution
NC	Curtis Shedd	29	White	Murder	3/23/1951
NC	James Hall	36	White	Rape/murder	3/29/1951
NC	John Rogers	NA	Black	Rape/robbery/ murder	4/27/1951
NC	John Roman	28	Black	Rape/robbery/ murder	6/6/1952
NC	Lafayette Miller	22	Black	Murder	5/1/1953
NC	Raleigh Spiller	NA	Black	Rape	5/29/1953
NC	Clyde Brown	NA	Black	Rape	5/29/1953
NC	Bennie Daniels	NA	Black	Murder	11/6/1953
NC	Lloyd Daniels	NA	Black	Murder	11/6/1953
NC	Richard Scales	29	Black	Rape/murder	7/15/1955
NC	Robert Conner	NA	Black	Robbery/murder	7/13/1956
NC	Ross McAfee	42	Black	Burglary/ attempted rape	11/22/1957
NC	Julius Bunton	21	Black	Robbery/murder	2/28/1958
NC	Matthew Bass	43	Black	Rape	12/5/1958
NC	Theodore Boykin	32	Black	Rape/robbery/ murder	10/27/1961
NC	David Lawson	38	White	Robbery/murder	6/15/1994
NC	Ricky Lee Sanderson	38	White	Rape/murder	1/30/1998
NM	David Nelson	NA	White	Robbery/murder	1/8/1960
NV	Gee Jon	29	Asian/ Pacific Islander	Murder	2/8/1924
NV	Stanko Jukich	29	White	Murder	5/21/1926
NV	Robert H. White	41	White	Robbery/murder	6/2/1930
NV	Luis Ceja	28	Hispanic	Murder	9/4/1931
NV	John Hall	52	White	Murder	11/28/1932
NV	Ray Elmer Miller	34	White	Murder	5/8/1934
NV	Joseph Behiter	56	White	Rape/murder	7/13/1934
NV	Luther Jones	33	White	Robbery/murder	1/26/1937
NV	Domenico Nadal	47	Hispanic	Murder	1/17/1939
NV	Burton F. Williamson	43	White	Murder	11/21/1939
NV	Wilson H. Boyd	44	Black	Murder	5/28/1940
NV	John A. Kramer	64	White	Murder	8/28/1942
NV	Floyd L. McKinney	34	White	Robbery/murder	11/27/1943
NV	Raymond Plunkett	38	White	Murder	6/30/1944
NV	Floyd Loveless	17	White	Murder	9/29/1944
NV	Albert E. Sala	38	White	Robbery/murder	8/23/1946
NV	Paul Skaug	26	White	Burglary/murder	1/10/1947
NV	David Blackwell	19	White	Murder	4/22/1949

(continued)

State	Name	Age	Race	Offense	Date of Execution
NV	Laszlo Varga	24	White	Rape/murder	6/7/1949
NV	Eugene Gambetta	46	White	Murder	10/18/1949
NV	James Williams	32	Black	Murder	8/24/1950
NV	Theodore Gregory	40	White	Murder	1/29/1951
NV	Gregorio Arellano	28	Hispanic	Murder	7/24/1951
NV	Comingo Echevarria	60	Hispanic	Murder	11/13/1952
NV	Clayton Fouquett	41	White	Kidnapping/ robbery/murder	4/13/1953
NV	Ferdinand Bourdiais	27	White	Robbery/murder	4/23/1953
NV	Frank Pedrini	35	White	Murder	7/15/1954
NV	Leroy Linden	47	White	Murder	7/15/1954
NV	Earl Steward	42	NA	Murder	2/24/1960
NV	Thayne Archibald	22	White	Kidnapping/ robbery/murder	8/23/1961
NV	Jesse Bishop	46	White	Robbery/murder	10/23/1979
OR	Leroy McCarthy	26	White	Robbery/murder	6/20/1939
OR	Claude Cline	46	White	Robbery/murder	7/26/1940
OR	James Thomas	19	White	Robbery/murder	10/30/1941
OR	John Soto	17	Hispanic	Robbery/murder	3/20/1942
OR	William Wallace	54	White	Murder	2/26/1943
OR	Harvey Cunningham	38	Black	Murder	3/6/1944
OR	Richard Layton	36	White	Murder	12/8/1944
OR	Robert Folkes	24	Black	Rape/murder	1/5/1945
OR	Walter Higgins	32	White	Robbery/murder	1/15/1945
OR	Henry Merten	31	White	Robbery/murder	1/15/1945
OR	Andrew Dennis	45	White	Murder	2/2/1946
OR	Kenneth Bailey	26	White	Murder	9/13/1946
OR	Wardell Henderson	27	Black	Robbery/murder	1/23/1948
OR	Wayne Long	26	White	Robbery/murder	8/8/1952
OR	Frank Payne	52	White	Robbery/murder	1/9/1953
OR	Morris Leland	22	White	Rape/murder	1/9/1953
OR	Albert Karnes	24	White	Robbery/murder	1/30/1953
OR	Leroy McGauhey	40	White	Murder	8/20/1962
WY	Perry Carroll	36	White	Murder	8/13/1937
WY	Stanley Lantzer	38	White	Murder	4/19/1940
WY	Cleveland Brown Jr.	27	Black	Rape/murder	11/17/1944
WY	Henry Ruhl	35	White	Robbery/murder	4/27/1945*
WY	Andrew Pixley	22	White	Rape/murder	12/10/1965

SOURCE: Adapted from M. Watt Espy and John Ortiz Smykla, *Executions in the United States, 1608–2002: The Espy File* [computer file], compiled by M. Watt Espy and John Ortiz Smykla, University of Alabama (Ann Arbor, MI: Inter-University Consortium for Political and Social Research, 2004), and other sources.

* federal prisoner executed by state

Notes

ABBREVIATIONS IN NOTES

ADS	*Arizona Daily Star*
AJS	*American Journal of Sociology*
AM	*American Mercury*
AR	*Arizona Republican*
CA	*Chemical Age*
CCDA	*Carson City Daily Appeal*
CLJDN	*Clarion Ledger/Jackson Daily News*
DI	*Dearborne (Michigan) Independent*
DP	*Denver Post*
FB	*Fresno Bee*
GDG	*Gastonia (North Carolina) Daily Gazette*
HMH	*Hagerstown Monthly Herald*
JAH	*Journal of American History*
JAMA	*Journal of the American Medical Association*
JCPT	*Jefferson City Post-Tribune*
JIEC	*Journal of Industrial Engineering Chemistry*
KCS	*Kansas City Star*
LADJ	*Los Angeles Daily Journal*
LAHE	*Los Angeles Herald Examiner*
LAT	*Los Angeles Times*

LD	*Literary Digest*
NCHQ	*North Carolina Historical Quarterly*
NHSQ	*Nevada Historical Society Quarterly*
NSJ	*Nevada State Journal*
NYEW	*New York Evening World*
NYHT	*New York Herald Tribune*
NYT	*New York Times*
OSE	*The Ogden (Utah) Standard-Examiner*
OT	*Oakland Tribune*
PEG	*Phoenix Evening Gazette*
PG	*Phoenix Gazette*
PR	*Pioche Record*
REG	*Reno Evening Gazette*
RGJ	*Reno Gazette Journal*
RMN	*Rocky Mountain News*
RNO	*Raleigh News & Observer*
RR	*Rawlins Republican*
RRB	*Rawlins Republican-Bulletin*
SB	*Sacramento Bee*
SDU	*San Diego Union*
SDUT	*San Diego Union-Tribune*
SFC	*San Francisco Chronicle*
SFCP	*San Francisco Call & Post*
SFE	*San Francisco Examiner*
SJMH	*San Jose Mercury Herald*
SMT	*San Mateo Times*
SSS	*Social Studies of Science*
TC	*Tucson Citizen*
TDC	*Tucson Daily Citizen*
TDT	*Tahoe Daily Tribune*
TT	*Tonopah Daily Times*
UCLR	*University of Colorado Law Review*
USPHR	*U.S. Public Health Reports*
WP	*Washington Post*
WSJ	*Winston-Salem Journal*

INTRODUCTION

1. Henry Friedlander, *The Origins of Nazi Genocide: From Euthanasia to the Final Solution* (Chapel Hill: University of North Carolina Press, 1995), p. 93.

2. Informed but brief mention of the lethal chamber and Nevada's first gassing appears in Edwin Black, *War Against the Weak: Eugenics and America's Campaign to Create a Master Race* (New York: Four Walls Eight Windows, 2003), p. 258.

3. Herbert Spencer, *Social Statics,* reprint (New York: Robert Schalkenback Foundation, 1970), pp. 58–60, 289–90.

4. Francis Galton, *Essays in Eugenics* (London: Eugenics Education Society, 1909), p. 35. Galton's conception is discussed in Alexandra Minna Stern, *Eugenic Nation: Faults and Frontiers of Better Breeding in Modern America* (Berkeley: University of California Press, 2005), p. 11.

5. Black, *War Against the Weak,* p. 21.

6. Stern, *Eugenic Nation,* pp. 16–17.

7. "Exterminating Agent for Vermin," filed by Gerhard Peters, Application May 26, 1939, Serial No. 276,021, in Germany, June 7, 1938, patent 2,344,105, U.S. Patent Office, March 14, 1944.

8. Friedlander, *Origins of Nazi Genocide,* p. 93.

9. See Adam Hochschild, *Bury the Chains: Prophets and Rebels in the Fight to Free an Empire's Slaves* (Boston: Houghton Mifflin, 2005); Claude Ribbe, *Napoleon's Crimes: A Blueprint for Hitler* (Oxford: Oneworld Publications, 2007), originally published in French as *Le Crime de Napoléon* in 2005.

10. *State of Nebraska v. Mata,* N.W.2d _, filed Feb. 8, 2008, No. S-05-1268; Adam Liptak, "Electrocution Is Banned in Last State to Rely on It," *NYT,* February 9, 2008.

11. Linda Greenhouse, "Justices to Enter the Debate over Lethal Injection," *NYT,* September 26, 2007; *Baze v. Rees,* No. 07–5439.

12. Professor Denno quoted in Rob Egelko, "Supreme Court to Review Lethal Injection Methods," *SFC,* September 26, 2007.

13. *Baze v. Rees,* 553 U.S. _ (2008).

14. Recent histories of the electric chair include Richard Moran, *The Executioner's Current* (New York: Knopf, 2003); Jill Jonnes, *Empires of Light* (New York: Random House, 2004); Mark Essig, *Edison and the Electric Chair: A Story of Light and Death* (New York: Walker & Co., 2003); and Craig Brandon, *The Electric Chair: An Unnatural American History* (Jefferson, NC: McFarland & Co., 1999).

15. Georg Rusche and Otto Kirchheimer, *Punishment and Social Structure* (New York: Columbia University Press, 1939), p. 5; Tony Platt and Paul Takagi, eds., *Punishment and Penal Discipline* (San Francisco: Crime and Social Justice, 1980), p. 13; Rusche, "Labor Market and Penal Sanction: Thoughts on the Sociology of Criminal Justice," trans. Gerda Dinwiddie, *Crime & Social Justice* (Fall/Winter 1978): 5. For a brief discussion of some of the rationales and theories of criminal punishment, see Scott Christianson, *With Liberty for Some: 500 Years of Imprisonment in America* (Boston: Northeastern University Press, 1998), pp. 309–13.

16. Rusche and Kirchheimer, *Punishment and Social Structure,* p. 5.

17. In 1922 Schweitzer delivered the Dale Memorial Lectures at Oxford University, and from them the following year appeared volumes 1 and 2 of his great work, *The Decay and Restoration of Civilization* and *Civilization and Ethics.* In 1936 he published the article "Reverence for Life" in the periodical *Christendom* 1 (1936): 225–39.

18. David Garland, *Punishment and Modern Society: A Study in Social Theory* (Chicago: University of Chicago Press, 1990), p. 153.

19. Michel Foucault, *The History of Sexuality, Volume I* (New York: Vintage, 1990), p. 95.

20. Garland, *Punishment and Modern Society,* pp. 106–9.

21. Ibid., chapters 6 and 7.

22. Jürgen Habermas, "Learning by Disaster? A Diagnostic Look Back on the Short 20th Century," *Constellations* 5(3) (1998): 307–20.

1. ENVISIONING THE LETHAL CHAMBER

1. Claude Bernard (1813–78), *De l'emploi de l'oxyde de carbone pour la détermination de l'oxygène au sang* (Compt. rend. de l'Acad. des sciences, meeting of September 6, 1858, vol. 47).

2. Peter D. Bryon, *Comprehensive Review in Toxicology for Emergency Technicians* (London: Informa Heath Care Press, 1996), p. 352. "Cyanide" refers to "a large number of compounds that contain the negatively charged cyanide ion: CN-. This ion consists of one carbon atom triple-bonded to one nitrogen atom. The negative charge primarily rests on the carbon atom. Cyanide can be found both as a gas and as a salt. When bound to hydrogen, it's referred to as hydrogen cyanide (HCN) and is a gas at room temperature. When bound to ions like sodium (Na+) or Potassium (K+), it's a salt and is a water-soluble solid. Its name varies depending on the ion it binds. KCN is potassium cyanide, for example" (Brian Harmon, "Technical Aspects of the Holocaust: Cyanide, Zyklon-B, and Mass Murder," 1994, http://nizkor.org/ftp.cgi/camps/auschwitz/cyanide/cyanide.001 [accessed September 11, 2007]).

3. "Executions at the Dog Pound," *NYT,* June 26, 1874.

4. J.R. McNeill, *Something New Under the Sun: An Environmental History of the Twentieth-Century World* (New York: W.W. Norton & Co., 2000), p. 66.

5. Benjamin Ward Richardson, "On the Painless Extinction of Life in the Lower Animals," *Scientific American Supplement* 476 (February 14, 1885). See also Edwin Black's excellent history of the eugenics movement, *War Against the Weak: Eugenics and America's Campaign to Create a Master Race* (New York: Four Walls Eight Windows, 2003), chapter 13. Black is practically the only American historian to date who has written in any detail about the significance of the lethal chamber.

6. When present in the air, carbon dioxide usually has no noticeable effect on humans at only 1–2 percent, but at 3 percent it causes breathing to become slightly more difficult, and at 5–6 percent it causes marked panting and head-

ache. At 10 percent there is extreme distress, and at 15 percent humans often slip into partial unconsciousness with narcotic poison effects. At 18 percent suffocation and death can occur, and at 25 percent or more rapid death.

7. H.G. Wells, *A Modern Utopia* (New York: Charles Scribner's Sons, 1905).

8. Robert Reid Rentoul, *Race, Culture; or, Race Suicide?* (London: Walter Scott Publishing Co., 1906), pp. 178, 179. See also Rentoul, "Proposed Sterilization of Certain Mental Degenerates," *AJS* 12(3) (November 1906): 319–27.

9. D.H. Lawrence, *Fantasia of the Unconscious* (New York: Thomas Seltzer, 1922), p. 144.

10. Black, *War Against the Weak*, p. 248.

11. These developments are outlined in ibid., pp. 247–50.

12. Scott Christianson, "Bad Seed or Bad Science? The Story of the Notorious Jukes Family," *NYT*, February 8, 2003.

13. Max Weber, "Politik als Beruf" (Politics as a Vocation), a lecture he gave in 1919, in Max Weber, *Political Writings*, ed. and trans. P. Lassman and R. Speirs (Cambridge: Cambridge University Press, 1944).

14. National Association for the Advancement of Colored People, *Thirty Years of Lynching in the United States, 1889–1918* (New York: NAACP, 1919; reprint, Negro Universities Press, 1969), pp. 7, 30–31, 45. See also Charles J. Ogletree and Austin D. Sarat, eds., *From Lynch Mobs to the Killing State: Race and the Death Penalty in America* (New York: New York University Press, 2006).

15. Margaret Werner Cahalan, *Historical Corrections Statistics in the United States, 1850–1984* (Rockville, MD: Bureau of Justice Statistics, U.S. Department of Justice, December 1986), p. 217. From 1890 to 1984 a total of 8,516 persons were legally executed and 3,543 were illegally lynched. About three-quarters of those lynched in that period were black. Although about 90 percent of those executed under state authority were executed for homicide, only 41 percent of those lynched were for homicide (ibid., 9).

16. Governor David Hill's inaugural address, January 6, 1885, David B. Hill Papers, New York State Library, Albany.

17. Richard Moran, *The Executioner's Current: Thomas Edison, George Westinghouse, and the Invention of the Electric Chair* (New York: Alfred A. Knopf, 2003), p. 248 n39.

18. R. Ogden Doremus, Clark Bell, J. Mount Bleyer, Charles F. Stillman, and Frank H. Ingram, "Report of the Committee on Best Method of Executing Criminals," *The Medico-Legal Journal* 5(1) (1888): 427–41. Bleyer is described in Moran, *Executioner's Current*, pp. 72–74.

19. Allan McLane Hamilton (1848–1919), *Recollections of an Alienist: Personal and Professional* (New York: George H. Doran Co., 1916).

20. Letter from Governor James G. Scrugham to Dr. J.W. Kime of Boulder Lodge Sanitarium, Fort Dodge, Iowa, April 9, 1924, in Governor Scrugham Papers, Nevada State Archives, Carson City, Nevada.

21. Moran, *Executioner's Current*, p. 110.

22. Quoted in "A New Form of Death Penalty," *NYT*, December 15, 1896.

23. Henry M. Boies, *Prisoners and Paupers: A Study of the Abnormal*

Increase of Criminals, and the Public Burden of Pauperism in the United States; the Causes and Remedies (New York: Putnam's, 1893), pp. 292–93.

24. W. Duncan McKim, *Heredity and Human Progress* (New York: G.P. Putnam's Sons, 1900), pp. 120, 168.

25. "72,000 Cats Killed in Paralysis Fear," *NYT*, July 26, 1916.

26. Madison Grant, *The Passing of the Great Race: The Racial Basis of European History* (New York: Charles Scribner's Sons, 1916). Grant's book later found an ardent fan in Adolf Hitler.

27. Carey McWilliams, *A Mask for Privilege: Anti-Semitism in America* (Boston: Little, Brown & Co., 1948), pp. 58–60.

28. Ian Dowbiggin, *A Merciful End: The Euthanasia Movement in Modern America* (New York: Oxford University Press, 2007).

29. William J. Robinson, *Eugenics, Marriage, and Birth Control* (New York: The Critic and Guide Company, 1917), pp. 74–76.

30. Paul Popenoe and Roswell Hill Johnson, *Applied Eugenics* (New York: Macmillan, 1918), p. 184.

31. Allan McLane Hamilton, *Recollections of an Alienist, Personal and Professional* (New York: George H. Doran, 1916), pp. 380–89.

2. FASHIONING A FRIGHTFUL WEAPON OF WAR

1. Robert Harris and Jeremy Paxman, *A Higher Form of Killing: The Secret History of Chemical and Biological Warfare* (New York: Random House, 2002), p. 3.

2. Anthony R. Hossack, first published in *Everyman at War*, edited by C.B. Purdom (New York: Dutton, 1930).

3. Rev. O.S. Watkins, quoted in Amos A. Fries and Clarence J. West, *Chemical Warfare* (New York: McGraw-Hill, 1921), p. 13.

4. Daniel Charles, *Master Mind: the Rise and Fall of Fritz Haber, the Nobel Laureate Who Launched the Age of Chemical Warfare* (New York: Ecco, 2005), pp. 162–63.

5. "Mars in White Smock," *Time*, March 8, 1937.

6. Curt Wachtel, *Chemical Warfare* (Brooklyn, NY: Chemical Publishing, 1941), p. 21.

7. "Mars in White Smock."

8. Fries and West, *Chemical Warfare*, p. 14.

9. Harris and Paxman, *A Higher Form of Killing*, p. 10.

10. See Thomas Hager, *The Alchemy of Air: A Jewish Genius, a Doomed Tycoon, and the Scientific Discovery That Fed the World but Fueled the Rise of Hitler* (New York: Harmony Books, 2008).

11. Fritz Stern, *Dreams and Delusions: The Drama of German History* (New York: Knopf, 1987), quoted in James G. Hershberg, *James B. Conant: Harvard to Hiroshima and the Making of the Nuclear Age* (New York: Knopf, 1993), p. 63.

12. Charles, *Master Mind*, p. 152. For more on Fritz Haber (1868–1934),

see Morris Goran, *The Story of Fritz Haber* (Norman: University of Oklahoma Press, 1967).

13. Joseph Borkin, *The Crime and Punishment of IG Farben* (New York: The Free Press, 1978), p. 18.

14. See Ludwig Fritz Haber, *The Poisonous Cloud: Chemical Warfare in the First World War* (Oxford: Clarendon Press, 1986).

15. Michael Pattison, "Scientists, Inventors and the Military in Britain, 1915–19," *SSS* 13(4) (November 1983): 526–27.

16. Gerhard Baader, Susan E. Lederer, Morris Low, Florian Schmaltz, and Alexander V. Schwerin, "Pathways to Human Experimentation, 1933–1945; Germany, Japan and the United States," *Osiris,* 2nd series, vol. 20, Politics and Science in Wartime: Comparative International Perspectives in the Kaiser Wilhelm Institute (2005), p. 212.

17. See Charles Howard Foulkes, *Gas! The Story of the Special Brigade* (London: William B. Blackwood & Sons, 1936); Donald Richter, *Chemical Soldiers: British Gas Warfare in World War I* (Lawrence: University Press of Kansas, 1992).

18. Daniel Patrick Jones, "The Role of Chemists in Research on War Gases in the United States During World War I," Ph.D. diss., University of Wisconsin, 1969, pp. 68–73, quoted in Hershberg, *James B. Conant,* p. 44.

19. "Mars in White Smock."

20. For an exception, see Rudyard Kipling, "Ground Torn by Shells, Grass Yellow from Shells," *LAT,* September 6, 1915.

21. Harris and Paxman, *A Higher Form of Killing,* p. 41. For a detailed study of the health effects of poison gas experimentation on sixty thousand U.S. soldiers in World War II, see Constance M. Pechura and David P. Rall, eds., *Veterans at Risk: The Health Effects of Mustard Gas and Lewisite* (Washington, DC: National Academy Press, March 1993).

22. Quoted in J. B. S. Haldane, *Callinicus: A Defense of Chemical Warfare* (New York: E.P. Dutton, 1925), p. 75. Haldane, a Communist and friend of Aldous Huxley, later became famous for his work in population genetics. Gas chamber experiments on sarin and other gases continued to be conducted at Porton Down well into the 1960s.

23. Cyanogen chloride was first prepared in 1787 by the action of chlorine upon hydrocyanic acid. Joseph Louis Gay-Lussac established its correct formula in 1815. It was not as poisonous as some chemical warfare agents used in World War I. The term "cyanogen" denotes a colorless toxic gas with an almondlike odor and is used to describe any substance that will form cyanide in the body (P. Kikilo and Andrew L. Ternay Jr., "Cyanogen Chloride—An Overview," www.du.edu/rmchd/documents/CYANOGENCHLORIDEforweb.doc, accessed September 16, 2006). Hydrogen cyanide (HCN) is a colorless or pale blue liquid or gas with a faint bitter almondlike odor that was used in capital punishment, first by several states in the United States and later by Germany.

24. Gertrud Woker, *The Next War, A War of Poison Gas* (Washington, DC: Women's International League for Peace and Freedom, 1927).

25. James B. Conant, "A Skeptical Chemist Looks into the Crystal Ball,"

September 5, 1951, JBC Speech file, JBC Presidential Papers, Harvard University Archives.

26. Bernhard C. Hesse, "Our Responsibilities," *JIEC* 8 (August 1916): 672.

27. Kathryn Steen, "Patents, Patriotism, and 'Skilled in the Art': USA v. the Chemical Foundation, Inc., 1923–1926," *Isis* 92 (2001): 95. See also Ludwig F. Haber, *The Chemical Industry, 1900–1930* (Oxford: Clarendon, 1971).

28. Daniel Patrick Jones, "The Role of Chemists in Research on War Gases."

29. See Records of the Chemical Warfare Service, Record Group 175, National Archives and Records Administration; Edward S. Farrow, *Gas Warfare* (New York: E.P. Dutton, 1920); Fries and West, *Chemical Warfare;* Benedict Crowell and Robert Forrest Wilson, *How America Went to War: An Account from Official Sources of the Nation's War Activities, 1917–1920* (New Haven, CT: Yale University Press, 1921); Victor Lefebure, *The Riddle of the Rhine: Chemical Strategy in Peace and War* (New York: The Chemical Foundation, 1923); Leo P. Brophy and George J.B. Fisher, *The Chemical Warfare Service: From Laboratory to Field* (Washington, DC: Office of the Chief of Military History, Department of the Army, 1959); Charles E. Heller, *Chemical Warfare in World War I: The American Experience, 1917–1918* (Ft. Leavenworth, KS: Combat Studies Institute, September 1984); Haber, *The Poisonous Cloud;* Harris and Paxman, *A Higher Form of Killing.*

30. These efforts are described in Charles L. Parsons, "The American Chemist in Warfare," *Science* 48 (1242) (October 18, 1918): 377–86.

31. Haber, *The Chemical Industry,* p. 224.

32. Brophy and Fisher, *The Chemical Warfare Service,* pp. 5–9. See also Gilbert F. Whittemore Jr., "World War I, Poison Gas Research, and the Ideals of American Chemists," *SSS* 5 (1975): 135–63.

33. Founded in 1910 to investigate poisonous and asphyxiating gases in mines, the Bureau of Mines offered its services to the Military Committee of the National Research Council (NRC) on February 8, 1917, shortly before war was declared on April 2.

34. Blase R. Dixon, "The Catholic University of America, 1909–1928: The Rectorship of Thomas Joseph Shahan," Ph.D. diss., Catholic University of America, 1972, p. 151.

35. Quoted in Joel A. Vilensky, *Dew of Death: The Story of Lewisite, America's World War I Weapon of Mass Destruction* (Bloomington: Indiana University Press, 2005), p. 17.

36. "Yandell Henderson," in *National Cyclopedia of American Biography* 36 (New York: J.T. White, 1950), p. 25.

37. George A. Burrell and Frank M. Siebert, "Experiments with Small Animals and Carbon Monoxide," *JIEC* 6 (March 1914): 241; W. Lee Lewis, "Some Features of Swimming Pool Control," *JIEC* 8 (October 1916): 914; Whittemore Jr., "World War I, Poison Gas Research," pp. 151–52.

38. "Christian Conscience and Poison-Gas," *LD,* January 8, 1921, p. 38.

39. Charles L. Parsons, "The American Chemist in Warfare," *JIEC* 10 (October 1918): 780.

40. Charles E. Roth, quoted in "American Chemical Industry Leaps Forward under the Spur of War," *Current Opinion*, November 1917, p. 349.

41. Amos A. Fries (1873–1963) is one of the great overlooked characters of the twentieth century. Born in a log cabin in Vernon County, Wisconsin, eight years after the end of the Civil War, Fries grew up in Missouri until the age of fifteen, when his family moved to Medford, Oregon. He graduated from West Point in 1898 and served as an engineer in the Army Corps of Engineers in the Philippines. In Puteaux, France, with the American Expeditionary Force in January 1918, Fries set up a major research laboratory and worked with several top scientific and industrial leaders to develop America's chemical warfare program. As a result of his efforts to advance gas warfare, Fries helped to make the United States a dominant military power and probably helped to shorten World War I, because the United States had planned to resort to massive use of chemical weapons against German civilians if the war had continued. After the war Fries commanded the army arsenal and chemical warfare storage facility in Maryland. He remains famous in military circles for his refusal to go along with international efforts to dismantle the gas service after the war, and for his political ability to amass power. On July 1, 1920, he became peacetime chief of the Chemical Warfare Service, replacing General William L. Sibert (the engineer who had also built the Panama Canal). Some historians know Fries best as a key player against pacifists, Reds, and internationalists in the wake of World War I. He devised a list of peacetime projects for the Chemical Warfare Service, including rat extermination, development of insecticides, extermination of locusts, production of gases for police uses, and secret laboratory experiments in several areas. His most famous activity involved the use of his Chemical Warfare Service office to conduct a propaganda campaign against "the worldwide Communist conspiracy," which he documented in something called the "Spider's Web Chart," which purported to show how all of the "leftist" groups such as the ACLU and the League of Women Voters were part of a massive Red conspiracy. Fries retired from the army in 1929. He had close ties to the American Defense Society, the American Legion, the Masons, the National Sojourners, the Military Order of the World War, and efforts to restrict immigration. He also worked with the KKK and other racist groups. In 1935, as president of the District Public School Association in Washington, D.C., Fries tried to ban the teaching of Communism in Washington schools and warned against subversive influence in education. From the mid-1930s to the mid-'50s he fought against Communist influence in education and was an original cold warrior and McCarthyite. A rabid anti-Semite, he was one of the first disseminators of the *Protocols of the Elders of Zion*. He advocated the use of poison gas at home, and coauthored a book about chemical warfare in 1921. His book *Communism Unmasked* defended fascist dictatorship. In the late 1930s he opposed sanctuary for Jews fleeing persecution in Europe and worked with the American Legion to fight the Jewish boycott of Nazi Germany. He also advocated the rearming of anti-Communist Nazi Germany. His wife, Elizabeth, was one of the leading socialites in Washington, D.C., and was also involved in many patriotic and right-wing causes. Much of this account is based on his unpublished papers and unpublished autobiography,

housed at the Division of Special Collections and University Archives, University of Oregon Library, in Eugene, Oregon.

42. Leo P. Brophy, "The Origins of the Chemical Corps," *Military Affairs* 20(4) (Winter 1956): 221.

43. Brophy and Fisher, *The Chemical Warfare Service,* p. 11.

44. Ibid., p. 13; Jones, "The Role of Chemists in Research," pp. 136–39; Hershberg, *James B. Conant,* p. 46.

45. Hershberg, *James B. Conant,* pp. 45–46; Harris and Paxman, *A Higher Form of Killing,* p. 35; Vilensky, *Dew of Death,* p. 18.

46. See James Bryant Conant, *My Several Lives: Memoirs of a Social Inventor* (New York: Harper & Row, 1970).

47. Joel A. Vilensky and Pandy R. Sinish, "The Dew of Death," *Bulletin of the Atomic Scientists* 60(2) (March–April 2004): 54–55. In 2005 an author who wrote about the site reported that "The building still houses CUA's chemistry department, and the ceilings of the basement laboratories (above the suspended ceilings of today) continue to shed even freshly applied paint because of the vapors absorbed from the work done there in 1918" (Vilensky, *Dew of Death,* p. 21).

48. Vilensky, *Dew of Death,* pp. 32–33.

49. W. Dwight Pierce to L.O. Howard, n.d., Correspondence on Body Lice, Vermin, Cooties, in Army, Tests and Recommendations, 1918, Correspondence and Reports Relating to a Study of Body Lice 1918, Records of the Bureau of Entomology and Plant Quarantine, RG 7 (Washington National Records Center, Suitland, MD), including "Report on Experiments Conducted on Oct. 16, 1918, Testing the Effect of Certain Toxic Gases on Body Lice and Their Eggs."

50. See the excellent article by Edmund P. Russell, "'Speaking of Annihilation': Mobilizing for War Against Human and Insect Enemies, 1914–1945," *JAH* 82 (March 1996): 1512–13.

51. Henry F. Pringle, "Profiles: Mr. President—I: James Bryant Conant," *New Yorker,* September 12, 1936, p. 24.

52. Vilensky, *Dew of Death,* p. 31.

53. Pringle, "Profiles: Mr. President," p. 24.

54. Vilensky, *Dew of Death,* p. 33.

55. Fries and West, *Chemical Warfare,* p. 49; "America Took Lead in Gas Production," *NYT,* May 11, 1919.

56. Richard Barry, "Vast U.S. Poison Gas Plant Was Working at Full Blast for 1919 Campaign," *NYT,* December 8, 1918; Harris and Paxman, *A Higher Form of Killing,* p. 35.

57. Farrow, *Gas Warfare.*

58. Barry, "Vast U.S. Poison Gas Plant." I have not been able to locate any empirical study specifically on the health effects of working in U.S. poison gas factories. See G.W. Beebe, "Lung Cancer in World War I Veterans: Possible Relation to Mustard Gas Injury and 1918 Influenza Epidemic," *Journal of National Cancer Institute* 10 (1958): 125–30. However, a study of 1,632 workers who manufactured mustard gas and lewisite in Japanese plants between 1927 and 1945 discovered mutagenic and carcinogenic effects with a notably

high incidence of lung cancer attributed to the inhalation of mustard gas. See Michio Yamakido, Shinichi Ishioka, Keiko Hiyama, and Akhiro Maeda, "Former Poison Gas Workers and Cancer: Incidence and Inhibition of Tumor Formation by Treatment with Biological Response Modifier N-CWS," *Environmental Health Perspectives* 104(3) (May 1996): 485–88.

59. Brophy, Miles, and Cochrane, *The Chemical Warfare Service,* p. 67.

60. Hershberg, *James B. Conant,* p. 47.

61. "America Took Lead in Gas Production."

62. Vilensky, *Dew of Death,* p. 44.

63. Ty Cobb, "My Life in Baseball: The True Record," quoted in Richard Gurtowski, "Remembering Baseball Hall of Famers Who Served in the Chemical Corps," *Army Chemical Review* (July–December 2005): 52.

64. Ibid., pp. 53–54.

65. Lieutenant Colonel Augustin M. Prentiss of the Chemical Warfare Service wrote in his book *Chemicals in War* (1937), considered the most thorough military treatise on chemical warfare, "Our offensive in 1919, in my opinion, would have been a walk to Berlin, due to chemical warfare. The campaign of 1919 would have been largely a chemical war." John Van Courtland Moon, "Controlling Chemical and Biological Weapons through World War II," in *Encyclopedia of Arms Control and Disarmament*, vol. 2, ed. Richard Dean Burns (New York: Charles Scribner's Sons, 1993), p. 662. For a laudatory review of Prentiss's book, see "Mars in White Smock." The *New York Times* reported on May 25, 1919, how two American airplanes carrying lewisite could have wiped out "every vestige of life—animal and vegetable—in Berlin. A single day's output would snuff out the millions of lives on Manhattan Island."

66. Barry, "Vast U.S. Poison Gas Plant."

67. Ibid.

68. Frederick J. Brown, *Chemical Warfare: A Study in Restraints* (Westport, CT: Greenwood Press, 1968), p. 47 n102.

69. For another account about the plans against Germany, see Edwin E. Slosson, "What Germany Escaped," *The Independent,* June 7, 1919, pp. 355–57, 381–83.

70. John Ellis and Michael Cox, *The World War I Data Book* (London: Aurum Press, 1993).

71. "Our Super-Poison Gas: First Story of Compound 72 Times Deadlier Than 'Mustard,' Manufactured Secretly by the Thousands of Tons," *NYT,* April 20, 1919; Vilensky, *Dew of Death,* p. 52; Hershberg, *James B. Conant,* p. 47; Frank P. Stockbridge, "War Inventions That Came Too Late," *Harper's* 11 (September 1919): 828–35.

72. Conant, *My Several Lives,* p. 49.

3. DEVISING "CONSTRUCTIVE PEACETIME USES"

1. Grinnell Jones, "Nitrogen: Its Fixation, Its Uses in Peace and War," *Quarterly Journal of Economics* 34(3) (May 1920): 391–431.

2. "Abandon Gas Weapon," *WP*, March 19, 1919; U.S. Congress, Senate, Committee on Military Affairs, *Reorganization of the Army*, part 1, 66th Cong., 1st sess. (Washington, DC: GPO, 1919), pp. 352–53.

3. Fries to J.D. Law, August 16, 1919, General Fries's file, Records of the Chemical Warfare Service, RG 175, National Archives.

4. Amos A. Fries to J.L. Clarkson, September 20, 1919, Clarkson Major J.L., General Fries's file, RG 175, National Archives.

5. Interview with Fries, cited in Leo P. Brophy, "The Origins of the Chemical Corps," *Military Affairs* 20(4) (Winter 1956), p. 225.

6. Fries and West, *Chemical Warfare* (New York: McGraw-Hill, 1921). See also Fries, "The Future of Poison Gas," *Current History* 15 (December 1921): 419–22; "United States Chemical Warfare Service," part 1, *Scientific American* 120 (March 29, 1919).

7. Part V, Section I, chapter I, Article 171, Versailles Treaty.

8. "Deadly Chemicals Are Made Useful and Harmless," *News-Sentinel* (Fort Wayne, Indiana), March 25, 1922.

9. "Army Chemists Turn to Peaceful Projects," *NYT*, February 11, 1922; Edmund P. Russell, *War and Nature: Fighting Humans and Insects with Chemicals from World War I to Silent Spring* (New York: Cambridge University Press, 2001) (see especially the chapter "Chemical Warfare in Peace").

10. "Toxic Gases to Help Industry," *NYT*, January 5, 1919.

11. Amos A. Fries, "Summary of Marine Piling Investigation," *Chemical Warfare* 11 (1925): 11–15.

12. "Army Invents Mask Against All Poisons," *NYT*, April 3, 1923.

13. Fries in 1922, quoted in Edmund P. Russell, "'Speaking of Annihilation': Mobilizing for War against Human and Insect Enemies, 1914–1945," *JAH* 82 (March 1996): 1517.

14. Russell, *War and Nature*, p. 66, quoting Amos Fries, "Address before Chemical Industries Exposition, New York City," September 12, 1922.

15. L.O. Howard, "Entomology and the War," quoted in Russell, "'Speaking of Annihilation,'" p. 1513.

16. L.O. Howard, "The War against Insects: The Insecticide Chemist and Biologist in the Migration of Plant Pests," *CA* 30(1) (1922): 5–6.

17. "Army to 'Gas' the Boll Weevil in Cotton Fields of the South," *NYT*, January 29, 1921; "To Use Poison Gas on Boll-Weevil," *NYT*, September 13, 1922.

18. H.W. Walker and J.E. Mills, "Progress Report of Work of the Chemical Warfare Service on the Boll Weevil *Anthonomus Grandis*," *Journal of Economic Entomology* 12 (1927): 233.

19. See also "How Fumigation Methods for Fighting Scale Have Changed," *LAT*, April 3, 1921.

20. Russell, "'Speaking of Annihilation,'" pp. 1508–9. See also Will Allen, *The War on Bugs* (White River Junction, VT: Chelsea Green Publishing, 2008).

21. Department of Agriculture Bulletin 1149, cited in "Hydrocyanic Acid as Fumigant for Pests," *Gazette* (Bedford, PA), December 28, 1923.

22. United States War Department, *Annual Reports 1922—Report of the Secretary of War to the President* (Washington, DC, 1923), p. 282.

23. "Says War Gas Leaves No Bad After Effect," *NYT,* November 12, 1923.

24. L.O. Howard, "The Needs of the World as to Entomology," *Smithsonian Institution Annual Report, 1925* (Washington, DC: Smithsonian, 1925), p. 370.

25. "Army Chemists Use Poison Gases on Disease; Grip, Pneumonia, Paresis Said to Be Cured," *NYT,* May 2, 1923.

26. H.S. Gasser, "Arthur S. Lovenhart," *Science Press* 70 (October 4, 1929): 317–21.

27. Joel A. Vilensky, *Dew of Death: The Story of Lewisite, America's World War I Weapon of Mass Destruction* (Bloomington: Indiana University Press, 2005), pp. 64–65. According to Vilensky, "This collaborative effort between the Department of Chemistry at Northwestern University and the Department of Pharmacology at the University of Wisconsin eventually led to the 1930s discovery of an arsenic-based drug, Mapharsen, which became a very successful antisyphilitic treatment."

28. John Walker Harrington, "Poison Gas Fumes Now Aid Medicine," *NYT,* May 27, 1923.

29. "Chlorine Gas, War Annihilator, Aids President's Cold," *WP,* May 21, 1924; *NYT,* May 22, 1924.

30. "Gen. Fries Defends Chlorine Treatment," *NYT,* January 6, 1925.

31. "Scientific Warfare Aids Man, Teachers Are Told," *WP,* November 30, 1924.

32. *NYT,* October 27, 1921.

33. "Gas Routs Burglars: Indiana Bank Vault Had Been Prepared for Attack," *NYT,* July 8, 1925; Vilensky, *Dew of Death,* pp. 65–66.

34. National Safety Council, from www.nsc.org/ehc/chemical/Hydrocya.htm (accessed May 8, 2008).

35. Cyanides comprise a wide range of compounds of varying degrees of chemical complexity and toxicity. Hydrogen cyanide was used in the fumigation of ships, railroad cars, large buildings, grain silos, and flour mills, as well as in the fumigation of peas and seeds in vacuum chambers. Other cyanides, such as sodium and potassium cyanide, are solid or crystalline hygroscopic salts widely used in ore extracting processes for the recovery of gold and silver, electroplating, case-hardening of steel, base metal flotation, metal degreasing, dyeing, printing, and photography. United Nations Environment Programme, *Hydrogen Cyanide and Cyanides: Human Health Aspects* (Geneva: World Health Organization, 2004). Hydrocyanic acid gas (HCN) was discovered as a fumigant for insect-control purposes in 1886 and first used to control insects in greenhouses in 1894; in 1898 it began to be used in some homes for insect control; in 1905 it was advocated for control of the cigarette beetle; in 1912 it began to be used for ship fumigation and was adopted by the U.S. Department of Health as a standard fumigant. Liquid hydrogen cyanide began to be tested for insect control purposes in 1915; in 1917 HCN fumigation methods were developed for control of insects affecting greenhouse ornamental plants,

and liquid hydrocyanic acid gas was introduced commercially. Agricultural Research Service, U.S. Department of Agriculture, *Chronological History of the Development of Insecticides and Control Equipment from 1854 through 1954* (Washington, DC: U.S. Department of Agriculture, 1954).

36. G.A. Roush, ed., *The Mineral Industry: Its Statistics, Technology, and Trade during 1920* (New York: McGraw-Hill, 1921), p. 314; Alan Lougheed, "The Anatomy of an International Cartel: Cyanide, 1807–1927," *Prometheus* 19(1) (2001): 4, 9.

37. "Head of German Society Is Held for Activities," *Syracuse Herald*, July 12, 1918. Today DEGUSSA remains best known for its manufacture of Zyklon-B, the poison gas used to exterminate millions of prisoners in Nazi concentration camps. In 1922 DEGUSSA took over DEGESCH (Deutsche Gesellschaft für Schädlingsbekämpfung, or the German Society for Pest Control). DEGESCH was the successor to the War Ministry's Technical Committee for Pest Control headed by Fritz Haber, which had concentrated on methods of killing lice in trenches, barracks, and submarines, and set the safety rules and standards for use of various pesticides. In 1920 DEGESCH had been converted into a corporation owned by a consortium of chemical firms. Peter Hayes, *From Cooperation to Complicity: Degussa in the Third Reich* (Cambridge: Cambridge University Press, 2004), chapter 1.

38. Alan Lougheed, "Anatomy of an International Cartel," p. 3.

39. Hayes, *From Cooperation to Complicity*, p. 6. See also K.D. Friedberg and H.A. Schwarzkopf, "The Exhalation of Hydrocyanic Acid in Cyanide Poisoning" (in German), *Archives of Toxicology* 24 (1969): 235–42.

40. "Alien Enemies' Property Sold," *LAT*, July 19, 1919.

41. Ibid. "Wants Judge Impeached: Ex-Federal Tax Employee Accuses Meekins, Once Miller's Counsel," *NYT*, May 8, 1926.

42. Arthur Altridge, "Sidelights on Alien Property," *The Searchlight on Congress* 71(1) (June 30, 1922): 19. Miller resigned as alien property custodian in 1925, and in 1927 he was convicted of defrauding the U.S. government.

43. Roessler & Hasslacher Chemical Company circular from 1916, reprinted in G. A. Roush, ed., *The Mineral Industry: Its Statistics, Technology, and Trade during 1916* (New York: John Wiley & Sons, 1917), p. 24.

44. Roush, ed., *The Mineral Industry: Its Statistics, Technology, and Trade during 1920*, p. 314.

45. American Cyanamid, Annual Reports to the Board of Directors, 1916–21, Princeton University Library; Roush, ed., *The Mineral Industry: Its Statistics, Technology, and Trade during 1920*, p. 314.

46. Ibid., 313.

47. Ibid., p. 314.

48. "German Firm Seeking Duty," *LAT*, February 14, 1921, p. 15.

49. Ibid.

50. Ibid.

51. R.W. Hodgson, "How Fumigation Methods for Fighting Scale Have Changed," *LAT*, April 3, 1921.

52. "Los Angeles Buyers Invading Nevada," *LAT*, November 7, 1920.

53. Guy Louis Rocha, "An Outline of Capital Punishment in Nevada,"

Nevada State Archives and Records, Nevada State Prison Inmate Case Files, updated on September 26, 1997.

54. The abolitionist states to that point had included Michigan (1846–), Rhode Island (1852–), Wisconsin (1853–), Iowa (1872–78), Maine (1876–83, 1887–), Colorado (1897–1901), Kansas (1907–35), Minnesota (1911–), Washington (1913–19), Oregon (1914–20), North Dakota (1915–), South Dakota (1915–39), Tennessee (1915–16), Arizona (1916–18), and Missouri (1917–19). Margaret Cahalan, *Historical Corrections Statistics in the United States, 1850–1984* (Rockville, MD: U.S. Department of Justice, Bureau of Justice Statistics, December 1986), p. 13.

55. *Nevada State Journal,* February 8, 1924. Curran was born in Woburn, Massachusetts, on June 26, 1886. His father was a prominent Boston attorney, and he was educated in Massachusetts, at the Ecole Alsacienne in France, and at Boston University School of Law, where he studied with Lothrop Stoddard (the white supremacist author and agitator against the "yellow peril") and graduated in 1909. Curran was admitted to the bar in Arizona but suffered ill health and moved to Nevada and California before returning to Battle Mountain, Nevada, where he served as district attorney of Lander County. After practicing law in Reno and other locations in 1920, he served as secretary to Senator Key Pittman (D-Nevada) during the Cox-Harding campaign. In 1922 he moved to practice law in Fresno, California, and he later served as deputy district attorney of Los Angeles. See Lilbourne Alsip Winchell, *History of Fresno County; the San Joaquin Valley* (Fresno: A.H. Cawston, 1933), p. 246. During World War I he had joined the army but failed to qualify for the aviation branch. Governor Scrugham Papers, Nevada State Archives.

56. *Las Vegas Age,* March 19, 1921; *PR,* March 25, 1921; *NSJ,* March 29, 1921; *CCDA,* January 6, 1923; *REG,* January 18, 1924; Loren B. Chan, "Example for the Nation: Nevada's Execution of Gee Jon," *NHSQ* 18(2) (Summer 1975): pp. 95, 104.

57. Nevada Legislature, Assembly, *Journal of the Assembly,* 30th sess. (1921): 247, 301, 314, Nevada Legislature, Senate, *Journal of the Senate,* 30th sess. (1921): 255, 257, 262, 272; *Nevada Statutes* (1921): ch. 246; *CCDA,* March 29, 1921.

58. From a two-page, unpublished typescript in the Nevada State Prison Papers, File 2320, Nevada State Archives.

59. "Nevada to Use Gas to Execute Criminals," *NYT,* March 18, 1921; "Signs Nevada Law for Lethal Execution," *NYT,* March 29, 1921. Boyle corresponded with Adolph Lewisohn, the famous philanthropist and mining tycoon who was president of the NCPPL based at Columbia University, about capital punishment.

60. *PR,* August 19, 1921.

61. "Painless and Yet Horrible," *NYT,* January 30, 1922.

62. "Huge Profits Charge Made," *LAT,* May 4, 1922. Pittman's background is described in Betty Glad, *Key Pittman: The Tragedy of a Senate Insider* (New York: Columbia University Press, 1986); and Fred Israel, *Nevada's Key Pittman* (Lincoln: University of Nebraska Press, 1963). Founded in 1882, Roessler & Hasslacher Chemical Company had its corporate head-

quarters in New York and plants in Perth Amboy and Niagara Falls. It merged with E.I. DuPont de Nemours and Company in 1930.

63. "Farm Bloc Victor in Tariff Fights," *NYT,* May 30, 1922.

64. C.R. DeLong, "The Import and Export Trade in Chemicals," *JIEC* 16(1) (January 1924): 83.

65. C.R. DeLong, "The Chemical Division of the United States Tariff Commission," *JIEC* 16(6) (June 1924): 610.

66. "Defeat of Cyanide Duty Saves Mines Big Sum," *REG,* May 30, 1922.

67. "American Cyanamid: Fourth-Largest U.S. Chemical Company," *Fortune* 22 (September 1940): 66–71.

68. Articles of Incorporation of the California Cyanide Company, Secretary of State records, book 450 at page 1xx, California State Archives, Sacramento. F.W. Braun arrived in Los Angeles in the early part of the century to sell drugs and chemicals wholesale. "Men interested in developing fumigation brought their troubles to me," he wrote. "I did not know much about cyanide, and at that time I knew nothing whatsoever of fumigation, but I believed that I knew how to push the buttons and pull the strings so as to get not only the information but the goods." Braun Corporation, *School of Fumigation . . . Held at Pomona, California, August 9–13, 1915* (Los Angeles: Braun Corporation, 1915), p. 43.

69. See, e.g., "2 Die in Vain Effort to Rescue Another in Gas-Filled Ship," *NYT,* July 14, 1921.

70. See Alfred J. Hillier, "Albert Johnson, Congressman," *Pacific Northwest Quarterly* 36 (July 1945): 193–211.

71. "Problems to Be Attacked by the Conference," *LD* 71 (November 12, 1921): 1. See also Will Irwin, *The Next War: An Appeal to Common Sense* (New York: Dutton, 1921).

72. "Hears War Gas Is Made Abroad," *NYT,* May 25, 1922. See also Kenneth D. Ackerman, *Young J. Edgar: Hoover, the Red Scare, and the Assault on Civil Liberties* (New York: Carroll & Graf, 2007); Joseph W. Bendersky, *The "Jewish Threat": Anti-Semitic Politics of the U.S. Army* (New York: Basic Books, 2000).

73. "Our Army Drops Gas as Treaty Provides," *NYT,* July 13, 1922.

74. U.S. Congress, Senate, *Congressional Record,* 67th Cong., 2nd sess., 1922, 62, part 5: 4230.

75. "Urges Free Speech for Army Officers," *NYT,* March 25, 1923; Bendersky, *The "Jewish Threat,"* pp. 162, 199.

76. "Says Fries's Critics Are Led by Moscow," *NYT,* April 5, 1923; "Lions Back Fries's Slap at Pacifists," *WP,* April 5, 1923; "Fries' Stand on Defense Endorsed by Lions Club," *WP,* April 12, 1923.

77. "Anti-War Council Denies Red Taint," *NYT,* April 14, 1923.

78. See Lucia Maxwell, "Spider Web Chart: The Socialist-Pacifist Movement in America Is an Absolutely Fundamental and Integral Part of International Socialism," *DI* 24 (March 22, 1924): 11.

79. Daniel P. Jones, "American Chemists and the Geneva Protocol," *Isis* 71(3) (September 1980): 433–35. The single most influential article was Winford Lee Lewis, "Poison Gas and the Pacifists," *The Independent* 115 (1925):

289–91, 308. Lewis was famous as the inventor of lewisite, which was said to be the most deadly weapon in the history of mankind at the time.

80. Jones, "American Chemists and the Geneva Protocol," p. 428.

81. "Arms Conference Interests Chemists," *LAT,* November 28, 1921.

4. STAGING THE WORLD'S FIRST GAS EXECUTION

1. *State of Nevada v. Gee Jon and Hughie Sing,* Justice Court of Mina Township, Mineral County, Nevada, September 9, 1921, pp. 5, 19–20, 22, 28, 30, 39, located in criminal case file no. 56, District Court Clerk, Mineral County, Hawthorne, Nevada. Barbara Parker Weber, "Lethal Gas Execution: Nevada's Daring Experiment," *Nevada Appeal* (Tahoe), February 7, 1999.

2. Loren B. Chan, "Example for the Nation: Nevada's Execution of Gee Jon," *NHSQ* 18(2) (Summer 1975): 91–92, 102. See also Stanford M. Lyman, *The Asian in the West,* Social Sciences and Humanities Publication no. 4 (Reno and Las Vegas: Desert Research Institute, University of Nevada System, 1970), pp. 123–25. From 1912 to 1923 California newspapers carried hundreds of articles about tong fighting activities.

3. Although the term "yellow peril" had been around since the nineteenth century, it had particular resonance in the American West in the 1920s, after the publication of Lothrop Stoddard's screed *The Rising Tide of Color against World-Supremacy* (New York: Charles Scribner's Sons, 1920). In 1913 and 1922 California passed alien land laws that were originally aimed at the Japanese but later amended in 1923 and 1927 to cover all Asians. Arizona, Idaho, Oregon, Washington, and Montana also enacted similar laws. As aliens under these measures, Chinese were ineligible for citizenship and denied the right to buy or own land. These laws were not declared unconstitutional until 1947. The 1924 Immigration Act would bar any Chinese women from entering the United States for permanent residence.

4. Nevada, Seventh Judicial District Court, County of Mineral, *State of Nevada v. Gee Jon and Hughie Sing,* trial transcript, 28030 November, December 1–3, 1921, pp. 212–14; *NSJ,* August 31, 1921; Confidential file no. 2321, Nevada State Prison, Nevada State Archives, Carson City (hereafter NSP-2321); Chan, "Example for the Nation," pp. 92, 103.

5. Confidential file no. 2320, Nevada State Prison, Nevada State Archives, Carson City (hereafter NSP-2320).

6. Chan, "Example for the Nation." 90–106.

7. *TT,* January 26, 1924.

8. *CCDA,* January 26, 1922; "To Die by Lethal Gas," *NYT,* January 28, 1922.

9. *CCDA,* January 26, 1921; January 27, 1921; March 29, 1921; February 27, 1922.

10. "Painless and Yet Horrible," *NYT,* January 30, 1922.

11. *The State of Nevada v. Gee Jon and Hughie Sing,* 46 Nev. 418, 211 P. 276, 30 A.L.R. 1443 (1923).

12. Raymond Hartmann, "The Use of Lethal Gas in Nevada Executions," *St. Louis Law Review* 8 (April 1923): 168.

13. Chan, "Example for the Nation"; *NSJ*, July 6, 1923; July 8, 1923; Nevada, Attorney General, *Biennial Report*, 1923–1924, p. 196.

14. *CCDA*, July 27, 1923; August 14, 20–21, and 31, 1923; September 5 and 29, 1923; *NSJ*, August 21, 1923; Chan, "Example for the Nation."

15. William Kennett to Jay H. White, December 27, 1923, case no. 2547, Nevada Supreme Court Clerk, Carson City; Chan, "Example for the Nation," pp. 96–97, 104.

16. *CCDA*, January 16, 1924; Chan, "Example for the Nation," pp. 97, 104.

17. *REG*, January 11 and 22, 1924; *NSJ*, January 25, 1924; Chan, "Example for the Nation."

18. Chartered in 1919, the American Legion had already grown to become a formidable force in American politics, contributing to the formation of the Veterans Bureau (later known as the Department of Veterans Affairs) and spearheading the campaign against "the Reds," or Communists. In 1923 its national commander, Alvin Owsley, publicly endorsed the new movement of fascism that had been started by Benito Mussolini.

19. *REG*, August 19, 1922. Scrugham's career is described in A.D. Hopkins and K.J. Evans, "James Scrugham (1880–1945), Governor on Wheels," in *Portraits of the Men and Women Who Shaped Las Vegas* (Las Vegas: Stephens Press, 2005). Some of Dickerson's gubernatorial papers are housed in the Nevada State Archives.

20. *NSJ*, January 8, 1924.

21. *REG*, January 3, 1924.

22. *NSJ*, January 8, 1924.

23. *LAT*, February 1, 1924.

24. *RGJ*, March 13, 1977.

25. Biennial Report of the Warden of the Nevada State Prison, 1923–1924, p. 3, in Governor Scrugham Papers, Nevada State Archives; *(Canandaigua, NY) Daily Messenger*, February 8, 1924.

26. As for the prison staff handling this type of cyanide: *(Elmira, NY) Chronicle-Telegram*, January 22, 1924. Prison staff and witnesses were doubtless aware that at that time hydrocyanic acid was being used extensively as a fumigant to destroy insects and rodents, and this usage had very recently been studied by the U.S. Department of Agriculture to determine the quantity of the fumigant that was absorbed and retained in various foodstuffs. Results of the investigation were given in Department Bulletin 1149, which had just been issued. The report did not offer any conclusions as to the safety of fumigated foods. See "Hydrocyanic Acid as a Fumigant for Pests," *(Bedford, PA) Gazette*, December 28, 1923. Given the federal government's condoning of HCN for fumigation of foodstuffs, it might appear there did not seem to be any lasting residual danger from HCN contamination of the death house or its equipment.

27. "Condemns Delays in Execution," *LAT*, January 29, 1924.

28. Letter from Major Charles R. Alley to Attorney General, State of

Nevada, January 30, 1924, Nevada State Prison Files, file 2320, Nevada State Archives.

29. *Fallon Standard,* January 16, 1924.

30. *(Elmira, NY) Chronicle Telegram,* January 22, 1924.

31. *CCDA,* January 25, 1924; Chan, "Example for the Nation," pp. 98–99, 104. See also "Gas Execution Is Inaugurated," *LAT,* February 9, 1924.

32. *REG,* January 28, 1924. Hughie would remain imprisoned at Carson City until his parole in 1938. Chan, "Example for the Nation," pp. 99, 104–5.

33. *CCDA,* February 4–5, 1924; *NSJ,* February 5, 1924. Two warden-appointed medical doctors, Dr. John E. Pickard of Reno and Dr. Anthony Huffaker of Carson City, the prison physician, examined Gee and declared him sane. *Young China,* February 7, 1924.

34. Gilbert Schenk, "Cyanogas Calcium Cyanide for the Control of Insects Infesting Grain in Storage Bins," in *Research in the Development of Cyanogas Calcium Cyanide* (n.p.: American Cyanamid Co., 1926), pp. 3–41.

35. *NSJ,* March 9, 1924. Two years earlier Water Heerdt in Germany had perfected a process for packing the volatile hydrogen cyanide in its principal product, a fumigant called Zyklon, in tins filled with small absorbent pellets. These stabilized the chemical until the cans were opened and the pellets were dumped, at which point the contents vaporized and would serve to block the transfer of oxygen to any warm-blooded organism in the vicinity. This product, known as Zyklon-B, amounted to a major technological breakthrough and rapidly enjoyed commercial success. Zyklon-B would have been safer to transport and easier to use in the Nevada execution because it didn't require the additional step of dipping into an acid solution, but Zyklon-B was not available on the West Coast.

36. *REG,* January 26, 1924; *NSJ,* March 9, 1924.

37. *REG,* January 26, 1924.

38. *CCDA,* January 15 and 28, 1924; *SFCP,* January 22, 1924; *REG,* January 26, 1924; February 5, 1924; Chan, "Example for the Nation," pp. 99, 105. In 1923–24 American Cyanamid conducted a series of experiments in an attempt to use liquefied HCN to fumigate grain elevators, but it proved difficult to get the poison to distribute evenly throughout the bin of grain. American Cyanamid Co., *Research in the Development of Cyanogas Calcium Cyanide,* pp. 3–41.

39. *NSJ,* February 5, 1924.

40. *NSJ,* February 7, 1924.

41. Ibid.

42. "Ready with Death Gas," *LAT,* February 7, 1924. The men who quit were identified as Harry James, John Gulling, Ed Kofed, and Richard Savage. *NSJ,* February 7, 1924.

43. "Nevada Will Execute Slayer by Gas Today," *NYT,* February 8, 1924; *NSJ,* February 8, 1924; *Chung Sai Yat Po,* February 8, 1924.

44. *NSJ,* February 7, 1924.

45. *(Canandaigua, NY) Daily Messenger,* February 8, 1924.

46. *REG,* February 7, 1924.

47. *Clearfield (PN) Progress,* February 8, 1924.

48. "Reprieved in Gas Cell," *LAT,* February 8, 1924.

49. Interestingly, the execution was scheduled to occur about a month before the deadline for disabled World War I veterans to present their claims for compensation to the United States Veterans Bureau. In other words, anyone who claimed to have suffered ill health as a result of poison gas related to their military service had little time left to establish they had been harmed. *NSJ,* March 9, 1924.

50. *NSJ,* February 9, 1924.

51. "Gas Kills Convict Almost Instantly," *NYT,* February 9, 1924. Born in Pioche in 1877, Turner had served as sheriff of Lincoln County and was a former federal marshal.

52. *NSJ,* February 9, 1924.

53. For the most detailed journalistic account of the execution, see *NSJ,* February 9, 1924.

54. Ibid.

55. Delos A. Turner to Chief of Chemical Warfare Service, U.S. War Department, February 1924, NSP-2320; *Young China,* February 9, 1924; *NSJ,* February 9, 1924; *SJMH,* February 9, 1924; *NYT,* February 9, 1924; Chan, "Example for the Nation," pp. 100, 105.

56. Biennial Report of the Warden of the Nevada State Prison, 1923–1924, p. 4; Chan, "Example for the Nation," pp. 100, 105.

57. *NSJ,* February 9, 1924.

58. Biennial Report of the Warden of the Nevada State Prison, 1923–1924, pp. 3–4. See also *REG,* February 8, 1924; *SFE,* February 9, 1924; *SJMH,* February 9, 1924; Chan, "Example for the Nation," pp. 100, 105.

59. *SFC,* February 9–10, 1924.

60. *NSJ,* February 9, 1924.

61. *REG,* February 8, 1924; *SFC,* February 9, 1924; Chan, "Example for the Nation," pp. 100, 105; *NSJ,* February 9, 1924.

62. Delos A. Turner, M.D., to Warden, Nevada State Prison, February 16, 1924, Nevada State Prison file 2320, Nevada State Archives.

63. "Witnesses Agree Lethal Gas Death Is Painless," *OSE,* February 10, 1924.

64. *NSJ,* March 7, 1924.

65. Ibid.

66. Turner to Chief of Chemical Warfare Service, February 1924, NSP-2320.

67. Copeland C. Burg, "New Style Cage," *Ogden (UT) Standard-Examiner,* February 10, 1924.

68. Ibid.

69. "Witnesses Agree Lethal Gas Is Painless."

70. "Law Held Success; State Claims Life for Life by Novel Method Used for First Time in History at Carson City; End Comes Quietly, Without Pain to Tong Killer," *NSJ,* February 9, 1924.

71. *NSJ,* February 9, 1924.

72. *SJMH,* February 9, 1924.

73. *NYT,* February 9, 1924.

74. "Execution by Gas," *LD*, March 1, 1924.

75. "Against Execution by Gas," *NYT*, February 10, 1924.

76. "Tong Clamor to Be Stilled," *LAT*, February 13, 1924.

77. *Biennial Report of the Warden of the Nevada State Prison, 1923–1924*, p. 4.

78. *SFCP*, February 9, 1924; "Lethal Gas Act to Be Retained," *REG*, February 27, 1925; "Lethal Gas Holds in Nevada," *NYEW*, April 9, 1925.

79. "Gas Chamber to Claim Another," *LAT*, April 26, 1926; "Slayers Await Sleeping Death," *OSE*, May 17, 1926; "Lethal Chamber Ready," *LAT*, May 19, 1926.

80. "Nevada Girl's Slayer Put to Death by Gas," *NYT*, May 22, 1926.

81. Associated Press, "Trotsky Sees War as American Aim," *NYT*, April 21, 1924.

82. See Robert G. Waite, "Law Enforcement and Crime in America: The View from Germany, 1920–40," in *Criminal Justice History*, ed. Louis A. Knafla, vol. 13 (Westport, CT: Greenwood Press, 1993), pp. 191–216 (quotation on p. 192); Nikolaus Wachsmann, *Hitler's Prisons: Legal Terror in Nazi Germany* (New Haven, CT: Yale University Press, 2004), p. 364.

83. Cyril Brown, "New Popular Idol Rises in Bavaria," *NYT*, November 21, 1922.

84. Robert O. Paxton, *The Anatomy of Fascism* (New York: Alfred A. Knopf, 2005), p. 218.

85. Roger Eatwell, *Fascism: A History* (New York: Penguin, 1995), pp. 13–14.

86. Associated Press, "Help from America to Bavarian Fascisti," *NYT*, December 11, 1922; "Berlin Hears Ford Is Backing Hitler," *NYT*, December 20, 1922.

87. "Germany Checks Effort to Form 'Klan' There," *NYT*, September 10, 1925.

88. Ernst ("Putzi") Hanfstaengl, *Hitler: The Missing Years* (London: Eyre & Spottiswoode, 1957); Carlos Widmann, "Play It Again, Putzi," *Der Spiegel* 10/8, March 1999, p. 60. Some of his papers are housed at the University of Maryland Archives.

89. John Toland, *Adolf Hitler*, vol. 1 (Garden City, NY: Doubleday, 1976), p. 195; Ian Kershaw, *Hitler: 1889–1936 Hubris* (New York: W.W. Norton, 2000), pp. 217–18.

90. Philipp Gassert and Daniel S. Mattern, *The Hitler Library: A Bibliography* (Westport, CT: Greenwood Press, 2001). Madison Grant, *Die Eroberung eines Kontinents order die Verbreitung der Rassen in Amerika*, trans. Else Mez (Berlin: Alfred Metzner, 1937). With a foreword by Nazi race scientist Eugen Fischer, the book was published in the United States as *Conquest of a Continent*.

91. Unpublished autobiography of Leon F. Whitney, 1971, Whitney Papers, American Philosophical Society, pp. 204–5.

92. "Hitler Tamed by Prison," *NYT*, December 21, 1924.

93. Ernst Hanfstaengl, "My Leader," *Colliers*, August 4, 1934.

94. Hanfstaengl, *Hitler: The Missing Years*, pp. 113–18. See also Neil

Baldwin, *Henry Ford and the Jews: The Mass Production of Hate* (New York: Public Affairs, 2002), p. 172.

95. Hanfstaengl describes this Hitler mannerism in Walter C. Langer, *The Mind of Adolf Hitler: The Secret Wartime Report* (New York: Signet, 1972), p. 44.

96. Lucy S. Dawidowicz, *The War Against the Jews, 1933–1945* (New York: Bantam Books, 1975), p. 3.

97. Toland, *Adolf Hitler,* vol. 2, p. 802.

98. Edwin Black, *War Against the Weak: Eugenics and America's Campaign to Create a Master Race* (New York: Four Walls Eight Windows, 2003), p. 275.

5. "LIKE WATERING FLOWERS"

1. "The New Lethal Gas House at the Nevada State Penitentiary, and the Method in Use for the Administration of the Gas to Capital Offenders," unpublished description sent by Nevada Warden M.R. Penrose to I.W. Winsmore, January 17, 1935, Board of Charities and Reform, Penitentiary, Gas Chamber file, Wyoming State Archives, Rawlins.

2. Peter Hayes, *From Cooperation to Complicity: Degussa in the Third Reich* (Cambridge: Cambridge University Press, 2004), pp. 6–7.

3. U.S. Patent 1,502,190.

4. Roessler & Hasslacher Chemical Co., *Zyklon B for the Control of Insects and Rodents Causing Great Economic Losses* (New York: Roessler & Hasslacher, July 1929).

5. Neil Spencer Marinovich, "American Industry and Finance, and German Rearmament: A Case Study of Standard Oil, Dupont, and General Motors and Their Relations with Interessengemeinschaft-Farbenindustrie Aktiengesellschaft," M.A. thesis, Eastern Michigan University, 1995, p. 14 n105. U.S. Patent 2,120,204 describes the American Cyanamid Zyklon discoids.

6. An American pesticide trade publication from 1928 noted the following:

> "The dangers of the use of hydrocyanic acid are increased by the fact that some people are unable to smell its peculiar almond odour and hence have no warning of its presence. In Germany, where hydrocyanic acid is often employed as a house fumigant, this difficulty has been overcome by the addition to the gas of an irritant component which will facilitate its detection. For this purpose, a trade preparation Zyklon (Cyclon) was introduced consisting of 90 parts of 'cyancarbonic ester' (probably methyl cyanoformate, CN.COOCH2) and 10 parts of 'chlor-carbonic ester.' It was claimed that this material, was an efficient substitute for hydrocyanic acid. More recently, this material has been replaced by 'Zyklon B,' which consists of a 'carrier' of kieselguhr impregnated with liquid hydrocyanic acid and a volatile irritant. Herzog has shown that kieselguhr is able to absorb half its weight of liquid hydrocyanic acid. The product is stored in airtight tins and, on being strewn on the ground, the hydrocyanic acid is slowly evolved. According to Staehelin, the irritant poison present increases the respiratory activity of the insect and enhances the toxic effects of the hydrocyanic acid." Hubert Martin, *The Scientific Principles of Plant Protection* (New York: Longmans Green & Co., 1928), p. 179.

7. For a startling account of the delousing of Mexican immigrants, see David Dorado Romo, *Ringside Seat to a Revolution: An Underground History of El Paso and Juarez: 1893–1923* (El Paso, TX: Cinco Puntos Press, 2005).

8. Oliver McKee Jr., "He Watches over the Nation's Health," *NYT,* June 10, 1928; quoted in Alexander Cockburn, "Zyklon B on the U.S. Border," *The Nation,* July 9, 2007.

9. See, e.g., Dr. Gerhard Peters, "Blausäure zur Schädlingsbekämpfung" (Stuttgart: Ferdinand Enke, 1933), p. 64. The title means "Hydrocyanic Acid for Pest Control."

10. J.R. Ridlon, "Experiments with Certain Fumigants Used for the Destruction of Cockroaches," *USPHR* 46(28) (July 10, 1931): 1572–78. This was one of many such reports the agency issued in 1931.

11. C.L. Williams, "The Air Jet Hydrocyanic Acid Sprayer," *USPHR* 46(30) (July 24, 1931).

12. C.L. Williams, "Report on Some Tests of the Use of a New Cyanogen Product in Ship Fumigation," *USPHR* 46(35) (August 28, 1931).

13. F. Flury, "Über Kampfgasvergiftungen I. Über Reizgase," *Z. Gesamte Experimentelle Medizin* 13 (1921): 1–15; F. Haber, "Zur Geschichte des Gaskrieges," in *Fuenf Vortraege aus den Jahren, 1920–1923* (Berlin: Julius Springer, 1924), pp. 76–92, as described in Hanspeter Witschi, "Some Notes on the History of Haber's Law," *Toxicological Sciences* 50 (1999): 164–68.

14. American Cyanamid, *Research in the Development of Cyanogas Calcium Cyanide* (n.p.: American Cyanamid Co., 1926).

15. "World Dye Trust Laid to 8 Big Firms," *NYT,* May 15, 1942.

16. See Gerard Colby, *DuPont Dynasty: Behind the Nylon Curtain* (Secaucus, NJ: Lyle Stuart, 1984); Charles Higham, *Trading with the Enemy: An Exposé of the Nazi-American Money Plot 1933–1949*. The plot was confirmed by the Dickstein-McCormack Committee, which held hearings on the subject. See House of Representatives, Special Committee on Un-American Activities, "Investigation of Nazi Propaganda Activities and Investigation of Certain Other Propaganda Activities," 73rd Cong., 2nd Sess., November 24, 1934.

17. http://heritage.dupont.com/floater/fl_randh/floater.shtml (accessed March 17, 2007).

18. Roessler & Hasslacher Chemical Company, *Fumigation of Flour Mills by Hydrocyanic Acid Gas Generated from "Cyanegg," Cyanide of Sodium 96–98%* (New York: Roessler & Hasslacher, 1929).

19. http://heritage.dupont.com/floater/fl_randh/floater.shtml (accessed March 17, 2007); Alan Lougheed, "The Anatomy of an International Cartel, 1897–1927," *Prometheus* 19(1) (2001): 6–7.

20. Robert Hauptman and Susan Hubbs Motin, *The Holocaust: Memories, Research, Reference* (Binghamton: Haworth Press, 1998), pp. 105–6.

21. Gerard Colby Zilg, *DuPont: Behind the Nylon Curtain* (Englewood Cliffs, NJ: Prentice-Hall 1974), p. 304.

22. U.S. Patent 2,120,204, application April 27, 1936, and patented June 7, 1938.

23. See, e.g., American Cyanamid, *Zyklon Discoids: Fumigation Manual* (New York: American Cyanamid, 1942).

24. "White Is Executed in Nevada by Gas," *NYT,* June 3, 1930.

25. Edward E. Hamer, M.D., "The Execution of Robert H. White by Hydrocyanic Acid Gas," *JAMA* 95 (August 30, 1930): 661–62.

26. "Nevada's Gas House," *Outlook* 155 (October 1930): 256.

27. See, e.g., P.J. Zisch, "Lethal Gas a Means of Asphyxiating Capital Offenders," *Medico-Legal Journal,* January–February 1931, p. 36; Anthony M. Turano, "Capital Punishment by Lethal Gas," *AM* 29 (1933): 91–93. See also Stuart Banner, *The Death Penalty: An American History* (Cambridge, MA: Harvard University Press, 2002), pp. 196–205.

28. "Head Severed from Body as Trap Is Sprung," *PEG,* February 21, 1930; "Brief Funeral Rites for Eva Dugan Attended Only by Prison Heads," *AR,* February 22, 1930; "Lethal Chamber Replaces Rope," *ADS,* March 15, 1931; "Lethal Gas, Which Replaces Rope in Arizona, Makes Execution Painless," *TDC,* March 18, 1931.

29. House Joint Resolution No. 4, amending Section 22, Article XXII of the state constitution, received by the secretary of state on March 15, 1933. Arizona Constitution, art. 22, sect. 22.

30. Crane McClennen, "Capital Punishment in Arizona," *Arizona Attorney,* October 1992, p. 19.

31. Alan Goldberg, *Hooded Empire: The Ku Klux Klan in Colorado* (Urbana: University of Illinois Press, 1981); Lee Casey, "When the Klan Controlled Colorado," *RMN,* June 17–19, 1946.

32. "Cañon City Klan Organized," *The Rocky Mountain Klansman* 1 (January 20, 1924).

33. Stephen J. Leonard, *Lynching in Colorado, 1859–1919* (Boulder: University Press of Colorado, 2002), p. 3.

34. "Eddie Ives Ends 40 Years of Crime in Three States on Gallows at Cañon City," *RMN,* January 11, 1930; "Belongia Goes to Death Gladly in Gas Chamber," *DP,* June 22, 1935; Michael L. Radelet, "Capital Punishment in Colorado, 1859–1972," *UCLR* 74(3) (2003): 961–62.

35. Act of March 31, 1933, ch. 61, 1933 Colo. Sess. Laws, 420–22; "Governor Signs Gas Bill," *RMN,* April 1, 1933.

36. Diana Andersen, "Warden Roy Best," Local History Center, Cañon City Public Library, 2002.

37. The state was becoming more sophisticated in determining the precise lethality of the chamber. In May 1930 Nevada's public health officer, Dr. E.E. Hamer, announced that he planned to utilize a special stethoscope with an extended tube over the heart of the next convict to be executed in the state's gas chamber, in order to test the actions of the heart and lungs of someone who was undergoing lethal gassing. "Doctors Will Study Man Being Executed," *NYT,* June 1, 1930.

38. "2,500 for Death House," *RMN,* June 15, 1933; Maurice Leckenby,

"State Pen Death Chamber Nearing Completion Here," *RMN,* September 24, 1933.

39. Thomas J. Noel and Kevin E. Rucker, *Eaton Metal Products: The First 80 Years* (Denver, CO: A.B. Hirschfeld Press, n.d.). Timothy J. Travis, president of Eaton, declined to be interviewed for this project and would not allow research into his company's records about the gas chamber.

40. "Execution Chamber Styles," *RMN,* February 27, 1938; Cary Stiff, "Denverite 'Refined' Death," *DP,* September 15, 1966; Bill Pardue, "Denver Firm Receives Inquiries on Gas Chambers," *RMN,* December 6, 1976; Cary Stiff, "The Death House by the Side of the Road," *DP,* May 16, 1971; *Empire Magazine,* May 16, 1971, pp. 17–22.

41. A detailed description of the Eaton design is available in Appendix 1.

42. Walden E. Sweet, "Young Wife's Plea for Mercy Fails to Save Kelley from Death Chamber," *DP,* June 19, 1934.

43. "Boy Is Told He Must Die in Gas Chamber," *NYT,* December 30, 1933.

44. Lorena Hickok, *One Third of a Nation: Lorena Hickok Reports on the Great Depression,* ed. Richard Lowitt and Maurine Beasley (Champaign, IL: University of Illinois Press, 1983), pp. 285–86, recounted in Radelet, "Capital Punishment in Colorado," p. 989.

45. Charles T. O'Brien, "Kelley Executed in New Gas Cell," *DP,* June 23, 1934.

46. Ibid.; "Death by Gas: 90¢," *Time,* July 2, 1934.

47. *Hernandez v. State,* 43 Ariz. 424 (1934).

48. "Youthful Slayers Executed," *St. John's Herald,* July 12, 1934.

49. "Arizona Has Double Lethal Gas Execution," *New Castle (PA) News,* July 6, 1934; *AR,* July 6, 1934.

50. McClennen, "Capital Punishment in Arizona," p. 19.

51. "Kisses Executed Man, Is Mysteriously Ill," *NYT,* July 12, 1936.

52. McClennen, "Capital Punishment in Arizona," pp. 17–21.

53. "Burglars Murder Colorado Farmer and Schoolboy and Wound Woman; Fiends Shoot Three Then Pour Kerosene on Them and Light It," *DP,* February 28, 1934; "Defense Suddenly Rests in Trial of Pacheco Brothers," *DP,* March 30, 1934; Wallis M. Reef, "Two Brothers Die for Brutal Murder," *RMN,* June 1, 1935.

54. "Ex-Convict Murders Colorado Rancher and Wounds His Wife," *DP,* December 17, 1934; "Murderer Offers Brain to Science," *DP,* June 20, 1935; "Belongia Goes to Death Gladly in Gas Chamber," *DP,* June 22, 1935.

55. "Posses Encircle Slayers of Sheriff in Colorado," *RMN,* July 16, 1935; Jack Carberry, "McDaniels Shows Remorse and Fear on Execution Day," *DP,* February 14, 1936; "Otis McDaniels Walks Smiling to Gas Chamber to Die as Double Slayer," *RMN,* February 15, 1936.

56. *RNO,* May 2, 1935. The best source on the history of North Carolina's lethal gas executions is Katrina Nannette Seitz, "The Transition of Methods of Execution in North Carolina: A Descriptive Social History of Two Time Periods, 1935 & 1983," Ph.D. diss., Virginia Polytechnic Institute and State University, Blacksburg, 2001.

57. *RNO,* March 27, 1935.

58. *RNO*, April 4, 1935; Journal of the House of Representatives of the General Assembly of the State of North Carolina, 1935; *RNO*, May 2, 1935.

59. *RNO*, May 2, 1935.

60. "Lethal Gas Bill Will Become Law: Almost Made a Bad Slip," *GDG*, April 25, 1935; "Death Gas Assailed as Cruel," *NYT*, December 8, 1935.

61. "New Execution Method to Be Tried," *Middletown (NY) Times Herald*, December 23, 1935.

62. Quoted in David Margolick, "Save Me, Joe Louis!" *LAT*, November 7, 2005.

63. *RNO*, January 24, 1936.

64. *RNO*, January 25, 1935; February 1, 1935; Virginius Dabney, "Use of Death Gas Stirs Carolinians," *NYT*, February 2, 1936. See also Trina Seitz, "The Killing Chair: North Carolina's Experiment in Civility and the Execution of Allen Foster," *NCHQ* 81(1) (2004): 1–35.

65. David Margolick, "Save Me, Joe Louis!"

66. *RNO*, January 25, 1936.

67. *RNO*, January 27, 1936.

68. Seitz, "Transition of Methods," p. 130.

69. Associated Press, "Slayer Executed by Gas," *NYT*, February 1, 1936; *RNO*, February 1, 1936.

70. Associated Press, "Two Die in Gas Chamber," *NYT*, February 8, 1936.

71. *RNO*, February 1, 1936; Judge M.H. Patel, unpublished opinion, No. C-92–1482, *Fierro v. Gomez*, 77 F.3d 301 (9th Cir. 1996).

72. *RNO*, February 1, 1936.

73. *RNO*, February 13, 1936.

74. Associated Press, "Executed in Lethal Chamber," *NYT*, March 28, 1936.

75. Associated Press, "Two Die in Gas Chamber," *NYT*, August 22, 1936.

76. Associated Press, "Slayer of Co-Ed Dies in Lethal Gas Room," *NYT*, December 12, 1936.

77. Guy B. Johnson, "The Negro and Crime," *The Annals* 217 (September 1941): 93–104; H. Garfinkel, "Inter- and Intra-Racial Homicides," *Social Forces* 27 (1949): 370–81.

78. The *Winston-Salem Journal* of December 8–12, 2002, produced a prize-winning series, "Lifting the Curtain on a Shameful Era," about North Carolina's eugenic sterilization program.

79. *RNO*, February 19, 1938.

80. Quoted in the *Salisbury Herald*, July 4, 1938.

81. Letter dated October 14, 1938, from Robert L. Thompson, Private Secretary to the Governor, Letters and Papers of Clyde Roarke Hoey, 1937–41, *Messages to the General Assembly*, p. 49, cited in Seitz, "The Transition of Methods," pp. 193–94.

82. *Arridy v. People*, 82 P.2d 757 (Colo. 1938); *People ex rel. Best v. Eldred*, 86 P.2d 248 (Colo. 1938).

83. Associated Press, "Witness Dies after Execution," *NYT*, August 15, 1937.

84. Quoted in Robert Perske, *Deadly Innocent?* (Nashville: Abingdon Press, 1995), pp. 126–7.

85. Associated Press, "Cardiogram Shows Death," *NYT,* October 1, 1939.

86. "Asphyxiation Preferable," *RR,* January 24, 1935.

87. "Gas Execution Fight Rages," *LAT,* January 3, 1937.

88. "Wyoming Prison Gets New 'Tank' for Executions," *Evening Independent,* November 11, 1936.

89. United Press, "First Gas Execution in Wyoming Prison," *JCPT,* August 13, 1937; "Perry Carroll Executed at 12:16 A.M. Today," *RRB,* August 13, 1937.

90. *Wyoming Eagle,* April 19, 1940.

91. Colorado had abolished the death penalty from 1897 to 1901, Oregon from 1914 to 1920, Arizona from 1916 to 1918, and Missouri from 1917 to 1919.

92. "Senate Measure Stops Hangings, Substitutes Gas in State Prison," *JCPT,* April 15, 1937.

93. "Missouri Uses Gas Chamber," *(Monessen, PA) Daily Independent,* September 17, 1937.

94. "Wardens See Gas Death in Carson City, Disagree on California Adoption," *SFC,* November 30, 1932.

95. "Lethal Gas Chamber for Book Worms," *NYT,* January 1, 1933.

96. "Churchmen Launch Fight on Lynching," *NYT,* December 4, 1933.

97. "Nazi Units in United States List 1,000 Aliens; Admit Their Aim Is to Spread Propaganda," *NYT,* March 23, 1933.

98. "6,000 Watch As Mob Hang Slayers of Brooke Hart," *NYT,* November 27, 1933; "Governor Rolph Backs San Jose Lynching as Kidnap Warning," *NYT,* November 28, 1933.

99. Alfred M. Beck, *Hitler's Ambivalent Attaché: Lt. Gen. Friedrich von Boetticher in America, 1933–1941* (Washington, DC: Potomac Books, 2005).

100. "Lethal Gas Takes Place of Gibbet as Death Penalty," *SFC,* May 8, 1937.

101. United Press, *Mansfield (OH) News Journal,* April 14, 1938.

102. Joan Smith, "The Return of the Big Green Death Machine," *San Francisco Examiner Image Magazine,* January 8, 1989.

103. Clinton T. Duffy Collection, Marin County Museum, San Rafael, California, quoted in Alan Bisbort, *"When You Read This, They Will Have Killed Me": The Life and Redemption of Caryl Chessman, Whose Execution Shook America* (New York: Carroll & Graf, 2006), p. 327.

104. "Denver Firm Makes Lethal Gas Chambers," *DP,* February 27, 1938.

105. "Pro or Con: Execution by Lethal Gas?" *Reader's Digest,* December 1937, pp. 56–58.

106. "Killers Executed in Gas Chamber," *SFC,* December 3, 1938; "Spectators Sickened as Two Die in Death Cell," *LAT,* December 3, 1938.

107. *SFE,* December 3, 1938, quoted in Bisbort, *"When You Read This,"* p. 328.

108. Chrisanne Beckner, "Darkness on the Edge of Campus: University's

Philanthropic 'Godfather' Was Mad about Eugenics," *Sacramento News & Review,* February 19, 2004.

109. Tony Platt, "The Frightening Agenda of the American Eugenics Movement," *History News Network,* July 7, 2003, http://hnn.us (accessed September 4, 2009).

110. Alexandra Minna Stern, *Eugenic Nation: Faults & Frontiers of Better Breeding in Modern America* (Berkeley: University of California Press, 2005), p. 118.

111. United Press, "Gas Chamber Is Installed," *Valley Sunday Star-Monitor-Herald,* August 22, 1937.

112. See Gary Murrell, *Iron Pants: Oregon's Anti-New Deal Governor, Charles Henry Martin* (Pullman: Washington State University Press, 2000).

113. "Two Slayers Die in Gas Chamber," *OSE,* January 15, 1945.

114. Associated Press, "Adam Richetti Executed, Last of Floyd Gang," *KCS,* October 7, 1938; Missouri Department of Corrections Records; "Author Claims Lethal Gas Isn't Humane as Hanging," *JCPT,* November 14, 1938.

6. PILLAR OF RESPECTABILITY

1. See, e.g., Kai Bird, *The Chairman: John J. McCloy and the Making of the American Establishment* (New York: Simon and Schuster, 1992); Thomas Alan Schwartz, *America's Germany: John J. McCloy and the Federal Republic of Germany* (Cambridge, MA: Harvard University Press, 1991); Walter Isaacson and Evan Thomas, *The Wise Men: Six Friends and the World They Made* (New York: Simon & Schuster, 1997); Alan Brinkley, "The Most Influential Private Citizen in America," *Harpers,* February 1983, pp. 31–46; "'We Know the Russians,'" *Time,* June 20, 1949. The John J. McCloy Papers are located at Amherst College.

2. Quoted in Isaacson and Thomas, *Wise Men,* p. 122.

3. "'We Know the Russians.'"

4. Paul Warburg (1868–1932) was a Jewish-German-American banker who helped found the U.S. Federal Reserve system, the Council on Foreign Relations, and many other key institutions. He also served on the board of the American IG Farben Chemical Company. McCloy also worked closely with his son, the banker and diplomat James P. Warburg.

5. The firm also had offices in Washington, D.C., and Paris. *The Martindale-Hubbell Law Directory, 71st Annual edition, Vol. I* (New York: Martindale-Hubbell, 1939), p. 1031.

6. Isaacson and Thomas, *Wise Men,* p. 122.

7. Howard Watson Ambruster, *Treason's Peace: German Dyes and American Dupes* (New York: Beechhurst Press, 1947), pp. 328–29, 345, 366, 370, 386, 411.

8. On IG Farben, see Joseph Borkin, *The Crime of IG Farben* (New York: The Free Press, 1978); Joseph Borkin and Charles Welsh, *Germany's Master Plan* (New York: Duell, Sloan & Pearce, 1943); Ambruster, *Treason's Peace;* Richard Sasuly, *IG Farben* (New York: Boni & Gaer, 1947); Peter Hayes,

Industry and Ideology: IG Farben in the Nazi Era (Cambridge: Cambridge University Press, 1987); John V.H. Dippel, *Two Against Hitler* (New York: Praeger, 1992); and Diarmuid Jeffreys, *Hell's Cartel: The Rise and Fall of IG Farben* (London: Bloomsbury, 2008).

9. See Ray Eldon Hiebert, *Courtier to the Crowd: The Story of Ivy Lee and the Development of Public Relations* (Ames: Iowa State University Press, 1966); U.S. Congress, House of Representatives, Special Committee on Un-American Activities, *Investigation of Nazi Propaganda Activities and Investigation of Certain Other Propaganda Activities,* 74th Cong., 1st sess., Report no. 153 (Washington, DC: U.S. Government Printing Office, 1934).

10. Quoted in Jules Witcover, *Sabotage at Black Tom* (Chapel Hill: University of North Carolina Press, 1989), p. 301.

11. See Bird, *The Chairman,* book 1.

12. Robert Paul Browder and Thomas G. Smith, *Independent: A Biography of Lewis W. Douglas* (New York: Alfred A. Knopf, 1986), p. 111.

13. As president of Harvard, Conant had been criticized for his tolerance of anti-Semitism. In 1934 he allowed the alumnus Ernst "Putzi" Hanfstaengl, a member of Hitler's inner circle, to participate in numerous welcoming events at the university; he also maintained a tight quota on Jewish admissions and never publicly criticized the Nazis for their treatment of Jews. In 1933 Conant corresponded with the chemical director of DuPont (a Harvard alumnus) about whether to hire a renowned organic chemist who happened to be Jewish. Conant advised that the candidate was "certainly very definitely of the Jewish type—rather heavy," probably dogmatic, with "none of the earmarks of genius," and he recommended against the hiring. See Stephen H. Norwood, "Legitimating Nazism: Harvard University and the Hitler Regime, 1933–1937," *American Jewish History* 92 (June 2004); E.K. Bolton to Dr. James B. Conant, September 8, 1933, and James B. Conant to Dr. E.K. Bolton, September 13, 1933, box 31, James B. Conant Presidential Papers, Harvard University Archives, Pusey Library, Cambridge.

14. Browder and Smith, *Independent,* pp. 119–20.

15. Most of this information comes directly from DEGUSSA's own website, www.degussa-history.com (accessed on May 25, 2006).

16. Browder and Smith, *Independent,* chapter 10.

17. Ibid., pp. 124–26.

18. Hans Zinsser, *Rats, Lice and History* (Boston: Little, Brown & Co., 1935).

19. Zinsser's mentor, Dr. Charles Nicolle of the Pasteur Institute in Tunis, had been the first to prove that lice from rats were the carrier of typhus, for which Nicolle received the Nobel Prize in 1928. See Naomi Baumslag, *Murderous Medicine: Nazi Doctors, Human Experimentation, and Typhus* (Westport, CT: Praeger, 2005), pp. 12–13.

20. The American Polish Relief Expedition of the U.S. Army was one of the units that attacked the lice using mobile delousing field columns that moved from town to town.

21. Alexander Cockburn, "Zyklon B on the Border," *The Nation,* June 21, 2007. Peters also wrote a book about Zyklon-B; see Dr. Gerhard Peters,

"Blausäure zur Schädlingsbekämpfung" (Hydrocyanic Acid for Pest Control) (Stuttgart: Ferdinand Enke, 1933), which is available on the web at www.holocaust-history.org/works/peters-1933/. The patent referred to is number 2,344,105, patented by the U.S. Patent Office on March 14, 1944.

22. "Der ewige Jude," *Unser Willie und Weg* 10 (1940): 54–55.

23. See Guenter Lewy, *The Nazi Persecution of the Gypsies* (New York: Oxford University Press, 2000).

24. Alexis Carrel, *Man, the Unknown* (New York: Doubleday, 1935), p. 391. See also Alexis Carrel, *Reflections on Life,* trans. Antonia White (London: H. Hamilton, 1952). To date, biographers have given him strongly favorable treatment, largely overlooking his racism and his role as a fascist member of the Vichy government.

25. Associated Press, "German Jurists Shocked," *NYT,* August 9, 1927.

26. Robert G. Waite, "Law Enforcement and Crime in America: The View from Germany, 1920–1940," in *Criminal Justice History,* vol. 13, ed. Louis A. Knafla (Westport, CT: Greenwood Press, 1993), 191–215.

27. "Against Reich Executions," *NYT,* November 2, 1928; Guido Enderis, "Legal Right to Kill Proposed in Reich," *NYT,* May 19, 1929.

28. Frederick T. Birchall, "Nazis Riot in Court as 5 Are Condemned for Murder of Reds," *NYT,* August 23, 1932.

29. Otto D. Tolischus, "2 Americans Face Secret Reich Trial," *NYT,* November 16, 1934.

30. Associated Press, "Death for Pacifists," *NYT,* April 20, 1935; see also Richard J. Evans, *Rituals of Retribution: Capital Punishment in Germany, 1600–1987* (New York: Oxford University Press, 1996).

31. General Amos Fries to Cong. Samuel Dickstein, March 21, 1933, University of Oregon Library, Fries Papers, box 3; Joseph W. Bendersky, *The "Jewish Threat": Anti-Semitic Politics of the U.S. Army* (New York: Basic Books, 2000), pp. 245–46.

32. See Edwin Black, *War Against the Weak: Eugenics and America's Campaign to Create a Master Race* (New York: Four Walls Eight Windows, 2003); and Stefan Kühl, *The Nazi Connection: Eugenics, American Racism, and German National Socialism* (New York: Oxford University Press, 1994).

33. "Eugenicists Hail Their Progress as Indicating Era of Supermen," *NYHT,* August 28, 1932.

34. Black, *War Against the Weak,* pp. 314–15.

35. Kühl, *Nazi Connection,* pp. 86–88.

36. Foster Kennedy, "Euthanasia: To Be or Not to Be?" *Colliers,* May 20, 1939, pp. 15–16; "Mercy Death Law Ready for Albany," *NYT,* February 14, 1939.

37. Foster Kennedy, "The Problem of Social Control of the Congenital Defective: Education, Sterilization, Euthanasia," *American Journal of Psychiatry* 99 (July 1942): 13–16.

38. Black, *War Against the Weak,* p. 309; see also Edwin Black, *IBM and the Holocaust: The Strategic Alliance Between Nazi Germany and America's Most Powerful Corporation* (New York: Crown Publishers, 2001).

39. G.L. Steer, "Ethiopians Suffer in Biggest Air Raid," *NYT,* March 26, 1936.

40. German Olympic propaganda, quoted in Kühl, *Nazi Connection,* pp. 88, 135.

41. Sam Knight, "The Tragic Story of Wallace Hume Carothers," *Financial Times,* November 29, 2008.

42. "W. Douglas Heads McGill University," *NYT,* October 5, 1937.

43. "11 Concerns Named as Nitrate Trust," *NYT,* December 4, 1940.

44. "Produces Chemical Here: DuPont Starts First U.S. Output of Potassium Cyanide," *NYT,* December 5, 1940.

45. "Vast Reich Funds Hunted in Inquiry into Drug Business," *NYT,* April 11, 1941.

46. "World Dye Trust Laid to 8 Big Firms," *NYT,* May 15, 1943. American Cyanamid was fined $453,451, a large fine considering that its net profit the previous year was $5.6 million.

47. Borkin and Welsh, *Germany's Master Plan,* p. 90.

48. "German Cartels Reported Boring In," *NYT,* September 13, 1944.

49. Quoted in Isaacson and Thomas, *Wise Men,* p. 186.

50. Browder and Smith, *Independent,* p. 158.

51. See Peter Irons, *Justice at War: The Story of the Japanese American Internment Cases* (New York: Oxford University Press, 1983).

7. THE RISING STORM

1. Svend Ranulf, *Moral Indignation and Middle Class Psychology* (New York: Schocken Books, 1964 [1938]).

2. Charles E. Silberman, *Criminal Violence, Criminal Justice* (New York: Random House, 1978), p. 30.

3. Walter White, quoted in Gunnar Myrdal, *An American Dilemma: The Negro Problem and Modern Democracy* (New York: Harper & Row, 1944), p. 563.

4. Edwin H. Sutherland, *Principles of Criminology,* 3rd ed. (New York: J.B. Lippincott, 1939), pp. 560–62.

5. National Commission on Law Observance and Enforcement, *Lawlessness in Law Enforcement* (Washington, DC: U.S. Government Printing Office, 1931).

6. See Haywood Patterson and Earl Conrad, *Scottsboro Boy* (New York: Doubleday, 1950).

7. *Brown v. Mississippi,* 297 U.S. 278 (1936).

8. Sutherland, *Principles of Criminology,* pp. 120–21.

9. John R. Larkins, *The Negro Population of North Carolina: Social and Economic* (Raleigh: North Carolina State Board of Charities and Public Welfare, 1944), p. 51.

10. See esp. Myrdal, *An American Dilemma,* which cites many such studies.

11. Paul M. Green, "A Rape, a Two-Day Trial, a Mistake," *RNO*, June 6, 1999.

12. *State v. Peele*, 220 N.C. 83, 16 S.E.2d 449 (1941); *Record on appeal*, No. 145, N.C. Supreme Court (1941); *RNO*, October 11, 1941; Paul M. Green, "Innocent in North Carolina," *Trial Briefs*, April 2000, p. 10.

13. *Buck v. Bell*, 274 U.S. 200, 207 (1927).

14. Radelet, "Capital Punishment in Colorado, 1859–1972," *UCLR* 74(3) (2003).

15. "Woman Executed in Gas Chamber," *NYT*, November 22, 1941; Kevin Roderick, "Last Steps and Words on Death Row," *LAT*, March 28, 1990.

16. Floyd Loveless, the prisoner executed in Nevada on September 29, 1944, had been only fifteen years old when he committed the murder for which he was sentenced to death. Floyd Loveless file, Nevada State Prison Inmate Case Files, Nevada State Library and Archives, Carson City, Nevada.

17. Kevin Roderick, "Last Steps and Last Words on Death Row," *LAT*, March 28, 1990.

18. Prime Minister's Personal Minute, dated June 7, 1944, in Guenther W. Gellermann, *Der Krieg, der nicht stattfand* (Koblenz: Bernard & Graefe Verlag, 1986), pp. 249–51.

19. Committee on Veterans' Affairs, 103d Cong., 2nd sess., *Is Military Research Hazardous to Veterans' Health? A Staff Report Prepared for the Committee on Veterans' Affairs* (Washington, DC: United States Senate, December 8, 1994).

8. ADAPTED FOR GENOCIDE

1. Richard Breitman, *The Architect of Genocide: Himmler and the Final Solution* (New York: Alfred A. Knopf, 1991), pp. 166, 289 n95, citing Gerhard Peters's affidavit, United States National Archives, War Crimes, Record Group 238, Microform Series T-301/R 99/700, NI-12111.

2. Hitler's euthanasia order read as follows:

> Berlin, 1 September 1939 [but actually predated from October 1]
>
> Reichsleiter Bouhler and Dr. Brandt, M.D., are charged with the responsibility of enlarging the authority of certain physicians to be designated by name in such a manner that persons who, according to human judgment, are incurable can, upon a most careful diagnosis of their condition of sickness, be accorded a mercy death.
>
> [signed] A. Hitler

3. Robert Jay Lifton, *The Nazi Doctors: Medical Killing and the Psychology of Genocide* (New York: Basic Books, 1986), pp. 62–70; Robert N. Proctor, *Racial Hygiene: Medicine under the Nazis* (Cambridge, MA: Harvard University Press, 1988), pp. 114–15, 177–79.

4. Henry Friedlander, *The Origins of Nazi Genocide: From Euthanasia to the Final Solution* (Chapel Hill: University of North Carolina Press, 1995), pp. 94–96.

5. Lifton, *Nazi Doctors;* Friedlander, *Origins of Nazi Genocide.*

6. National Archives and Records Administration, National Archives Building, Washington, D.C., Nuremberg Documents, RG 238: interrogation of Karl Brandt, October 1, 1945, P.M., p. 7.

7. Testimony of Viktor Brack, U.S. Military Tribunal, Transcript of the Proceedings in Case 1, p. 7652, quoted in Friedlander, *Origins of Nazi Genocide,* p. 88.

8. Arno J. Mayer, *Why Did the Heavens Not Darken: The "Final Solution" in History* (New York: Pantheon, 1988); Friedlander, *Origins of Nazi Genocide;* Lifton, *Nazi Doctors.*

9. Friedlander, *Origins of Nazi Genocide,* p. 115.

10. Mayer, *Why Did the Heavens Not Darken.*

11. Edwin Black, *War Against the Weak: Eugenics and America's Campaign to Create a Master Race* (New York: Four Walls Eight Windows, 2003), p. 337.

12. See Friedlander, *Origins of Nazi Genocide.*

13. DEGESCH, "Directives for the Use of Prussic Acid (Zyklon) for the Destruction of Vermin (Disinfestation)," NI-9912, as cited in Jean-Claude Pressac, *Auschwitz: Technique and Operation of the Gas Chambers* (New York: Beate Klarsfeld Foundation, 1989), p. 18.

14. Eugen Kogon, Hermann Langbein, and Adalbert Rückerl, *Nazi Mass Murder: A Documentary History of the Use of Poison Gas,* trans. Mary Scott and Caroline Lloyd-Morris (New Haven, CT: Yale University Press, 1993), p. 139.

15. Friedlander, *Origins of Nazi Genocide,* p. 287. See also American Cyanamid and Chemical Corporation, *Military Fumigation Manual: Zyklon Discoids for Insect Control* (New York: American Cyanamid, 1944).

16. Harry W. Mazal, "Zyklon-B: A Brief Report on the Physical Structure and Composition," www.holocaust-history.org/auschwitz/zyklonb/ (accessed May 4, 2009).

17. Testimony of *SS-Unterscharführer* Pery Broad, describing gassing in Krema I in Auschwitz, quoted in Rudolf Höss, Pery Broad, and Johann Paul Kremer, *KL Auschwitz as Seen by the SS,* trans. Constantine FitzGibbon (New York: Howard Fertig, 1984), p. 176.

18. Quoted in Yitzhak Arad, *Belzec, Sobibor, Treblinka: The Operation Reinhard Death Camps* (Bloomington: Indiana University Press, 1987), p. 9.

19. Testimony of Hans Stark, registrar of new arrivals in the Auschwitz death camp, quoted in E. Klee, W. Dressen, V. Riess, *The Good Old Days* (New York: The Free Press, 1988), p. 255.

20. Friedlander, *Origins of Nazi Genocide,* p. 287.

21. Breitman, *Architect of Genocide.*

22. *Die Zeit,* January 9, 1998.

23. Peter Novick, *The Holocaust in American Life* (Boston: Houghton Mifflin, 1999), p. 24.

24. On what the German people knew, see Daniel Jonah Goldhagen, *Hitler's Willing Executioners: Ordinary Germans and the Holocaust* (New York: Alfred A. Knopf, 1996).

25. Ibid., p. 198.

26. "Mann Bids Reich Break Nazi Yoke: Author Warns German People to Act Before Ever-Growing World Hatred Engulfs You," *NYT,* December 7, 1941.

27. United Press, untitled report, dateline Stockholm, Sweden, *NYT,* June 27, 1942.

28. "Poles Ask U.S. to Seize Nazis," *NYT,* July 10, 1942.

29. Paul Jacobs, *Is Curly Jewish?* (New York: Reader's Digest Press, 1965), p. 15.

30. "Poland in Appeal on Nazi Outrages," *NYT,* November 28, 1942.

31. Milton Bracker, "Polish Executions Put at 3,200,000," *NYT,* July 27, 1943.

32. Goldhagen, *Hitler's Willing Executioners,* p. 194.

33. Victor Cavendish-Bentinck Minute, August 23, 1943, Public Record Office, FO 371/34551.

34. "1943 Timeline," www.holocaustchronicle.org/StaticPages/462.html (accessed August 13, 2007).

35. "Dewey for Offset to Anti-Semitism," *NYT,* March 29, 1944.

36. Joseph M. Levy, "Jews in Hungary Fear Annihilation," *NYT,* May 10, 1944.

37. "Czechs Report Massacre," *NYT,* June 20, 1944.

38. Joseph W. Bendersky, *The "Jewish Threat": Anti-Semitic Politics of the U.S. Army* (New York: Basic Books, 2000), pp. 338–40.

39. See especially David S. Wyman, *The Abandonment of the Jews: America and the Holocaust, 1941–1945* (New York: Pantheon, 1984).

40. Kai Bird, *The Chairman: John J. McCloy and the Making of the American Establishment* (New York: Simon & Schuster, 1992); Joseph Finder, "Ultimate Insider, Ultimate Outsider," *NYT,* April 12, 1992; Robert N. Rosen, *Saving the Jews: Franklin D. Roosevelt and the Holocaust* (New York: Basic Books, 2006), pp. 405–6.

41. Interview with Jan Karski, quoted in Doris Kearns Goodwin, *No Ordinary Time: Franklin and Eleanor Roosevelt: The Home Front in World War II* (New York: Touchstone, 1995), p. 516.

42. Peter Novick, *Holocaust in American Life,* pp. 55–56.

43. W.H. Lawrence, "Nazi Mass Killing Laid Bare in Camp," *NYT,* August 30, 1944.

44. "3,000,000 Jews Executed," *NYT,* November 13, 1944.

45. Bendersky, *"Jewish Threat,"* p. 350.

46. William Casey, *The Secret War Against Hitler* (Washington, DC: Regnery Gateway, 1988), p. 218.

47. Gene Currivan, "Forced Tour at Buchenwald," *NYT,* April 18, 1945.

48. Affidavit of Karl von Heider, Frankfurt a/M., Grillparzerstr. 83, Nuernberg Military Tribunal, Vol. VII, p. 455, The Mazal Library, www.mazal.org/archive/nmt/07/NMT07-T0455.htm (accessed May 25, 2007).

49. "Nazi Death Factory Shown in Film Here," *NYT,* April 28, 1945.

50. Bendersky, *"Jewish Threat,"* pp. 352–58.

51. Joel Sack, *Dawn over Dachau* (New York: Shengold Publishers, 1990).

I appreciate having had the opportunity to interview Joel Sack, a Dachau survivor, in September 1990.

52. Report of Earl G. Harrison, August 1945, pp. 2, 12, Harry S. Truman Library, Independence, MO, Harry S. Truman Papers, Official Files, box 127.

53. Carey McWilliams, *A Mask for Privilege: Anti-Semitism in America* (Boston: Little, Brown & Co., 1948), p. 164.

54. Rebecca West, "Rebecca West at Nuremberg," from *The New Yorker,* 1946, reprinted in Louis L. Snyder and Richard B. Morris, eds., *A Treasury of Great Reporting* (New York: Simon & Schuster, 1962), p. 707.

55. See Telford Taylor, *The Anatomy of the Nuremberg Trials* (New York: Knopf, 1992); Joseph E. Persico, *Nuremberg: Infamy on Trial* (New York: Viking Press, 1994).

56. Pressac, *Auschwitz;* Peter Hayes, *From Cooperation to Complicity: Degussa in the Third Reich* (Cambridge: Cambridge University Press, 2004); Lifton, *Nazi Doctors,* p. 160.

57. Franz von Papen, *Memoirs,* trans. Brian Connell (London: Andre Deutsch, 1952), p. 563; see also Giles MacDonogh, *After the Reich: The Brutal History of the Allied Occupation* (New York: Basic Books, 2007).

58. See, e.g., WO 235–12, Case 12, Bergen-Belsen and Auschwitz Concentration Camps Case (Lueneburg Tribunal), 11 vols., National Archives, London.

59. WO 235–83, Case 71, Bruno Tesch, Karl Weinbacher, and Joachim Drosihn (Hamburg Tribunal), National Archives, London.

60. Some defenders of Dr. Tesch, Holocaust deniers, later pointed out that hydrogen cyanide had also been used in large quantities for fumigation, including by the U.S. military. See, e.g., American Cyanamid and Chemical Corporation, Military Fumigation Manual, 1944, cited by William B. Lindsey, "Zyklon B, Auschwitz, and the Trial of Dr. Bruno Tesch," *Journal of Historical Review* 4(3) (1983): 261–303.

61. See J.H. Barrington, ed., *The Zyklon B Trial: Trial of Bruno Tesch and Two Others* (London: n.p., 1948); and Joseph Borkin, *The Crime and Punishment of IG Farben* (New York: The Free Press, 1978). Incidentally, the National Archives in San Francisco contains an investigative case file (RG 175) concerning a series of contracts made by the Chemical Warfare Service with the American Cyanamid and Chemical Corporation in the 1940s.

62. *American Jewish Year Book, 1956,* available at http://69.20.59.207/AJC_DATA/files/1956_10_centralEurope.pdf (accessed December 1, 2008).

63. John V.H. Dippel, *Two Against Hitler: Stealing the Nazis' Best-Kept Secrets* (New York: Praeger, 1992), pp. 84–85. I am indebted to Dr. Dippel for sharing his research with me.

64. Records of the Office of Strategic Services, Record Group 226, U.S. Archives and Records Administration, College Park, Maryland.

65. After the war, Hoffmann was dragooned into working in chemical warfare for the British at Porton Down and for the Americans at Edgewood Arsenal. See Jonathan B. Tucker, *War of Nerves: Chemical Warfare from World War I to Al-Qaeda* (New York: Pantheon, 2006), pp. 116, 117, 160.

66. Dippel's book *Two Against Hitler* covers these relationships.

67. Dippel, *Two Against Hitler,* p. 85; Robert D. Murphy, *Diplomat among*

Warriors: The Unique World of a Foreign Service Expert (Garden City, NY: Doubleday, 1964), pp. 245, 247–48, 273; Respondek, report on the Kaiser Wilhelm Society, p. 2, Max Planck Gesellschaft, Berlin Archives and Library.

68. Dippel, *Two Against Hitler,* p. 84.

69. McCloy interview, cited in Jean Edward Smith, *Lucius D. Clay: An American Life* (New York: Henry Holt & Co., 1990), pp. 211, 730.

70. U.S. Congress, Senate Committee on the Judiciary, Internal Security Subcommittee, *Morgenthau Diary (Germany)* (Washington, DC: U.S. Government Printing Office, 1965), vol. 1, pp. 573–74.

71. See Bird, *The Chairman.*

72. Rosemary Sponner, "Private Citizen Mrs. McCloy," *Information Bulletin,* June 1950, p. 11.

73. "'We Know the Russians,'" *Time,* June 20, 1949.

74. See Thomas Alan Schwartz, *America's Germany: John J. McCloy and the Federal Republic of Germany* (Cambridge, MA: Harvard University Press, 1991).

75. Finder, "Ultimate Insider, Ultimate Outsider."

76. Herbert H. Haines, *Against Capital Punishment: The Anti–Death Penalty Movement in America, 1972–1994* (New York: Oxford University Press, 1996), pp. 10–11.

9. CLOUDS OF ABOLITION

1. For a shocking account of the postwar treatment of German prisoners of war and relocated civilians, of which an estimated two million perished, see Giles MacDonogh, *After the Reich: The Brutal History of the Allied Occupation* (New York: Basic Books, 2007).

2. Marie Gottschalk, *The Prison and the Gallows: The Politics of Mass Incarceration in America* (New York: Cambridge University Press, 2006), p. 250; Royal Commission on Capital Punishment, 1949–53, *Report* (London: HMSO, September 1953); Harry Elmer Barnes and Negley K. Teeters, *New Horizons in Criminology* (New York: Prentice-Hall, 1954), p. 352.

3. Novick, *The Holocaust in American Life* (Boston: Houghton Mifflin, 1999), pp. 85–87.

4. See Sam Roberts, *The Brother: The Untold Story of Atomic Spy David Greenglass and How He Sent His Sister, Ethel Rosenberg, to the Electric Chair* (New York: Random House, 2001).

5. Elaine Ross, quoted in Ronald Radosh and Joyce Milton, *The Rosenberg File: A Search for the Truth* (New York: Holt, Rinehart & Winston, 1983), p. 329.

6. Letter from Julius Rosenberg to Emanuel Block, June 19, 1953, Sing Sing death house files, New York State Archives.

7. Arthur Miller, "The Crucible and the Execution, A Memoir," in *The Rosenbergs: Collected Visions of Artists and Writers,* ed. Rob A. Okun (New York: Universe Books, 1988), p. 87.

8. *People v. Daugherty,* quoted in Ivan Solotaroff, *The Last Face You'll*

Ever See: The Private Life of the American Death Penalty (New York: HarperCollins, 2001), p. 8.

9. Barnes and Teeters, *New Horizons in Criminology,* p. 350.

10. 1951 Okla. Sess., Laws 17 §1 (lethal gas); Bob Gregory, "They Died for Their Sins," *Oklahoma Monthly,* November 1979, p. 73; Deborah Denno, "Getting to Death: Are Executions Constitutional?" *Iowa Law Review* 82 (1996–97): 457.

11. David M. Oshinsky, *"Worse than Slavery"; Parchman Farm and the Ordeal of Jim Crow Justice* (New York: The Free Press, 1996), pp. 228–29.

12. Inventor Thomas Clyde Williams filed his patent on September 2, 1955, and the U.S. Patent Office issued patent no. 2,802,462 on August 13, 1957.

13. Frank Pittman, Associated Press, "8 States Use Gas Chamber in Execution of Condemned," *Bridgeport (CT) Sunday Post,* January 2, 1955.

14. Associated Press, "Killer Dies in Miss. Gas Chamber," *Lima (OH) News,* March 4, 1955. (The Gallego execution did not prove to be a very good deterrent. Decades later Gallego's son, Gerald Armond Gallego, was convicted as a serial murderer in Nevada, and he was executed by lethal injection on July 18, 2002.) Gerald Gallego's execution is described in Solotaroff, *Last Face You'll Ever See,* pp. 65–66.

15. "Mobster Dies in Miss. Gas Chamber," *FB,* January 17, 1958.

16. "Maryland May Use Gas Execution Chamber," *Connellsville (PA) Daily Courier,* January 15, 1949; "Killer to Die for Slaying," *HMH,* October 9, 1957.

17. Solotaroff, *Last Face You'll Ever See,* p. 220.

18. Larry Hall, Associated Press, "Kidnapers Pay with Lives," *The Lincoln (NE) Star,* December 18, 1953.

19. *SB,* April 20, 1998; Roderick, "Last Steps and Last Words on Death Row," *LAT,* March 28, 1990. See also Byron E. Eshelman and Frank Riley, *Death Row Chaplain* (Englewood Cliffs, NJ: Prentice-Hall, 1962). The quote is from Warden Warren Wilson, in Ian Gray and Moira Stanley, *A Punishment in Search of a Crime: Americans Speak Out Against the Death Penalty* (New York: Avon Books, 1989), p. 122.

20. A *San Francisco Chronicle* reporter attending the 1955 execution of Walter Thomas Byrd at San Quentin later recalled, "The methodical, even detached and deliberate performance of his tasks, designed to minimize or eliminate the human drama that is taking place, stood out in sharp contrast to the execution itself." Declaration of Arthur Hoppe, April 15, 1992, exhibit 18, vol. 1, *Fierro v. Gomez.*

21. Declaration of John M. Steiner, Ph.D., April 1992, exhibit 33, vol. 1, *Fierro v. Gomez.*

22. "Abbott Executed!" *SMT,* March 15, 1957.

23. Harold V. Streeter, Associated Press, "Barbara Graham Dies in San Quentin Gas Chamber," *FB,* June 3, 1955. Another witness, a police officer, later declared that seeing Graham and two others put to death that day convinced him that "death by lethal gas is cruel and undignified." Robert H. Coveney, April 15, 1992, exhibit 10, vol. 1, *Fierro v. Gomez.*

24. Harry Kreisler, "Conversation with Robert Wise," Institute of Interna-

tional Studies, U.C. Berkeley, February 28, 1998, at http://globetrotter.berkeley.edu/conversations/Wise/wise-con6.html (accessed May 22, 2006). See also Bosley Crowther, "Screen: Vivid Performance by Susan Hayward," *NYT*, November 19, 1958. In 1969 another popular movie picturing San Quentin's gas chamber was released. *Una sull'altra* (also known as *Perversion Story*), directed by Lucio Fulci, was filmed in the actual death house.

25. Harry Minott, United Press, "Death Penalty Foes to Step up Fight," *Cedar Rapids (IA) Gazette*, September 12, 1955. Sara Ehrmann (1895–1993) was a major figure in the abolitionist movement who got involved through the Sacco and Vanzetti case. The author interviewed her by telephone in 1984. She joined the Massachusetts Council for the Abolition of the Death Penalty in 1927 and assumed leadership of the American League to Abolish Capital Punishment in 1949. Founded in 1925, the latter had originally been based in New York. She was also active in many Jewish organizations, including the American Jewish Committee. She is profiled in Gray and Stanley, *Punishment in Search of a Crime*, pp. 231–36. Many of her papers are located in the Northeastern University Archives in Boston.

26. See Ralph Blumenthal's celebrated biography, *Miracle at Sing Sing: How One Man Transformed the Lives of America's Most Dangerous Prisoners* (New York: St. Martin's Press, 2004).

27. See Clinton T. Duffy with Al Hirshberg, *88 Men and 2 Women* (New York: Pocket Books, 1963); Clinton T. Duffy, as told to Dean Jennings, *The San Quentin Story* (New York: Doubleday, 1950); Gladys Duffy with Blaise Whitehead Lane, *Warden's Wife* (New York: Popular Library, 1963).

28. Duffy and Hirshberg, quoted in Adelaide H. Villmoare, "Through the Looking Glass of Teaching: The Death Penalty and the Political Culture of Detached Passions," *Richmond Journal of Law & Public Interest* 6(1) (Spring 2001).

29. Quoted in Alan Bisbort, "*When You Read This, They Will Have Killed Me": The Life and Redemption of Caryl Chessman, Whose Execution Shook America* (New York: Carroll & Graf, 2006), p. 118.

30. Caryl Chessman, San Quentin Extreme Penalty File, #66565, California State Archives, Sacramento.

31. Bisbort, "*When You Read This,*" pp. 84–85.

32. See, e.g., William J. Kunstler, *Beyond a Reasonable Doubt? The Original Trial of Caryl Chessman* (New York: William Morrow, 1961); Milton Machlin and William R. Woodfield, *Ninth Life* (New York: Putnam, 1961), which concluded that Chessman was innocent; and Frank J. Parker, *Caryl Chessman: The Red Light Bandit* (Chicago: Nelson-Hall, 1975), which found him guilty.

33. Bisbort, "*When You Read This,*" chapter 4. See also Theodore Hamm, *Rebel and a Cause: Caryl Chessman and the Politics of the Death Penalty in Postwar California, 1948–1974* (Berkeley: University of California Press, 2001).

34. Bisbort, "*When You Read This,*" chapter 5.

35. David Lamson, *We Who Are About to Die: Prison as Seen by a Condemned Man* (New York: Charles Scribner's Sons, 1935); Bernard Butcher,

"Was It Murder?" *Stanford Magazine,* January–February 2000. The film *We Who Are about to Die,* directed by Christy Cabanne and starring Preston Foster, is considered one of the classic early movies about prison, death row, and wrongful conviction.

36. Caryl Chessman, *Cell 2455, Death Row: A Condemned Man's Own Story* (New York: Permabooks, 1960). The movie of the same title was released by Columbia Pictures. For a discussion of Chessman's book in the context of prison literature, see Hamm, *Rebel and a Cause,* pp. 69–75.

37. John Barkham, Syndicated Review, *Saturday Review,* May 1954.

38. Chessman's books included *Trial by Ordeal* (Englewood Cliffs, NJ: Prentice-Hall, 1955); *The Face of Justice* (Englewood Cliffs, NJ: Prentice-Hall, 1957); and *The Kid Was a Killer* (Greenwich, CT: Gold Medal Books, 1960).

39. Arnaldo Cortesi, "Spare Chessman, Vatican Implores," *NYT,* February 19, 1960; "Chessman's Stay Hailed in Europe," *NYT,* February 20, 1960; United Press International, "Demonstrations Planned," *NYT,* February 20, 1960.

40. E.W. Kenworthy, "Chessman Uproar Persists in Capital," *NYT,* February 21, 1960; C.P. Trussell, "U.S. Scored Anew in Chessman Case," *NYT,* February 23, 1960; "Nixon Criticized on Death Penalty," *NYT,* February 28, 1960.

41. "Death Penalties Decline in World," *NYT,* May 3, 1960.

42. U.S. House, Subcommittee No. 2 of the Committee on the Judiciary, "Abolition of Capital Punishment," 86th Congress, 2nd Sess. (May 5, 1960), p. 27.

43. Lawrence E. Davies, "Chessman, in a Prison Interview, Sees 50–50 Chance of Clemency," *NYT,* May 1, 1960.

44. Lawrence E. Davies, "Caryl Chessman Executed; Denies His Guilt to the End," *NYT,* May 3, 1960; quoted from Harold V. Streeter, Associated Press, "Reporter Lets You 'See' an Execution," *Wisconsin State Journal,* May 3, 1960; Bisbort, "*When You Read This,*" pp. 359–64.

45. Affidavit of John R. Babcock, April 12, 1992, exhibit 1, vol. 1, *Fierro v. Gomez,* Plaintiffs' Trial Exhibits.

46. William L. O'Neill, *Coming Apart: An Informal History of America in the 1960s* (Chicago: Quadrangle Books, 1971), pp. 276–77.

47. Hamm, *Rebel and a Cause,* pp. 137–44.

48. Homer Bigart, "Eichmann's Tape Depicts Killings," *NYT,* April 20, 1961. See also *Eichmann Interrogated: Transcripts from the Archives of the Israeli Police,* ed. Jochen von Lang in collaboration with Claus Sibyll, trans. Ralph Manheim (New York: Vintage Books, 1984).

49. Homer Bigart, "Eichmann to See Preview of Death-Camp Films," *NYT,* May 28, 1961; Homer Bigart, "Eichmann Is Unmoved in Court as Judges Pale at Death Films," *NYT,* June 9, 1961.

50. H.R. Trevor-Roper, "'Eichmann Is Not Unique,'" *NYT,* September 17, 1961.

51. Hannah Arendt, *Eichmann in Jerusalem: The Banality of Evil* (New York: Viking, 1963).

52. Albert Camus, "Reflections on the Guillotine," in *Resistance, Rebellion and Death,* trans. Justin O'Brien (New York: Modern Library, 1960).
53. Novick, *Holocaust in American Life.*
54. James W.L. Park, quoted in Gray and Stanley, *Punishment in Search of a Crime,* p. 128.
55. "Bar Owner Wants to Purchase Death Unit," *(Eugene, OR) Register-Guard,* January 14, 1965.

10. THE BATTLE OVER CAPITAL PUNISHMENT

1. Robert M. Bohm, "American Death Penalty Opinion, 1936–1986: A Critical Examination of the Gallup Polls," in *The Death Penalty in America: Current Research,* ed. Robert M. Bohn (Cincinnati, OH: Andersen Publishing, 1991), p. 116, table 8.1.
2. Margaret Werner Cahalan, *Historical Corrections Statistics in the United States, 1850–1984* (Rockville, MD: U.S. Department of Justice, December 1986), p. 18, table 2–7; President's Commission on Law Enforcement and the Administration of Justice, *The Challenge of Crime in a Free Society* (New York: Avon Books, 1968), p. 352; "Stirrings on Death Row," *Time,* April 21, 1967.
3. Like earlier gassings, these executions were not pretty either. An Arizona corrections officer and former Korea combat war veteran who witnessed the execution of Pat McGee on March 8, 1963, later reported it was "one of the most vicious and inhumane acts I have ever witnessed . . . pure agony," and said he became a heavy drinker to try to forget it. Affidavit of Carl Behrens, April 15, 1992, exhibit 4, vol. 1, *Fierro v. Gomez.*
4. "Stirrings on Death Row."
5. Ibid.; Chaplain Byron E. Eshelman, quoted in Ian Gray and Moira Stanley, *A Punishment in Search of a Crime: Americans Speak Out Against the Death Penalty* (New York: Avon Books, 1989), p. 154. For more on Mitchell's execution, see "Mitchell Executed as Pickets March; Controversy Rages over Death Issue," *Chico Enterprise Record,* April 12, 1967; "Mitchell Yells, Dies in Gas Cell," *OT,* April 12, 1967; "Killer Dies in Gas Chamber; Suicide Try Fails," *Redwood City Tribune,* April 12, 1967; "Killer Dies Shouting; Carried to San Quentin Gas Chamber," *SFE,* April 12, 1967; "Pleas Fail—Mitchell Goes to Death," *The Independent,* April 12, 1967; "Mitchell Is Executed for Killing Officer," *SB,* April 12, 1967; "Police Slayer Dies in Gas Chamber: Execution State's First Since '63," *LAT,* April 13, 1967; "58 Watch Execution of Policeman's Killer," *SDU,* April 13, 1967; "Execution!" *Santa Cruz Sentinel,* April 13, 1967; "Mitchell Collapses at the Gas Chamber," *SFC,* April 13, 1967; "Police Slayer Dies in Gas Chamber," *LAT,* April 13, 1967.
6. Declaration of Howard Brodie, April 11, 1992, exhibit 8, vol. 1, *Fierro v. Gomez.* I deeply appreciate Mr. Brodie's courtesy and cooperation in allowing me to reproduce one of his drawings in this book.
7. Declaration of Charles Raudenbaugh, April 15, 1992, exhibit 28, vol. 1, *Fierro v. Gomez.*

8. James W.L. Park, quoted in Gray and Stanley, *Punishment in Search of a Crime*, pp. 126–27.

9. "No. 77," *Time*, June 9, 1967.

10. Gary P. Stiff II, "Executive Log," *Time*, June 23, 1967.

11. Deborah W. Denno, "Getting to Death: Are Executions Constitutional?" *Iowa Law Review* 82 (1996–97): 321.

12. *Weems v. United States*, 217 U.S. 349 (1910).

13. Margaret J. Radin, "The Jurisprudence of Death: Evolving Standards for the Cruel and Unusual Punishments Clause," *University of Pennsylvania Law Review* 126 (1978): 997.

14. *Trop v. Dulles*, 356 U.S. 86, 101 (1958).

15. *Rudolph v. Alabama*, 375 U.S. 889, 890, 891 (1963).

16. For a discussion of how the legal revolution affected prisoners and vice versa, see Scott Christianson, *With Liberty for Some: 500 Years of Imprisonment in America* (Boston: Northeastern University Press, 1998), pp. 252–58.

17. Chaplain Eshelman, in Gray and Stanley, *Punishment in Search of a Crime*, p. 153.

18. See Steven C. Tauber, "On Behalf of the Condemned? The Impact of the NAACP Legal Defense Fund on Capital Punishment Decision Making in the U.S. Courts of Appeals," *Political Research Quarterly* 51(1) (1998): 191–219.

19. *Maxwell v. Bishop*, 385 U.S. 690 (1967); Bob Woodward and Scott Armstrong, *The Brethren: Inside the Supreme Court* (New York: Simon & Schuster, 1979), pp. 205–6, 210.

20. Anthony Amsterdam, quoted in "The Death Penalty: Cruel and Unusual?" *Time*, January 24, 1972. For an excellent profile of Amsterdam, see Nadya Labi, "A Man Against the Machine," *NYU Law School Magazine*, Autumn 2007.

21. Michael Meltsner, *Cruel and Unusual: The Supreme Court and Capital Punishment* (New York: Random House, 1973), pp. 281–82.

22. *Furman v. Georgia*, 408 U.S. 238 (1972).

23. Ibid. (Brennan, J., with the majority).

24. Ibid. at 404 (Burger, C.J., dissenting).

25. For a follow-up study on what happened to the inmates who were resentenced, see James W. Marquart and Jonathan R. Sorensen, "A National Study of the *Furman*-Commuted Inmates: Assessing the Threat to Society from Capital Offenders," *Loyola of Los Angeles Law Review* 23(1) (November 1989): 5–28.

26. Franklin E. Zimring and Gordon Hawkins, "Capital Punishment and the Eighth Amendment: Furman and Gregg in Retrospect," *U.C. Davis Law Review* 18(4) (Summer 1985): 927.

27. Bertram H. Wolfe. *Pileup on Death Row* (Garden City, NY: Doubleday, 1973), p. 384; Gottschalk, *The Prison and the Gallows: The Politics of Mass Incarceration in America* (New York: Cambridge University Press, 2006), p. 219.

28. 1973 R.I. Pub. Laws 280 §1 (lethal gas). The 1973 law made the death

penalty mandatory for anyone who committed murder while confined in an adult correctional institution or state reformatory for women.

29. "They Shoot Horses, Don't They," *Time,* October 8, 1973.

30. *Gregg v. Georgia,* 428 U.S. 153, 168–69 (1976).

31. Ibid., at 186–87.

32. See Norman Mailer, *The Executioner's Song* (New York: Warner Books, 1980), a masterpiece about the place of Gilmore's execution in American culture.

33. Gottschalk, *Prison and the Gallows,* pp. 224–25.

34. For a study of the constitutionality of various execution methods and the rise of lethal injection, see Denno, "Getting to Death"; and "When Legislatures Delegate Death: The Troubling Paradox Behind State Uses of Electrocution and Lethal Injection and What It Says about Us," *Ohio State Law Journal* 63(1) (2002): 63–260. Also see the following early articles about lethal injection: Scott Christianson, "Needle Executions: The 'Civilized' Way to Kill," Pacific News Service, September 26, 1977; "This Won't Hurt a Bit," *Mother Jones,* January 1978, p. 6; "Execution by Lethal Injection," *Criminal Law Bulletin,* January–February 1979, pp. 69–78; and "Killing with Kindness," *Playboy,* April 1979, p. 65.

35. Reverend Clyde Johnston, quoted in *Austin American-Statesman,* June 12, 1977.

11. "CRUEL AND UNUSUAL PUNISHMENT"?

1. Schwarzschild, in Ian Gray and Moira Stanley, *A Punishment in Search of a Crime: Americans Speak Out Against the Death Penalty* (New York: Avon Books, 1989), 291–98.

2. See David von Drehle, *Among the Lowest of the Dead: The Culture of Death Row* (New York: Times Books, 1995).

3. Ann Salisbury, "'I'm Not Afraid. I'm Jesse Bishop,'" *LAHE,* August 23, 1979; Associated Press, "Prison Psychiatrist Counsels Patients at a Gas Chamber," *NYT,* May 11, 1978.

4. Wallace Turner, "Murderer in Casino Executed in Nevada," *NYT,* October 23, 1979.

5. Declaration of Tad Dunbar, exhibit 14, vol. 1, *Fierro v. Gomez.*

6. *Gray v. Lucas,* 463 U.S. 1237 (1983).

7. Quoted in *James Gomiez and Daniel Vasquez v. United States District Court for the Northern District of California et al.,* "On Application to Vacate Stay" (April 21, 1992), Supreme Court of the United States (Docket No. A-767), Justices Stevens and Blackmun dissenting.

8. E.R. Shipp, "Killer of 3-Year-Old Mississippi Girl Executed after Justices Reject Plea," *NYT,* September 3, 1983; Associated Press, "Father Says Execution Won't Erase His Memories," *NYT,* September 3, 1983.

9. Ivan Solotaroff, *The Last Face You'll Ever See: The Private Life of the American Death Penalty* (New York: HarperCollins, 2001), pp. 56–57.

10. United Press International, "Mississippi's Gray Steel Chamber Was

Built in 1955 to Replace a Traveling Electric Chair and Executioner T. Berry Bruce Has Been on Hand Every Time It Was Used," September 1, 1983. See also "Eerie, Emotional, Unsettling; For All Who Asked, a Diary of Gray's Execution," *CLJDN,* September 4, 1983; "After Years of Legal Delays, Death Came in Just Minutes," *CLJDN,* September 2, 1983; "Eyewitness Account—He Fought It," *CLJDN,* September 2, 1983; "Killer of Girl, 3, Dies in Gas Chamber," *SFC,* September 2, 1983; "Mississippi Looks for Ways to 'Refine' Execution Process," *Chicago Sun-Times,* September 3, 1983; "Gray Died Quickly, Officials Maintain," *CLJDN,* September 3, 1983; "Gray's Lawyer Calls Gas Death Cruel," *Post Herald,* September 3, 1983; "Prison Official Calls for Reform after Witnessing Grisly Execution," *LADJ,* September 5, 1983; United Press International, "Southern Horizons," September 14, 1983; Solotaroff, *Last Face You'll Ever See.*

11. Affidavit of Dennis N. Balske, April 13, 1992, vol. 1, exhibit 2, *Fierro v. Gomez.*

12. Solotaroff, *Last Face You'll Ever See,* p. 90.

13. Affidavit of Daniel Lohwasser, April 15, 1992, vol. 1, exhibit 21, *Fierro v. Gomez.*

14. 1979 N.M. Laws 150 §8 (lethal injection); N.M. Stat. Ann. §31–14–11 (Michie 1978). The 1979 law expressly did not apply to offenses committed prior to July 1, 1979. See 1979 N.M. Laws 150 §10; 1983 Nev. Stat. 601 §1 (lethal injection); 1983 N.C. Sess. Laws 678 §1 (lethal gas, or lethal injection at the condemned's election; lethal gas if the condemned fails to choose a method); N.C. Gen. Stat. §15–187 (1983). Quote of Representative Warner from Guy Munger, "The Grim History of N.C. Executions," *RNO Perspective,* March 4, 1984. Nev. Rev. Stat. 176 §176.355(1) (1983) (amended 1995). The 1983 law did not expressly indicate retroactivity. See *State v. Quinn,* 623 P.2d 630 (Or. 1981), in which the Oregon Supreme Court found the state law unconstitutional. Then in 1984 Oregon adopted lethal injection. 1984 Or. Laws 3 §7 (lethal injection); Or. Rev. Stat. §137.473(1) (1985). The 1984 law did not expressly indicate retroactive operation. 1984 Miss. Laws 448 §2 (lethal injection; lethal gas if the condemned's death sentence was imposed prior to the Act's effective date); 1984 R.I. Pub. Laws 221 §1 (death penalty abolished); 1984 Wyo. Sess. Laws 54 §1 (lethal injection); Wyo. Stat. Ann. §7–13–904(a) (Michie 1984). The 1984 act did not expressly indicate retroactivity. See 1988 Colo. Sess. Laws 113 §1 (lethal injection); 1988 Mo. Laws p. 985 §A (lethal gas or lethal injection; statute leaves unclear at whose election); Mo. Rev. Stat. §546.720 (1988). The 1988 law also did not expressly indicate retroactivity.

15. William B. Lindsey, "Zyklon B, Auschwitz, and the Trial of Dr. Bruno Tesch," *Journal of Historical Review* 4(3) (1983): 261–303.

16. Documents regarding this case may be found at www.shamash.org/holocaust/denial/mervsIHR.txt (accessed May 2, 2009).

17. Mark Weber, "William Lindsey," *Journal of Historical Review* 13(3) (1992): 21.

18. "An Englishman Abroad," in Gray and Stanley, *Punishment in Search of a Crime,* pp. 171–86; United Press International, "The Mississippi Execu-

tioner," May 17, 1987; "Johnson Execution Places Media in Newsmaker Role," *The Panolian,* May 27, 1987; Christopher Hitchens, "Minority Report," *The Nation,* August 29, 1987, p. 150.

19. "Evans Is Executed at Parchman," *CLJDN,* July 8, 1987; Associated Press, "Texas and Mississippi Executions Are Carried out after Pleas Fail," *NYT,* July 9, 1987.

20. Solotaroff, *Last Face You'll Ever See,* pp. 169–70.

21. Affidavit of Robert R. Marshall, April 14, 1992, exhibit 23, vol. 1, *Fierro v. Gomez.*

22. United Press International, "Edwards Executed for Convenience Store Murder," June 21, 1989; Associated Press, "Man Who Called His Trial Unjust Is Executed for Mississippi Killing," *NYT,* June 22, 1989. See also "Miss. Robber Executed," *Newsday,* June 22, 1989, pp. 16, 18; "Mississippi Store-Clerk Executed," *Facts on File World News Digest,* July 14, 1989; Solotaroff, *Last Face You'll Ever See,* pp. 178–79.

23. Martin Garbus, *Courting Disaster: The Supreme Court and the Unmaking of American Law* (New York: Times Books, 2002), pp. 50–51.

24. *McCleskey v. Kemp.* 107 S.Ct. 1756 (1987).

25. David C. Baldus, George Woodworth, and Charles A. Pulaski Jr., "Monitoring and Evaluating Contemporary Death Sentencing Systems: Lessons from Georgia," *University of California at Davis Law Review* 18(4) (Summer 1985): 1401.

26. *McCleskey v. Kemp,* at 1765, 1769.

27. *People v. Anderson,* 493 P.2d 880, 889 (Cal. 1992) (declaring the state's death penalty law unconstitutional under the state prohibition against cruel and unusual punishment). The new law enacted was 1992 Cal. Stat. 558 §2 (lethal gas or lethal injection at the condemned's election; lethal gas if the condemned fails to choose a method); Cal. Penal Code §3604(a–c) (West 1941) (amended 1992). Ariz. Const. Art. XXII, §22 (1992) (lethal injection or lethal gas at the condemned's election if the condemned was sentenced to death for an offense committed prior to the act's effective date; lethal injection if the preenactment condemned fails to choose a method); Ariz. Rev. Stat. Ann. §13–704(a–b) (1978) (amended 1993). In Maryland, 1994 Md. Laws 5 §1 (lethal injection); 1994 Md. Laws 5 §2 (lethal injection, or lethal gas at the condemned's election, if the condemned's death sentence was imposed prior to the act's effective date; lethal injection if the preenactment condemned fails to choose a method); Md. Ann. Code, art. 27, §71 (1957) (amended 1994); Md. Ann. Code art. 27 §627 (1957) (amended 1994).

28. See "Life of Violence Ends Violently," *TC,* April 6, 1992; "Witnessing a 'Medieval' Execution," *AR,* April 5, 1992; "Where and How an Inmate Is Executed," *AR,* April 5, 1992; "Don Harding Put to Death, 1st State Execution Since '63," *AR,* April 6, 1992; "Harding's Death Raises Questions on Gas Chamber," *AR,* April 7, 1992; "Harding's Slow Death Renews Death Penalty Debate," *PG,* April 7, 1992; and "Woods Says He Didn't See Finger Gesture," *PG,* April 7, 1992.

29. Affidavit of Reverend Ralph Fowler, April 15, 1992, exhibit 15, vol. 1, *Fierro v. Gomez.*

30. Affidavit of Donna Leone Hamm, April 14, 1992, exhibit 16, vol. 1, *Fierro v. Gomez.*

31. "Arizona Executes Killer; State Gripped by Grisly Accounts," *LAT,* April 7, 1992.

32. "Gruesome Death in Gas Chamber Pushes Arizona Towards Injections," *NYT,* April 25, 1992; "Switch to Lethal Injection Gets an OK in Arizona," *SFCE,* April 25, 1992; "Arizona Likely to Switch from Gas to Injection: 'Humane' Measure Gains Support after Harris Execution," *Sunday San Francisco Examiner/Chronicle,* April 26, 1992; "Arizona House Approves Switch in Execution Method," *San Francisco Daily Journal,* April 27, 1992; "Bad Luck on Gallows Led State to Replace Hanging," *AR,* January 5, 1993; "Lethal Injection: Most Relatives of Victims Don't Want Killers to Suffer," *PG,* February 24, 1993.

33. The text of some of this correspondence is contained in the *Fierro v. Gomez* exhibit materials.

34. Daniel B. Vasquez, "Trauma Treatment: Helping Prison Staff Handle the Stress of an Execution," *Corrections Today* 55(4) (July 1993): 70, 72.

35. *Gomez v. United States District Court for the Northern District of California,* 503 U.S. 653, 655 (1992).

36. *Gomez v. California,* 503 U.S. 653, 654 (1992).

37. See Charles M. Sevilla and Michael Laurence, "Thoughts on the Cause of the Present Discontents: The Death Penalty Case of Robert Alton Harris," *UCLA Law Review* 40(2) (1992): 345–79.

38. Declaration of Craig W. Haney, Ph.D., exhibit 38, vol. 1, *Fierro v. Gomez.*

39. Dan Morain, "Witness to the Execution: A Macabre, Surreal Event," *LAT,* April 22, 1992; Larry Hatfield, "Witness' Report: Banal and Macabre," *SFE,* April 22, 1992; Richard Polito, "Harris Saga Finally Ends," *Marin Independent Journal,* April 22, 1992; Sam Stanton, "Eyewitness: Harris' Violent Life Ends Quickly," *SB,* April 22, 1992; Tamara Welch, "Writer's Eyewitness Report," *Bakersfield Californian,* April 22, 1992; "San Quentin Pre-Execution Activity Log," two-page execution summary for Robert Harris from the Warden's Execution Book, California State Archives.

40. "Video of a California Execution Is Destroyed," *NYT,* February 13, 1994. Dutch filmmakers later made a documentary using testimonials by several witnesses to the Harris execution. *Procedure 769* was released in 1996 and shown on public TV in Europe and the United States.

41. Declaration of Craig W. Haney.

42. See, e.g., Steven G. Calabresi and Gary Lawson, "Equity and Hierarchy: Reflections on the Harris Execution," *Yale Law Journal* 102 (1992): 255; Evan Caminker and Erwin Chemerinsky, "The Lawless Execution of Robert Alton Harris," *Yale Law Journal* 102 (1992): 225; Judge Stephen Reinhardt, "The Supreme Court, The Death Penalty, and the Harris Case," *Yale Law Journal* 102 (1992): 205; Wendy Lesser, *Pictures at an Execution: An Inquiry into the Subject of Murder* (Cambridge, MA: Harvard University Press, 1993), pp. 24–187; Deborah W. Denno, "Getting to Death: Are Executions Constitutional?" *Iowa Law Review* 82 (1996–97): 319.

43. Affidavit of Paul V. Benko, April 14, 1992, exhibit 7, vol. 1, *Fierro v. Gomez.*

44. Affidavit of Gloria H. Lyon, April 7, 1992, exhibit 22, vol. 1, *Fierro v. Gomez.*

45. "California Suit Challenges State's Use of Gas Chamber," *NYT,* October 25, 1993.

46. Kevin Fagan, "Mason Died as He Said He Would," *SFC,* August 25, 1993; Marsha Ginsburg, "Eyewitness: No Dignity in Gas Chamber," *OT,* August 24, 1993; Anne Krueger, "Killer Executed," *SDUT,* August 24, 1993; Sam Stanton and Cynthia Hubert, "Mason Gets His Wish, Is Put to Death," *SB,* August 24, 1993; David K. Li, "Watching Mason's Death," *OT,* August 25, 1993; David K. Li, "The Mason Saga Is Far from Over," *OT,* August 25, 1993; Tracie Reynolds, "Mason Left Note, 'Went Out Tough,'" *OT,* August 25, 1993; San Quentin Pre-Execution Activity Log, *Fierro v. Gomez* exhibit copy of EKG tape produced during the execution of David Mason.

47. The U.S. Supreme Court had recently set standards proposed by *Daubert v. Merrell Dow Pharm., Inc.,* 509 U.S. 579 (1993) (adopting the following standard from Federal Rules of Evidence. 702: "If scientific, technical, or other specialized knowledge will assist the trier of fact to understand the evidence or to determine a fact in issue" an "expert may testify thereto").

48. Some examples of articles consulted from the medical literature are J. Wexler, J.L. Whittenberger, and P.R. Dumke, *The Effect of Cyanide on the Electrocardiogram of Man* (Washington, DC: Clinical Research Section of Medical Division, Chemical Warfare Service, 1946), pp. 163–73; F.A. Pirzada, W.B. Hood, J.V. Messer, and O.H.L. Bing, "Effects of Hypoxia, Cyanide, and Ischaemia on Myocardial Contraction: Observations in Isolated Muscle and Intact Heart," *Cardiovascular Research* 9 (1975): 38–45; J.B. Brierly, "Comparison Between Effects of Profound Arterial Hypotension, Hypoxia, and Cyanide on the Brain of Macaca Mulatta," in *Advanced Neurology,* ed. B.S. Meldrum and C.D. Marsden (New York: Raven Press, 1975), pp. 213–21; B. Ballantyne, "Toxicology of Cyanides," in *Clinical and Experimental Toxicology of Cyanides* (Bristol, England: Wright Publications, 1987), pp. 41–126.

49. See, e.g., Chris Lambers, "State Scrambling to Get Gas Chamber Tested," *ADS,* December 15, 1991; James Bandler, "Fred Leuchter: Killing Time and Death's Efficiency Expert," *In These Times,* June 20–July 3, 1990; "An 'Expert' on Executions Is Charged with Fraud," *NYT,* October 24, 1990; Ron Rosenbaum, *Travels with Dr. Death and Other Unusual Investigations* (New York: Penguin, 1991); and Stephen Trombley, *The Execution Protocol: Inside America's Capital Punishment Industry* (New York: Crown, 1992). Two acclaimed documentary films have been made about Leuchter: Trombley's *The Execution Protocol,* released in 1992, and *Mr. Death: The Rise and Fall of Fred A. Leuchter,* by Errol Morris, released in 1999.

50. *R. v. Zündel,* 37 O.A.C. 354 (1990) (Canada).

51. See, e.g., Fred A. Leuchter, with a foreword by David Irving, *The Leuchter Report: The First Forensic Examination of Auschwitz* (London:

Focal Point Publications, 1989); Fred A. Leuchter and Robert Faurisson, "The Second Leuchter Report," *Journal of Historical Review* 10(3) (Fall 1990); Fred A. Leuchter, *The Third Leuchter Report: A Technical Report on the Execution Gas Chamber at Mississippi State Penitentiary Parchman, Mississippi* (Toronto: Samisdat Publishers, 1989); Fred A. Leuchter, *The Fourth Leuchter Report: An Engineering Evaluation of Jean-Claude Pressac's Book, "Auschwitz: Technique and Operation of the Gas Chambers"* (Hamilton, Ontario: History Buff Books and Video, 1991); Fred A. Leuchter, Robert Faurisson, and Germar Rudolf, *The Leuchter Reports: Critical Edition* (Chicago: Theses & Dissertations Press, 2005).

52. Some of this videotape was later used by Errol Morris in his documentary movie.

53. Affidavit of Marshall L. Dayan, February 9, 1999. A copy was provided to the author by Mr. Dayan.

54. *Fierro v. Gomez,* 865 F.Supp. 1387 (N.D. Cal. 1994).

55. Ibid.

56. See Denno, "Getting to Death," pp. 342–43, for cites.

57. *Fierro v. Gomez,* 865 F.Supp. at 1400.

58. See *In re Petition of Donald Thomas,* 155 F.R.D. 124, 126–28 (D.Md. 1994).

59. *Fierro v. Gomez,* 77 F.3d 301 (9th Cir. 1996).

60. Denno, "Getting to Death."

61. See *Gomez v. Fierro,* 117 S. Ct. 285 (remanding for reconsideration in light of changed statute), *vacating on other grounds,* 77 F.3d 301 (9th Cir. 1996).

62. Martin Kady II, "Putting a Face on the Politics of Death," *Washington Business Journal,* May 17, 2002.

12. THE LAST GASP

1. For a description of the crime and prior proceedings, see *State v. LaGrand,* 734 P.2d 563 (Ariz. 1987), and *LaGrand v. Stewart,* 133 F.3d 1253 (9th Cir.), cert. denied, 119 S. Ct. 422 (1998).

2. Mark Shaffer, "No Reprieve for German Killer: International Focus on Ariz. Case," *AR,* February 24, 1999.

3. *LaGrand (Karl) v. Stewart,* 173 F.3d 1144 (9th Cir. 1999).

4. *Stewart v. LaGrand,* 526 U.S. 115 (1999).

5. See William J. Aceves, "Case Concerning the Vienna Convention on Consular Relations (Federal Republic of Germany v. United States), Provisional Measures Order," *American Journal of International Law* 93(4) (October 1999): 924–28.

6. "German Executed in Arizona, Legal Challenge Fails," CNN.com, March 5, 1999.

7. Roger Cohen, "U.S. Execution of German Stirs Anger," *NYT,* March 5, 1999.

8. Denno, a leading authority on the constitutionality of execution meth-

ods, argues that "*Fierro* and other execution methods cases, while reaching the right result, fail to provide a sufficiently comprehensive Eighth Amendment standard for determining the constitutionality of any execution method." Deborah W. Denno, "Getting to Death: Are Executions Constitutional?" *Iowa Law Review* 82 (1996–97): 321.

Select Bibliography

Adam, Uwe Dietrich. "The Gas Chambers." In *Unanswered Questions: Nazi Germany and the Genocide of the Jews,* edited by François Furet. New York: Schocken Books, 1989.

Addison, James T. *Story of the First Gas Regiment.* Boston: Houghton Mifflin, 1919.

Allen, Michael Thad. "The Devil in the Details: The Gas Chambers of Birkenau, October 1941." *Holocaust and Genocide Studies* 16(2) (2002): 189–216.

Auld, Maj. S. J. M. *Gas and Flame.* London: Doran & Co., 1918.

Bache, William. *An Inaugural Experimental Dissertation, Being An Endeavour to Ascertain the Morbid Effects of Carbonic Acid Gas, or Fixed Air, on Healthy Animals, and the Manner in Which They Are Produced.* Philadelphia: T. Dobson, 1794.

Banner, Stuart. *The Death Penalty: An American History.* Cambridge, MA: Harvard University Press, 2002.

Beard, Kristina F. Comment, "Five Under the Eighth: Methodology Review and the Cruel and Unusual Punishments," 51 *Miami Law Review* 445 (1997).

Bedau, Hugo Adam, ed. *The Death Penalty in America, 3rd ed.* New York: Oxford University Press, 1982.

Bendersky, Joseph W. *The "Jewish Threat": Anti-Semitic Politics of the U.S. Army.* New York: Basic Books, 2000.

Bird, Kai. *The Chairman: John J. McCloy and the Making of the American Establishment.* New York: Simon & Schuster, 1992.

Black, Edwin. *IBM and the Holocaust: The Strategic Alliance Between Nazi Germany and America's Most Powerful Corporation.* New York: Crown Publishers, 2001.

———. *War Against the Weak: Eugenics and America's Campaign to Create a Master Race*. New York: Four Walls Eight Windows, 2003.

Boies, Henry M. *Prisoners and Paupers: A Study of the Abnormal Increase of Criminals, and the Public Burden of Pauperism in the United States; the Causes and Remedies*. New York: Putnam's, 1893.

Borkin, Joseph. *The Crime and Punishment of IG Farben*. New York: The Free Press, 1978.

Bowers, Carol. "Loving Cecile: the Strange Case of Stanley Lantzer." *Annals of Wyoming* 69(3) (Summer 1997).

Brandon, Craig. *The Electric Chair: An Unnatural American History*. Jefferson, NC: McFarland & Co., 1999.

Breitman, Richard. *The Architect of Genocide: Himmler and the Final Solution*. New York: Alfred A. Knopf, 1991.

Brierly, J.B. "Comparison between Effects of Profound Arterial Hypotension, Hypoxia, and Cyanide on the Brain of Macaca Mulatta." In *Advances in Neurology*, edited by B.B. Meldrum and C.D. Marsden, 213–21. New York: Raven Press, 1975.

Brinkley, Alan. "The Most Influential Private Citizen in America." *Harpers*, February 1983, 31–46.

Brophy, Leo P. "The Origins of the Chemical Corps," *Military Affairs*, 20(4) (Winter 1956): 217–26.

Brophy, Leo P., and George J.B. Fisher. *The Chemical Warfare Service: From Laboratory to Field*. Washington, DC: Office of the Chief of Military History, Department of the Army, 1959.

Brown, Edmund G., with Dick Adler. *Public Justice, Private Mercy: A Governor's Education on Death Row*. New York: Weidenfeld & Nicholson, 1989.

Brown, Frederic. *Chemical Warfare: A Study in Restraints*. Westport, CT: Greenwood Press, 1968.

Browning, Christopher R. *The Path to Genocide: Essays on Launching the Final Solution*. Cambridge: Cambridge University Press, 1992.

Cabana, Donald A. *Death At Midnight: Confessions of an Executioner*. Boston: Northeastern University Press, 1996.

Cahalan, Margaret Werner. *Historical Corrections Statistics in the United States, 1850–1984*. Rockville, MD: U.S. Department of Justice, Bureau of Justice Statistics, December 1986.

Carlson, Elof Axel. *The Unfit: A History of a Bad Idea*. Cold Spring Harbor, NY: Cold Spring Harbor Laboratory Press, 2001.

Carrel, Alexis. *Man, the Unknown*. New York: Doubleday, 1935.

Chambers, Robert W. *The King in Yellow*. London: F. Tennyson Neely, 1895.

Chan, Loren B. "Example for the Nation: Nevada's Execution of Gee Jon." *Nevada Historical Society Quarterly* 18(2) (Summer 1975): 90–106.

Charles, Daniel. *Master Mind: The Rise and Fall of Fritz Haber, the Nobel Laureate Who Launched the Age of Chemical Warfare*. New York: Ecco, 2005.

Chessman, Caryl. *Cell 2455, Death Row: A Condemned Man's Own Story*. New York: Permabooks, 1960.

———. *The Kid Was a Killer*. Greenwich, CT: Gold Medal Books, 1960.

———. *Trial by Ordeal*. Englewood Cliffs, NJ: Prentice-Hall, 1955.

Christianson, Scott. "Bad Seed or Bad Science: The Story of the Notorious Jukes Family." *New York Times*, February 8, 2003.

———. *Condemned: Inside the Sing Sing Death House*. New York: New York University Press, 1999.

———. "Executions by Lethal Injection." *Criminal Law Bulletin* 15(1) (January–February 1979): 69–78.

———. *With Liberty for Some: 500 Years of Imprisonment in America*. Boston: Northeastern University Press, 1998.

Cobb, Ty. *My Life in Baseball: The True Record*. Omaha: University of Nebraska Press, 1993.

"Company Gives Gas to a Deadly Memory." *Rocky Mountain News*, February 19, 1990.

Conant, James Bryant. *My Several Lives: Memoirs of a Social Inventor*. New York: Harper & Row, 1970.

Dawidowicz, Lucy. *The War Against the Jews, 1933–1945*. New York: Bantam Books, 1975.

Denno, Deborah W. "Getting to Death: Are Executions Constitutional?" *Iowa Law Review* 82 (1996–97): 319–464.

Dickerson, D.S. *Biennial Report of the Warden of the State Penitentiary 1923–1924*. Carson City, NV: State Printing Office, 1925.

Dippel, John V.H. *Two Against Hitler: Stealing the Nazis' Best-Kept Secrets*. New York: Praeger, 1992.

Dowbiggin, Ian. *A Merciful End: The Euthanasia Movement in Modern America*. New York: Oxford University Press, 2007.

DuBois, Josiah E. *The Devil's Chemists: 24 Conspirators of the International Farben Cartel Who Manufacture Wars*. Boston: Beacon Press, 1952.

Duffy, Clinton T., as told to Dean Jennings. *The San Quentin Story*. New York: Doubleday, 1950.

Duffy, Clinton T., with Al Hirshberg. *88 Men and 2 Women*. New York: Doubleday, 1962.

Dwork, Debórah, and Robert Jan van Pelt. *Auschwitz: 1270 to the Present*. New York: W.W. Norton & Co., 1996.

Elks, Martin A. "The 'Lethal Chamber': Further Evidence for the Euthanasia Option." *Mental Retardation* 31(4) (August 1993).

Engelbrecht, H.C. *Merchants of Death*. New York: Dodd, Mead & Co., 1984.

Eshelman, Byron E., with Frank Riley. *Death Row Chaplain*. Englewood Cliffs, NJ: Prentice-Hall, 1962.

Essig, Mark. *Edison and the Electric Chair: A Story of Light and Death*. New York: Walker & Co., 2003.

"Execution by Gas." *Literary Digest* 80 (March 1, 1924): 17.

Feig, Konnilyn G. *Hitler's Death Camps: The Sanity of Madness*. New York: Holmes & Meier, 1981.

"Firm's Steel Egg Resumes Life as Chamber of Death." *Rocky Mountain News*, April 23, 1992.

Foucault, Michel. *Discipline and Punish: The Birth of the Prison*, translated by Alan Sheridan. New York: Pantheon Books, 1977.

———. *Power/Knowledge—Selected Interviews and Other Writings 1972–1977*, ed. Colin Gordon. Brighton: Harvester Press, 1980.

Foulkes, Charles Howard. *Gas! The Story of the Special Brigade*. London: William B. Blackwood & Sons, 1936.

Freinkel, A., Koopman, C., and D. Spiegel. "Dissociative Symptoms in Media Eyewitnesses of an Execution." *American Journal of Psychiatry* 151 (1994): 1335–39.

Friedlander, Henry. *The Origins of Nazi Genocide: From Euthanasia to the Final Solution*. Chapel Hill: University of North Carolina Press, 1995.

Friedländer, Saul. *Kurt Gerstein: The Ambiguity of Good*. New York: Alfred A. Knopf, 1967.

Fries, Amos A., and Clarence J. West. *Chemical Warfare*. New York: McGraw-Hill, 1921.

Gardner, Martin R. "Executions and Indignities—An Eighth Amendment Assessment of Methods of Inflicting Capital Punishment," 39 *Ohio Law Journal* 96 (1978).

Garland, David. *Punishment and Modern Society: A Study in Social Theory*. Chicago: University of Chicago Press, 1990.

Garth, Bryant G., and Austin Sarat. *How Does Law Matter?* Evanston: Northwestern University Press, 1998.

"Gas Kills Convict Almost Instantly." Associated Press, February 8, 1924, in *New York Times*, February 9, 1924.

Glass, James M. *"Life Unworthy of Life": Racial Phobia and Mass Murder in Hitler's Germany*. New York: Basic Books, 1997.

Goins, Craddock. "The Traveling Executioner." *American Mercury* (January 1942): 93–97.

Goldhagen, Daniel Jonah. *Hitler's Willing Executioners: Ordinary Germans and the Holocaust*. New York: Alfred A. Knopf, 1996.

Goran, Morris. *The Story of Fritz Haber*. Norman: University of Oklahoma Press, 1967.

Gray, Ian, and Moira Stanley. *A Punishment in Search of a Crime: Americans Speak Out Against the Death Penalty*. New York: Avon Books, 1989.

Grim, Randy. *Miracle Dog: How Quentin Survived the Gas Chamber to Speak for Animals on Death Row*. Loveland, CO: Blue Ribbon Books, 2005.

Gurtowski, Richard. "Remembering Baseball Hall of Famers Who Served in the Chemical Corps." *Army Chemical Review* (July–December 2005): 52–54.

Haber, Ludwig Fritz. *The Poisonous Cloud: Chemical Warfare in the First World War*. Oxford: Clarendon Press, 1986.

Habermas, Jürgen. "Learning by Disaster? A Diagnostic Look Back on the Short 20th Century." *Constellations* 5(3) (1998): 307–20.

Hager, Thomas. *The Alchemy of Air: A Jewish Genius, a Doomed Tycoon, and the Scientific Discovery That Fed the World but Fueled the Rise of Hitler*. New York: Harmony Books, 2008.

Hamilton, Allan McLane. *A Manual of Medical Jurisprudence, with Special Reference to Diseases and Injuries of the Nervous System*. New York: Bermingham & Co., 1883.

———. *Recollections of an Alienist: Personal and Professional.* New York: George H. Doran Co., 1916.

Hamm, Theodore. *Rebel and a Cause: Caryl Chessman and the Politics of the Death Penalty in Postwar California, 1948–1974.* Berkeley: University of California Press, 2001.

Hammond, James W. *Poison Gas: The Myths Versus Reality.* Westport, CT: Greenwood Press, 1990.

Harris, Robert, and Jeremy Paxman. *A Higher Form of Killing: The Secret History of Chemical and Biological Warfare.* New York: Random House, 1982.

Hart, Jordana. "Death Machine Builder under Scrutiny for Nazi Gas Report." *Boston Globe,* October 1, 1990.

Hartmann, Raymond. "The Use of Lethal Gas in Nevada Executions." *St. Louis Law Review* 8 (April 1923): 164–68.

Hayes, Peter. *From Cooperation to Complicity: Degussa in the Third Reich.* New York: Cambridge University Press, 2004.

———. *Industry and Ideology: IG Farben in the Nazi Era.* New York: Cambridge University Press, 1987.

Heller, Major Charles E. *Chemical Warfare in World War I: The American Experience, 1917–1918.* Ft. Leavenworth, KS: Combat Studies Institute, September 1984.

Hershberg, James. *James B. Conant: Harvard to Hiroshima and the Making of the Nuclear Age.* New York: Alfred A. Knopf, 1993.

Hilberg, Raul. *The Destruction of the European Jews,* rev. ed., 3 vols. New York: Holmes & Meier, 1985.

Hill, H.W., and W.S. Landis. "The Analysis of Complete Fertilizers Containing Cyanamid." *Journal of Industrial & Engineering Chemistry* 6(1) (1914): 20–22.

Hounshell, David A., and John Kenly Smith. *Science and Corporate Strategy: DuPont R & D, 1902–1980.* New York: Cambridge University Press, 1988.

"House Panel Approves Bill to Eliminate Gas Executions." Associated Press, in *Winston Salem Journal,* June 5, 1998.

Hylton, A.R. *The History of Chemical Warfare Plants and Facilities in the United States, Studies on the Technical and Control Aspects of Chemical and Biological Weapons,* vol. 4. Kansas City, KS: Midwest Research Institute for the U.S. Arms Control and Disarmament Agency, November 1972.

Jeffreys, Diarmuid. *Hell's Cartel: The Rise and Fall of IG Farben.* London: Bloomsbury, 2008.

Johnston, Harold. *A Bridge Not Attacked: Chemical Warfare Civilian Research During World War II.* Singapore: World Publishing Co., 2003.

Jones, Daniel Patrick. "American Chemists and the Geneva Protocol." *Isis* 71(3) (September 1980): 426–40.

———. "The Role of Chemists in Research on War Gases in the United States during World War I." Ph.D. diss., University of Wisconsin, 1969.

Jonnes, Jill. *Empires of Light: Edison, Tesla, Westinghouse, and the Race to Electrify the World.* New York: Random House, 2004.

Kendall, James. *Breathe Freely! The Truth About Poison Gas.* London: G. Bell and Sons, 1938.

Kevles, Daniel J. *In the Name of Eugenics: Genetics and the Uses of Human Heredity.* Cambridge, MA: Harvard University Press, 1985.

Kogon, Eugen, Herman Langbein, and Adalbert Rückerl, eds. *Nazi Mass Murder: A Documentary History of the Use of Poison Gas,* translated by Mary Scott and Caroline Lloyd-Morris. New Haven, CT: Yale University Press, 1993.

Kühl, Stefan. *The Nazi Connection: Eugenics, Racism, and German National Socialism.* New York: Oxford University Press, 1994.

Kunstler, William M. *Beyond a Reasonable Doubt? The Original Trial of Caryl Chessman.* New York: William Morrow, 1961.

Labi, Nadya. "A Man Against the Machine." *NYU Law School Magazine,* Autumn 2007.

"LaGrand Dies in State Gas Chamber: Killer Executed Despite Protests from Germany." *Arizona Republic,* March 4, 1999.

Lamott, Kenneth. *The Chronicles of San Quentin: The Biography of a Prison.* New York: David McKay Co., 1962.

Laqueur, Walter. *The Terrible Secret: Suppression of the Truth About Hitler's "Final Solution."* Boston: Little, Brown & Co., 1980.

Lederer, Susan E. *Subjected to Science: Human Experimentation in America before the Second World War.* Baltimore, MD: Johns Hopkins University Press, 1995.

Lefebure, Victor. *The Riddle of the Rhine: Chemical Strategy in Peace and War.* New York: The Chemical Foundation, 1923.

"Lethal Chamber Essential to Eugenics." *London Daily Express,* March 4, 1910.

Leuchter, Fred A., Jr. *The Fourth Leuchter Report: An Engineering Evaluation of Jean-Claude Pressac's Book "Auschwitz: Technique and Operation of the Gas Chambers."* Hamilton, Ontario: History Buff Books and Video, 1991.

———. *The Leuchter Report: The First Forensic Examination of Auschwitz.* London: Focal Point Publications, 1989.

———. *The Third Leuchter Report: A Technical Report on the Execution Gas Chamber at Mississippi State Penitentiary Parchman, Mississippi.* Toronto: Samisdat Publishers, 1989.

Leuchter, Fred A., Jr., and Robert Faurisson. "The Second Leuchter Report." *Journal of Historical Review* 10(3) (Fall 1990).

Leuchter, Fred A., Jr., Robert Faurisson, and Germar Rudolf. *The Leuchter Reports: Critical Edition.* Chicago: Theses and Dissertations, 2005.

Levy, Richard H. "The Bombing of Auschwitz Revisited: A Critical Analysis." *Holocaust and Genocide Studies* 10 (Winter 1996): 267–98.

Lifton, Robert Jay. *The Nazi Doctors: Medical Killing and the Psychology of Genocide.* New York: Basic Books, 1986.

Lindsey, William B. "Zyklon B, Auschwitz, and the Trial of Dr. Bruno Tesch." *Journal of Historical Review* 4(3) (1983): 261–303.

Lougheed, Alan. "The Anatomy of an International Cyanide Cartel: Cyanide, 1897–1927." *Prometheus* 19(1) (2001).

Margolick, David. "'Save Me, Joe Louis!'" *Los Angeles Times,* November 7, 2005.

Maxwell, Lucia. "Spider Web Chart: The Socialist-Pacifist Movement in America Is an Absolutely Fundamental and Integral Part of International Socialism." *The Dearborn Independent* 24, March 22, 1924.

Mazal, Harry W. "Zyklon-B: A Brief Report on the Physical Structure and Composition." Available at www.holocaust-history.org/auschwitz/zyklonb/ (accessed May 4, 2009).

McKim, W. Duncan. *Heredity and Human Progress.* New York: G.P. Putnam's Sons, 1900.

"Monge's Death Gripped Witnesses." *Denver Post,* October 14, 1997.

Moran, Richard. *The Executioner's Current: Thomas Edison, George Westinghouse, and the Invention of the Electric Chair.* New York: Alfred A. Knopf, 2003.

Morris, Errol. *Mr. Death: The Rise and Fall of Fred A. Leuchter, Jr.* Documentary film, Channel Four Films, 1999.

Mott, Maryann. "Animal Gas Chambers Draw Fire in U.S." *National Geographic,* April 11, 2005.

Müller-Hill, Benno. *Murderous Science: Elimination by Scientific Selection of Jews, Gypsies, and Others in Germany, 1933–1945,* translated by George R. Fraser. Cold Spring Harbor, NY: Cold Spring Harbor Laboratory Press, 1998.

Murrell, Gary. *Iron Pants: Oregon's Anti–New Deal Governor, Charles Henry Martin.* Pullman: Washington State University, 2000.

"Nevada's Gas House." *Outlook* 155 (June 18, 1930): 255–56.

Note, "Constitutional Law—Eighth Amendment—Ninth Circuit Holds California's Lethal Gas Method of Execution Unconstitutional—*Fierro v. Gomez.*" *Harvard Law Review* 110 (1997): 971.

Novick, Peter. *The Holocaust in American Life.* Boston: Houghton Mifflin, 1999.

Ornstein, G. "Liquid Chlorine." *Journal of Industrial and Engineering Chemistry* 8 (March 1916): 288.

Parker, Frank J. *Caryl Chessman: The Red Light Bandit.* Chicago: Nelson-Hall, 1975.

"Perry Carroll Executed at 12:16 A.M. Today." *Republican-Bulletin* (Rawlins, Wyoming), August 13, 1937.

Persico, Joseph. *Eleventh Month, Eleventh Day, Eleventh Hour: Armistice Day, 1918, World War I and Its Violent Climax.* New York: Random House, 2005.

Perske, Robert. *Deadly Innocent?* Nashville: Abingdon Press, 1995.

Pickett, F.N. *Don't Be Afraid of Poison Gas: Hints for Civilians in the Event of a Poison Gas Attack.* London: Simpkin Marshall, 1934.

Pirzada, F.A., W.B. Hood, J.V. Messer, and O.H.L. Bing. "Effects of Hypoxia, Cyanide, and Ischaemia on Myocardial Contraction: Observations in Isolated Muscle and Intact Heart." *Cardiovascular Research* 9 (1975): 38–45.

Popenoe, Paul, and Roswell Hill Johnson. *Applied Eugenics.* New York: Macmillan, 1918.

Prentiss, A.M. *Chemicals in War: A Treatise on Chemical Warfare.* New York: McGraw-Hill, 1937.

Pressac, Jean Claude. *Auschwitz: Technique and Operation of the Gas Chambers.* New York: Beate Klarsfeld Foundation, 1989.

Price, Richard M. *The Chemical Weapons Taboo.* Ithaca, NY: Cornell University Press, 1997.

"Pro and Con: Execution by Lethal Gas." *Reader's Digest,* December 1937, 56–59.

Proctor, Robert. *Racial Hygiene: Medicine under the Nazis.* Cambridge, MA: Harvard University Press, 1988.

Radelet, Michael L. "Capital Punishment in Colorado, 1859–1972." *University of Colorado Law Review* 74(3) (2003): 885–1008.

Rawson, Tabor. *I Want to Live! The Analysis of a Murder.* New York: Signet, 1958.

Reed, Germaine M. *Crusading for Chemistry: The Professional Career of Charles Holmes Herty.* Athens: University of Georgia Press, 1995.

Rentoul, Robert. *Race Culture; Or, Race Suicide?* London: Walter Scott Publishing Co., 1906.

Riley, Brendan. "Old Execution Chamber May Never Be Used Again." *Las Vegas Review-Journal,* August 18, 2002.

Roderick, Kevin. "Last Steps and Last Words on Death Row." *Los Angeles Times,* March 28, 1990.

Rosenbaum, Eli M. "German Company Got Crematorium Patent." *New York Times,* July 27, 1993.

Rusche, Georg, and Otto Kirchheimer. *Punishment and Social Structure.* New York: Columbia University Press, 1939.

Russell, Edmund. "'Speaking of Annihilation': Mobilizing for War against Human and Insect Enemies." *Journal of American History* 82 (March 1996): 1505–29.

———. *War and Nature: Fighting Humans and Insects with Chemicals from World War I to* Silent Spring. New York: Cambridge University Press, 2001.

Sarat, Austin D. *When the State Kills: Capital Punishment and the American Condition.* Princeton, NJ: Princeton University Press, 2001.

Sarat, Austin D., ed. *Pain, Death, and the Law.* Ann Arbor: University of Michigan Press, 2001.

Sasuly, Richard. *IG Farben.* New York: Boni & Gaer, 1947.

Schrift, Alan. *Modernity and the Problem of Evil.* Bloomington: Indiana University Press, 2004.

Sexton, Steve. "Five Executions Included 'Roughest, Toughest.'" *Elko Daily Free Press,* May 8, 2000.

Slotten, Hugh R. "Humane Chemistry or Scientific Barbarism? American Responses to World War I Poison Gas, 1915–1930." *Journal of American History* 77(2) (September 1990): 476–98.

Smith, Jean Edward. *Lucius D. Clay: An American Life.* New York: Henry Holt & Co., 1990.

Solotaroff, Ivan. *The Last Face You'll Ever See: The Private Life of the American Death Penalty*. New York: HarperCollins, 2001.

Spiers, Edward M. *Chemical Weaponry: A Continuing Challenge*. New York: St. Martin's Press, 1989.

Stiff, Cari. "Looking Back: The Death House by the Side of the Road." *Denver Post Empire Magazine*, May 16, 1971, 17–22.

Tauber, Steven C. "On Behalf of the Condemned? The Impact of the NAACP Legal Defense Fund on Capital Punishment Decision Making in the U.S. Courts of Appeals." *Political Research Quarterly* 51(1) (1998): 191–219.

Taylor, William Banks. *Brokered Justice: Race Politics and Mississippi Prisons*. Columbus: Ohio State University Press, 1993.

———. *Down On Parchman Farm*. Columbus: Ohio State University Press, 1999.

Trials of War Criminals before the Nuremberg Military Tribunals under Control Council Law No. 10 (Green Series), 14 vols. Washington, DC: U.S. Government Printing Office, 1950–52.

Trombley, Stephen. *The Execution Protocol*. New York: Crown, 1992.

Tucker, Jonathan B. *War of Nerves: Chemical Warfare from World War I to Al-Qaeda*. New York: Pantheon, 2006.

Turano, Anthony M. "Capital Punishment by Lethal Gas." *American Mercury* 29 (May 1933): 91–93.

U.S. Congress, House Committee on Immigration and Naturalization. *Temporary Suspension of Immigration*, 66th Cong., 3rd sess., 1920, House Report no. 1109.

———. 67th Cong., 4th sess., 1923, House Report no. 1621.

———. Hearings. *Restrictions on Immigrations*. 68th Cong., 1st sess., 1924. House Report no. 350.

U.S. Congress, Senate, Committee on Immigration. Hearings. *Emergency Immigration Legislation*. 66th Cong., 3rd sess., 1921.

———. Hearings. *Selective Immigration Legislation*. 68th Cong., 1st sess., 1924.

U.S. Congress, Senate, Hearings: *Special Committee Investigating the Munitions Industry, pursuant to S.206*. 74th Congress, 2nd sess., 1936.

U.S. Military Intelligence Reports: Surveillance of Radicals in the United States, 1917–1941. Microfilm. Frederick, MD, 1984.

"Used by German Scientists to Kill Crop Pests." *New York Times*, January 12, 1936.

Van Ness, Richard. *The History of the U.S. Army Medical Service Corps*. St. Louis, MO: U.S. Army, n.d.

van Pelt, Robert Jan. *The Case for Auschwitz: Evidence from the Irving Trial*. Bloomington: Indiana University Press, 2002.

Vilensky, Joel A. *The Dew of Death: The Story of America's World War I Weapon of Mass Destruction*. Bloomington: Indiana University Press, 2005.

Vilensky, Joel A., and Pandy R. Sinish. "The Dew of Death." *Bulletin of the Atomic Scientists* 60(2) (March–April 2004): 54–60.

Wachtel, Curt. *Chemical Warfare*. Brooklyn, NY: Chemical Publishing, 1941.

Waite, Robert G. "Law Enforcement and Crime in America: The View from Germany, 1920–1940." In *Criminal Justice History,* vol. 13, ed. Louis A. Knafla. 191–215. Westport, CT: Greenwood Press, 1992.

Weber, Barbara Parker. "Lethal Gas Execution: Nevada's Daring Experiment." *Nevada Appeal* (Tahoe), February 7, 1999.

Wexler, J., J.L. Whittenberger, and R.P. Dumke. "The Effect of Cyanide on the Electrocardiogram of Man." *Clinical Research Section of Medical Division, Chemical Warfare Service,* 1946: 163–73.

Whaley, Sean. "Nevada Executes Killer." *Las Vegas Review-Journal,* October 5, 1998.

Whitmore, Julie. *A History of Colorado State Penitentiary, 1871–1940.* Cañon City, CO: Printing Plus Press, July 1983.

Whittemore, Gilbert F., Jr. "World War I, Poison Gas Research, and the Ideals of American Chemists." *Social Studies of Science* 5(2) (May 1975): 135–63.

Wise, Robert. *I Want to Live!* Feature film, United Artists (1958).

Woker, Gertrud. *The Next War, A War of Poison Gas.* Washington, DC: Women's International League for Peace and Freedom, n.d.

Wyman, David S. *The Abandonment of the Jews: America and the Holocaust, 1941–1945.* New York: Pantheon, 1984.

Zinsser, Hans. *Rats, Lice and History.* Boston: Little, Brown & Co., 1935.

Zisch, P.J. "Lethal Gas as a Means of Asphyxiating Capital Offenders." *Medico-Legal Journal,* January–February 1931, 26.

Index

Text: 10/13 Sabon
Display: Sabon, Franklin Gothic
Compositor: BookMatters, Berkeley
Printer and binder: Maple-Vail Book Manufacturing Group